Or s

The Magazine c lral

A quality publication offering intelligent, informative and interesting articles aimed at Catholics and non-Catholics alike, as well as all those who visit and worship at the mother church of England & Wales.

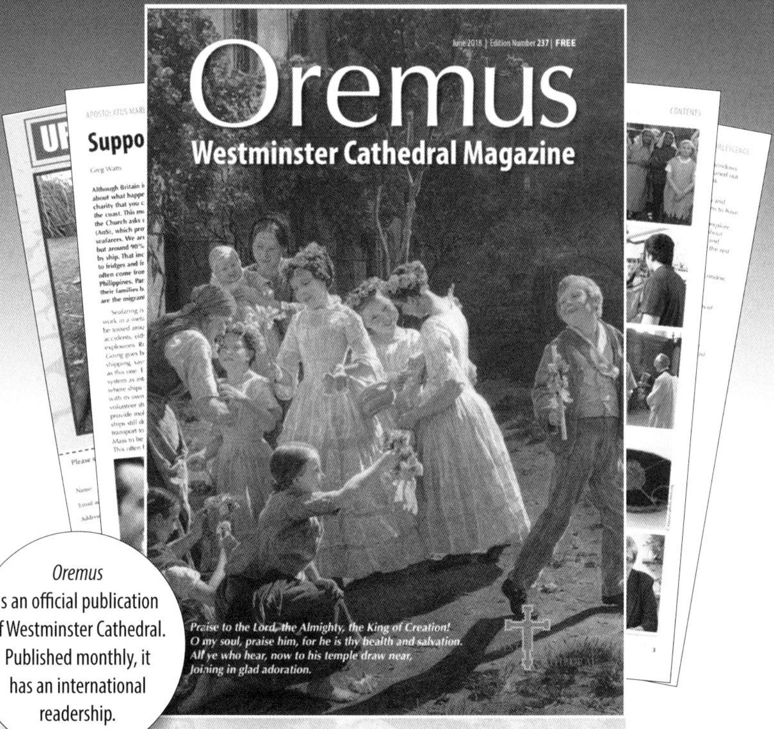

Oremus is an official publication of Westminster Cathedral. Published monthly, it has an international readership.

Available FREE from the Cathedral

or online: ***www.westminstercathedral.org.uk*** *or* ***www.issuu.com***

See the magazine for postal rates

T: **020 7790 9052** | E: **oremus@westminstercathedral.org.uk**

Oremus, Cathedral Clergy House, 42 Francis Street, London SW1P 1QW

Westminster Year Book 2019

67th Edition

Patrons of the Diocese

Our Blessed Lady Immaculate, 8 December;
St Joseph, 19 March; St Peter, Prince of the Apostles, 29 June;
and St Edward the Confessor, 13 October.
Consecration to the Sacred Heart of Jesus 17 June 1873.

The Westminster Year Book
Archbishop's House, Ambrosden Avenue
London SW1P 1QJ
Editor: Fr John Scott
Tel: 020 7798 9370
Email: wyb@rcdow.org.uk

Published with authority by Westminster Roman Catholic Diocese Trustee
Compilation completed 31 October 2018. Information is correct at the time of going to print.

The Diocese of Westminster
comprises the London Boroughs
north of the River Thames
and west of Waltham Forest and Newham,
the Borough of Spelthorne, and the County of Hertfordshire

Unless stated otherwise,
all email addresses in this publication
are formed as follows:
Individuals: firstname+surname@rcdow.org.uk,
e.g. francesmurphy@rcdow.org.uk
Parishes: parish@rcdow.org.uk,
e.g. abbotslangley@rcdow.org.uk

Front cover:
On 29 September 2018 the Seminarians of Allen Hall and
Students of St Edmund's College, Ware celebrated
in the collegiate church of Saint-Pierre, Douai
the 450th Anniversary of their foundation by Cardinal Allen.

Perfect-bound ISBN 978-0-9956262-3-2
Ring-bound ISBN 978-0-9956262-4-9

CONTENTS

Printed on paper from responsible sources

Dear Brothers and Sisters in Christ

In September, tens of thousands of people gathered in Liverpool for *Adoremus,* the first National Eucharistic Congress since that of 1908 in London. This was the largest gathering of Catholics in England and Wales since the Papal Visit of 2010. Those present in Liverpool will remember clearly that the outdoor Blessed Sacrament Procession coincided with a downpour. Perhaps the penitential edge which this brought was not inappropriate, in view of difficulties that have been brought into particularly sharp focus of late. Alongside the penance, though, was a sense, certainly not of triumphalism, but of joy that cannot easily be dislodged: joy that we walked with one another, and with the Lord.

It was right that we brought emotions and needs of every kind to our Eucharistic Lord. In the Blessed Sacrament we find, truly, 'a home for every heart', restless or peaceful, yearning or serene. Here we are offered an ear, always open to us, into which we may trustingly tell whatever tale we wish. A visit to the Blessed Sacrament, long or short, is always time well spent.

If *Adoremus* played its part in deepening knowledge of and love for Our Lord, it will have done valuable service. But love for Christ needs to flourish for more than three days a century! In every Catholic church, Jesus is there for us, truly present in the Blessed Sacrament. We are particularly blessed in our new Shrine of the Blessed Sacrament, the Church of Corpus Christi, Maiden Lane which I was privileged to inaugurate in June. May it become a place of pilgrimage and a focus of devotion for many; I encourage you warmly to visit yourself.

When we receive Holy Communion, we are nourished spiritually with a gift not just for our own benefit, but to be shared. As Catholics, we have a vision of humanity healed and restored to the intrinsic beauty that God wills for every person. Christ gave himself on the Cross so that death might be overcome, and in the Blessed Sacrament he gives himself to transform our lives, so that we in turn may give generously of ourselves to all around us.

Pope Francis sent this message of greeting and blessing to *Adoremus*: 'With a deeper awareness of the Real Presence of Christ among us, may each of you hear afresh the summons of the Lord to share this saving joy in practical concern for the material and spiritual needs of the poorest of our brothers and sisters.' That is a challenge for us all, in 2019 and beyond!

+ Vincent Nichols

Section I

FRANCIS

BISHOP OF ROME, VICAR OF JESUS CHRIST

Successor of St Peter (Prince of the Apostles), Supreme Pastor of the Universal Church, Primate of Italy, Archbishop and Metropolitan of the Province of Rome, Sovereign of the State of the Vatican City, Servant of the Servants of God

His Holiness Pope Francis (Jorge Mario Bergoglio SJ)

Born in Buenos Aires, Argentina 17 December 1936.

Ordained Priest 13 December 1969.

Ordained Titular Bishop of Auca and Auxiliary Bishop of Buenos Aires 27 June 1992.

Appointed Co-adjutor Archbishop of Buenos Aires 3 June 1997.

Installed as Archbishop of Buenos Aires 28 February 1998.

Created Cardinal Priest of San Roberto Bellarmino 21 February 2001.

Elected Pope 13 March 2013.

Inaugurated 19 March 2013.

© Photo: Alexander Balzanella

THE HIERARCHY IN ENGLAND AND WALES

Dates shown below are of Episcopal Ordination and Translation.

The Cardinal is addressed as **His Eminence**; Archbishops as **The Most Reverend**; and Bishops as **The Right Reverend**.

THE PROVINCE OF WESTMINSTER

WESTMINSTER Cardinal Vincent Nichols (1992; 2009)
Archbishop's House, Ambrosden Avenue SW1P 1QJ
Auxiliary Bishops John Sherrington (2011), Nicholas Hudson (2014), Paul McAleenan (2016), John Wilson (2016)
BRENTWOOD Alan Williams SM (2014)
Cathedral House, Ingrave Road, Brentwood, Essex CM15 8AT
Bishop Emeritus Thomas McMahon (1980)
EAST ANGLIA Alan Hopes (2003; 2013)
The White House, 21 Upgate, Poringland, Norwich NR14 7SH
NORTHAMPTON Peter Doyle (2005)
Bishop's House, Marriott Street, Northampton NN2 6AW
Bishop Emeritus Leo McCartie (1977; 1990)
NOTTINGHAM Patrick McKinney (2015)
Bishop's House, 27 Cavendish Road East, The Park, Nottingham NG7 1BB

THE PROVINCE OF BIRMINGHAM

BIRMINGHAM Bernard Longley (2003; 2009)
Archbishop's House, 8 Shadwell Street, Birmingham B4 6EY
Auxiliary Bishops David McGough (2005), William Kenney CP (1987; 2006), Robert Byrne (2014)
Retired Auxiliary Bishop Philip Pargeter (1990)
CLIFTON Declan Lang (2001)
St Ambrose, North Road, Leigh Woods, Bristol BS8 3PW
SHREWSBURY Mark Davies (2010; 2011)
Bishop's House, Laburnum Cottage, 97 Barnston Road, Barnston, Wirral L61 1BW
Bishop Emeritus Brian Noble (1995)

THE PROVINCE OF CARDIFF

CARDIFF George Stack (2001; 2011)
Archbishop's House, 43 Cathedral Road, Cardiff CF1 9HD
MENEVIA Tom M Burns SM (2002; 2008)
Convent Street, Swansea SA1 2BX
Bishops Emeriti Daniel J Mullins (1970; 1987), Mark Jabalé OSB (2000; 2001)
WREXHAM Peter Brignall (2012)
Bishop's House, Sontley Road, Wrexham, Clywd LL13 7EW
Bishop Emeritus Edwin Regan (1994)

THE PROVINCE OF LIVERPOOL

LIVERPOOL Malcolm McMahon OP (2000, 2014)
Archbishop's House, 19 Salisbury Road, Cressington Park, Liverpool L19 0PQ
Archbishop Emeritus Patrick Kelly (1984; 1986)
Auxiliary Bishop Tom Williams (2003)
Retired Auxiliary Bishop Vincent Malone (1989)
HALLAM Ralph Heskett CSsR (2010; 2014)
75 Norfolk Road, Sheffield S2 2SZ
Bishop Emeritus John Rawsthorne (1981; 1997)
HEXHAM & NEWCASTLE Seamus Cunningham (2009)
Bishop's House, East Denton Hall, 800 West Road, Newcastle-upon-Tyne NE25 2BJ
LANCASTER Paul Swarbrick (2018)
Cathedral House, Balmoral Road, Lancaster LA1 3BT
Bishops Emeriti Patrick O'Donoghue (1993; 2001), Michael Campbell OSA (2008)
LEEDS Marcus Stock (2014)
Bishop's House, 13 North Grange Road, Leeds LS6 2BR
Bishop Emeritus Arthur Roche (2001; 2004), Archbishop *ad personam*
MIDDLESBROUGH Terry Drainey (2008)
Bishop's House, 16 Cambridge Road, Middlesbrough, Cleveland TS5 5NN
Bishop Emeritus John Crowley (1992)
SALFORD John Arnold (2006; 2014)
Wardley Hall, Worsley, Manchester M28 5ND
Bishop Emeritus Terence Brain (1991; 1997)

THE PROVINCE OF SOUTHWARK

SOUTHWARK Peter Smith (1995; 2010)
Archbishop's House, 150 St George's Road SE1 6HX
Archbishops Emeriti Michael G Bowen (1970, 1977), Kevin McDonald (2001; 2003)
Auxiliary Bishops Paul Hendricks (2006), Patrick Lynch SS.CC (2006)
Retired Auxiliary Bishops Howard Tripp (1980), John Hine (2001)
ARUNDEL & BRIGHTON Richard Moth (2009; 2015)
High Oaks, Old Brighton Road North, Pease Pottage, West Sussex RH11 9AJ
PLYMOUTH Mark O'Toole (2014)
Bishop's House, 31 Wyndham Street West, Plymouth, Devon PL1 5RZ
Bishop Emeritus Christopher Budd (1986)
PORTSMOUTH Philip Egan (2012)
Bishop's House, Bishop Crispian Way, Portsmouth PO1 3HG
Bishop Emeritus Crispian Hollis (1987; 1988)

THE BISHOPRIC OF THE FORCES

BISHOP OF THE FORCES Paul Mason (2016; 2018)
Wellington House, St Omer Barracks, Thornhill Road, Aldershot, Hants GU11 2BG

THE APOSTOLIC NUNCIATURE

APOSTOLIC NUNCIO His Excellency Archbishop Edward Adams, Titular Archbishop of Scala (1996, 2017)
54 Parkside SW19 5NE Tel: 020 8944 7189 Fax: 020 8947 2494

THE BISHOPS' CONFERENCE OF ENGLAND AND WALES

General Secretary Fr Christopher Thomas
Catholic Bishops' Conference of England and Wales, 39 Eccleston Square SW1V 1BX
Tel: 020 7901 4815 Fax: 020 7901 4819 Email: christopher.thomas@cbcew.org.uk
Web: www.catholicchurch.org.uk
Registered in England and Wales
Company Number: 4734592 Registered Charity Number: 109748239

The Secretariat of the Conference consists of the office of the General Secretary and a number of departments whose work focuses on the work of the Bishops of England and Wales. These are Christian Life and Worship, Christian Responsibility and Citizenship, Catholic Education and Formation, Dialogue and Unity, Evangelisation and Catechesis, and International Affairs. Further information on their work, and contact details, can be found on the website.

The Bishops' Conference also has a number of agencies and offices, for which entries can be found in Section 6, under Catholic Societies and Organisations, and Other Useful Addresses:

Apostleship of the Sea
Catholic Agency for Overseas Development
Catholic Association for Racial Justice
Catholic Communications Network
Catholic Education Service
Catholic Safeguarding Advisory Service
Catholic Social Action Network
National Office for Vocation

They have been there for us... Let's be there for them...

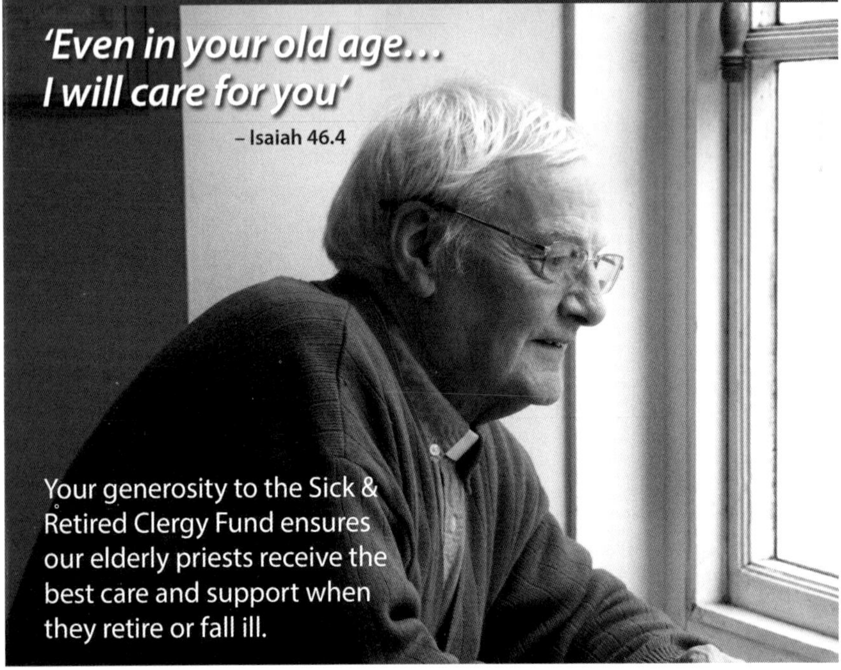

Diocese of Westminster

Registered charity no. 233699

To find out how to become a regular supporter, or make a one-off donation, please contact our Supporter Engagement Manager on **020 7798 9353** or you can donate online at **www.rcdow.org.uk/donations**

Section 2

PATRONS, SAINTS AND BLESSED

Here are listed the Diocesan Patrons and other Saints and Blessed associated with Westminster. The Liturgical Calendar can be found on page 297.

PATRONS

19 March
St Joseph
On 10 December 1898, at the request of Cardinal Vaughan, St Joseph was added as a patron of the diocese. Blessed Pius IX had already declared him to be Patron of the Universal Church (1870) and Cardinal Vaughan himself had a great devotion to him. As a young priest he had founded St Joseph's Society for the Foreign Missions and established a National Shrine of St Joseph at Mill Hill (now at St Michael's Abbey, Farnborough). This patronage of St Joseph was thought appropriate since, as Vaughan noted, 'the Church itself is the expansion of the Holy Family'.

29 June
St Peter, Prince of the Apostles
The inclusion of St Peter among our diocesan patrons testifies to the age-old devotion shown by English men and women to the 'Prince of the Apostles'. From an early date English pilgrims flocked to Rome to visit his tomb and it was King Ine of Wessex who is thought to have initiated the Peter's Pence collection to support the papacy. Many churches were dedicated to the chief of the apostles, including Westminster Abbey. On 29 June 1893 England was re-consecrated to St Peter.

13 October
St Edward the Confessor, King (1003-66)
King of England from 1042, St Edward was famed for his piety, alms-giving and the building of Westminster Abbey. He died on 5 January 1066 and the resulting Norman and Saxon claims to the succession were fought out on the battlefield of Hastings. Canonised in 1161, St Edward's incorrupt body was translated to a new shrine on 13 October 1163 (the origin of his present feast day). His cult flourished in the Middle Ages and he was considered one of the patrons of England. Pope Benedict XVI prayed before his shrine on 17 September 2010, alongside the Archbishop of Canterbury, and called St Edward 'a model of Christian witness and an example of that true grandeur to which the Lord summons his disciples'.

8 December
Our Blessed Lady Immaculate
Our Blessed Lady Immaculate was the original primary patron of the diocese. There are several local Marian shrines within the diocese, including Our Lady of Graces at Tower Hill, Our Lady of Muswell Hill, Our Lady of Warwick Street and Our Lady of Westminster. Our Lady of Willesden in particular was an important Marian shrine for Londoners on the eve of the Protestant Reformation. Although the statue of Our Lady was destroyed in 1538, the shrine was restored in 1892. Since then, Our Lady of Willesden has become the focus of Marian devotion in the diocese and during the Marian Year Rally at Wembley Stadium on 3 October 1954 Cardinal Griffin solemnly crowned the statue before a crowd of over 90,000.

Moreover, the shrine is unusual in having been visited by two canonised saints: St Thomas More and (in the 1950s) St Josemaria Escriva, the founder of Opus Dei.

SAINTS

15 February

St Claude de la Colombière, Priest (1641-82)

St Claude was a Jesuit chaplain to Mary of Modena, then Duchess of York and wife of the future James II, at St James' Palace between 1676 and 1679. Before coming to London he was the spiritual director of St Margaret Mary at Paray-le-Monial. He became a great proponent of modern devotion to the Sacred Heart of Jesus and the Catholics of London were one of the first to receive it. Nearly two hundred years later, on 17 June 1873, the diocese was consecrated to the Sacred Heart. St Claude was banished to France at the time of the 'Popish Plot' and died on 15 February 1682. He was canonised by St John Paul II on 31 May 1992.

19 April

St Alphege, Bishop & Martyr (c.953-1012)

St Alphege started life as a monk in Gloucestershire and Somerset, but despite trying to live a solitary life his talents were soon recognised and he became successively Abbot of Bath, Bishop of Winchester and (in 1005) Archbishop of Canterbury. In 1011 he was captured and imprisoned by the Danish invaders ('Vikings'). When he refused to let his ransom be paid, he was killed at Greenwich; according to tradition, the Danes threw bones at him from their table during a banquet and then one of them struck him on the head with an axe. He was buried at St Paul's Cathedral, where his shrine was visited by many pilgrims, before being moved to Canterbury in 1023. St Thomas Becket prayed to St Alphege just before his own martyrdom in Canterbury Cathedral.

24 April

St Erconwald, Bishop (d. 693)

Born to a rich family, St Erconwald founded the Abbeys of Chertsey (where he was Abbot) and Barking (where his sister, St Ethelburga, was Abbess). In 675 he became Bishop of London - a medieval hymn calls him *Lux Lundoniae* ('light of London'). His final years were plagued by poor health, but he was transported around his diocese in a wooden litter or cart. He was buried at St Paul's Cathedral. In the present diocesan calendar, St Erconwald is kept with the first Bishop of London, St Mellitus, on 24 April.

24 April

St Mellitus, Bishop (d. 624)

St Mellitus was sent to England by St Gregory the Great in 601 to assist the mission of St Augustine. In 604 he was consecrated first Bishop of London. However, he was expelled under St Ethelbert's pagan son, King Saeberht, and eventually became third Archbishop of Canterbury (619). He died on 24 April 624 and was buried at Canterbury. In the present diocesan calendar, St Mellitus is kept with St Erconwald on 24 April.

22 June (celebrated 20 June)

St Alban, Protomartyr (d. c. 209)

St Alban is the earliest British Christian that we know by name. He was a prominent citizen of Verulamium (a town later renamed St Albans), who hid a priest fleeing from persecution. So impressed was he by the priest's example that he took instruction and was baptised. When the soldiers came to search for the priest, Alban put on the fugitive's cloak and was arrested and beheaded – the punishment reserved for Roman citizens. A cult quickly grew up around the martyr – St Germanus, Bishop of Auxerre, visited his shrine in 429 and spread his cult on the continent. Pilgrims visited his shrine in St Albans Abbey until the Reformation. Perhaps the most astonishing thing about St Alban is that he may have suffered as early as 209, testifying to the early existence of Christianity in Britain.

16 November

St Edmund of Abingdon, Bishop (c.1175-1240)

Educated at Oxford and Paris, St Edmund started off as an academic and pioneer of scholasticism. In 1222 he became Treasurer of Salisbury and, in 1233, Archbishop of Canterbury. As Metropolitan, he became known as a defender of the Church's rights, which often brought him into conflict with the king. He died on his way to see the Pope on 16 November 1240 and was buried at Pontigny. He is the patron of St Edmund's College, Ware, which was for many years the location of the diocesan seminary. Several other Archbishops of Canterbury are remembered in our diocesan calendar – Ss Laurence (d.619), Dunstan (909-88) and Theodore (d.690) (3 February) – stressing the links between Canterbury and Westminster. Indeed, the arms of the See of Westminster are similar to those of Canterbury, although there is a red instead of blue background (or 'field') and there is no cross above the pallium.

29 December

St Thomas of Canterbury, Bishop and Martyr (1118-70)

St Thomas Becket was born in Cheapside and entered the service of the Archbishop of Canterbury. He was soon noticed by Henry II, who became a close friend and appointed him Chancellor (1155). St Thomas lived a worldly life, like many in his station, until becoming Archbishop of Canterbury in 1162 when, in the saint's own words, he went from being 'a patron of play-actors and a follower of hounds to being a shepherd of souls'. Taking his responsibilities seriously and living an austere life, he was careful to defend the rights and prerogatives of the Church. Inevitably his relationship with the king began to suffer and for six years he lived as an exile in the French towns of Pontigny and Sens. Returning to England at the end of 1170, he was murdered in his own Cathedral by four of Henry's knights on 29 December (his feast day). The king did penance and Canterbury soon became one of the most popular shrines in Europe. St Thomas was quickly canonised by Alexander III in 1173 and, in more recent times, was proclaimed Patron of the English Secular Clergy.

THE MARTYRS OF THE SIXTEENTH AND SEVENTEENTH CENTURIES

Many of these men and women had London connections – some ministered in the diocese, others were brought to the capital for trial and execution. Among the sites of martyrdom in London are Tyburn, Clerkenwell, Fleet Street, Gray's Inn, Isleworth, Lincoln's Inn Fields, Mile End Green, St Paul's Churchyard, Shoreditch, Smithfield and Tower Hill. Of special importance are the following martyrs:

4 May
St Richard Reynolds (c.1492-1535)
Born in Devon and educated at Cambridge, St Richard joined the Bridgettine community at Syon Abbey, Isleworth in 1513. Famed for his holiness and learning, Ss Thomas More and John Fisher consulted him over Henry VIII's divorce. He was arrested in the spring of 1535 and, refusing to take the Oath of Supremacy, was taken to the Tower together with the three Carthusian Priors. He suffered with them at Tyburn on 4 May.

11 May
The Carthusian Martyrs (1535)
The London Charterhouse (founded 1371) was one of the great religious houses of pre-Reformation London. At the break with Rome, the monks remained loyal to the Pope. The three English Carthusian Priors (including St John Houghton of London) suffered on 4 May 1535. Some other members of the Charterhouse (Bl Sebastian Newdigate, Humphrey Middlemore and William Exmew) were martyred on 25 May; others died in prison. Traditionally the diocese kept their feast on 11 May.

27 June
St John Southworth (d.1654)
St John Southworth's significance for our diocese lies in the discovery of his body at Douai in 1927 and his subsequent translation to Westminster Cathedral in 1930. He acts as a representative figure for the many priests who courageously worked in London in the sixteenth and seventeenth centuries, at the risk of imprisonment and execution. Southworth was trained at Douai and worked in Lancashire and London. Together with the Jesuit St Henry Morse (1595-1645), Southworth cared for the victims of the 1636 plague at great personal risk. Spending many years in prison, he was finally hung, drawn and quartered at Tyburn on 28 June 1654, together with two counterfeiters. Westminster has traditionally kept his feast on 27 June because 28 June (the day of his martyrdom) is already occupied by St Irenaeus and the Vigil of Ss Peter and Paul.

6 July (celebrated 22 June)

St Thomas More (1478-1535)
Born in Milk Street in Cheapside (near the birthplace of St Thomas Becket), he studied at Oxford and Lincoln's Inn and followed a successful career as lawyer, politician and humanist scholar. Henry VIII appointed him Lord Chancellor in 1529 but More resigned three years later as pressure was put on him to support the king's divorce. His refusal to take the Oath of Supremacy led to his imprisonment and execution on Tower Hill on 6 July 1535, a few weeks after the martyrdom of his friend St John Fisher, Bishop of Rochester. He was a devoted family man, twice-married and father of four. His beloved 'great house' in Chelsea was situated near Allen Hall. St Thomas More was canonised by Pius XI in 1935 and has since been proclaimed Patron of Politicians.

BLESSED

9 October

Blessed John Henry Newman, Priest (1801-90)
Cardinal Newman is normally associated with the West Midlands but it is often forgotten that he was born a Londoner. He was born at 88 Old Broad Street (in the City) on 21 February 1801 and moved the following year to 17 Southampton Street (now Southampton Place). The Newman family lived there until 1816. Blessed John Henry went to school in Ealing before entering Trinity College, Oxford as an undergraduate. Newman was a leading force in the Oxford Movement within the Church of England until his search for truth led him to the Catholic Church. He was received into the Church by Blessed Dominic Barberi at Littlemore on 9 October 1845. He set up the Oratory of St Philip Neri in England and spent most of the remainder of his life in Birmingham. After many disappointments and trials, he was created a Cardinal by Leo XIII in 1879 in recognition of his theological work and personal witness. Newman died on 11 August 1890.

29 October

The Blessed Martyrs of Douai College (1577-1679)
Cardinal Allen founded the English College, Douai, in 1568 to train new recruits for the priesthood. This was crucial to the survival of English Catholicism. Over 160 of the priests trained at Douai are now recognised as martyrs, led by the proto-martyr, St Cuthbert Mayne (1577). This is of special significance to the diocese, since St Edmund's, Ware and Allen Hall claim continuity with Douai.

THE ARCHBISHOP

His Eminence Cardinal Vincent Nichols

Born Crosby, Liverpool 8 November 1945. Ordained Priest in Rome on 21 December 1969 for the Archdiocese of Liverpool. Appointed assistant priest in St Mary's Parish, Wigan and chaplain to the Sixth Form College and St Peter's High School in 1971. Ordained Bishop of the titular see of Othona and Auxiliary Bishop of Westminster on 24 January 1992. Translated to Birmingham as Archbishop on 29 March 2000, and to Westminster on 21 May 2009. Created Cardinal Priest of the Most Holy Redeemer and St Alphonsus Liguori on 22 February 2014.

SECTION 2

Archbishop's House, Ambrosden Avenue SW1P 1QJ
Tel: 020 7798 9033 Fax: 020 7798 9077
Email: cardinalnichols@rcdow.org.uk Web: www.rcdow.org.uk/cardinal

Private Office of the Cardinal Archbishop

Private Secretary to the Cardinal Fr Alexander Master
Tel: 020 7798 9041 Email: privatesecretary@rcdow.org.uk

PA to the Cardinal's Private Office (Correspondence) Ellen Dunleavy
Tel: 020 7798 9039 Email: ellendunleavy@rcdow.org.uk

PA to the Cardinal's Private Office (Diary) Maura McBride
Tel: 020 7931 6007 Email: mauramcbride@rcdow.org.uk

Press Enquiries

Press Secretary to the Cardinal Alexander DesForges
Tel: 020 7798 9045 Email: alexander.desforges@cbcew.org.uk

Archbishop's House Reception

Tel: 020 7798 9033 Email: abhreception@rcdow.org.uk
Gillian Reid Email: gillianreid@rcdow.org.uk,
Michael Holmes

Sisters responsible for the Cardinal's Household

La Sagesse
Tel: 020 7798 9398

THE AUXILIARY BISHOPS AND VICAR GENERAL

The Right Rev John Sherrington Titular Bishop of Hilta
Born Leicester 5 January 1958. Ordained Priest 13 June 1987.
Ordained Bishop 14 September 2011 by Archbishop Vincent Nichols.
Archbishop's House, Ambrosden Avenue SW1P 1QJ Tel: 020 7798 9060
PA Virginia Utley **Tel: 020 7798 9075 Email: virginiautley@rcdow.org.uk**

The Right Rev Nicholas Hudson Titular Bishop of St Germans
Born Hammersmith 14 February 1959. Ordained Priest 19 July 1986.
Ordained Bishop 4 June 2014 by Cardinal Vincent Nichols.
Archbishop's House, Ambrosden Avenue SW1P 1QJ Tel: 020 7931 6061
PA Julie McMahon **Tel: 020 7798 9381 Email: juliemcmahon@rcdow.org.uk**

The Right Rev Paul McAleenan Titular Bishop of Mercia
Born Belfast 15 July 1951. Ordained Priest 8 June 1985.
Ordained Bishop 25 January 2016 by Cardinal Vincent Nichols.
Archbishop's House, Ambrosden Avenue SW1P 1QJ Tel: 020 7931 6062
PA Rebecca Goode **Tel: 020 7798 9023 Email: rebeccagoode@rcdow.org.uk**

The Right Rev John Wilson Titular Bishop of Lindisfarne
Born Sheffield 4 July 1968. Ordained Priest 29 July 1995.
Ordained Bishop 25 January 2016 by Cardinal Vincent Nichols.
Archbishop's House, Ambrosden Avenue SW1P 1QJ Tel: 020 7798 9043
PA Rebecca Goode **Tel: 020 7798 9023 Email: rebeccagoode@rcdow.org.uk**

Mgr Martin Hayes
Vicar General
Archbishop's House, Ambrosden Avenue SW1P 1QJ
Tel: 020 7931 6076 Email: martinhayes@rcdow.org.uk
PA Paola Greco **Tel: 020 7798 9151 Email: pgreco@rcdow.org.uk**

THE DIOCESE OF WESTMINSTER AND CATHEDRAL CHAPTER

ARCHBISHOP'S COUNCIL

The Cardinal Archbishop, Auxiliary Bishops, Vicar General, Judicial Vicar, Chair of the Council of Priests, Private Secretary, Chief Operating Officer/Financial Secretary (attends for non-clergy matters).

THE WESTMINSTER ROMAN CATHOLIC DIOCESE TRUST is the charitable trust through which the activities of the Diocese are conducted. Established by a trust deed dated 1 November 1940, it is registered under the Charities Act 1993 **(Registration No 233699).** The Trustees are also the **FINANCE COMMITTEE** (Canon 492, CIC)
Trustees The Cardinal Archbishop and Auxiliary Bishops; Mgr Séamus O'Boyle; Mgr Martin Hayes; Lord Brennan; Miss Leslie Ferrar; Mrs Ruth Kelly; Mr Christopher Kembell; and Mr Andrew Ndoca. **Secretary** Mr Paolo Camoletto.

FINANCE BOARD (with responsibilities delegated from the Trustees)
Chair Bishop John Sherrington; Bishop Nicholas Hudson; Bishop Paul McAleenan; Bishop John Wilson; Mgr Martin Hayes; Mr John Gibney; Mr Andrew Ndoca. **In attendance** Mr Paolo Camoletto; Mrs Marta Luiz.

METROPOLITAN CATHEDRAL CHAPTER (est. 19 June 1852)
(Canons 377, 463, 503-10, CIC)
The Chapter assembles at Archbishop's House for a meeting once a month, generally on the first Tuesday, after which Vespers and Capitular Mass are celebrated in the Cathedral for the intentions of the Diocese.

Provost Canon Michael Brockie; **Secretary** Canon Patrick Browne; **Treasurer** Canon Colin Davies; **Theologian** Canon John O'Leary; **Penitentiary** Canon Anthony Dwyer; **M.C.** Canon Daniel Cronin; Canon Michael Munnelly; Mgr Canon Paul McGinn; Canon Robert Plourde; Canon Stuart Wilson; Canon Christopher Tuckwell; Canon Paschal Ryan; Canon Peter Newby; Canon Shaun Lennard; Canon Terence Phipps; Canon Roger Taylor; Canon Alexander Sherbrooke; Canon Gerard King.

Provost Emeritus Mgr Canon Frederick Miles; **Canons Emeriti** Canon Richard Marriott; Canon Philip Cross; Canon Bernard Scholes; Canon Edward Matthews; Canon Vincent Berry; Mgr Canon Henry Turner; Mgr Canon Thomas Egan.

SECTION 2

CONSULTATIVE BODIES

COLLEGE OF CONSULTORS (Canon 502, CIC)
Functions are entrusted to the Cathedral Chapter.

COUNCIL OF DEANS
Chair The Cardinal Archbishop; Auxiliary Bishops; Vicar General; Deans; Chair of Council of Priests; Private Secretary

COUNCIL OF PRIESTS (Canons 495-501, CIC)
President The Cardinal Archbishop
Chair Mgr James Curry **Secretary** Fr Daniel Humphreys

HISTORIC CHURCHES COMMITTEE
Particular Pastoral Responsibility Bishop John Wilson

Under the Ecclesiastical Exemption provision of the Town and Country Planning Act, listed churches are exempt from the requirement to obtain from their local authority Listed Building Consent for works of repair and refurbishment, providing they obtain approval from the local Historic Churches Committee. These regulations have been confirmed by the Bishops' Conference of England and Wales in its 1999 'Directory on the Ecclesiastical Exemption from Listed Building Control'.

Chair Fr Peter Harris **St Joseph's, 3 Windhill, Bishop's Stortford CM23 2ND Tel: 01279 654063**
Secretary Chris Fanning **Historic Churches Committee, c/o Property Services Office, St Joseph's Grove NW4 4TY Tel: 020 8457 6540 / 07885 768889**
Administrative Secretary Lesley McNealis **Tel: 020 8457 6532**
Committee Members
Fr Peter Harris (Chair), Mgr James Curry (Vice-Chair), Fr Andrew Cameron-Mowat SJ, Paolo Camoletto, Andrew Derrick, Clive Horscroft, Bruce Kirk, Paul Moynihan, Canon Peter Newby, Mark Price, Paul Velluet, Bishop John Wilson; Chris Fanning (Secretary), Lesley McNealis (Administrative Secretary)

LITURGY COMMISSION
Particular Pastoral Responsibility Bishop John Wilson

The Commission is charged by the Cardinal Archbishop to assist him in promoting liturgical renewal and on-going liturgical formation in the Diocese. It is to establish policy for the ordering of churches and to approve such. It also has oversight of principal diocesan liturgies.
Chair Fr Allen Morris **Email: allenmorris@rcdow.org.uk Web: www.rcdow.org.uk/liturgy**
Chair of Art and Architecture Committee Canon Peter Newby **Tel: 020 8892 3902**

MASTER OF CEREMONIES for the Cardinal Archbishop Paul Moynihan

MASTERS OF CEREMONIES for the Diocese Fr Agustin Conesa; Fr Michael Dunne; Fr James Neal; Fr David Reilly; Fr Antonio Ritaccio; Fr Gerard Skinner; Fr Mark Vickers; Fr Sławomir Witoń; Rev Gordon Nunn (Deacon)

AGENCY FOR EVANGELISATION

Particular Pastoral Responsibility Bishop Nicholas Hudson

Working under the banner of 'Proclaim: Building Missionary Parishes', the Agency for Evangelisation provides assistance to parish communities in developing local evangelising initiatives and programmes of Adult Faith Formation, Sacramental Catechesis, the Rite of Christian Initiation of Adults (RCIA), Parish Religious Education for Children and support for Marriage and Family Life at all stages.

Director Fr Christopher Vipers **Tel: 020 7798 9157 Email: chrisvipers@rcdow.org.uk**
Vaughan House, 46 Francis Street SW1P 1QN
Administrative Assistant Warren Brown **General Enquiries Tel: 020 7798 9152**
Email: evangelisation@rcdow.org.uk Web: www.rcdow.org.uk/evangelisation

Evangelisation
Evangelisation Co-ordinator Rev Adrian Cullen
Tel: 020 7798 9150 Email: adriancullen@rcdow.org.uk

Catechesis
The Catechesis Support Team oversees the provision of formation, resources, training and the certification of parish catechists in all parishes of the diocese for Baptism preparation, First Confession, Holy Communion, Confirmation, RCIA, Parish-based Religious Education for Children, Children's Liturgy, and initial and ongoing training and formation of parish catechists.
Email: catadmin@rcdow.org.uk
Catechesis Advisers for Deaneries and Parishes
Mary Crowley **Tel: 020 7931 6090 Email: marycrowley@rcdow.org.uk**
Anna Dupelycz **Tel: 020 7798 9026 Email: annadupelycz@rcdow.org.uk**

Adult Faith Formation and Faith Sharing Resources
Adult Faith Formation Advisor Ausra Cane **Tel: 020 7931 6078**
Email: ausracane@rcdow.org.uk / smallgroups@rcdow.org.uk

Marriage and Family Life
The team provides support for marriage preparation, marriage enrichment and for seriously-troubled marriages. Working alongside existing groups, we promote a renewed culture of the Gospel of Life within parishes, schools and the wider community. We develop resources and arrange for speakers on pastoral care of the family, including up-to-date comment on and access to research and authoritative teaching in bio- and medical ethics. Support is offered for the catechesis of parents and for instilling greater confidence in them as the primary educators within the home – the domestic church.
Co-ordinator Rev Roger Carr-Jones **Tel: 020 7798 9363**
Email: rogercarrjones@rcdow.org.uk
Administrative Assistant Charlotte McNerlin **Tel: 020 7931 6064**
Email: charlottemcnerlin@rcdow.org.uk / family@rcdow.org.uk

SECTION 2

Marriage Enrichment Weekend Programme
Web: www.loving4life.co.uk

ARCHIVES

Particular Pastoral Responsibility Bishop John Sherrington

Archivist Fr Nicholas Schofield (Uxbridge)
Administrative Archivist Susannah Rayner
Archives Assistant Judi McGinley
16a Abingdon Road W8 6AF
Tel: 020 7938 3580 Email: archivist@rcdow.org.uk
Open by appointment (Mon, Tue, 10-12.30pm, 1.30-5pm)

CARITAS WESTMINSTER

Particular Pastoral Responsibility Bishop Paul McAleenan

ADVISORY COMMITTEE

Chair Bishop Paul McAleenan; Daniel Belloso; Paolo Camoletto; Siobhan Garibaldi; Mick McAteer; Sarah Macken; Andrew Ndoca; Fr Mark Woodruff.

Caritas Westminster is the diocesan social action and engagement agency. We seek to bring about a society where everyone lives a life of dignity and worth by enabling Catholic communities to identify and respond to all forms of poverty and social exclusion. We run three of our own projects for some of the most marginalised people in our society, and offer grants for individuals in crisis and for social action projects in the Diocese of Westminster.

Vaughan House, 46 Francis Street SW1P 1QN Tel: 020 7931 6077
Email: caritaswestminster@rcdow.org.uk Web: www.caritaswestminster.org.uk

Director	John Coleby	Tel: 020 7798 9357
Assistant Director	Jackie Tominey	Tel: 020 7931 6077
Communications Assistant	Martha Behan	Tel: 020 7798 9030
Volunteer Co-ordinator	Awaiting appointment	Tel: 020 7931 6077
Development Worker	Silvana Dallanegra	Tel: 07921 471506
Development Worker	Sue Day	Tel: 07525 812513
Development Worker	Anna Gavurin	Tel: 07801 572434
Development Worker	Finola Ryan	Tel: 07525 812518
Development Worker	Elizabeth Wills	Tel: 07877 902313
Social Enterprise Manager	Elena Bologna	Tel: 07803 410815

THE ST JOHN SOUTHWORTH CARITAS FUND

Through the Fund, Caritas Westminster provides grants to individuals in crisis and to social action projects in the Diocese.
Vaughan House, 46 Francis Street SW1P 1QN Tel: 020 7798 9063

Administrator Elke Springett
Email: caritasgrants@rcdow.org.uk **Web:** www.caritaswestminster.org.uk/grants

CARITAS DEAF SERVICE

Working with Deaf, Deafblind and Hard of Hearing people of all ages to enable them to participate fully in the life of the Church and share their gifts.

St Joseph's Pastoral Centre, St Joseph's Grove NW4 4TY Textphone: 020 732 8340
SMS: 07779 341 136 Fax: 020 8203 9745 Email: michelleroca@rcdow.org.uk
Web: www.caritaswestminster.org.uk/deafservice

Director	Shell (Michelle) Roca	**Tel: 020 8457 6536**
Assistant	Sarah Metcalfe	**Tel: 020 8457 6535**

Signs of Hope – Deaf Counselling Service

Offers counselling to Deaf and Hard of Hearing people and their relatives in sign language or English. Mini-loop system available.

Tel/SMS: 07534 570 429 Email: signsofhope@rcdow.org.uk

CARITAS ST JOSEPH'S

Supporting people with intellectual disabilities, their families and friends.

St Joseph's Pastoral Centre, St Joseph's Grove NW4 4TY
Email: enquiries@stjoseph.org.uk Web: www.stjoseph.org.uk

Centre Manager	Gail Williams	**Tel: 020 8202 3999**

CARITAS BAKHITA HOUSE

Accommodation and support for women escaping human trafficking and modern slavery.

Email: bakhitahouse@rcdow.org.uk
Web: www.caritaswestminster.org.uk/bakhitahouse

Service Manager	Karen Anstiss	**Tel: 020 7931 6045**

SEIDS Social Innovation and Enterprise Hub

The Hub is a social enterprise community centre offering a unique ecosystem of resources, ispiration and collaboration opportunities for those who have a credible enterprise idea.

Email: hello@seids.org.uk Web: www.seids.org.uk

SEIDS Hub Manager	Elena Bologna	**Tel: 020 3026 2502**

SEIDS Property Services

SEIDS Property Services provides high-quality painting and decorating, and general maintenance services at an affordable price across the diocese of Westminster.

Email: pawelszkolnik@rcdow.org.uk Web: seids.org.uk

Manager Pawel Szkolnik

SECTION 2

CHANCERY

Archbishop's House, Ambrosden Avenue SW1P 1QJ
For *Celebrets* please email: celebret@rcdow.org.uk

Chancellor Fr Jeremy Trood MA, JCL
Email: jeremytrood@rcdow.org.uk
Vice-Chancellor Brenda Roberts MA (Canon Law)
Tel: 020 7798 9037 Email: brendaroberts@rcdow.org.uk
Chancery Assistant Laura Dale BA(Hons), MTh
Tel: 020 7931 6042 Email: lauradale@rcdow.org.uk

CLERGY AND CONSECRATED LIFE

ALLEN HALL SEMINARY (Douai 1568; Old Hall Green 1793; Chelsea 1975)

Particular Pastoral Responsibility Bishop John Sherrington

28 Beaufort Street SW3 5AA Tel: 020 7349 5600 Fax: 020 7349 5601
PA to the Rector Mrs Helena Duckett Tel: 020 7349 5786
Email: allenhall@rcdow.org.uk Web: www. allenhall.org.uk

Formation Staff:

Rector (resident)	Canon Roger Taylor	Tel: 020 7349 5627
Vice-rector / Dean of Studies (resident)	Rev Dr Michael O'Boy	Tel: 020 7349 5608
Formation Advisor	Fr Lorenzo Andreini	Tel: 020 7724 8643
Formation Advisor (resident)	Rev Dr Michael Doyle	Tel: 020 7349 5610
Formation Advisor (resident)	Fr John Hemer MHM	Tel: 020 7349 5618
	Sr Bernadette Hunston SCSJA	Tel: 020 7349 5786
Pastoral Director / Formation Advisor (resident)	Fr William Nicol	Tel: 020 7349 5617
Spiritual Director (resident)	Canon Stuart Wilson	Tel: 020 7349 5620

See page 190 for a list of those currently training for priesthood in the Diocese of Westminster.

COMMITTEE FOR THE WELFARE OF SICK AND RETIRED PRIESTS

Particular Pastoral Responsibility Bishop Paul McAleenan

Chair Canon Gerard King
Healthcare Visitor Sr Clement Doran RGN, RMN Tel: 020 7798 9154 / 07817 143353

DECEASED CLERGY ASSOCIATION

Vaughan House, 46 Francis Street SW1P 1QN
Registrar Mgr John Conneely Tel: 020 7798 9003

EASTERN CATHOLIC CHURCHES

Episcopal Vicar Mgr John Conneely Tel: 020 7798 9003

SECTION 2

ETHNIC CHAPLAINCIES
Particular Pastoral Responsibility Bishop Paul McAleenan

Episcopal Vicar Fr David Irwin **Tel: 020 7935 4420 / 07786 769392 (Co-ordinator for Westminster, Brentwood and Southwark)**

ONGOING FORMATION OF CLERGY
Episcopal Vicar for Ongoing Formation of Clergy Canon Peter Newby
Ongoing Formation of Junior Clergy Fr Gerard Skinner

PASTORAL CARE FOR CHAPLAINCIES See relevant entries in Section 3 for details

PERMANENT DIACONATE
Particular Pastoral Responsibility Bishop Paul McAleenan

Vaughan House, 46 Francis Street SW1P 1QN Tel: 020 7798 9360
Director of Diaconate Programme
Rev Anthony Clark **Tel: 020 8455 9822 Email: anthonyclark@rcdow.org.uk**
Assistant Directors
Rev Adrian Cullen **Tel: 01920 462140 Email: adriancullen@rcdow.org.uk**
Rev Don Hopkins **Tel: 01707 855255 Email: donhopkins@rcdow.org.uk**

VICAR FOR RELIGIOUS
Episcopal Vicar Fr Tom O'Brien a.a. **16 Nightingale Road, Hitchin SG5 1QS**
Tel: 01462 459126 Email: vfr@rcdow.org.uk
Team members Sr Brigid Collins RSM, Sr Rachel Harrington SND, Sr Monica O'Brien SM, Sr Margaret Barrett DC

VOCATION TO PRIESTHOOD IN THE DIOCESE OF WESTMINSTER
See page 38 below for full information and contact details.

COUNCIL OF CENSORSHIP

Secretary Fr Terry Tastard **St Mary's Church House, 279 High Road N2 8HG**
Tel: 020 8883 4234 Email: terrytastard@rcdow.org.uk
For applications and information concerning the *Nihil obstat* and *Imprimatur.*
Please allow two months for examination of proofs.

DIOCESAN CURIA

Moderator of the Curia Bishop John Sherrington
Chief Operating Officer Paolo Camoletto

Based in ARCHBISHOP'S HOUSE
Ambrosden Avenue SW1P 1QJ Tel: 020 7798 9033

PRINT ROOM
Email: printroom@rcdow.org.uk

Manager	David Darby	**Tel: 020 7798 9380**
Assistant	Rudy Rodrigues (Tue-Thu)	**Tel: 020 7798 9380**

Based in VAUGHAN HOUSE
46 Francis Street SW1P 1QN Tel: 020 7798 9009
Receptionists Warren Brown (am) Ronita Fernandes (pm)

COMMUNICATIONS

Communications Officer	Marie Saba	Tel: 020 7798 9031
Communications Assistant	Sharon Pinto	Tel: 020 7798 9178
Communications Assistant	Martha Behan	Tel: 020 7798 9030
Diocesan Website		Tel: 020 7798 9031

Email: communications@rcdow.org.uk
Westminster Information (published in the middle of each month)

Editor	Fr Jeremy Trood	

Westminster Record (Diocesan newspaper, published monthly every first Sunday)

Editor	Mgr Mark Langham	
Advertising in the Record	Andrea Black / David Whitehead	Tel: 0161 908 5301

Email: andrea.black@thecatholicuniverse.com, david.whitehead@thecatholicuniverse.com

Distribution queries	Michelle Jones	Tel: 0161 908 5330

Email: michelle.jones@thecatholicuniverse.com

Westminster Year Book	Fr John Scott	Tel: 020 7798 9370

Email: wyb@rcdow.org.uk

DATA PROTECTION OFFICER	Mathew D'Souza	Tel: 020 7798 9099

FINANCIAL SECRETARY and CHIEF OPERATING OFFICER	Paolo Camoletto	Tel: 020 7798 9036
Executive Assistant	Anna Duncan	Tel: 020 7798 9160

FINANCE

Finance Director	Marta Luiz	Tel: 020 7798 9174
PA	Mary Ann D'Cruz	Tel: 020 7798 9170
Financial Controller	Ksenija Glover	Tel: 020 7931 6096
Financial Accounting Manager	Gisele Mantsounga	Tel: 020 7798 9161
Accounts Assistant	Eimear Keegan	Tel: 020 7798 9163
Accounts Assistant	Anita Lobo	Tel: 020 7798 9171
Accounts Assistant	Ross Miller	Tel: 020 7798 9388
Accounts Assistant	Kanchan Merai	Tel: 020 7798 9089
Management and Reporting Manager	Agnes Dabrowska	Tel: 020 7798 9360
Management and Reporting Accountant	Santhi Kurup	Tel: 020 7931 6006
(covering maternity leave for	Abiola Seweje)	
Management and Reporting Accountant	Gabriela Szkolnik	Tel: 020 7798 9169
Parish Finance Officer	Margaret Brady	Tel: 020 7798 9197
School Projects Supervisor	Marisa Borgerth	Tel: 020 7798 9176

SECTION 2

School Projects Assistant	Loan Tran	Tel: 020 7798 9016

FUNDRAISING AND STEWARDSHIP

Director of Development	Matt Parkes	Tel: 020 7798 9375
Development Manager	Awaiting appointment	Tel: 020 7798 9353
Fundraising Officer (Parishes)	João Tavares	Tel: 020 7798 9159
Supporter Care Manager	Eszter Croitor-Tifan	Tel: 020 7798 9025 / 020 7798 9099
Senior Supporter Care Officer	Francisca Yawson	Tel: 020 7798 9351
Supporter Care Officer	Maria Da Silva	Tel: 020 7798 9088

HUMAN RESOURCES

Director of Human Resources	Ann Hayward	Tel: 020 7798 9166
Senior Human Resources Adviser	Julie Dauncey	Tel: 020 7798 9167
Payroll Officer	Charmaine Daley	Tel: 020 7798 9172
Pensions Administrator	Anthony Williams	Tel: 020 7798 9162
Administrative Assistant	Madelayne Lang	Tel: 020 7798 9158

INFORMATION & COMMUNICATION TECHNOLOGY

Manager	Rod de Silva	Tel: 020 7798 9165
Systems Administrator	Daniel Prasanna	Tel: 020 7798 9050
ICT Support / Help Desk	Andrew Baptista	Tel: 020 7798 9164

PARISH SUPPORT TEAM - Parish Finance and Gift Aid Support, Internal Auditors

Team Manager Marie Ryan Tel: 07889 537138 Email: marieryan@rcdow.org.uk
Harrow Deanery

Alison Gartlan Tel: 07736 293640 Email: alisongartlan@rcdow.org.uk
Brent, Hillingdon and Hounslow Deaneries; School Gift Aid Auditor

Dagmara Jakubowska Tel: 07736 272832 Email: dagmaraj@rcdow.org.uk
Barnet, Chaplaincies, Hackney, Haringey and Tower Hamlets Deaneries

Pascal Kwo Tel: 07808 362937 Email: pascalkwo@rcdow.org.uk
Lea Valley and St Albans Deaneries; School Gift Aid Auditor

Beverley Meakes Tel: 07736 272830 Email: beverleymeakes@rcdow.org.uk
Enfield, Islington, Stevenage and Watford Deaneries

Richard Robinson Tel: 07790 472716 Email: richardrobinson@rcdow.org.uk
Hammersmith & Fulham, Kensington & Chelsea and Upper Thames Deaneries

Elizabeth Wills Tel: 07877 902313 Email: elizabethwills@rcdow.org.uk
Marylebone, North Kensington and Westminster Deaneries

Margaret Wilson Tel: 07395 793676 Email: margaretwilson@rcdow.org.uk
Camden and Ealing Deaneries

SCHOOL BUILDING FUNDRAISING

Manager	John Lee	Tel: 020 7798 9168

Based in ST JOSEPH'S, HENDON
St Joseph's Centre, St Joseph's Grove NW4 4TY

PROPERTY

Director	Clive Horscroft	Tel: 020 8457 6538
Estates Surveyor	Carol Haigh	Tel: 020 8457 6534
Estates Building Surveyor	James Keegan	Tel: 020 8457 6542
Estates Building Surveyor	Awaiting appointment	Tel: 020 8457 6542
Technical Administrator	Anthony Williams	Tel: 020 8457 6541

Senior Parish Buildings Surveyor and
Secretary, Historic Churches Committee

	Chris Fanning	Tel: 020 8457 6540 / 07885 768889
Secretary / PA to Chris Fanning	Roz Freedland	Tel: 020 8457 6593
Property Secretary / HCC Admin / Property Archives	Lesley McNealis	Tel: 020 8457 6532

ECUMENISM

Particular Pastoral Responsibility Bishop John Wilson

Ecumenical activity in the Diocese is very much rooted at the local level, with numerous clergy and laity involved in a variety of ecumenical bodies and projects that are too many to list here. In addition to this local ecumenical engagement:

Cardinal Vincent Nichols attends London Church Leaders;

Bishop John Sherrington (North London), **Bishop Nicholas Hudson** (Central and East London) and **Bishop Paul McAleenan** (Hertfordshire) all support the Church leaders' groups in their areas.

Mgr Harry Turner is Ecumenical Chaplain at St. Albans Abbey.

EDUCATION AND FORMATION

Particular Pastoral Responsibility Bishop John Wilson

THE DIOCESAN EDUCATION COMMISSION

is appointed by the Cardinal Archbishop as a decision-making body which acts in his name. It is responsible to him in all areas relating to education in schools and colleges set out in Canon law and English law. It is responsible to the Diocesan Trustees for the financial aspects of providing and maintaining Catholic education in the Diocese. Through its Chair, the Education Commission liaises with the Cardinal Archbishop, his Auxiliary Bishops and the Diocesan Trustees. It liaises with schools and colleges mainly through the Director of Education and the staff of the Education Service.

Members of the Commission
Chair Bishop John Wilson, Mr John Asgian, Mrs Lisa Barton, Mr Edward Conway, Fr Michael Dunne, Mrs Kate Griffin, Mrs Juliette Jackson, Mrs Pamela Singh OBE
In attendance Director of Education, Chief Operating Officer **Secretary** Linette Blackmore

THE EDUCATION SERVICE

works to the Diocesan Education Commission in providing professional support for Catholic Schools and Colleges, Head Teachers, Principals and Governing Bodies.

Vaughan House, 46 Francis Street SW1P 1QN
Tel: 020 7798 9005 Fax: 020 7798 9013
Email: education@rcdow.org.uk Web: https://education.rcdow.org.uk

Director of Education (Diocesan Schools Commissioner)	John Paul Morrison	Tel: 020 7798 9005
Deputy Director of Education	Amanda Crowley	Tel: 020 7798 9005
Chief Inspector	Jane Goring	Tel: 020 7798 9005
Assistant Director (Strategic Operations)	Mike Pittendreigh	Tel: 020 7798 9005
Assistant Director (Capital Strategy and Pupil Placement)	Nigel Spears	Tel: 020 7798 9005
Education Officer (Legal & Policy)	Mary Ryan	Tel: 020 7798 9005

Advisers for Catholic Education (Primary)

Elaine Arundell	Tel: 020 7798 9005
Grace Anderson	Tel: 020 7798 9005
Tony Gorton (from January 2019)	Tel: 020 7798 9005
Theresa O'Sullivan	Tel: 020 7798 9005
Diana Roberts	Tel: 020 7798 9005

Advisers for Catholic Education (Secondary)

Trisha Hedley	Tel: 020 7798 9005
Claire O'Neill	Tel: 020 7798 9005

Office Manager & PA to the Director	Linette Blackmore	Tel: 020 7798 9193
Governance Co-ordinator	Greeny Longville-Ancel	Tel: 020 7798 9187
Office Administrator	Carol Campbell	Tel: 020 7798 9005
Events & Marketing Co-ordinator	Francis Leeder	Tel: 020 7798 9189

Co-ordinator of School Chaplains
Fr David Reilly — Tel: 020 7798 9005

INTERFAITH

Particular Pastoral Responsibility Bishop John Wilson

Vaughan House, 46 Francis Street SW1P 1QN Tel: 020 7931 6028
Email: westminsterinterfaith@rcdow.org.uk

Director Rev Jon Dal Din
Tel: 07889 536957 / 07527 758729 Email: jondaldin@rcdow.org.uk
Co-ordinator for North London Sr Elizabeth O'Donohoe HC
Tel: 020 7272 8048 Email: eodonohoe@btinternet.com

JUSTICE AND PEACE

Particular Pastoral Responsibility Bishop Nicholas Hudson

JUSTICE & PEACE COMMISSION

The Commission exists to promote action and reflection on peace and social justice in parishes, in the light of the Gospel and Catholic Social Teaching.

4 Vincent Road N15 3QH Tel: 020 8888 4222 Fax: 020 8888 4333
Email: justiceandpeace@rcdow.org.uk Web: www.rcdow.org.uk/justiceandpeace
Chair Fr Joe Ryan
Co-ordinator Awaiting appointment
Youth Worker Awaiting appointment
Commission Members Maggie Beirne, Lauri Clarke, Santana Luis, Fr Tom O'Brien AA, Sr Elizabeth O'Donohoe HC, Tony Sheen, Edmund Tierney, Dr David Toorawa.
Parish Contacts for details of parish Justice and Peace contacts, see page 165

METROPOLITAN TRIBUNAL

Vaughan House, 46 Francis Street SW1P 1QN Tel: 020 7798 9003

Judicial Vicar Mgr John Conneely JCL
Assistant Judicial Vicar Canon Michael Brockie JCL
Canonical Assistant Alicia Sloan JCL
Judges Canon Vincent Berry, Sr Rachel Harrington SND JCD, Fr Gerard Quinn STL, Alicia Sloan JCL, Fr Jeremy Trood JCL,
Defenders of the Bond Fr Dominic Byrne JCD, Sr Isabel MacPherson SND JCD, Paul Robbins JCL
Advocates Fr Noel Barber SJ, Francesca Knox
Tribunal Assistant Matthew Gillespie
Auditors Mr Nathan Paine-Davey, Mrs Margaret Dixon, Mrs Jo O'Neill, Fr Dennis F P Touw Tempelmans-Plat

PILGRIMAGES

HOLY LAND

Director Fr Paul McDermott
186 St John's Road, Boxmoor HP1 1NR Tel: 01442 391759

LOURDES

Director Fr Dennis F P Touw Tempelmans-Plat
60 Rylston Road SW6 7HW Tel: 020 7835 4040

SECTION 2

For volunteer helpers aged 16+ interested in the diocesan pilgrimage to Lourdes **contact** Katrina Lavery, Youth Director **Tel: 07921 409402**

WALSINGHAM
DIRECTOR Fr John McKenna
82 Union Street, Barnet EN5 4HZ Tel: 020 8449 3338

Pilgrimage Co-ordinator Elizabeth Uwalaka **Vaughan House, 46 Francis Street SW1P 1QN Tel: 020 7798 9173 Email: elizabethuwalaka@rcdow.org.uk**

SAFEGUARDING SERVICE

Vaughan House, 46 Francis Street SW1P 1QN Email: safeguarding@rcdow.org.uk

Episcopal Vicar for Safeguarding Mgr Séamus O'Boyle
Tel: 020 7226 3277 Email: seamusoboyle@rcdow.org.uk
Safeguarding Co-ordinator Eva Edohen
Tel: 020 7798 9350 Email: evaedohen@rcdow.org.uk
PA, Team Administrator and Commission Secretary Gabriele Sedda
Tel: 020 7798 9356 Email: gabrielesedda@rcdow.org.uk
Safeguarding Officer Natalie Creswick
Tel: 020 7798 9359 Email: nataliecreswick@rcdow.org.uk
Safeguarding Support Officer Arianna Sommariva
Tel: 0207 798 9358 Email: ariannasommariva@rcdow.org.uk
DBS Administrator Jackie Krobo
Tel: 020 7798 9352 Email: jackiekrobo@rcdow.org.uk

Westminster Safeguarding Commission Chair Peter Houghton
Email: peterhoughton@rcdow.org.uk

VOCATION TO PRIESTHOOD IN THE DIOCESE OF WESTMINSTER

Particular Pastoral Responsibility Bishop John Sherrington

PRIESTS' TRAINING FUND (PTF)
Chair Bishop John Sherrington
The Fund **(Registration No 312528)** supports the work of vocations to the priesthood, formation of priests and on-going clergy formation.

VOCATIONS PROMOTER
Canon Stuart Wilson **Allen Hall, 28 Beaufort Street SW3 5AA**
Tel: 020 7349 5620 / 07515 065696 Email: vocationspromoter@rcdow.org.uk

ASSISTANT VOCATIONS PROMOTER
Fr Michael Maguire **247 High Road W4 4PU Tel: 020 8994 2877**
Email: vocations@rcdow.org.uk
All initial enquiries about the call to priesthood should be made to Canon Stuart or Fr Michael.

VOCATIONS DIRECTOR

Canon John O'Leary The Presbytery, St Mellitus Church, Tollington Park N4 3AG
Tel: 020 7272 3415 Email: vocationsdirector@rcdow.org.uk

The Vocations Director is responsible for helping men prepare for selection and placement in Seminary.

Email: vocations@rcdow.org.uk Web: www.rcdow.org.uk/vocations
Twitter: @westminsterVoca Facebook: westminsterVocations

WESTMINSTER YOUTH MINISTRY

Particular Pastoral Responsibility Bishop Nicholas Hudson

Director of Youth Ministry
Andrzej Wdowiak Tel: 020 3757 2502 Email: andrzejwdowiak@rcdow.org.uk
Diocesan Youth Chaplain
Fr Mark Walker Tel: 020 3757 2519 Email: markwalker@rcdow.org.uk
Communications and Events
James Kelliher Tel: 020 3757 2517 Email: jameskelliher@rcdow.org.uk

1. Centre for Youth Ministry, 125 Waxwell Lane, Pinner HA5 3EP
Tel: 020 3757 2516 Email: youth@rcdow.org.uk Web: http://dowym.com

Manager
Rebekah Curran Tel: 020 3757 2516 Email: rebekahcurran@rcdow.org.uk
Youth Support Team
Dominic Cunliffe Tel: 020 3757 2517 Email: dominiccunliffe@rcdow.org.uk
Awaiting appointment Tel: 020 3757 2516 Email:

2. SPEC, Waxwell House, 125 Waxwell Lane, Pinner HA5 3EP
Tel: 020 3757 2500 Email: spec@rcdow.org.uk Web: http://dowym.com/spec
SPEC is the diocesan day and residential retreat centre for young people in our parishes and schools.

Manager
Awaiting appointment Tel: 020 3757 2502 Email:
Retreats and Formation Manager
JJ Hussem Tel: 020 3757 2503 Email: jjhussem@rcdow.org.uk
Administration and Operations Manager
Sara Rhodes Tel: 020 3757 2500 Email: sararhodes@rcdow.org.uk
Enquiries and Bookings Tel: 020 3757 2500 Email: spec@rcdow.org.uk

CATHOLIC CHILDRENS SOCIETY (CRUSADE OF RESCUE, FOUNDED 1859)

73 St Charles Square W10 6EJ Tel:020 8969 5305 Fax: 020 8960 1464
Email: info@cathchild.org.uk Web: www.cathchild.org.uk
Chief Executive Officer Rosemary Keenan BA, DSA, DASS, CQSW, MA, PhD

The Catholic Children's Society (CCS) works across the diocese to support disadvantaged children and families. Services include:

SCHOOL COUNSELLING & THERAPY

CCS's ConnectEd counselling and therapy service supports the mental health and emotional wellbeing of thousands of children each year. Qualified and experienced counsellors/therapists work on-site in over 70 primary, secondary and special schools.
Contact Greg Brister **Head of Service Development & Communications**
Email: gregb@cathchild.org.uk

MENTAL HEALTH TRAINING

Expert training delivered to school staff, clergy and other members of the children's workforce, helping enhance their skills to identify and support children experiencing mental health issues. Examples of topics covered include: mental health awareness and promoting positive mental health; introduction to attachment theory; working with challenging and hard-to-reach children. Bespoke training is also available.
Contact Jo Trickett **Mental Health Trainer Email: joannet@cathchild.org.uk**

RAINBOWS BEREAVEMENT SUPPORT PROGRAMME

Training for school staff so they can deliver support groups for pupils who have experienced separation, bereavement and loss.
Contact Katrina Avery **Rainbows Registered Director Email: katrinaa@cathchild.org.uk**

CRISIS FUND

A special fund providing emergency financial assistance for families in immediate need. Applications can be made by Headteachers and Parish Priests.
Contact Duty Manager **Email: reception@cathchild.org.uk**

GRENFELL CRISIS FUND

A fund to deliver material and therapeutic help to all those affected by the Grenfell Tower fire. Applications can be made by Headteachers and Parish Priests.
Contact Duty Manager **Email: reception@cathchild.org.uk**

FAMILY CENTRE BASED SERVICES

Qualified Early Years staff operate in two centres to help disadvantaged families. Services include an Ofsted-rated 'Outstanding' nursery, drop-in, after school groups, holiday play-schemes and trips, a toy library, welfare advice and information.

St Francis Family Centre 34 Wades Place E14 0DE
Contact Margaret Wilkinson **Centre Co-ordinator**
Tel: 020 7987 8257 Email: margaretw@cathchild.org.uk

St Mark's Stay & Play, St Mark's Road W10 6BZ
Contact Sandra Mullings **Drop-in Worker Tel: 020 8960 2970 (Noon – 4pm)**

POST ADOPTION & AFTERCARE
Although no longer an adoption agency, we offer support, counselling and advice to former adoptees, their adopters and birth families. We also provide information to those formerly in our care.
Contact Irena Lyczkowska **Post-Adoption Manager Email: irenal@cathchild.org.uk**

OTHER RESOURCES

MINISTRY TO ALIENATED CATHOLICS

The purpose of the apostolate is to be a practical sign that the Church is reaching out to alienated Catholics and to allow them to voice any hurt or grievance.
Fr Francis Wahle **Tel: 020 7487 5956 Email: francis@wahle.plus.com**

PARLIAMENTARY ROMAN CATHOLIC DUTY PRIEST

Canon Pat Browne is, by kind permission of the Speaker, available for the celebration of the Sacraments and pastoral care of Peers, MPs and Staff of the Palace of Westminster.
Holy Apostles Church, 47 Cumberland Street SW1V 4LY
Tel: 07988 441691 Email: patbrowne@rcdow.org.uk

CARDINAL HUME CENTRE

The Centre welcomes homeless young people, and individuals and families in need from all backgrounds. Our specialist teams help individuals and families access the support, and gain the skills they need, to overcome poverty and the threat of homelessness. We run a range of specialist services on-site: advice and assessment; family and young people's services; housing and welfare rights advice and advocacy; learning and employment services; immigration advice and representation; and residential services for homeless young people. There is also a GP surgery on site and a charity shop in Horseferry Road. The Centre is supported by regular volunteers who work in different roles across the Centre and play an integral part in all that we do. Volunteer opportunities include teaching English, digital inclusion support, working in the charity shop and supportive roles in various clubs for families and children. Vacancies and role descriptions are listed on the website.

Chair of Trustees Robert Arnott **Chief Executive** George O'Neill **Community Fundraiser** Stephen Currid **Volunteer Co-ordinators** Flora Swartland / Emily Hynes
Partnership Manager Hilary Nightingale **Surgery:** Sr Dr Mary Hickey MBE
3-7 Arneway Street SW1P 2BG Tel: 020 7222 1602
Email: info@cardinalhumecentre.org.uk Web: www.cardinalhumecentre.org.uk

PROVIDENCE ROW

For homeless or vulnerably housed people, finding employment and housing opportunities can feel like an uphill battle, even more so if affected by health, mental health or substance misuse issues. Providence Row works with more than 1,600 people a year in East London, offering an integrated service of crisis support, advice, recovery and learning and training programmes. It helps those who are so often excluded from mainstream services gain the support and opportunities they need to help create a safer, healthier life off the streets.

Chief Executive Tom O'Connor **The Dellow Centre, 82 Wentworth Street E1 7SA**
Tel: 020 7375 0020 Email: info@providencerow.org.uk
Web: www.providencerow.org.uk

THE PASSAGE

Our mission is to provide resources which encourage, inspire and challenge homeless people to transform their lives. We undertake street outreach work in Westminster, including the area around Westminster Cathedral and Victoria stations, which has the highest incidence of people sleeping outside in the UK. The Resource Centre provides food, showers, laundry and clothing store facilities, as well as addressing health, education, employment, housing and welfare rights issues. The hostels help give people additional support when they first move from the streets, including some of the longest-term rough sleepers. The Passage's Home for Good project enables volunteers to support former rough sleepers across London. In summary, the Passage helps people to stop living on the streets and supports them as they move into places of their own, and helps many to return to employment.

Chief Executive Mick Clarke **St Vincent's, Carlisle Place SW1P 1NL**
Tel: 020 7592 1850 Fax: 020 7592 1870 Email: info@passage.org.uk
Web: www.passage.org.uk

Section 3

DEANERIES

The name of the Auxiliary Bishop or Episcopal Vicar with particular pastoral responsibility is given in brackets.

1. BARNET (Bishop John Sherrington)
Barnet, Burnt Oak, Cricklewood, Edgware, Finchley Church End, Finchley East, Finchley North, Golders Green, Grahame Park, Hendon, Hendon West, Mill Hill, New Barnet, Whetstone
Dean Fr John McKenna (Barnet) Tel: 020 8449 3338

2. BRENT (Bishop John Sherrington)
Dollis Hill, Kensal Rise, Kingsbury Green, Neasden, Stonebridge, Wembley 1, Wembley 2, Wembley 3, Willesden, Willesden Green
Dean Fr Stephen Willis (Willesden) Tel: 020 8965 4935

3. CAMDEN (Bishop Nicholas Hudson)
Camden Town, Hampstead, Haverstock Hill, Kentish Town, Kilburn, Kilburn West, Lebanese Church, Somers Town, Swiss Cottage
Dean Fr Thomas Skeats OP (Haverstock Hill) Tel: 020 7482 9224

4. EALING (Bishop John Wilson)
Acton, Acton East, Acton West, Ealing, Greenford, Hanwell, Northfields, Perivale, Polish Church 3, Southall
Dean Fr Jim Duffy (Northfields) Tel: 020 8567 5421

5. ENFIELD (Bishop John Sherrington)
Cockfosters, Cuffley, Edmonton, Enfield, New Southgate, Palmers Green, Ponders End, Potters Bar
Dean Fr Sławomir Witoń (Enfield) Tel: 020 8363 2569

6. HACKNEY (Bishop Nicholas Hudson)
Clapton, Clapton Park, Hackney, Homerton, Hoxton, Kingsland, Manor House, Stoke Newington
Dean Fr David Evans (Hackney) Tel: 020 8985 2496

7. HAMMERSMITH & FULHAM (Bishop John Wilson)
Brook Green, Fulham1, Fulham 2, Hammersmith, Parsons Green, Polish Church 2, Shepherd's Bush, White City
Dean Fr Richard Andrew (Brook Green) Tel: 020 7603 3832

8. HARINGEY (Bishop John Sherrington)
Muswell Hill, Stamford Hill, Stroud Green, Tottenham, West Green, Wood Green
Dean Fr Sean Carroll (Stroud Green) Tel: 020 8340 3394

SECTION 3

9. HARROW (Bishop John Sherrington)
Harrow-on-the-Hill, Harrow North, Harrow South & Northolt, Headstone Lane, Kenton, Pinner, Stanmore, Sudbury, Wealdstone
Dean Canon Michael Munnelly (Stanmore) Tel: 020 8954 1299

10. HILLINGDON (Bishop John Wilson)
Eastcote, Harefield, Hayes, Hillingdon, Northwood, Ruislip, Ruislip South, Uxbridge, West Drayton, Yeading
Dean Fr Nicholas Schofield (Uxbridge) Tel: 01895 233193

11. HOUNSLOW (Bishop John Wilson)
Brentford, Chiswick, Cranford, Feltham, Grove Park, Gunnersbury, Heathrow Airport, Heston, Hounslow, Isleworth, Osterley
Dean Fr Gerard Quinn (Brentford) Tel: 020 8560 1671

12. ISLINGTON (Bishop Nicholas Hudson)
Archway, Bunhill Row, Clerkenwell, Copenhagen Street, Highbury, Highgate, Holloway, Islington, Polish Church 1, Tollington Park
Dean Mgr Seamus O'Boyle (Islington) Tel: 020 7226 3277

13. KENSINGTON AND CHELSEA (Bishop John Wilson)
Chelsea 1, Chelsea 2, Fulham Road, Kensington 1, Kensington 2, Oratory
Dean Fr Patrick Ryall OSM (Fulham Road) Tel: 020 7352 6965

14. LEA VALLEY (Bishop Paul McAleenan)
Bishop's Stortford, Buntingford, Cheshunt, Hertford, Hoddesdon, Old Hall Green & Puckeridge, Waltham Cross, Ware
Dean Fr Peter Harris (Bishop's Stortford) Tel: 01279 654063

15. MARYLEBONE (Bishop Nicholas Hudson)
Farm Street, Marylebone, Ogle Street, St John's Wood, Spanish Place, Ukrainian Cathedral, University Chaplaincy
Dean Fr Stephen Wang (University Chaplaincy) Tel: 020 7387 6370

16. NORTH KENSINGTON (Bishop John Wilson)
Bayswater, Harrow Road, Kensal New Town, Notting Hill, Paddington, Queensway, St Charles Square
Dean Fr Gerard Skinner (Notting Hill) Tel: 020 7727 7968

17. ST ALBANS (Bishop Paul McAleenan)
Berkhamsted, Borehamwood, Borehamwood North, Harpenden, Hemel Hempstead Boxmoor, Hemel Hempstead East, Hemel Hempstead North, Hemel Hempstead West, London Colney, Radlett, Redbourn, St Albans, St Albans South, Shenley, Tring, Wheathampstead
Dean Fr Dominic McKenna (Borehamwood Parishes) Tel: 020 8953 1294

18. STEVENAGE (Bishop Paul McAleenan)
Baldock, Hatfield, Hatfield South, Hitchin, Knebworth, Letchworth, Royston, Stevenage Bedwell, Stevenage Old Town, Stevenage Shephall, Welwyn Garden City, Welwyn Garden City Digswell and Welwyn Garden City East
Dean Fr Norbert Fernandes (Welwyn Garden City) Tel: 01707 323234

19. TOWER HAMLETS (Bishop Nicholas Hudson)
Bethnal Green, Bow, Bow Common, Commercial Road, German Church, Limehouse, Lithuanian Church, Mile End, Millwall, Poplar, Tower Hill, Underwood Road, Wapping
Dean Fr Keith Stoakes (Limehouse/Poplar) Tel: 020 7987 4523

20. UPPER THAMES (Bishop John Wilson)
Ashford, Hampton Hill, Hampton-on-Thames, St Margarets-on-Thames, Shepperton, Staines-upon-Thames, Stanwell, Sunbury-on-Thames, Teddington, Twickenham, Whitton
Dean Fr Philip Dyer-Perry (Staines-upon-Thames) Tel: 01784 452381

21. WATFORD (Bishop Paul McAleenan)
Abbots Langley, Bushey, Carpenders Park, Chipperfield, Chorleywood, Croxley Green, Garston, Mill End & Maple Cross, Rickmansworth, Watford, Watford North
Dean Awaiting appointment Tel:

22. WESTMINSTER (Bishop Nicholas Hudson)
(City) Ely Place, Italian Church, Lincoln's Inn Fields, Moorfields;
(West End) Cathedral, Covent Garden, French Church, Pimlico, Soho Square, Warwick Street
Dean Canon Alexander Sherbrooke (Soho Square) Tel: 020 7437 2010

23. ETHNIC CHAPLAINCIES (Fr David Irwin)
Dean Fr Petras Tverijonas (Lithuanian Church) Tel: 020 7739 8735

SECTION 3

PARISH MAP

The diocesan website features an interactive map-based search facility on which you can search for Catholic parishes and schools, and explore the geography of the Diocese on Google Maps.

Please visit
www.rcdow.org.uk/virtual

Parishes in the Diocese of Westminster

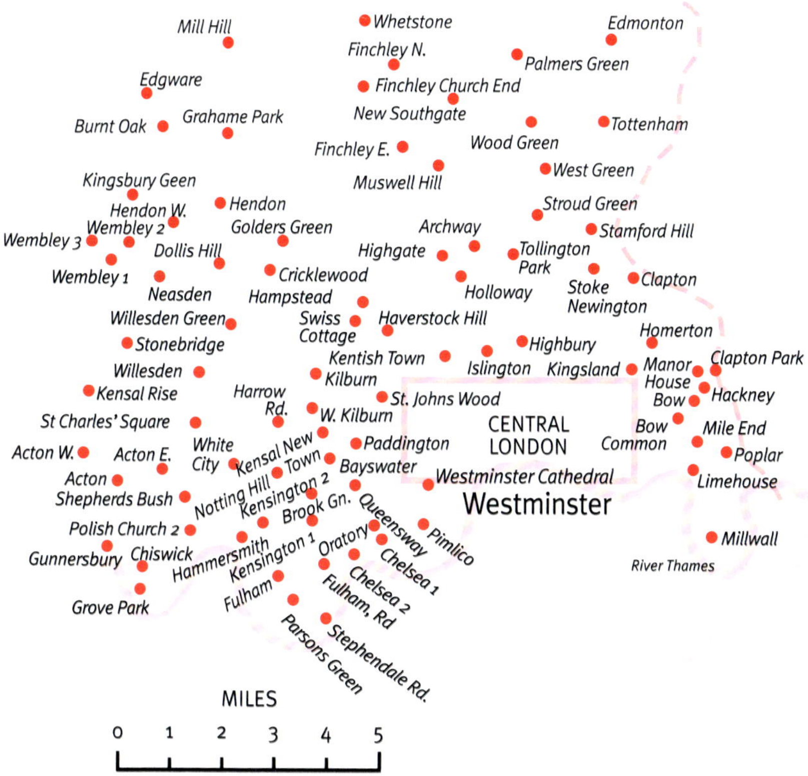
Mill Hill
Whetstone
Edmonton
Finchley N.
Palmers Green
Edgware
Finchley Church End
New Southgate
Burnt Oak
Grahame Park
Tottenham
Finchley E.
Wood Green
Muswell Hill
West Green
Kingsbury Geen
Hendon W.
Hendon
Stroud Green
Wembley 2
Golders Green
Archway
Stamford Hill
Wembley 3
Dollis Hill
Highgate
Tollington Park
Wembley 1
Cricklewood
Clapton
Neasden
Hampstead
Holloway
Stoke Newington
Willesden Green
Swiss Cottage
Haverstock Hill
Homerton
Stonebridge
Highbury
Kentish Town
Islington
Kingsland
Manor House
Clapton Park
Willesden
Kilburn
Bow
Hackney
Kensal Rise
Harrow Rd.
St. Johns Wood
St Charles' Square
W. Kilburn
CENTRAL LONDON
Bow Common
Mile End
Acton W.
Acton E.
White City
Kensal New Town
Paddington
Poplar
Acton
Bayswater
Westminster Cathedral
Limehouse
Shepherds Bush
Notting Hill
Kensington 2
Brook Gn.
Westminster
Queensway
Pimlico
Polish Church 2
Millwall
Gunnersbury
Chiswick
Hammersmith
Kensington 1
Oratory
Chelsea 1
River Thames
Chelsea 2
Fulham
Fulham, Rd
Grove Park
Parsons Green
Stephendale Rd.
MILES
0 1 2 3 4 5

Parishes in London

Camden Town
Copenhagen St.
Somers Town
Polish Ch. 1
Lithuanian Ch.
University Chaplaincy
Hoxton
Clerkenwell
Bunhill Row
Bethnal Grn.
Italian Ch.
Marylebone Rd.
Underwood Rd.
Spanish Pl.
Ogle St.
Ely Pl.
German Ch.
Soho Sq.
Lincoln's Inn Fields
Moorfields
Ukrainian Ch.
Commercial Rd.
French Ch.
Warwick St.
Tower Hill
River Thames
Covent Garden
Wapping
Farm St.

Parishes in Central London

SECTION 3

PARISH DIRECTORY

1. Within the Diocese the parishes are grouped in deaneries. The deaneries, with their component parishes, are listed on the preceding pages.

2. + Indicates a church registered for marriages.

3. Each parish entry gives the name of the parish, the title of the church, the postal address, telephone number, email address and website, the road in which it is situated, and its deanery reference (***in italic bold type***). Dates in parentheses refer to its founding, the building of the church and its consecration. London postal addresses indicate the name of the road and postcode. Hertfordshire and Middlesex addresses include the name of the nearest town. Details of all parishes can be found at **parish.rcdow.org.uk/parishname**.

4. The name highlighted in **red** is that of the Parish Priest. Priests are listed by name only; degrees etc. can be found in the alphabetical list of clergy in Section 4.

5. Diocesan email addresses are formed thus: **firstname+surname@rcdow.org.uk**.

6. The first Mass of Sunday celebrated on Saturday evening, or the first Mass of a Holy Day celebrated on the evening of the preceding day, is indicated thus:
   Sunday Mass (Sat 6pm), 8, 9, ... **Holy Day Mass** (Vigil 8pm), 10, 11 .....
   Different timetables will apply at Christmas, Easter and on Public Holidays; enquire at the church.

7. Times of services shown are a.m. (i.e. 11.15), unless specifically indicated as p.m. (i.e. 6pm).

8. For Ecumenical or Justice and Peace contacts, ring the parish office. A list of Justice and Peace contacts is also given at the end of this Section.

9. Parish details are followed by relevant mission institutions, houses of female and male religious, then other public institutions (e.g. hospitals). These are served by priests of the parish unless otherwise stated.

10. Facilities for physically disabled and/or hearing impaired people are indicated after the name of the church by the following symbols:
    A Access only (ramps, etc)
    ♿ Full facilities (access, plus disabled access lavatory)
    👂 Loop System for hearing-aid users
    S Mass celebrated regularly in Word and Sign, and/or Confession in Sign Language; enquire for details and times.

WESTMINSTER CATHEDRAL + METROPOLITAN CATHEDRAL OF THE MOST PRECIOUS BLOOD

Sunday Mass (6pm Sung) 8, 9, 10.30 (Choir), 12noon (Sung), 5.30pm (Sung), 7pm; **Holy Day Mass** (Vigil 5.30pm, Choir), 7, 8, 10.30 (Latin), 12.30pm, 1.05pm, 5.30pm (Choir); **Weekday Mass** Mon-Fri 7, 8, 10.30 (Latin), 12.30pm, 1.05pm, 5.30pm (Choir); **Saturday Mass** 8, 9, 10.30 (Latin, Choir), 12.30pm; **Public Holidays** Mass 10.30, 12.30pm, 5pm

Divine Office: Morning Prayer Sun 10, Mon-Fri 7.40, Sat 10; **Vespers** Sun 3.30pm with **Benediction** (Choir), Mon-Fri 5pm (Choir, except Tue), Sat 5.30pm; **Public Holidays** Morning Prayer 10; ***No Vespers***

Confession Sat 10.30-6.30pm, Sun 11-1pm, 4.30pm-7pm, Mon-Fri 11.30-6pm, **Public Holidays** 11-1pm

Opening times Mon-Fri 7-7pm; Sat 8-7pm, Sun 7-7.45pm; **Public Holidays** 8-5.30pm

Victoria Street SW1P 1LT; Clergy House is at 42 Francis Street SW1P 1QW
Clergy House Reception open Mon-Fri 8-7pm, Sat, Sun 10-1pm
Enquiries Tel: 020 7798 9055; Times of services Tel: 020 7798 9097
Email: chreception@rcdow.org.uk Web: www.westminstercathedral.org.uk
Victoria Station (BR/TfL)
Westminster Deanery (1903; cons 28 June 1910)

Administrator Canon Christopher Tuckwell Tel: 020 7798 9374
PA Elizabeth Arnot Tel: 020 7798 9062

Cathedral Chaplains:
Fr Daniel Humphreys (Sub-Administrator) Tel: 020 7798 9180
Fr Julio Albornoz Tel: 020 7931 6097
Fr Andrew Bowden Tel: 020 7798 9373
Fr Michael Donaghy Tel: 020 7798 9048
Fr Andrew Gallagher (Precentor) Tel: 020 7798 9098
Fr Rajiv Michael Tel: 020 7798 9055
Fr Michael Quaicoe Tel: 020 7798 9055
Fr John Scott (Registrar) Tel: 020 7931 6041

Sub-Administrator's Intern Oliver Delargy Tel: 020 7798 9179
Precentor's Assistant Lorcán Keller Tel: 020 7798 9058

Music Department:
Email: music@westminstercathedral.org.uk
Master of Music Martin Baker Tel: 020 7798 9066
Assistant Master of Music Peter Stevens Obl OSB Tel: 020 7931 6091
Organ Scholar Jonathan Allsopp Tel: 020 7798 9378
Music Administrator Madeline Smith (Mon, Wed-Fri) Tel: 020 7798 9057
Email: musicadmin@rcdow.org.uk

SECTION 3

Cathedral Choir School, Ambrosden Avenue SW1P 1QH Tel: 020 7798 9081
Head Neil McLaughlan **Chaplain** Fr Andrew Gallagher

Cathedral Manager Peter McNulty **Tel: 020 7798 9064**
Retail and Procurement Manager Ansuya Padhiar
Head of Security Alistair Calton **Tel: 020 7798 9014 / 07801 572433**
Works Manager Neil Fairbairn **Tel: 020 7798 9054**
Works Assistant Caroline Keogh **Tel: 020 7798 9053**

Franciscan Sisters of Our Lady of Victories, Cathedral Clergy House Tel: 020 7798 9067
Srs Francisca Belo, Maria Celeste da Silva Pontes, Joanina Do Rego, Angelina Moniz

Friends of Westminster Cathedral
Director Christina White **Tel: 020 7798 9059**

***Oremus*, the magazine of Westminster Cathedral Tel: 020 7798 9052**

Registry Tel: 020 7798 9376 Email: registrar@rcdow.org.uk

Sacred Heart Church, Horseferry Road SW1P 2EF (Parochial Chapel of Ease)
Enquiries Fr John Scott **Tel: 020 7931 6041**
Sunday Mass 11, 4pm (Croatian); **Weekday Mass** Thu 12.30pm

• **Daughters of Charity, St Vincent's, Carlisle Place SW1P 1NL**
Tel: 020 7834 4004 Fax: 020 7630 5467
Email: carlisleplace@btconnect.com Web: www.daughtersofcharity.org.uk
also **94a Horseferry Road SW1P 2EE Tel: 020 7222 6485**
Email: horseferryroaddc@gmail.com
Srs Louise Callen, Bernie Geary, Mary Mitchell, Irene Sweeney
• **Vincentian Care Plus** (Care of Elderly in Own Home) Srs Margaret Bannerton, Anne O'Mahony
• **Cardinal Hume Centre, 3-7 Arneway Street SW1P 2BG Tel: 020 7222 1602**
Web: www.cardinalhumecentre.org.uk
Director George O'Neill
• **The Passage, St Vincent's, Carlisle Place SW1P 1NL Tel: 020 7592 1850**
Web: www.passage.org.uk
Chief Executive Mick Clarke
• **The Gordon Hospital Tel: 020 8746 8733**
• **St Paul's Bookshop Managing Director** Fr Francy Kochupaliathil SSP
Morpeth Terrace SW1P 1EP Tel: 020 7828 5582 Fax: 020 7828 3329

ABBOTS LANGLEY + ST SAVIOUR

Sunday Mass (Sat 5pm), 8.30, 11.30; **Holy Day Mass** 10, 7pm; **Weekday Mass** Mon-Fri 10; **Exposition** *Ist Fri only* 10.30-12noon; **Holy Hour** and **Benediction** *Ist Sunday only* 4 pm, with **Confession** available; **Confession** Sat 4.15-4.45pm & on request

Salvatorians (SDS) Fr Richard Mway-Zeng, Fr Christopher Luoga (clergy also serve Chipperfield)
The Presbytery, 96 The Crescent, Abbots Langley, Watford WD5 0DS
Tel: 01923 266177 (Presbytery)
Email: abbotslangley@rcdow.org.uk Web: parish.rcdow.org.uk/abbotslangley
Watford Deanery (1928; 1963)

ACTON + OUR LADY OF LOURDES

Sunday Mass (Sat 7pm), 9, 10.30, 12noon, 6pm; **Holy Day Mass** 10, 7pm; **Weekday Mass** Mon-Sat 10, Fri 10, 7pm; **Confession** Sat 10.30, 6-7pm & on request

Congregation of the Sacred Hearts of Jesus and Mary (SS.CC) Fr Fergal Maguire (resident at 85 Old Oak Common Lane W3 7DD), Fr Fintan Crotty, Fr Ultan Naughton; Rev Tito Pereira (Deacon)
5 Berrymead Gardens W3 8AA Tel: 020 8992 2014
Email: acton@rcdow.org.uk Web: parish.rcdow.org.uk/acton
On High Street, between Town Hall and Horn Lane.
Ealing Deanery (1878; 1902; cons 17 May 1961)

• Medical Mission Sisters (Generalate) (SCMM), 41 Chatsworth Gardens W3 9LP
Tel: 020 8992 6444 Email: generalate@medicalmissionsisters.org.uk
Web: www.medicalmissionsisters.org
• Religious Sisters of Charity, Caritas, 4 Buxton Gardens W3 9LQ Tel: 020 8992 8550 also 9 Rosemont Road W3 9LU Tel: 020 8992 4461
Email: rsocacton@gmail.com Web: www.religioussistersofcharity.org
• Damien Centre (Acton Homeless Concern), 3-5 Church Road W3 8BU
Tel: 020 8993 6096
• Emmaus House (Acton Homeless Concern), 1 Berrymead Gardens W3 8AA
Tel: 020 8992 5768

ACTON EAST + ST AIDAN OF LINDISFARNE

Sunday Mass (Sat 6.30pm), 9, 11 (Sung), 1pm (Gheez Rite); **Holy Day Mass** 10, 7.30pm; **Weekday Mass** 10, also Wed 6.30 pm; **Exposition** Sat 5.30-6.15pm, with **Benediction** 6.15pm; **Confession** Sat 5.30-6.15pm

Congregation of the Sacred Hearts of Jesus and Mary (SS.CC) Fr Fergal Maguire, Fr Christopher McAneny (resident at 372 Uxbridge Road W5 3LH)
85 Old Oak Common Lane W3 7DD Tel: 020 8743 5732
Email: actoneast@rcdow.org.uk Web: parish.rcdow.org.uk/actoneast
On Old Oak Common Lane just off Western Avenue (A40) at Savoy Circus, 1 min East Acton Stn
Ealing Deanery (1922; 1961; cons 31 October 1972)

Parish Office Mon, Wed, Fri 10.30-12noon
Head Server Donald Allwright **Tel: 020 8992 7616**
Music Co-ordinator Amy Cotton **Tel: 020 8743 5732**

• **Infant Jesus Sisters, 16 East Acton Lane W3 7EG Tel: 020 8248 9458** Sr Pat Armato; also at **30 Sunningdale Avenue W3 7NS Tel: 020 8743 0116**
• **HMP Wormwood Scrubs Chaplain** Fr Chima Ibekwe **(See HM Prison Service)**
• **Hammersmith, Queen Charlotte's & Chelsea Hospitals**
Sunday Mass 11.30; **Weekday Mass** Tue 12.30pm
Chaplains Fr Giles Pinnock, Fr Gerard O'Brien **Tel 020 3313 4574**

ACTON WEST + THE HOLY FAMILY

Sunday Mass (Sat 6pm), 8.45, 10 (Polish), 11.15, 12.45pm (Iraqi, Chaldean Rite); **Holy Day Mass** as announced; **Weekday Mass** as announced; **Exposition** and **Benediction** *First Fri only* after 10 Mass; **Rosary** ***in May and October only*** after weekday Mass; **Confession** Sat 9.45-10, 5.30-5.45pm

Fr Neil Reynolds
The Presbytery, Vale Lane W3 0DY Tel: 020 8992 1308
Email: actonwest@rcdow.org.uk Web: parish.rcdow.org.uk/actonwest
Closest Stns: North Ealing or West Acton
Ealing Deanery (1967; cons 1 April 2017)

• **Franciscan Missionaries of Mary, 26 Inglis Road W5 3RL**
Tel: 020 8992 0802 Email: fmmealing@yahoo.co.uk
• **IBVM, 21 Twyford Avenue W3 9PY Tel: 020 8993 6931**
Email: magdalenibvm@gmail.com
Srs Mary Agnes Idiong, Magdalen O'Neill, Gill Regnard, Josette Zammit-Mangion
• **Congregation of the Sacred Hearts of Jesus and Mary (SS.CC), 372 Uxbridge Road W5 3LH Tel: 020 8992 5941 Web: www. ssccpicpus.com**
Frs Kenneth Barnes, Derek Laverty, Chris McAneny
• **Focolare Movement, 57 Twyford Avenue W3 9PZ**

ARCHWAY + ST GABRIEL OF OUR LADY OF SORROWS A

Sunday Mass (Sat 6.30pm), 9, 11.30 (with Children's Liturgy), 6.30pm; **Meditative Rosary** precedes each Sunday Mass, with **Exposition** Sun 10.30-11.30; **Holy Day Mass** 12noon, 7pm; **Weekday Mass** Mon-Sat 12noon; **Healing Mass, Holy Hour** and **Benediction** ***First Fri only*** 12 noon; **Confession** Sat 11.30, 6pm & on request

Spiritans (CSSp) Fr Ugo Ikwuka, Fr Vincent Waiga, Fr Oliver Ugwu (in residence, Hospital Chaplain)
15 St John's Villas N19 3EE Tel: 020 7272 8195
Email: archway@rcdow.org.uk Web: parish.rcdow.org.uk/archway
Between Upper Holloway Stn (BR) and Archway Stn (TfL)
Islington Deanery (1928; cons 1967)

• Marist Sisters, 17 St John's Villas N19 3EE Tel: 020 7272 1079
• Ugandan Martyrs Catholic Community
Mass *Last Sunday of the month* 3pm

ARNOS GROVE, N11: *SEE NEW SOUTHGATE*

ASHFORD + ST MICHAEL S

Sunday Mass (Sat 6pm), 9.15, 11, 6pm; **Holy Day Mass** 9.15, 7pm; **Weekday Mass** Mon, Tue, Wed, Fri, Sat 9.15; **Exposition** Sat 9.45-10.15; **Confession** Sat 10.15-10.45

Mgr James Overton
112 Clarendon Road, Ashford TW15 2QD Tel: 01784 252230
Email: ashford@rcdow.org.uk Web: parish.rcdow.org.uk/ashford
Corner of Fordbridge Road & Clarendon Road, close to the War Memorial
Upper Thames Deanery (1906; 1928; cons 19 November 2006)

• HMP Bronzefield Chaplain Karen Connaughton (See HM Prison Service)

BALDOCK + HOLY TRINITY AND ST AUGUSTINE OF CANTERBURY A

Sunday Mass (Sat 6.30pm), 8.30, 10.30 (Sung), 3pm (Extraordinary Form, ***First Sun only)***; **Holy Day Mass** 10, 7.30pm; **Weekday Mass** Mon-Thu 10; **Holy Hour** Sat 5.15-6.15pm; **Confession** Sat 5.45-6.15pm

Fr Denis Sarsfield
Holy Trinity Church, London Road, Baldock SG7 6LQ Tel: 01462 893127
Email: baldock@rcdow.org.uk Web: parish.rcdow.org.uk/baldock
Stevenage Deanery (1913; 1926; cons 17 December 1977)

BARNET + MARY IMMACULATE AND ST GREGORY THE GREAT A

Sunday Mass (Sat 6.30pm), 8, 9.30, 11.15, 6.30pm; **Sunday Holy Half Hour** 5.45pm, but **Holy Hour** 5.15pm ***on First Sunday only***; **Holy Day Mass** (Vigil 7.30pm), 10, 7.30pm; **Weekday Mass** Mon-Sat 10; **Confession** Sat 6-6.30pm

Fr John McKenna, Fr Arnel Tadeo (in residence)
82 Union Street, Barnet EN5 4HZ Tel: 020 8449 3338
Email: barnet@rcdow.org.uk Web: parish/rcdow.org.uk/barnet
Barnet Deanery (1849; 1860; cons 15 December 1931; new church cons 8 December 1977; renewed church cons 3 September 2017)
Pastoral Assistant Mary Boland

• Barnet Hospital
Chaplain Fr Arnel Tadeo Tel: 0845 111 4000
• Poor Clares, Poor Clare Monastery, 102 Galley Lane, Arkley, Barnet EN5 4AN
Tel: 020 8449 8815 Fax: 020 8441 5458 Email: stclaresarkley@yahoo.co.uk
Web: www.arkleypoorclares.weebly.com
Chaplain Awaiting appointment
• Sisters of Christian Instruction, Summerhill, Leecroft Road, Barnet EN5 2TH
Tel: 020 8440 1853 Email: stgildasbarnet@yahoo.co.uk

SECTION 3

BAYSWATER + ST MARY OF THE ANGELS A

Sunday Mass (Sat 6pm), 9.30 (Family), 11 (Portuguese), 12.30pm, 6pm; ***Summer Sunday Mass*** (Sat 6pm), 11, 6pm; **Holy Day Mass** 10, 7pm; **Weekday Mass** 10 and **Exposition** Mon-Sat 9-9.50; **Confession** Sat 10.30-11, 5.30-6pm & on request

Mgr Keith Barltrop, Fr Richard Price (in residence)
The Presbytery, Moorhouse Road W2 5DJ Tel: 020 7229 0487 Fax: 020 7229 3223
Email: bayswater@rcdow.org.uk Web: www.humilitas.org
West of junction of Westbourne Grove & Chepstow Road, via Artesian Road
North Kensington Deanery (1857; cons 4 November 2007)

• Convent of the Assumption, St Catherine's, 7 Pembridge Square W2 4EQ
Tel: 020 7792 0623 Email: Shafto38@hotmail.com
• Sisters of Sion, 34 Chepstow Villas W11 2QZ Tel: 020 7229 6266 (Community)
Email: sionbayswater@gmail.com Web: www.sistersofourladyofsion.org
Sion Centre for Dialogue and Encounter, Conference Centre and Jewish/Christian Library Study Days and Reading/Library Resources Tel: 020 7313 8286
Email: sioncentrefordialogue@gmail.com Web: sioncentre.org
• Comboni Missionaries (MCCJ), 16 Dawson Place W2 4TJ
Tel: 020 7229 7059 Email: benitodemarchi@hotmail.com, anzioli47@hotmail.com
Web: www.comboni.org.uk
Frs Angelo Anzioli (Superior), Louis Mawoulolo Kouevi Adjétey, Carmine Curci, Benito De Marchi, Pasquino Panato
• Pembridge House, 29 Pembridge Square W2 4DS Tel: 020 7221 0588
Pastoral care entrusted to the Prelature of Opus Dei
• **Courage** Support group for those experiencing same-sex attraction and who wish to live a chaste life in accordance with the Church's teaching. **Contact** the **Parish Priest** or london.courage@gmail.com

BERKHAMSTED + SACRED HEART CHURCH A

Sunday Mass 8.30, 10.15; **Holy Day Mass** as announced; **Weekday Mass** Tue, Fri, Sat 10; **Liturgy of the Word** with **Holy Communion** Wed 10; **Holy Hour** with **Exposition** and **Benediction** follows Sat Mass; **Confession** Sat 10.30-11.15

Fr David Burke (also serves Tring)
Sacred Heart Church, Park Street, Berkhamsted HP4 1HX Tel: 01442 863845
Email: berkhamsted@rcdow.org.uk Web: parish.rcdow.org.uk/berkhamsted
Off Berkhamsted High Street (north side)
St Albans Deanery (1909; 1967)

BETHNAL GREEN + OUR LADY OF THE ASSUMPTION

Sunday Mass (Sat 6.30pm), 9.30, 11.30 (all with Children's Liturgy), 2.15pm (Chinese), 5pm (Tagalog, ***4th Sun only***); **Holy Day Mass** 7.30 (Priory Chapel), 12.15pm, 6.30pm; **Weekday Mass** Mon-Fri 12.15pm; Sat 9.30; **Exposition** Wed 11-12noon; **Confession** Sat 5.45-6.15pm

Assumptionists (a.a.) Fr Justin Kasereka, Fr Ricky Montanez, Fr Erik Samson; Br Joseph Quoc Cuong Tran;
Fr Joseph Liang (in residence)
Assumption Priory, Victoria Park Square E2 9PB Tel: 020 8980 1968
Email: bethnalgreen@rcdow.org.uk Web: parish.rcdow.org.uk/bethnalgreen
Just off main road, close to Bethnal Green Stn (TfL)
Tower Hamlets Deanery (1901; 1912)

• Chinese Community Fr Joseph Liang Tel: 020 8709 5281 / 07753 471611
Email: josephliang1998@gmail.com; Amy Lou (Mandarin & Cantonese-speaking)
Tel: 07878 582111 Email: amyfclou@hotmail.com

BISHOP'S STORTFORD + ST JOSEPH AND THE ENGLISH MARTYRS

Bishop's Stortford, + St Joseph and the English Martyrs: **Sunday Mass** (Sat 6pm), 9, 11, 6pm; **Holy Day Mass** 9.30, 7.30pm; **Weekday Mass** Mon-Fri 9.30, **Confession** (also **Exposition**) Sat 5.15-5.45pm
Much Hadham, + Shared Church of St Andrew and Holy Cross: **Sunday Mass** 11.15
Sawbridgeworth, Most Holy Redeemer: **Sunday Mass** 9
Live streaming from St Joseph's at **www.churchservices.tv/bishopsstortford**

Fr Peter Harris, Fr Carlos Quito
St Joseph's, 3 Windhill, Bishop's Stortford CM23 2ND Tel: 01279 654063
Email: bishopsstortford@rcdow.org.uk Web: parish.rcdow.org.uk/bishopsstortford
St Andrew and Holy Cross, Church Lane, Much Hadham SG10 6DH; Most Holy Redeemer, Sayesbury Road, Sawbridgeworth CM21 0ED
Lea Valley Deanery (St Joseph's: 1900; 1906; cons 19 June 1906; Much Hadham 1939; Sawbridgeworth 1940)
Parish Administrator Debbie Jackson

• Daughters of the Cross of Liège, St Elizabeth's Centre, South End, Much Hadham SG10 6EW Tel: 01279 843451 Email: enquiries@stelizabeths.org.uk
Web: www.stelizabeths.org.uk
52 week residential Special School, FE College and Adult Residential Care Home for those with severe epilepsy, autism and other complex medical needs. St Elizabeth's also has a 5-bedded Respite Care Unit for people aged 18+ with epilepsy.
Srs Annette Clemence (Superior), Patricia Ainsworth, Mary Gaffney, Gillian Price
Sunday Mass 11; **Holy Day Mass** 5.30pm; **Weekday Mass** Mon, Wed, Fri 8, Tue, Thu 5.30pm
Chaplain Fr Paul Arnold Tel: 01279 842145
• Herts and Essex Community Hospital
• Rivers Hospital

BOREHAMWOOD + ST TERESA OF THE CHILD JESUS

Sunday Mass (Sat 6pm), 10; **Holy Day Mass** 7, 9.15; **Weekday Mass** Mon, Tue, Thu, Fri 9.15; **Rosary** Thu after 9.15 Mass, Fri 6.30pm; **Confession** Sat 11-11.30 and 5-5.40pm
Live streaming from St Teresa's at **www.churchservices.tv/borehamwood**

SECTION 3

Fr Dominic McKenna, Fr Antonio Pineda (clergy also serve Borehamwood North)
291 Shenley Road, Borehamwood WD6 1TG Tel: 020 8953 1294
Email: borehamwood@rcdow.org.uk
Web: www.catholicparishesofborehamwood.wordpress.com
Opposite Hertsmere Civic Offices
St Albans Deanery (1925; 1962; cons 27 September 1978)
Parish Administrator Sue Partington

BOREHAMWOOD NORTH + SS JOHN FISHER AND THOMAS MORE

Sunday Mass 8.30, 12noon; **Holy Day Mass** 7.30pm; **Weekday Mass** and **Confession** see times for St Teresa's

Fr Dominic McKenna, Fr Antonio Pineda (clergy resident at 291 Shenley Road, Borehamwood WD6 1TG Tel: 020 8953 1294),
28 Rossington Avenue, Borehamwood WD6 4LA
Email: borehamwood@rcdow.org.uk
Web: www.catholicparishesofborehamwood.wordpress.com
St Albans Deanery (1955; 1958; cons 27 October 1992)

- Daughters of Divine Love, Villa Scalabrini, Green Street, Shenley WD7 9BB
Tel: 020 3730 1824
Srs M Jennifer Ekeigwe, M Roseline Ezeifo, M ChisimdinOnwuka, M Elonna Ugochukwu
- Scalabrini Fathers, Villa Scalabrini, Green Street, Shenley WD7 9BB
Tel: 020 8207 5713 Fr Alberto Vico CS

BOW + OUR LADY REFUGE OF SINNERS AND ST CATHERINE OF SIENA A

Sunday Mass (Sat 6pm), 9.30 (Sung), 11.30 (Family), 6pm; **Holy Day Mass** 10, 7pm; **Weekday Mass** Mon, Tue, Wed 10, Fri 12noon; **Exposition** 11, with **Benediction** 11.45 *on First Fri only*; **Confession** and **Exposition** Sat 5-5.30pm, with **Rosary** 5.30pm and **Benediction** 5.45pm

Fr F. Javier Ruiz-Ortiz
177 Bow Road E3 2SG Tel/Fax: 020 8980 3961
Email: bow@rcdow.org.uk Web: parish.rcdow.org.uk/bow
Tower Hamlets Deanery (1869; 1870)

- Columban Sisters, 6/8 Ridgdale Street E3 2TW
Tel: 020 8980 3017 Web: www.columbansisters.org Srs Margaret Holleran, Kate Midgley, Lucia Park, Anne Marie Smith

BOW COMMON + THE HOLY NAME AND OUR LADY OF THE SACRED HEART

English: **Sunday Mass** 9.15; **Holy Day Mass** as announced; **Weekday Mass** Thu 9.15; *Vietnamese:* **Sunday Mass** 12noon; **Holy Day Mass** as announced; **Weekday Mass** Mon, Tue 10, Thu, Fri 8pm, Sat 10; **Confession** before Mass or by arrangement

Fr Simon Thang Duc Nguyen
117 Bow Common Lane E3 4AU Tel: 020 7987 3477
Email: bowcommon@rcdow.org.uk Web: parish.rcdow.org.uk/bowcommon
Tower Hamlets Deanery (1892; 1894; cons 30 June 1894)

• Vietnamese Chaplaincy Tel: 020 7987 3477 **Chaplains** Fr Simon Thang Duc Nguyen (**Tel: 07920 044275**), Fr Tam Huu Nguyen, Fr Van Dien Nguyen, Rev Paul Song Trong Ly (Deacon)

BOXMOOR: *SEE HEMEL HEMPSTEAD*

BOXMOOR: SEE HEMEL HEMPSTEAD

BRENTFORD + ST JOHN THE EVANGELIST A

Sunday Mass (Sat 6.30pm), 9.30, 11.30; **Holy Day Mass** 9, 7.30pm; **Weekday Mass** as announced; **Confession** and **Exposition** Sat 5.30-6.15pm

Fr Gerard Quinn
44 Boston Park Road, Brentford TW8 9JF Tel: 020 8560 1671
Email: brentford@rcdow.org.uk Web: parish.rcdow.org.uk/brentford
North side of Great West Road (A4); approach via Windmill Road
Hounslow Deanery (1856; cons 1866)

• Poor Servants of the Mother of God, St Mary's Convent, 10 The Butts, Brentford TW8 8BQ Tel: 020 8847 4800 Email: kathleen.coleman@psmgs.org.uk
Chaplain Fr Hilary Crewe
Maryville Care Home Tel: 020 8560 7124
• Missionaries of Africa (MAfr) (White Fathers), 64 Little Ealing Lane W5 4XF
Tel: 020 8799 5010 Email: lelsuperior@mafrgb.org.uk
Frs Richard Calcutt, Joseph Cummins, Thomas Cummins, Matthew Hannon, Peter Kelly, Terence Madden (Provincial **Tel: 020 8799 5012**), Francis Nolan, Aylward Shorter, George Smith, Denis Starkey (Treasurer **Tel: 020 799 5011**), Gerry Stones, Christopher Wallbank (Superior **Tel: 020 8799 5037**), Edward Woo; Br Patrick O'Reilly
• Hungarian Chaplaincy, 62 Little Ealing Lane W5 4EA Tel: 020 8566 0271
Fr János Csicsó
• Clayponds Hospital

BROOK GREEN + HOLY TRINITY A

Sunday Mass (Sat 6pm), 8.30, 10, (Family), 11.30 (Solemn), 1pm (Syriac Rite), 6pm; **Holy Day Mass** 9.30, 12.30pm, 6pm; **Weekday Mass** 9.30, 6pm, followed by **Rosary** Mon-Fri; **Exposition** *First Fri only* 3-6pm, Sat 5-6pm; **Confession** Sat 10-10.30, 5.15-5.45pm

Fr Richard Andrew, Fr Mark Dunglinson, Mgr Nizar Semaan (in residence, Syriac Catholic Chaplaincy)
41 Brook Green W6 7BL Tel: 020 7603 3832
Email: brookgreen@rcdow.org.uk Web: www.holytrinityw6.org
Off Hammersmith Road (north side) between Hammersmith Broadway & Olympia.
Hammersmith & Fulham Deanery (1851;1853; cons 2 June 1866)

SECTION 3

Catechetical Co-ordinator Sr Jenefer Glencross OSU
Parish Administrator Mrs Anja Huynh

• Sisters of Nazareth, Nazareth House, 169-175 Hammersmith Road W6 8DB
Tel: 020 8748 3549 Web: www.sistersofnazareth.com
Chaplain Awaiting appointment
• Society of the Holy Child Jesus, 42 Batoum Gardens W6 7QD Tel: 020 7602 9265
• Society of the Sacred Heart (Paris), 3 Bute Gardens W6 7DR (Provincial House)
Tel: 020 8748 9353 Email: sshprovincial@btopenworld.com
Web: www.societysacredheart.org.uk Sr Jane Maltby (Provincial)
11 Bute Gardens W6 7DR Tel: 020 8748 9887 Web: societysacredheart.org.uk
• St Joseph's House, 42 Brook Green W6 7BW Tel: 020 7603 9817

BUNHILL ROW + ST JOSEPH

Sunday Mass 11.30; **Holy Day Mass** 7pm; **Weekday Mass** Wed 12.05pm; **Confession** Sun 11.15-11.30
Moorfields: **Sunday Mass** 10; **Holy Day Mass** (Vigil 7pm) 8.05, 12noon, 12.30 pm, 1.05pm, 5.30pm; **Weekday Mass** Mon-Fri 8.05, 1.05pm; **Exposition** as announced; **Confession** Mon-Fri 12.30-12.50pm, 1.30-1.50pm

Priest in Charge Fr Christopher Vipers, Fr Andrew Jaxa-Chamiec (clergy also serve Moorfields and are resident at **4/5 Eldon Street EC2M 7LS Tel: 020 7247 8390**)
15 Lamb's Passage, off Bunhill Row EC1Y 8LE
Email: bunhillrow@rcdow.org.uk Web: www.stjosephsbunhillrow.co.uk
In small street linking Bunhill Row to Errol Street; 3 mins from entrance to Barbican Centre, beside City University Business School; nearest TfL Stns Barbican, Moorgate, Old Street
Islington Deanery (1856; 1901)
Quiet Garden Mon-Fri 8-6pm (Open Easter-Sept)

• Moorfields Eye Hospital

BUNTINGFORD + ST RICHARD OF CHICHESTER

Sunday Mass 9.15 (with term time Children's Liturgy, *2nd & 4th Sun only*) ; **Holy Day Mass** 7pm; **Weekday Mass** Tue, Thu 9.30, Fri 10.30, with **Exposition** and **Benediction** 11-11.30, Sat 9.30; **Confession** Sat 10.30-11
Old Hall Green and Puckeridge **Sunday Mass** (Sat 6pm, Puckeridge); 11.15 (Old Hall Green); **Holy Day Mass** 10.30 (Puckeridge); **Weekday Mass** Wed 10.30 (Puckeridge); **Confession** Sat 5.15-5.45pm (Puckeridge)

Fr Cyril Chiaha (also serves Old Hall Green and Puckeridge)
3 Station Road, Buntingford SG9 9HT Tel: 01763 271471
Email: buntingford@rcdow.org.uk Web: parish.rcdow.org.uk/buntingford
Lea Valley Deanery (1912; 1914; cons 5 June 1940)

BURNT OAK + THE ANNUNCIATION A

Sunday Mass (Sat 6.30pm), 9, 10.30, 12noon; **Holy Day Mass** 9, 2pm (Annunciation Junior School), 7.30pm; **Weekday Mass** Mon 7.30, Tue-Fri 9, Sat 10, with **Morning Prayer** 20 mins before Mass and **Rosary** after; **Exposition** Wed 9.30-10.30; **Novena** Tue 7pm; **Confession** Sat 10.30-11, 5.30-6.15pm

Canon Colin Davies
4 Thirleby Road, Burnt Oak, Edgware HA8 0HQ Tel: 020 8959 1971
Email: burntoak@rcdow.org.uk Web: parish.rcdow.org.uk/burntoak
Off Gervase Road, close to Burnt Oak Stn (TfL)
Barnet Deanery (1928)

• Edgware Community Hospital
Chaplain Awaiting appointment Tel: 020 8952 2381

BUSHEY AND OXHEY + SACRED HEART OF JESUS AND ST JOHN THE EVANGELIST A

Sunday Mass (Sat 6pm), 8.30, 10.30 (Sung), 6pm; **Holy Day Mass** 9, 7.30pm; **Weekday Mass** Mon (**Eucharistic Service**) 9.15, Tue 7.30pm, Wed-Fri 9.15; **Confession** Sat 11-11.30, 5-5.30pm & on request

Fr James McNicholas
Sacred Heart Presbytery, London Road, Bushey WD23 1BA Tel: 020 8950 2077
Email: busheyandoxhey@rcdow.org.uk Web: www.busheyrc.org.uk
Ten minutes walk up Chalk Hill from Bushey BR Stn
Watford Deanery (1863; 1959; cons 20 September 1977)
Sacred Heart Parish Centre Tel: 07925 979414

• Dominican Sisters, Rosary Priory, 93 Elstree Road, Bushey Heath WD23 4EE
Tel: 020 8950 1148 (Convent) 020 8950 6065 (Generalate)
Web: www.dominicansisters.co.uk
• Heath House, Birchville Court

CAMDEN TOWN + OUR LADY OF HAL

Sunday Mass (Sat 6pm), 8.30, 10 (Family), 12noon (Solemn), 5pm (Portuguese); **Holy Day Mass** 9.30, 12noon, 7pm; **Weekday Mass** Mon-Sat 12noon; **Holy Hour and Benediction** Fri 12.30-1.30pm; **Confession** Fri 12.45-1.15pm, Sat 11-11.30, 5.15-5.45pm

Fr John Hai Pham, Fr Christopher Connor (in residence, School Chaplain), Fr Mark Elliott-Smith (in residence, Ordinariate), Fr Sebastian Chamakala John (in residence, Syro-Malabar Chaplaincy), Fr Colin McLean (in residence, retired)
165 Arlington Road NW1 7EX Tel: 020 7485 2727
Email: camdentown@rcdow.org.uk Web: parish.rcdow.org.uk/camdentown
Camden Deanery (1933; cons 1984)
Parish Administrator Judith Murphy

CANARY WHARF CATHOLIC CHAPLAINCY: *SEE MILLWALL*

CARPENDERS PARK AND SOUTH OXHEY + ST JOSEPH A

Sunday Mass (Sat 6pm), 8.30, 10.30; **Weekday Mass** Tue (**Healing Mass**) 6pm, Wed-Fri 9.15; **Confession** Sat 5.30pm, Tue 6.30pm

Priest in Charge Fr Stephen Hewitt
St Joseph's Church, Oxhey Drive, South Oxhey, Watford WD19 7SW
Tel: 020 8428 2774
Email: carpenderspark@rcdow.org.uk Web: parish.rcdow.org.uk/carpenderspark
Off Prestwick Road, close to Carpenders Park Stn - on South Oxhey side of railway line
Watford Deanery (1952; 1960; cons 1981)
Pastoral Associate Jacqueline Faria
Children & Family Worker Donna Osborne

• The Fairways Old People's Home, Pinewood Lodge Old People's Home

CHELSEA 1 + ST MARY CADOGAN STREET A

Sunday Mass (Sat 6.30pm), 10, 11.30, 6.30pm; **Holy Day Mass** 12noon, 7pm; **Weekday Mass** Mon 10.30 (Royal Hospital), Tue, Thu, Fri 12noon; **Exposition** Fri 11-11.45; **Confession** Sat 5.45-6.15pm

Fr Shaun Middleton, Mgr Martin Hayes (in residence)
Presbytery & Communication address: St Mary's Rectory, Draycott Terrace SW3 2BG
Tel: 020 7589 5487
(Church address: Cadogan Street SW3 2QR)
Email: chelsea1@rcdow.org.uk Web: parish.rcdow.org.uk/chelseastmary
Corner of Cadogan Street and Draycott Terrace
Kensington & Chelsea Deanery (1798; 1811; 1879; cons 12 June 1882)
Royal Hospital, Chelsea

• Daughters of the Cross, St Wilfrid's Convent, 29 Tite Street SW3 4JX
Tel: 020 7351 5339 (Convent and Home) Tel: 020 7351 2117 (Provincialate)
Email: maureen.obrien@stwilfridssw3.org.uk Web: www.daughtersofthe cross.org.uk
Chaplain Fr William Wilby Tel: 020 7351 5339 ext 381
• Dawliffe Hall, 1-2 Chelsea Embankment SW3 4LG Tel: 020 7351 0719
Pastoral care entrusted to Prelature of Opus Dei
• Lister Hospital
• Royal Hospital, Chelsea

CHELSEA 2 + OUR MOST HOLY REDEEMER AND ST THOMAS MORE

Sunday Mass (Sat 6.30pm), 10 (Family), 11 (Sung Latin), 12.15pm, 6.30pm; **Holy Day Mass** 8, 6.30pm; **Weekday Mass** Mon-Fri 8, Sat and Public Holidays 10; **Morning Prayer** Mon-Fri 7.30, Sat and Sun 9.30; **Evening Prayer** Sat and Sun 6pm; **Confession** Sat 10.30-11, 5.30-6pm

Canon Paschal Ryan
7 Cheyne Row SW3 5HS Tel: 020 7352 0777 Fax: 020 7352 4223
Email: chelsea2@rcdow.org.uk Web: www.holyredeemerchelsea.org.uk
North of Albert Bridge, off Oakley Street
Kensington & Chelsea Deanery (1892; 1895; cons 21 June 1905)

- Diocesan Seminary: see entry for Allen Hall in Section 2
- Chelsea Court Place Residential and Day Memory Care

CHESHUNT + ST PAUL A

Sunday Mass (Sat 5pm) 9, 11; **Holy Day Mass** 9.30, 8pm; **Weekday Mass** Mon-Wed, Fri 9.30 ; **Mass for parents bereaved of children** 9.30 *17th of every month;* **Mass for Carers** 9.30 *First Fri;* **Exposition** Fri 9; **Confession** Sat 4.15-4.45pm

Priest in Charge Fr Clement Nyarko
17 Churchfield Path, off Church Lane, Cheshunt EN8 9EG Tel: 01992 629878
Email: cheshunt@rcdow.org.uk Web: parish.rcdow.org.uk/cheshunt
Lea Valley Deanery (1998)

CHIPPERFIELD + OUR LADY MOTHER OF THE SAVIOUR A

Sunday Mass (Sat 6.30pm), 10; **Holy Day Mass** 12 noon; **Weekday Mass** Tue, Fri 10 (subject to change); **Confession** before any Mass & on request

Salvatorians (SDS) Fr Richard Mway-Zeng, Fr Noel Keane (in residence) (clergy also serve Kings Langley, Bovingdon and Sarratt)
Catholic Church, Dunny Lane, Chipperfield WD4 9DB (Clergy resident at the Presbytery at Abbots Langley Tel: 01923 266177)
Email: chipperfield@rcdow.org.uk Web: parish.rcdow.org.uk/chipperfield
Watford Deanery (1978; 1988; cons 11 October 1989)

- Bovingdon, HM Prison The Mount Chaplain Kim Davey (See HM Prison Service)

CHISWICK + OUR LADY OF GRACE AND ST EDWARD

Sunday Mass (Sat 6.30pm), 8.30, 9.45 (Family), 11 (Sung), 12.15pm, 6.30pm; **Holy Day Mass** 10, 12.30pm, 7.30pm, **Weekday Mass** 10, 12.30pm (as announced); **Exposition** Mon-Fri 3-4pm, Sat 5-6pm; **Benediction** Mon-Fri 4pm, Sat 6pm; **Confession** Sat 11-12noon, 5-6pm & on request

Fr Michael Dunne, Fr Michael Maguire (clergy also serve Gunnersbury)
247 High Road W4 4PU Tel: 020 8994 2877 Fax: 020 8987 8332
Email: chiswick@rcdow.org.uk Web: www.ourladyofgracechiswick.org
Main road, corner of Chiswick High Road and Duke's Avenue
Hounslow Deanery (1852; 1886; cons 10 October 1904)
Administrator Sharon Bowden

- Comboni Missionary Sisters (Community), 2 Chiswick Lane W4 2JF
Tel: 020 8994 0449 Email: trinircastellano@gmail.com

SECTION 3

Comboni Centre for Spirituality and Mission, 2 Chiswick Lane W4 2JF
Tel: 020 8994 1220 Email: combonicentre16@gmail.com
• Missionary Sisters of the Immaculate (PIME), Regina Pacis Convent, 10 Chiswick Lane W4 2JE Tel: 020 8994 2053 Email: msilondon@aol.com Web: www.mdipime.org

CHORLEYWOOD + ST JOHN FISHER ♿

Sunday Mass (Sat 6pm), 9; **Holy Day Mass** as announced; **Weekday Mass** Tue, Fri 9.30; **Exposition** 1st Sat 5.30-5.55pm; **Confession** on request & by appointment

Mill End: **Sunday Mass** (Sat 6pm), 10.30; **Holy Day Mass** as announced; **Weekday Mass** Mon, Wed 9.30; **Exposition** Sat 5.30-5.55pm; **Confession** on request & by appointment

Rickmansworth: **Sunday Mass** 8.30, 11, 6pm; **Holy Day Mass** 9.30, 8pm; **Weekday Mass** Mon, Tue, Thu, Fri 9.30, Sat 10; **Exposition** and **Confession** Sat 10.30-11.30

Fr Shaun Church, Fr Damian Ryan (clergy also serve Mill End and Rickmansworth and are resident at **5 Park Road, Rickmansworth WD3 1HU Tel: 01923 773387**)
Hill Cottage, Shire Lane, Chorleywood, Rickmansworth WD3 5NH
Email: rickmansworth@rcdow.org.uk Web: parish.rcdow.org.uk/chorleywood
Close to shopping centre & Stn
Watford Deanery (1955)

CLAPTON + ST SCHOLASTICA A

Sunday Mass (Sat 6pm), 10, 11.45, 6pm; **Holy Day Mass** 9.05, 7pm; **Weekday Mass** Mon-Fri 9.05, preceded by **Exposition** 8-9; Fri 6.05pm, preceded by **Exposition** 5-6pm; Sat 10.05, preceded by **Exposition** 9-10; **Confession** Fri 5-6pm, Sat 9-10, 5-5.45pm

Fr Kingsley Arulananthem, Rev Kingsley Izundu (Deacon)
17 Kenninghall Road E5 8BS Tel: 020 8985 2178
Email: clapton@rcdow.org.uk Web: parish.rcdow.org.uk/clapton
Hackney Deanery (1862; 1962; cons 15 February 1987)

• **Servite Sisters, 12 Cleveleys Road E5 9JN Tel: 020 8880 0257**
Sr Petronia Williams
• **Servite Sisters Generalate, 1 Brownsea Court, 160 Clarence Road E5 8EF**
Sr Marie Thérèse Connor

CLAPTON PARK + ST JUDE

Sunday Mass (Sat 6pm), 9.30 (Sung), 11.30 (Sung); **Holy Day Mass** 9.30; **Weekday Mass** Tue-Sat 9.30; **Legion of Mary** Thu 5.30pm; **Prayer Group** Thu 7-8pm, **Confession** Sat 5.30-5.45pm and on request

Priest in Charge Fr Neil Hannigan
131 Glenarm Road E5 0NB (Church is at 76 Blurton Road E5 0NH)
Tel: 020 8525 1929
Email: claptonpark@rcdow.org.uk Web: parish.rcdow.org.uk/claptonpark
Off Chatsworth Road
Hackney Deanery (1964)

• Sisters of Mercy, 4 Hilsea Street E5 0SG Tel: 020 8986 3196
• Homerton University Hospital NHS Trust Tel: 020 8510 5555
Chaplain Fr George Donaghy Tel: 020 8510 5555 / 020 7739 5006
Sunday Mass 11

CLERKENWELL + ST PETER AND ST PAUL A

Sunday Mass (Sat 6.30pm) 9.45 (Sung), 12noon (Sung); **Holy Day Mass** 12.30pm; **Weekday Mass** Mon 12:30pm, Tue, Wed 8, Thu, Fri 12.30pm; **Confession** Sat 5.45pm & on request

Fr Ivano Millico
5 Amwell Street EC1R 1UL Tel: 020 7837 2094 Fax: 020 7837 2724
Email: clerkenwell@rcdow.org.uk Web: parish.rcdow.org.uk/clerkenwell
Islington Deanery (1842; 1847)
Secretary Helen Lebab

• Pallottine Missionary Sisters, 35 Wilmington Square WC1X 0EG Tel: 020 7837 3010
Email: bohr@talktalk.net Web: www.pallottinesisters-tanzania.org
• Royal National Throat, Nose & Ear Hospital

CLERKENWELL + ST PETER'S: *SEE ITALIAN CHURCH*

COCKFOSTERS + CHRIST THE KING

Sunday Mass (Sat 5.30pm), 9, 11; **Holy Day Mass** 11; **Weekday Mass** 11
Ecumenical Prayer Group Mon 8pm, Thu 11.30; **Confession** Sat 11.30, 5pm

Chemin Neuf (CCN) Fr Christophe Brunet, Fr Sebastian Ostrynski
29 Bramley Road N14 4HE Tel: 020 8449 6648
Email: cockfosters@rcdow.org.uk Web: parish.rcdow.org.uk/cockfosters
On main road, a few yards west of Oakwood Stn (TfL), junction with Peace Close
Enfield Deanery (1936; 1940)
Community Frs Christophe Brunet, Sebastian Ostrynski; Mme Hélène Guilbault

• Net for God Prayer Group Tue 8pm
• Cockfosters Centre for Spirituality Tel: 020 8449 6648
Web: www.cockfosterscs.org.uk
• Sr Louisa Poole SSL (Representative, CBCEW Ecumenical Environment Issues)
Flat 8, 34 Green Road N14 4AU Tel: 020 8441 2858
• Homes for Aged: Servite House, Sir Thomas Lipton's, The Chine, Elizabeth Lodge

COMMERCIAL ROAD + ST MARY AND ST MICHAEL

Sunday Mass (Sat 6pm), 9, 11; **Holy Day Mass** 9.30, & as announced; **Weekday Mass** Mon-Wed, Fri, 9.30; **Confession** Sat 5-5.30pm

Fr William Skehan, Fr Julien Matondo Mboko (in residence, Congolese Chaplaincy), Fr Aidan Sharratt (in residence, contact details below)
2 Lukin Street E1 0AA Tel: 020 7790 5911

SECTION 3

Email: commercialroad@rcdow.org.uk Web: parish.rcdow.org.uk/commercialroad
200 yards east of Watney Market
Tower Hamlets Deanery (1856; cons 4 December 1929)
(Fr Aidan Sharratt **Tel: 020 7790 0383**) (Congolese Chaplaincy **Tel: 020 7790 2211**)

• Sisters of Mercy, 88 Hardinge Street E1 0EB Tel: 020 7790 1459
Mass Thu, Sat 9.30
• Royal London Hospital (Whitechapel) Tel: 020 3416 5000
Chaplains Fr Rory Murphy IVD, Fr Andrew Jaxa-Chamiec **Tel: 020 3594 2070** Sr Andrena Mulligan SM
Emails: Rory.Murphy@bartshealth.nhs.uk, Andrew.Chamiec@bartshealth.nhs.uk

COPENHAGEN STREET + THE BLESSED SACRAMENT A

Sunday Mass 8.30, 11 (Family, Sung); **Holy Day Mass** 10.30, 7.30pm; **Weekday Mass** Mon-Wed, Sat 10.30; **Confession** Sun 8-8.25, 10.30-10.55

Islington: **Sunday Mass** (Sat 6pm), 9, 10.30 (Sung, with Children's Liturgy), 12noon (Sung), 6pm; **Holy Day Mass** 10, 12.30pm, 7.30pm; **Weekday Mass** 10; **Exposition** Sat 10.30-11.30; **Confession** Sat 10.30-11, 5.15-5.45pm

Mgr Séamus O'Boyle, Fr Allan Alvarado Gil, Fr Lawrence Milby (clergy also serve Islington and are resident at **39 Duncan Terrace N1 8AL Tel: 020 7226 3277**)
157 Copenhagen Street N1 0SR
Email: copenhagenstreet@rcdow.org.uk Web: parish.rcdow.org.uk/copenhagenstreet
Off Caledonian Road, half mile north of Kings Cross Stn (BR/TfL)
Islington Deanery (1916)

• School Sisters of Notre Dame, 41 Havelock Street N1 0DA Tel: 020 7837 8378
Email: ssnd27@yahoo.co.uk Web: www.ssnd.org and www.gerhardinger.org
Srs Miriam Bruder, Paulette Tomlinson

COVENT GARDEN (MAIDEN LANE) + CORPUS CHRISTI A

The Church is the Diocesan Shrine of the Most Blessed Sacrament (2018)
Sunday Mass (Sat 6pm), 9.30, 11.30; **Holy Day Mass** 8 (Extraordinary Form), 12.05pm, 1.05pm; **Weekday Mass** Mon-Fri 1.05pm, also Mon 6.30pm (Extraordinary Form), Bank Holidays 10; **Sodality of the Blessed Sacrament** *First Thu* 6.30pm; **Eucharistic Prayer Group** Wed 7pm; **Exposition** Mon, Wed-Fri 12-1pm; **Confession** 30 mins before each Mass & on request

Fr Alan Robinson
Corpus Christi Presbytery, Maiden Lane WC2E 7NB Tel: 020 7836 4700
Email: coventgarden@rcdow.org.uk Web: www.corpuschristimaidenlane.org.uk
Off Southampton Street, north of Strand; near Covent Garden
Westminster Deanery (1873; cons 18 October 1956)

CRANFORD + OUR LADY AND ST CHRISTOPHER

Sunday Mass (Sat 6pm), 8.30, 10.30, 1pm (Portuguese); **Holy Day Mass** as announced; **Weekday Mass** Mon, Tue, Thu-Sat 9.30, Wed 9; **Confession** Sat 5.15-5.45pm & on request

Fr Francis Press
32 High Street, Cranford, Hounslow TW5 9RG Tel: 020 8759 9136
Email: cranford@rcdow.org.uk Web: parish.rcdow.org.uk/cranford
Next to Holy Angels Church, opposite The Avenue
Hounslow Deanery (1967; 1970, cons 1979)

CRICKLEWOOD + ST AGNES

Sunday Mass (Sat 6.30pm), 9, 10.30, 12noon, 6.30pm; **Holy Day Mass** as announced; **Weekday Mass** Mon-Fri 9.15, Sat 10; **Confession** Sat 10.30-11, 5.30-6pm & on request

Fr John Buckley
35 Cricklewood Lane NW2 1HR Tel: 020 8452 2475
Email: cricklewood@rcdow.org.uk Web: parish.rcdow.org.uk/cricklewood
On A407, midway between A41 and Cricklewood Broadway (A5)
Barnet Deanery (1883; 1930)
Pastoral Assistant Elizabeth Sayer

- Dominican Sisters (St Rose's Convent, St Rose's Chapel, Prayer Garden and Poustinia), 160 Anson Road NW2 6BH Tel: 020 8830 7465 Email: raymundaop72@gmail.com
- Sisters of Mercy, 149 Walm Lane NW2 3AU Tel: 020 8450 7472
- Sisters of St Joseph of Peace, 157 Walm Lane NW2 3AY Tel: 020 8450 8859 Web: www.csjp.org

CROXLEY GREEN + ST BEDE A

Sunday Mass (Sat 6pm), 10, 6pm; **Holy Day Mass** 10, 7.30pm; **Weekday Mass** 10; **Confession** Sat 10.30

Fr John Wiley
185 Baldwins Lane, Croxley Green, Rickmansworth WD3 3LL Tel: 01923 231969
Email: croxleygreen@rcdow.org.uk Web: parish.rcdow.org.uk/croxleygreen
Watford Deanery (1958; cons 1975)

CUFFLEY + ST MARTIN DE PORRES A

Sunday Mass (Sat 5.30pm) 9, 11; **Holy Day Mass** 9.30, 8pm; **Weekday Mass** as announced; **Confession** Sat 10.30

Priest in Charge Fr Patrick Carroll
4 Church Close, Cuffley EN6 4LS Tel: 01707 873308
Email: cuffley@rcdow.org.uk Web: parish.rcdow.org.uk/cuffley
Enfield Deanery

SECTION 3

DOLLIS HILL + ST MARY AND ST ANDREW

Sunday Mass (Sat 7pm), 8.30, 10.30 (Family), 12noon (Sung); (***in August*** (7pm), 9, 11); **Holy Day Mass** as announced; **Weekday Mass** Mon-Thu 9.30; **Confession** Sat 12.30pm & on request

Fr Michael O'Doherty
216 Dollis Hill Lane NW2 6HE Tel: 020 8452 6158
Email: dollishill@rcdow.org.uk Web: parish.rcdow.org.uk/dollishill
Brent Deanery (1915; 1933)

EALING + ABBEY CHURCH OF ST BENEDICT

Sunday Mass (Sat 6pm, 8.30pm with Neocatechumenate Community in Chapel), 8, 9, 10.15 (Family, in Parish Centre), 10.30 (Sung), 12noon, 7pm; **Holy Day Mass** 7, 9.15, 6pm, 8pm; **Weekday Mass** 7, 9.15, 6pm; **Exposition** Thu 8.15-9pm, Fri 9.45-12.30pm; **Rosary** Mon-Sat 9.40; **Confession** Sat 10-11, 4-5pm, 7-7.30pm, Thu 8-8.30pm.
Divine Office: Matins 6, but Sat 6.30, (Sun Vigil on Sat 7.30pm); **Lauds** 7.35; **Conventual Mass** 7 (Sat 9.15, Sun 10.30); **Vespers** 6.35pm (Sat 5.30pm; Sun 6pm, with **Exposition**); **Compline** 8pm (except Sat and Sun)

Benedictines of the English Congregation (OSB) Dom Ambrose McCambridge, Dom Timothy Gorham (Sub Prior), Dom Dominic Taylor (Prior), Abbot Martin Shipperlee
Rev Alex Burke (Deacon), Rev Ian Edwards (Deacon), Rev Gordon Nunn (Deacon)
Ealing Abbey, Charlbury Grove W5 2DY
Parish Tel: 020 8862 2160 Parish Fax: 020 8862 2166
Email: ealingabbey@rcdow.org.uk Web: www.ealingabbey.org.uk
1/4 mile north of station and shops; local bus via Eaton Rise to Marchwood Crescent
Ealing Deanery (1897; 1899)
Monastery Tel: 020 8862 2100 Fax: 020 8862 2206
Email: ealingmonk@ealingabbey.org.uk
Other priests OSB in the community: Doms Alexander Bevan, Peter Burns, Gregory Chillman, Vincent Cooper, Andrew Hughes, James Leachman, Alban Nunn, Abbot Francis Rossiter, Dom Thomas Stapleford

- The Benedictine Institute, 74 Castlebar Road W5 2DD
Tel: 020 8862 2156 Fax: 020 8862 2133 Email: info@benedictine-institute.org
- Capitanio Sisters, Nile Lodge, Queen's Walk W5 1TJ
Tel: 020 8997 3933 Email: stbc.sisters@gmail.com
Srs Thresia Poulose (Superior), Giustina Contessa, Jessice Crasta, Sharon Crasta, Rosaline D'Souza, Patricia Olivera, Anna Maria Tiziani
- Little Company of Mary, Flat 10, Berkeley Court, 33 Gordon Road W5 2AE
Tel: 020 8810 4432 Email: jbugeja@aol.com
Sr Josephine Bugeja
- Medical Missionaries of Mary, 2 Denbigh Road W13 8PX Tel: 020 8998 1725
Email: mmmealing37@yahoo.co.uk Web: www.mmmworldwide.org
Srs Maureen Clarke, Ruth Percival, Mary Shephard

• Missionary Sisters of Our Lady of Africa, Flat 13 Montpelier Court, Montpelier Road W5 2QN Tel: 020 8998 6731 (Office), 020 8997 3166, 020 8810 7619
Regional Superior Email: ukmsolareg@btinternet.com Web: www.msolafrica.org
• Sisters of Charity of St Jeanne Antide, 6/8 Woodfield Road W5 1SJ
Tel: 020 8998 9549 Email: srstrion16@btinternet.com
• Sisters of the Holy Cross, 82 The Avenue W13 8LB Tel: 020 8997 2858
Email: holycross@hcengland.co.uk Web: www.holycrossengland.org.uk
• Sisters of the Resurrection, 18 Carlton Road W5 2AW
Tel: 020 8810 6241 Email: csr.englishregion@yahoo.co.uk
Srs Mary Pauline Hebron, Maria Janina Kwoczka, Faustina Lagodzinska, Catherine Nastala, Teresita Williams
also **84 Gordon Road W5 2AR Tel: 020 8998 8954**
Srs Mary Angela Coyne, Mary Kathleen Delaney, Maria Goretti Feeheny, Elizabeth Geraghty, Rachel Baj
• Columban Fathers (SSC), 12 Blakesley Avenue W5 2DW
Tel: 020 8997 0587 Fax: 020 3581 9676 Email: columbanlondon12@gmail.com
Web: www.columbans.co.uk
Frs Aodh O'Halpin (Superior), Gerard Markey, Eamonn O'Brien, Thomas Ryan
• Congregation of Marian Fathers, Divine Mercy Apostolate, 1 Courtfield Gardens W13 0EY
Tel: 020 8998 0925 Email: info@divinemercy.org.uk
Web: www.divinemercyapostolate.co.uk
Sunday Mass (Polish) 10; **Daily Mass** and **Divine Mercy Chaplet** (English) Mon-Fri 2.30pm *except first Fri*
Community Fr Andrzej Gowkielewicz, Fr Dariusz Mazewski
• Missionaries of Africa (White Fathers) (MAfr), 15 Corfton Road W5 2HP
Tel: 020 8601 7900 Email: corftonsuperior@mafrgb.org.uk
Frs John Gerrard (Superior), Michael Heap, Agustin Sawadogo, Edward Wildsmith; Br Nicholas Murphy

EASTCOTE + ST THOMAS MORE

Sunday Mass (Sat 6.30pm), 9.30 (Family), 11.30; **Holy Day Mass** 9.30, 7.30pm; **Weekday Mass** 9.30 (or **Liturgy of the Word with Holy Communion** as advised); **Confession** with **Exposition** Sat 10-10.30

Fr Martin Plunkett
32 Field End Road, Eastcote, Pinner HA5 2QT Tel: 020 8866 6581 Fax: 020 8429 2346
Email: eastcote@rcdow.org.uk Web: parish.rcdow.org.uk/eastcote
On main road, north of station and shops, just beyond Bridle Road junction
Hillingdon Deanery (1935; 1977; cons 6 February 1978)

• St Vincent's Nursing Home, Wiltshire Lane, Eastcote HA5 2NB
Tel: 020 8872 4900 Web: www. svnh.co.uk
Chaplain Fr Antoni Markowski MAfr
Tel: 020 8429 4778 Email: JAM5331@protonmail.com

SECTION 3

EDGWARE + ST ANTHONY OF PADUA

Sunday Mass (Sat 6.30pm), 10, 12noon, 6pm; **Holy Day Mass** 9, 7.30pm; **Weekday Mass** Mon-Fri 9, Tue 7.30pm (followed by **Devotions to St Anthony** and **Benediction**), Sat 10; **Exposition** Mon-Sat 8(am)-10pm, Sun 8-9.30, 7-10pm; **Confession** Sat 9.30-9.50, 5.30-6pm

Fr Robert Pachuta
5 Garratt Road, Edgware HA8 9AN Tel: 020 8952 0663 Office: 020 8951 5769
Email: edgware@rcdow.org.uk Web: parish.rcdow.org.uk/edgware
Off the A5 mid-way between the junctions with Station Road and Deansbrook Road
Barnet Deanery (1913;1931;1958)

- Daughters of Mary, Mother of Mercy, 16 St Margaret's Road, Edgware HA8 9UP Tel: 020 8958 8316
Srs Maria Resurrecta Nzeribe, Mary Chukwuma Okafor, Mary Stella Okeadu, Mary Bibiana Ononiwu, Mary Kyrian Ononiwu
- Dominican Sisters of St Catherine of Siena, St Albert's, 267 Hale Lane, Edgware HA8 8NW Tel: 020 8958 5622

EDMONTON + THE MOST PRECIOUS BLOOD AND ST EDMUND, KM

Sunday Mass (Sat 7pm), 8, 9.15, 10.30, 12noon, 2pm *in Igbo, 2nd Sun only*, 6.30pm; **Holy Day Mass** 9.15, 12noon, 7pm; **Weekday Mass** 9.15, 12noon; **Exposition** Sat 11-11.45; **Confession** Sat 11-11.45, 6-6.45pm

Missionary Society of St Paul (MSP) Fr Emmanuel Ogunnaike
115 Hertford Road N9 7EN Tel: 020 8803 6631 Fax: 020 8345 6495
Email: edmonton@rcdow.org.uk Web: www.stedmundsedmonton.co.uk
Corner of Croyland Road, 1/4 mile north of Edmonton Green
Enfield Deanery (1903; cons 17 May 1907)
Catechetical Co-ordinator Mike Boggis
Parish Secretary Susan Phagoo

- Handmaids of the Holy Child Jesus, Trinity House, 48 Cavendish Road N18 2LS Tel: 020 8803 3839 Email: trinityconventhouse@yahoo.com
Srs Judith Ube, Elisabeth Wills-Obong
and Ancilla Convent, 4 Woodstock Crescent N9 7LY 020 8804 4070
Sr Rita Etuk
- North Middlesex Hospital

ELY PLACE + ST ETHELDREDA

Sunday Mass 9, 11 (Sung Latin); **Holy Day Mass** 1pm; **Weekday Mass** Mon-Fri 1pm; **Confession** Weekdays 1.20pm and on request

Institute of Charity (IC) Fr Tom Deidun
14 Ely Place EC1N 6RY Tel: 020 7405 1061 Fax: 020 7405 7440
Email: elyplace@rcdow.org.uk Web: www.stetheldreda.com
Westminster Deanery (1252-1290; 1297; crypt re-opened 1876; upper church re-opened 1879)

ENFIELD + OUR LADY OF MOUNT CARMEL AND ST GEORGE ♿ 🦻 S

Our Lady of Mount Carmel and St George: Sunday Mass (Sat 6pm, 7.30pm with Neo-Catechumenate), 8, 9 (with Children's Liturgy), 10.30, 12noon, 6pm; **Holy Day Mass** 12.30pm, 7pm; **Weekday Mass** Mon-Fri 12.30pm, Sat 9.30; **Exposition** Sat 10-11, 5-5.45pm and *First Fri only* 9.30-6.30pm; **Rosary** Mon-Fri 12noon; **Confession** Sat 10-11, 5.15-5.45pm
Chapel of Ease: Sunday Mass 10, 3.30pm (Syro-Malabar, ***3rd Sun only***)
Holy Family Convent: Sunday Mass (Sat 6pm), 9 (Polish), 10.30 (Maronite); **Weekday Mass** Mon, Tue 7.30; **Exposition** Tue 7-8pm, Wed 8-9pm, Thu 4.45pm-5.45pm

Fr Sławomir Witoń, Fr Chinedu Udo, Rev Ronald Seery (Deacon)
45 London Road, Enfield EN2 6DS Tel: 020 8363 2569 Fax: 020 8342 0159
Email: enfield@rcdow.org.uk Web: www.catholicenfield.org
Main road, near Enfield Town Stn (Overground)
Enfield Deanery (1862; 1958; cons 16 July 1967)
Chapel of Ease: Our Lady of Walsingham and the English Martyrs, Holtwhites Hill, Enfield EN2 8HG
Catechetical Co-ordinator Sybil Lee Email: sybillee@rcdow.org.uk
Parish Secretary Susi Thompson (Mon-Thu)

• Fr Krzysztof Chaim, resident at Holy Family of Nazareth Convent, 52 London Road, Enfield EN2 6EN Tel: 07902 432343 (Polish Chaplain)
• Sisters of the Holy Family of Nazareth, 52 London Road, Enfield EN2 6EN Tel: 020 8363 4483 Web: www.nazarethfamily.org
• Chase Farm Hospital, Enfield Community Care Centre at St Michael's Hospital, BMI Cavell Hospital, BMI King's Oak Hospital

EUSTON, NW1: *SEE SOMERS TOWN*

FARM STREET + THE IMMACULATE CONCEPTION A 🦻

Sunday Mass (Sat 6pm), 8, 9.30 (Family), 11 (Sung Latin), 12.30pm, 5.30pm, Young Adults Mass 7pm; **Holy Day Mass** (Vigil 6pm), 8, 1.05pm, 6pm; **Weekday Mass** Mon-Fri 8, 1.05pm, 6pm, Sat 8 only, Bank Holiday 1.05pm only; **Exposition** Mon-Fri 12.30-1pm; **Confession** Mon-Sat 10 mins before Mass and on request, Sun before each Mass

Society of Jesus (SJ) Fr Dominic Robinson, Fr Chris Pedley
114 Mount Street W1K 3AH Tel: 020 7493 7811 Fax: 020 7495 6685
Email: farmstreet@rcdow.org.uk Web: www.farmstreet.org.uk
Opposite Carlos Place (south side, Grosvenor Square); and at Farm Street (off Berkeley Square)
Marylebone Deanery (1849, cons 1993)
Parish Administrator Scott George McCombe
Jesuits (SJ) Provincial Curia, 114 Mount Street W1K 3AH
Tel: 020 7499 0285 Fax: 020 7408 7111
Other members of Community: Frs Michael Beattie, Brendan Carmody, Damian Howard (Provincial), Patrick Hume, John Mahoney, Paul Nicholson (Superior), Adrian Porter, Robert Styles

SECTION 3

• **LGBT Catholics Westminster** meet on the 2nd and 4th Sunday evenings at Farm Street Church; **contact** Sherwyn Sicat, **lgbtcatholicswestminster@gmail.com,** or Mgr Keith Barltrop (**Chaplain**; *see Bayswater* **entry**).

FELTHAM + ST LAWRENCE

Sunday Mass (Sat 6pm), 9, 11, 1pm Polish, 3pm Ukrainian Liturgy ***2nd Sun only***; 6pm; **Holy Day Mass** 9.30, 12.15pm, 7.30pm; **Weekday Mass** Mon-Fri 9.30, Sat 12noon; **Confession** Sat 11-11.45, 5-5.45pm

Fr John Byrne, Fr Peter Shekelton, Rev Colin Macken (Deacon)
St Lawrence's Presbytery, The Green, Feltham TW13 4AF Tel: 020 8890 2367 / 07879 058732
Email: feltham@rcdow.org.uk Web: www.saintlawrences.org.uk
Set back on east side of High Street, not far from Feltham Stn
Hounslow Deanery (1910; 1934)
Pastoral Assistant Jordan Pullicino

• Sisters of Mercy, 35 Ruscombe Way, Feltham TW14 9NY Tel: 020 8751 0862
• HMYOI and Remand Centre **Chaplains** Barry Phillips-Devaney, Bridget Brinkley (See HM Prison Service)

FINCHLEY CHURCH END + ST PHILIP THE APOSTLE

Sunday Mass (Sat 6.30pm), 9.30 (Sung), 11.30 (Family), 6.30pm (Polish); **Holy Day Mass** 12noon, 7.30pm; **Weekday Mass** Mon, Tue, Thu-Sat 10; **Exposition** Sat 10.30-11; **Confession** Sat 10.30-11, 5.45-6.15pm

Fr John P. Dermody, Fr Marek Gałuszka (in residence)
Priests House, Gravel Hill N3 3RJ Tel: 020 8346 2459
Email: finchleychurchend@rcdow.org.uk Web: www.stphilipsfinchley.org.uk
Regent's Park Road near Finchley Central Stn, junction with Gravel Hill
Barnet Deanery (1918; 1933; cons 3 May 1975)

• Consolata Fathers (IMC), 3 Salisbury Avenue N3 3AJ
Tel: 020 8346 5498 Email: consolatafathers.uk@consolata.net
Frs Luis Tomas (Superior), Carlo Bonelli
• Finchley Memorial Hospital, Dell Field Court Nursing Home

FINCHLEY EAST + ST MARY

Sunday Mass (Sat 6pm), 8.30, 10 (Family), 12noon; **Holy Day Mass** 10, 7.30pm; **Weekday Mass** 10, with **Morning Prayer** 9.45; **Exposition** Thu 10.30-11, Sat 5.30-6pm; **Confession** Sat 10.30-11, 5.30-6pm

Fr Terry Tastard
279 High Road N2 8HG Tel: 020 8883 4234
Email: finchleyeast@rcdow.org.uk Web: www.stmaryseastfinchley.org
10 minutes walk from East Finchley Stn (TfL), heading north
Barnet Deanery (1898; 1953)

Secretary Yvonne Merola Email: finchleyeastsec@rcdow.org.uk
Director of Christian Education and Youth Holly Graham
Email: finchleyeastcatechist@rcdow.org.uk

• Sisters of Nazareth, Nazareth House, 162 East End Road N2 0RU
Tel: 020 8883 1104 Fax: 020 8444 3691 Email: superior.finchleyuk@nazarethcare.com
Larmenier Centre, Nazareth Care (Regional Office)
Chaplain Fr John Boland

FINCHLEY NORTH + ST ALBAN

Sunday Mass (Sat 6pm), 8.45 (Sung Latin), 10.15 (Family Mass with Children's Liturgy), 12noon (Folk); **Holy Day Mass** as announced; **Weekday Mass** 10 with **Morning Prayer** preceding, followed by **Rosary** until 11; **Exposition** *First Fri only* 10.30-11.30, each Sat 10.30-11.30; **Confession** Sat 10.45-11.15, 5.15-5.45pm

Priest in Charge Dom Bernard Akoeso OSB
51 Nether Street N12 7NN Tel: 020 8446 0224 Fax: 020 8343 7400
Email: finchleynorth@rcdow.org.uk Web: parish.rcdow.org.uk/finchleynorth
200 yds from Tally Ho Corner
Barnet Deanery (1903; 1909; cons 24 February 1995)
Key Catechist Ursula Morrissey

• Belarusian Catholic Mission: see under *Eastern Catholic Churches* at the end of this Section
• Care and Nursing Homes:
Abbeyfield, Acacia Lodge, Ashfield House, Barnet Temporary Unhoused, Clovelly House, Catherine Lodge, Elmhurst, Fernbank, Dr French Memorial, Grace House, The Grange, Hilton Lodge, Kenwood House, The Limes, Meadowside Home, Safestart Foundation, Torrington, Wimbush House, Woodlands
• North London Hospice

FRENCH CHURCH + NOTRE DAME DE FRANCE A

Sunday Mass - *all French* - (Sat 6pm), 10, 11.30; *Summer Sunday Mass* (Sat 6pm), 11.30; **Holy Day Mass** 12.15pm *English*, 6pm *English*, 7.30pm *French*; **Weekday Mass** 12.15pm except Tue, 6pm; **Confession** before & after Mass & by arrangement

Marists (SM) Fr Pascal Boidin
5 Leicester Place WC2H 7BX Tel: 020 7437 9363 Fax: 020 7440 2645
Email: frenchchurch@rcdow.org.uk Web: www.ndfchurch.org
Off north side of Leicester Square
Westminster Deanery (1865; 1868; 1955)
Community: Frs Pascal Boidin, Hubert Bonnet-Eymard, (Superior), Damien Diouf, Kevin Duffy (from Jan 2019); Br Ivan Vodopivec
Parish Administrator Philippine de Beauregard Tel: 020 7440 2642

SECTION 3

• Missionary Sisters of the Society of Mary SMSM, 34 Lisle Street WC2H 7BD
Tel: 020 3659 7836
Srs Marie-Emmanuel Fuchs, Catherine Jones

• Chaplaincy to the French Schools, 23 Cromwell Mews SW7 2JY
Florence Blagburn Tel: 020 7584 3006

FULHAM 1 + ST THOMAS OF CANTERBURY

Sunday Mass (Sat 5.30pm), 9, 10.30 (Family), 12noon, 3pm (Portuguese), 6pm; **Holy Day Mass** 9.30, 8pm; **Weekday Mass** Mon-Fri 9.30, Sat 10; **Exposition** Sat 10.30-11.30; **Confession** Sat 10.30-11.30, 6.15-6.45pm

Fr Dennis F P Touw Tempelmans-Plat, Fr Emmanuel Onwu
60 Rylston Road SW6 7HW Tel: 020 7385 4040
Email: fulham@rcdow.org.uk Web: www.stocf.wordpress.com
Hammersmith & Fulham Deanery (1847; cons 5 December 1969; recons 2006)

FULHAM 2 STEPHENDALE ROAD + OUR LADY OF PERPETUAL HELP A

Sunday Mass (Sat 6.30pm), 9, 11; **Holy Day Mass** as announced; **Weekday Mass** Mon 9, Tue 7pm, Wed 9, Thu 9.30, Fri 8; **Exposition** Thu 8.30; **Confession** Sat 5-6pm

Fr Bill Bowder
Parish House, 2 Tynemouth Street SW6 2QT Tel: 020 7736 4864 / 07598 878599
Email: stephendaleroad@rcdow.org.uk Web: parish.rcdow.org.uk/stephendaleroad
Sand's End: east of Wandsworth Bridge Road, south of New King's Road, southwest of Imperial Wharf
Hammersmith & Fulham Deanery (1922)
Parish Administrator Susan Keogh **Catechetical Co-ordinator** Jackie Charles
CAFOD Fabienne Noakes

FULHAM: *SEE ALSO PARSONS GREEN*

FULHAM ROAD + OUR LADY OF DOLOURS A

Sunday Mass (Sat 6.30pm), 8.30, 10 (Family), 11.15 (Spanish), 12.15pm, 7pm; **Holy Day Mass** (Vigil 6.30pm), 10, 6.30pm; **Weekday Mass** 10, 6.30pm; **Exposition** Mon-Fri 10.30-11.15; **Rosary** Wed 10.30-10.45; **Legion of Mary** Tue 7.15pm; **Confession** daily 6.15-6.30pm & on request, Sat 10.45-11.15, 6-6.30pm

Servites (OSM) Fr Patrick Ryall
St Mary's Priory, 264 Fulham Road SW10 9EL Tel: 020 7352 6965 Fax: 020 7351 9749
Email: fulhamroad@rcdow.org.uk Web: www.servitechurch.org
In Fulham Road, east of Redcliffe Gardens/Edith Grove traffic lights
Kensington & Chelsea Deanery (1864; 1875; cons 4 November 1953)
Community: Frs Patrick Ryall (Prior and Parish Priest), Paul Addison, Chris O'Brien (Formation Master), Patrick O'Connell, Allan Satur
Parish Sister Sr Clementina Wasike

• Sisters of the Cross and Passion (CP), 7 Stadium Street SW10 0PU Tel: 020 7352 6013
Srs Rita Cahill, Marcella Roe

• Sisters Hospitallers of the Sacred Heart (Spanish), St Teresa's Residential Care Home 40-46 Roland Gardens SW7 3PW Tel: 020 7373 5820, Provincialate Tel: 020 7373 3054 Email: provincial@hsc-uk.org Web: www.sisterhospitallers.org
• Chelsea & Westminster Hospital

GARSTON + OUR LADY AND ST MICHAEL

Sunday Mass (Sat 6pm), 8.30, 10, 12noon; **Holy Day Mass** 9.30, 7.30pm; **Weekday Mass** Mon-Wed, Fri 9.30; **Confession** Sat 5-5.50pm & on request

Fr Fortunato Pantisano, Rev Paul Quinn (Deacon)
Catholic Church, Crown Rise, Garston, Watford WD25 0NE Tel: 01923 673239
Email: garston@rcdow.org.uk Web: parish.rcdow.org.uk/garston
On A405 North Orbital Road, just south of St Albans Road junction
Watford Deanery (1954)
Parish Administrator Awaiting appointment Tel: 01923 673239 (Mon, Tue, Wed, Fri 9-12noon)

• Pembroke House, Langley House, Tenterden House, Allington Court

GERMAN CHURCH + ST BONIFACE

Sunday Mass (Sat 5pm, 1st & 3rd Sun), 11 (2nd, 4th & 5th Sun); **Confession** (German) by appointment

Fr Andreas Blum
47 Adler Street E1 1EE Tel: 020 7247 9529
Email: germanchurch@rcdow.org.uk Web: parish.rcdow.org.uk/germanchurch
Tower Hamlets Deanery (1809; 1875; cons 4 October 1925; recons 2 October 1960)

• Wynfrid House, 20 Mulberry Street E1 1EH
Tel: 020 7247 6110 Email: info@wynfridhouse.com
German Community Centre and Youth Hostel
Manager Anthony Perera
• St Boniface Secular Institute (English Region) & Lioba House German Hostel for Young People 42-44 Exeter Road NW2 4SB Tel: 020 8438 9628
Email: info.house42@yahoo.com Web: www.hostel-lioba-house.de
(see also *Willesden Green* entry) Barbara von Alten, Christa von Gleichenstein, Maria Lohre, Dr Eva Roettgers

GOLDERS GREEN + ST EDWARD THE CONFESSOR

Sunday Mass under review, see parish website **www.stedwardgg.uk**; **Holy Day Mass** (Vigil 7pm), 10, 7pm; **Weekday Mass** as announced; **Confession** Sat 10.30-11, 5.30-6pm & on request before & after Mass as available

Fr Antony Convery, Rev Anthony Clark (Deacon, non-resident,
Email: anthonyclark@rcdow.org.uk)
700 Finchley Road NW11 7NE Tel: 020 8455 1300
Email: goldersgreen@rcdow.org.uk Web: www.stedwardgg.uk

SECTION 3

On main road just north of Golders Green Stn (TfL)
Barnet Deanery (1909; 1915; cons 30 September 1931)

GRAHAME PARK + ST MARGARET CLITHEROW A

Sunday Mass (Sat 6.30pm), 9, 12noon; **Holy Day Mass** 9.15, 7pm; **Weekday Mass** Mon, Fri 7pm, Tue, Wed, Thu 9.15, Sat 12noon; **Exposition** Sat 5-6pm; **Novena** Mon after Mass; **Confession** Sat 10-12noon, 5-6pm

Fr Brian Griffiths
The Presbytery, Everglade Strand NW9 5PX Tel: 020 8205 6830
Email: grahamepark@rcdow.org.uk Web: parish.rcdow.org.uk/grahamepark
Off Great Strand (near RAF Museum)
Barnet Deanery (1970; 1973; cons 14 November 1998)

- Metropolitan Police Training School

GREENFORD + OUR LADY OF THE VISITATION

Sunday Mass (Sat 7pm), 8, 9, 10.30, 12noon, 7pm; **Holy Day Mass** 8.30, 12noon, 7.30pm; **Weekday Mass** Mon-Sat 12noon; **Confession** Sat 11-12noon, 6.15-6.45pm

Pallottine Fathers (SAC) Fr Eugene Lynch, Fr Thomas Daly, Fr Joseph McLoughlin, Fr Liam O'Donovan,
358 Greenford Road, Greenford UB6 9AN Tel: 020 8578 1363 Fax: 020 8813 2230
Email: greenford@rcdow.org.uk Web: parish.rcdow.org.uk/greenford
Main Road (A4127) south of Ruislip Road junction
Ealing Deanery (1928; 1937)
Catechetical Co-ordinator Henry Chichon

GROVE PARK + ST JOSEPH

Sunday Mass (Sat 6.30pm), 9, 11; **Holy Day Mass** (Vigil 7.30pm), 10, 7.30pm; **Weekday Mass** as announced; **Confession** Sat 11-11.30

Fr John Seabrook
1 Bolton Road W4 3TE Tel: 020 8994 6861
Email: grovepark@rcdow.org.uk Web: parish.rcdow.org.uk/grovepark
South A4, close to Chiswick Stn (BR), corner of Devonshire Gardens
Hounslow Deanery (1964; cons 23 February 1973)

GUNNERSBURY + ST DUNSTAN

Sunday Mass 10; **Weekday Mass** Tue, Thu 9.30 or as announced; **Confession** as announced

Fr Michael Dunne, Fr Michael Maguire (clergy also serve Chiswick and are resident at 247 High Road W4 4PU Tel: 020 8994 2877)
141 Gunnersbury Avenue W3 8LE
Email: gunnersbury@rcdow.org.uk Web: parish.rcdow.org.uk/gunnersbury
On North Circular Road (A406), 300 yards north of Chiswick roundabout
Hounslow Deanery (1931)

• Little Company of Mary (Provincialate), 93 Gunnersbury Avenue W5 4LR
Tel: 020 8993 6107 Web: www.lcmsisters.org
• Westpark, 1 Leopold Road W5 3PB Tel: 020 8992 3954
Pastoral care entrusted to the Prelature of Opus Dei Fr James Pereiro
• Woodlands, 12 Gunnersbury Avenue W5 3NJ Tel: 020 8992 4025
Pastoral care entrusted to the Prelature of Opus Dei

HACKNEY + ST JOHN THE BAPTIST

Sunday Mass (Sat 6pm), 9.30, 11.30; **Holy Day Mass** 9.30, 5.30pm (Latin), 7pm; **Weekday Mass** Mon 12noon (Hospice), Tue-Fri 12noon, Sat 10; **Confession** Sat 10.30

Fr David Evans
3 King Edward's Road E9 7SF Tel: 020 8985 2496
Email: hackney@rcdow.org.uk Web: parish.rcdow.org.uk/hackney
King Edward's Road, off Mare Street, north of St Joseph's Hospice
Hackney Deanery (1847; 1956; cons 14 June 1972)

• Religious Sisters of Charity, St Joseph's Convent, 36 Mare Street E8 4AD
Tel: 020 8525 4242 Email: rschackney@yahoo.co.uk Web: www.religioussistersofcharity.org
• Sisters of Charity of St Paul, 28 Warneford Street E9 7NG
Tel: 020 8986 2346 Email: b.devine@btinternet.com
Srs Bernie Devine, Dolores Bourke
• St Joseph's Hospice
Chaplain Fr Peter-Michael Scott Tel: 020 8525 3032

HAMMERSMITH + ST AUGUSTINE

Sunday Mass (Sat 6pm), 9, 10.30, 12.15pm, 6.30pm; **Holy Day Mass** 8, 12.15pm, 7pm; **Weekday Mass** 8 (not Sat), 12.15pm; **Exposition** Sat 10.30-12noon; **Confession** Sat 10.30-11.30; 5-5.45pm

Augustinians (OSA) Fr Gianni Notarianni
55 Fulham Palace Road W6 8AU Tel: 020 8748 3788
Email: hammersmith@rcdow.org.uk Web: www.saintaugustineshammersmith.org
South Hammersmith Broadway, just beyond flyover
Hammersmith & Fulham Deanery (1903; 1916; cons 1933)
Community Bishop Michael G Campbell (in residence); Frs Mark Minihane (Prior), Gianni Notarianni (Parish Priest), Fr Gladson Dabre (Director of Discernment Community and Vocations), Fr Jacob Choi
Discernment community for men Fr Gladson Dabre
Email: Vocations@theaugustinians.org Web: www.theaugustians.org
Parish Administrator Claudette Foley

• Austin Forum
Director Fr Gianni Notarianni Email: gianni@austin-forum.org
Austin Forum Project Manager and Order Communication Officer Marie Marin La Meslée Email: marie@austin-forum.org

SECTION 3

Administrator / Venue Manager Helen Murphy **Tel: 020 8748 3254**
Email: helen@austin-forum.org
• **Charing Cross Hospital, Chapel of the Holy Cross**
Sunday Mass 10; **Weekday Mass** Mon 1pm
Chaplains Fr Giles Pinnock, Fr Gerard O'Brien **Tel 020 3311 1056**

HAMPSTEAD + ST MARY

Sunday Mass (Sat 6.30pm), 8.30, 10, 11.30, 6.30pm; **Holy Day Mass** 10, 7.30pm; **Weekday Mass** as announced; **Confession** Sat 6-6.30pm & on request

Mgr Phelim Rowland
4 Holly Place NW3 6QU Tel: 020 7435 6678 Fax: 020 7435 8436
Email: hampstead@rcdow.org.uk Web: parish.rcdow.org.uk/hampstead
Near Hampstead Stn (TfL); via Church Row, lower end of Heath Street
Camden Deanery (1796; 1816; cons 1977)
Parish Administrator Mark Martinez **Email: markmartinez@rcdow.org.uk**
Pastoral Assistant Mary Stanier **Email: marystanier@rcdow.org.uk**

• **Sisters of St Dorothy 99 Frognal NW3 6XR**
International Students' Residence Tel: 020 7794 6893
Email: stdorothylondon@gmail.com Web: www.st.dorothys.talktalk.net
• **Sisters of St Marcellina, Hampstead Towers, 6 Ellerdale Road NW3 6BD**
Tel: 020 7435 0181 Email: sisters@stmarcellina.org.uk Web: stmarcellina.org.uk

HAMPTON HILL (AND UPPER TEDDINGTON) + ST FRANCIS DE SALES

Sunday Mass (Sat 6pm), 9, 11; **Holy Day Mass** (Vigil 7.30pm), 9.30; **Weekday Mass** as announced; **Confession** Sat 10-11 & before weekday Masses

Society of Christ (SChr) Fr Wojciech Stachyra
16 Wellington Road, Hampton Hill TW12 1JR Tel: 020 8977 1415
Email: hamptonhill@rcdow.org.uk Web: http://stfrancisdesales.co.uk/.
Upper Thames Deanery (1920; 1928; 1966; cons 18 December 1976)
Parish Secretary Mrs Rhona Chilvers (Tue, Wed, Fri mornings)

• **Laurel Dene Care Home, Hampton**

HAMPTON-ON-THAMES + ST THEODORE OF CANTERBURY

Sunday Mass (Sat 6.30pm), 8.30, 10.30; **Holy Day Mass** 9.30, 7.30pm; **Weekday Mass** as announced; **Exposition** Thu after morning Mass; **Confession** Sat 10-10.30, 5.45-6.15pm & on request

Fr Bernard Boylan
110 Station Road, Hampton-on-Thames TW12 2AS
Tel: 020 8979 3596 Fax: 020 8979 8854
Email: hamptononthames@rcdow.org.uk Web: parish.rcdow.org.uk/hamptononthames
Upper Thames Deanery (1927; 1986; cons 22 March 1987)
Parish Secretary Paul Danon (Thu, Fri)

• Poor Servants of the Mother of God (PSMG), 112 Station Road, Hampton-on-Thames TW12 2AS Tel: 020 8255 1106 Sr Marian Ward

HANWELL + OUR LADY AND ST JOSEPH A

Sunday Mass (Sat 6.30pm), 8, 10 (Sung Family), 12noon; **Holy Day Mass** 10, 7pm; **Weekday Mass** Mon-Wed, Fri 10; **Exposition** Sat 5-6pm; **Confession** Sat 5.30-6pm & on request

Fr Cristiano Braz

52 Uxbridge Road W7 3SU Tel: 020 8567 4056
Email: hanwell@rcdow.org.uk Web: parish.rcdow.org.uk/hanwell
On main road, corner of St George's Road (traffic lights)
Ealing Deanery (1853; 1967)
Parish Administrator Pam Sheridan
Catechetical Co-ordinator awaiting appointment

• Medical Mission Sisters, 8 Springfield Road W7 3JP
Email: mmsspringfield@gmail.com Web: www.medicalmissionsisters-uk.org
• Sisters of St Joseph of Peace, St Mary's Convent, 50 Uxbridge Road W7 3PP
Tel: 020 8567 8635
• Ealing Hospital, Southall: General Wing
Mass Wed 2pm
St Bernard's Wing

HAREFIELD + ST PAUL, MERLE AVENUE A

Sunday Mass (Sat 6.30pm), 9, 11, 5pm *2nd Sun only, Syro-Malabar Rite*; **Holy Day Mass** 9.15, 7pm; **Weekday Mass** Mon-Sat 9.15; **Confession** Sat after morning Mass & 6pm

Fr James Mulligan

St Paul's House, 2 Merle Avenue, Harefield UB9 6DG Tel: 01895 822365
Email: harefield@rcdow.org.uk Web: parish.rcdow.org.uk/harefield
Bus 331 Uxbridge, U9 Northwood; church in Merle Avenue off High Street at south end of shopping parade
Hillingdon Deanery (1963; 1965; ext 1983)

• Harefield Hospital, Courtfield, Rylstone, Bardom Court, Harefield Nursing Home, Cedar House, Coppermill Care Home

HARPENDEN + OUR LADY OF LOURDES

Sunday Mass (Sat 6pm), 8.30, 9.45 (Family), 11.30 (sung); **Holy Day Mass** 9.15, 6pm; **Weekday Mass** Mon, Tue, Wed, 9.15, Thu 11, Fri Liturgy of the Word & Holy Communion 9.15, Sat 10; **Novena** after Wed Mass; **Confession** Sat 10.30-11, 6.45-7.15pm

Canon Anthony Dwyer

1 Kirkwick Avenue, Harpenden AL5 2QH Tel: 01582 712245
Email: harpenden@rcdow.org.uk Web: parish.rcdow.org.uk/harpenden
Rothamsted Avenue; off High Street, up from Church Green
St Albans Deanery (1905; 1929; cons 28 May 1936)

SECTION 3

Office Administrator Melanie Armitage **Tel: 01582 712245**
Email: harpenden@rcdow.org.uk Office open 9.30-12.30pm, Mon-Thu
Parish Safeguarding Rep Sue Harkness

- **Dominican Sisters, 18 Kirkdale Road, Harpenden AL5 2PT Tel: 01582 712814**
- **Spire Hospital**

HARROW NORTH + ST JOHN FISHER A

Sunday Mass (Sat 6pm), 8.30, 10, 11.30; **Holy Day Mass** 9.30, 7pm; **Weekday Mass** Mon, Tue, Thu, Fri 9.30; **Exposition** Mon 8.15-9.15, ***First Fri only***, with **Benediction** 10-11; **Confession** Sat 5.15-5.45pm & by appointment

Fr Graham Stokes

80 Imperial Close, North Harrow HA2 7LW Tel: 020 8868 7531
Email: harrownorth@rcdow.org.uk Web: www.stjohnfisheronline.org.uk
Between North Harrow/Rayners Lane Stns, just south of The Ridgeway junction
Harrow Deanery (1939; cons 2014)
Fr Graham Stokes **Tel: 020 8429 5684**
Parish Administrator Claudia McHugh **Tel: 020 8429 5681 Email: claudiamchugh@rcdow.org.uk**
Catechist Kay O'Connor **Tel: 020 8429 5682 Email: kayoconnor@rcdow.org.uk**
Accounts Fiona Moreira **Tel: 020 8429 5683 Email: fionamoreira@rcdow.org.uk**

HARROW-ON-THE-HILL + OUR LADY AND ST THOMAS OF CANTERBURY

Sunday Mass (Sat 6pm), 8.30, 9.45 (Family), 11.15 (Sung), 6.30pm; **Holy Day Mass** 9.30, 8pm; **Weekday Mass** Mon 9.30, Tue 9.30 (Eucharistic Service), Wed 7pm, Thu, Fri 9.30; **Exposition** Sat 11.30-12noon; **Confession** Sat 11.30-12noon

Fr Guy Sawyer

22 Roxborough Park, Harrow-on-the-Hill HA1 3BE
Tel: 020 8422 2513 Fax: 020 8869 6896
Email: harrowonthehill@rcdow.org.uk Web: parish.rcdow.org.uk/harrowonthehill
Harrow Deanery (1873; 1894)
Parish Safeguarding Officer Desmond Gaynor **Tel: 01923 778987**
Parish Secretary Anna Byrne **Mon-Fri 9.30-12.30pm**
Pastoral Assistant Holly Cook **Tel: 07724 362853 Email: hollycook@rcdow.org.uk**

- **Sisters of St Mary of Namur, 1 Grafton Road, Harrow HA1 4QS Tel: 020 8424 8185 Email: srjudith@gmail.com**

HARROW SOUTH + ST GABRIEL & NORTHOLT + ST BERNARD

St Gabriel: Sunday Mass (Sat 6pm), 8.30, 10 (with Children's Liturgy), 12noon; **Holy Day Mass** 10; **Weekday Mass** Mon, Wed, Thu 10; **Exposition** Thu 10.30-11; **Confession** Sat 5.15-5.45pm
St Bernard: Sunday Mass 9, 11 (with Children's Liturgy), 5pm (Polish); **Holy Day Mass** 7.30pm; **Weekday Mass** Tue, Fri 10, Sat 9.30; **Exposition** Sat 10-11; **Confession** Sat 10.15-10.45

Fr James Neal (resident at St Bernard's), Fr David Lucuy Claros (resident at St Gabriel's)
The Presbytery, 17 Mandeville Road, Northolt UB5 5HE
Parish Office: 390b Northolt Road, South Harrow HA2 8EX Tel: 020 8864 5455
Email: harrowsouth@rcdow.org.uk Web: parish.rcdow.org.uk/harrowsouth

\+ St Gabriel's Church
390b Northolt Road, South Harrow HA2 8EX
On main road, south of South Harrow Stn, near junction with Park Lane
Harrow Deanery (1933; 2002; cons 2003)

\+ St Bernard's Church
17 Mandeville Road, Northolt UB5 5HE
On main road, between Target Roundabout & Northolt Stn
Harrow Deanery (1965; cons 2010)

• Sisters of St Louis, 67 Parkfield Road, South Harrow HA2 8LA Tel: 020 8248 3838

HARROW ROAD + OUR LADY OF LOURDES AND ST VINCENT DE PAUL

Sunday Mass (Sat 6pm), 11.30; **Holy Day Mass** as Weekday Mass, also 7pm; **Weekday Mass** Mon, Fri 10 (Tue, Thu 10 at Paddington); **Exposition** and **Benediction** Mon, Fri 9-10, Sat 5-6pm; **Confession** Sat 5-6pm

Fr Michael Jarmulowicz (also serves Paddington)
337 Harrow Road W9 3RB Tel: 020 7286 2170
Email: harrowroad@rcdow.org.uk Web: parish.rcdow.org.uk/harrowroad
East of Great Western Road junction; near Westbourne Park Stn
North Kensington Deanery (1876; 1912; 1975)
Parish Administrator Mrs Jennifer Ellis **Mon, Thu, Fri 9-1pm**

HARROW WEALD: *SEE WEALDSTONE*

HATCH END: *SEE HEADSTONE LANE*

HATFIELD + MARYCHURCH A

Sunday Mass (Sat 6pm), 11 (with Children's Liturgy); **Holy Day Mass** 9.30, 7.30pm; **Weekday Mass** Mon, Tue 9.30, Wed 7.30pm, Thu, Fri 9.30; **Divine Office** 20 mins before Weekday Mass; **Novenas** Tue: Our Lady of Perpetual Succour, Thu**Exposition** Fri after Mass; **Confession** Sat 5.15-5.45pm

Missionary Society of St Paul (MSP) Fr Livinus Onyebuchi, Fr Julius Otoaye (clergy also serve Hatfield South and are resident at St Peter's Presbytery, Bishop's Rise, Hatfield AL10 9HN Tel: 01707 262121)
26 Salisbury Square, Hatfield AL9 5JD Tel: 01707 262 439
Email: hatfield@rcdow.org.uk Web: parish.rcdow.org.uk/hatfield
Just off Great North Road (A1000), near BR Stn & Hatfield House
Stevenage Deanery (1930, 1971)

SECTION 3

Chapel of Ease: St Thomas More, Station Road, Welham Green
Sunday Mass 9.30; **Holy Day Mass** (Vigil 7.30pm)

HATFIELD SOUTH + ST PETER

Sunday Mass 9.15, 11 (with Children's Liturgy), Student Mass 6pm; **Holy Day Mass** 9.30, 7pm; **Weekday Mass** Mon, Tue, Wed, Fri 9.30, preceded by **Morning Prayer** 9.10, Thu 7pm, Sat 10.30; **Exposition** Sat 11-12noon, with **Benediction** 12noon; **Novena** Tue after Mass - Our Lady of Perpetual Help, Fri after Mass - Most Sacred Heart of Jesus; **Rosary** Wed after Mass; **Confession** Sat 11-12noon, 5-5.30pm

Missionary Society of St Paul (MSP) Fr Livinus Onyebuchi, Fr Julius Otoaye (also Chaplain to University of Hertfordshire) (clergy also serve Hatfield Marychurch)
St Peter's Presbytery, Bishop's Rise, Hatfield AL10 9HN Tel: 01707 262121
Email: hatfieldsouth@rcdow.org.uk Web: www.stpetershatfield.org
Half-mile from Comet Roundabout, via Cavendish Way
Stevenage Deanery (1959; 1961)

HAVERSTOCK HILL + OUR LADY OF THE ROSARY AND ST DOMINIC A

The Church is the Diocesan Shrine of the Most Holy Rosary (2016)

Sunday Mass (Sat 6pm), 8.30, 10 (Family), 12noon (Solemn Shrine Mass), 6pm; **Holy Day Mass** (Vigil 6pm), 7.30, 10, 6pm; **Weekday Mass** Mon-Fri 7.30, 6pm (Thu 6pm with **Vespers**), Sat 7.30, 10; **Morning Prayer** Mon-Fri 7, Sat, Sun 8; **Evening Prayer** Mon, Tu, Fri 6.45pm, Sun 5.30pm; **Exposition** Mon-Fri 5-5.45pm, also **Benediction** Thu 5.45pm, **Exposition** and **Rosary Procession** Sat 10.30; **Confession** Sat 10.30-11, 5.30-6.15pm, Sun 9.45-10.15, 11.45-12.15pm

Dominicans (OP) Fr Thomas Skeats (Tel: 020 7482 9224)
St Dominic's Priory, Southampton Road NW5 4LB
Tel: 020 7482 9210 Fax: 020 7482 9239
Email: haverstockhill@rcdow.org.uk Web: www.rosaryshrine.co.uk
Top of Malden Road, nearest TfL Stns Chalk Farm & Belsize Park.
Camden Deanery (1867; 1874; cons 1 August 1923)
Community: Frs Michael Dunn, Leo Edgar, Martin Ganeri (Provincial **Email: provincial@english.op.org**), Peter Harries, Oliver Keenan, Lawrence Lew, Rudolf Löwenstein, Thomas Skeats (Prior and Parish Priest)

• **Hospital Chaplain to UCLH NHS Trust** Fr Peter Harries **Tel: 020 7482 9216**
(Elizabeth Garrett Anderson Wing, Heart, National for Neurology & Neurosurgery and University College Hospitals)
Sunday Mass 9.45
• **Royal Free Hospital**
Tel: 020 7794 0500 Chaplain Fr John McCarthy **Tel: 020 7830 2742**

HAYES + THE IMMACULATE HEART OF MARY A

Sunday Mass (Sat 6.30pm), 8.30, 10, 12noon, 8.30pm; **Holy Day Mass** (Vigil 7.30pm), 12.15pm, 7.30pm; **Weekday Mass** Mon, Tue, Thu 8.15, Mon-Sat 12.15pm, Wed,

Fri 7.30pm; **Bank Holidays** 10; **Confession** (Spanish, Polish available) Sat 10.30-11.30, 5.45-6.15pm & by appointment

Claretian Missionaries (CMF) Fr Paul Smyth
Botwell House, Botwell Lane, Hayes UB3 2AB Tel: 020 8573 2544
Email: hayes@rcdow.org.uk Web: www.botwell.org.uk
In town centre, just off Coldharbour Lane/Station Road; near Hayes and Harlington Stn (BR)
Hillingdon Deanery (1912; 1954; 1961; cons 24 October 1972)
Community: Frs Joseph Katthula (from Dec 2018), Chris Newman, John O'Byrne, Paul Smyth (Major Superior), Krzysztof Stawicki
Pastoral Assistant Daniel Ortiz **Administrator** Michael Bagness **General Parish Assistant** Bridget Fahy **Tel: 020 8573 2544**
Claretian Pastoral Centre, Botwell House, Botwell Lane, Hayes UB3 2AB
Tel: 020 8573 2544

- Hayes Cottage Nursing Home

HEADSTONE LANE + ST THERESA OF THE CHILD JESUS

Sunday Mass (Sat 5pm), 10, 6pm; **Holy Day Mass** 9.30, 7.30pm; **Weekday Mass** Mon-Thu 9.30, Fri, Sat 10; **Exposition** and **Benediction** ***First Fri only*** 8.50-9.45; **Confession** Sat 10.30, with **Exposition** and **Benediction** 4-4.30pm

Fr Richard Parsons (Tel: 020 8864 8021)
22 Boniface Walk, Harrow HA3 6PU Tel: 020 8428 3260
Email: headstonelane@rcdow.org.uk Web: parish.rcdow.org.uk/headstonelane
Uxbridge Road, Hatch End, junction Headstone Lane; near Headstone Lane/Hatch End Stns
Harrow Deanery (1953)

HEATHROW AIRPORT + ST GEORGE'S CHAPEL

Sunday Mass 12.30pm - Chapel of St George; **Weekday Mass** Mon, Wed, Fri 12.30pm

Chaplain Fr Daniel Adayi CSSp Tel: 020 8745 4261 (in residence at Hounslow Parish, 94 Bath Road, Hounslow TW3 3EH **Tel: 020 8570 1693 ext 6**), Rev Robert Levett (Deacon) **Tel: 07882 491127**, Helen Baly, Sr Margaret Byrnes RSCJ, **Tel: 07751 285305**, Shaun Loader CSB, Elisangela Rivera MBA
Chapel of St George, Heathrow Airport, Central Terminal Area, Hounslow TW6 1BP
Tel: 020 8745 4261 Email: heathrowairport@rcdow.org.uk
Web: parish.rcdow.org.uk/heathrow
The Chapel is located in the central area close to London Underground, train and bus stations and the new Terminal 2, Queen's Terminal. Visitors using cars should park in Car Park 1a. From any point go to the Central Bus Station and locate Stand 17. From there turn left and follow the blue signs along the designated pathway to the Chapel next to the large stone wall.
Please contact the Chapel office for details of other services and airport locations during the week. Priests and groups who wish to celebrate Mass at the airport should contact the office, or a chaplain directly, in advance if possible. Multi-faith prayer rooms are to be found in all terminals, either airside or landside.
Hounslow Deanery (1968)

HEMEL HEMPSTEAD EAST PARISHES A ♿ 👂

Our Lady, Queen of All Creation: **Sunday Mass** (Sat 5pm), 10.30, 12noon; **Holy Day Mass** as announced; **Weekday Mass** Mon, Tue 10, Fri 6.30pm, Sat 10; **Exposition** Sat 10.30-11; **Confession** Sat 10.30-11

The Resurrection: **Sunday Mass** 9; **Holy Day Mass** as announced; **Weekday Mass** Thu 10; **Confession** before Mass

For Weekday Mass times, please check the parish newsletter at **www.hemelcatholic.org**

Fr Kim Addison
The Presbytery, Rant Meadow, Hemel Hempstead HP3 8PG Tel: 01442 210610

+ Our Lady, Queen of All Creation (Hemel Hempstead East)
The Presbytery, Rant Meadow, Hemel Hempstead HP3 8PG Tel: 01442 210610
Email: hemeleast@rcdow.org.uk Web: www.hemelcatholic.org
On dual carriageway A414 between M1 (exit 8) & town centre
St Albans Deanery (1955; 1987; cons 13 November 1987)

+ The Church of the Resurrection, Grovehill (Hemel Hempstead North)
9 Henry Wells Square, Grovehill, Hemel Hempstead HP2 6BJ (Postal address: The Presbytery, Rant Meadow, Hemel Hempstead HP3 8PG) Tel: 01442 210610
Email: hemeleast@rcdow.org.uk Web: www.hemelcatholic.org
Access from Washington Avenue into Turnpike Green
St Albans Deanery (Shared church, 1977)

HEMEL HEMPSTEAD WEST PARISHES A ♿ 👂

Boxmoor, Ss Mary and Joseph: **Sunday Mass** (Sat 6pm), 8.45, 11.45; **Holy Day Mass** as announced; **Weekday Mass** Wed, Fri 10; **Exposition** *1st Fri only* 10.30-11; **Confession** Sat 11-11.30

West, St Mark: **Sunday Mass** 8.45 (Ordinariate Rite), 10.15; **Holy Day Mass** as announced; **Weekday Mass** Wed 7.45pm (Ordinariate Rite); **Confession** before Mass

For Weekday Mass times, please check the parish newsletter at **www.hemelcatholic.org**

Fr Paul McDermott, Rev Simon Wright (Deacon)
186 St John's Road, Boxmoor HP1 1NR Tel: 01442 391759

+ Ss Mary and Joseph (Hemel Hempstead Boxmoor)
186 St John's Road, Boxmoor HP1 1NR Tel: 01422 391759
Email: hemelwest@rcdow.org.uk Web: www.hemelcatholic.org
St Albans Deanery (1890; 1938; 1951)

+ St Mark (Hemel Hempstead West)
Hollybush Lane, in the grounds of John F Kennedy Catholic School, Hemel Hempstead HP1 2PH

(Postal address: 186 St John's Road, Boxmoor HP1 1NR)
Email: hemelwest@rcdow.org.uk Web: www.hemelcatholic.org
St Albans Deanery (1977)

HENDON + OUR LADY OF DOLOURS A

Sunday Mass (Sat 6pm), 10, 12noon; **Holy Day Mass** as announced; **Weekday Mass** Mon-Wed 10, Thu 7.30, Fri 10, Sat 9; **Exposition**, then **Benediction** Sat 9.30-10; **Confession** Sat 9.30-10, 5.15-5.45pm and on request

Fr Tim Edgar
4 Egerton Gardens NW4 4BA Tel: 020 8202 0560 Fax: 020 8201 5636
Email: hendon@rcdow.org.uk Web: www.ourladyofdolours.org.uk
Off The Burroughs (opp. Town Hall), close to Watford Way (A41) & Hendon Central Stn (TfL)
Barnet Deanery (1849; 1863; cons 1927; recons 25 March 1966)

• Poor Handmaids of Jesus Christ, St Joseph's Convent, Westminster House, Watford Way NW4 4TY Tel: 020 8202 7626 Email: winifred.orourke@btinternet.com Web: www.poorhandmaidsofjesuschrist.org.uk
• Hendon Hospital

HENDON WEST + ST PATRICK

Sunday Mass 9.30, 12noon, 6pm, with **Exposition** 1.15-5.45pm; **Holy Day Mass** as announced; **Weekday Mass** Mon, Wed, Sat 10, Tue, Fri 7pm; **Our Lady of Perpetual Succour Novena** Tue 7.30pm; **Confession** Sat 10.30-11

Fr Donald Graham
167 West Hendon Broadway NW9 7EB Tel: 020 8202 5143
Email: hendonwest@rcdow.org.uk Web: parish.rcdow.org.uk/hendonwest
Hendon Broadway on main road (A5), 800 yds north of Staples Corner
Barnet Deanery (1964)

HERTFORD + THE IMMACULATE CONCEPTION AND ST JOSEPH

Sunday Mass (Sat 6pm), 8.30, 10.30 (Sung), 6pm; **Holy Day Mass** 7.30, 10 (at school in term time), 8pm; **Weekday Mass** Mon, Wed, 10, Tue, Fri, 12.15pm, Thu 7.30; **Exposition** Sat 5-5.45pm (***Stations of the Cross replace Exposition on Saturdays in Lent***); **Confession** Sat 10-10.30, 5.15-5.45pm

Canon Terence Phipps
23 St John's Street, Hertford SG14 1RX Tel: 01992 582109
Email: hertford@rcdow.org.uk Web: parish.rcdow.org.uk/hertford
Off Railway Sreet, close to Hertford East Stn (BR)
Lea Valley Deanery (Priory 1087-1539; 1848; 1858; cons 16 October 1866)

HESTON + OUR LADY QUEEN OF APOSTLES

Sunday Mass (Sat 7pm), 8, 9.30, 11.30, 3pm (Polish), 5.30pm; **Holy Day Mass** (Vigil 7pm), 9, 7pm; **Weekday Mass** 9, 7pm; **Exposition** Sat 9.30-10; **Novena** during Wed 7pm Mass; **Confession** Sat 9.30-10, 6.15-6.45pm & on request

SECTION 3

Society of Divine Vocations (SDV) Fr Luigi Morrone, Fr Vipin James, Fr Paul Rout OFM (in residence)
15 The Green, Heston Road, Heston TW5 0RL Tel: 020 8570 1818 Fax 020 8572 7861
Email: heston@rcdow.org.uk Web: parish.rcdow.org.uk/heston
Set back from main road, just south of motorway bridge
Hounslow Deanery (1928; 1929; 1964; cons 19 May 1974)
Fr Colin Whatling (retired) 2B Eton Avenue, Heston TW5 0HB Tel: 020 8606 9544
Heston Catholic Social Club (Pope John Centre) Tel: 020 8574 5411
Parish Halls (Parish Secretary) Tel: 020 8570 1818

HIGHBURY + ST JOAN OF ARC A

Sunday Mass (Sat 6pm), 9, 11, 2pm (Congolese Community); **Holy Day Mass** 9.15, 7.30pm; **Weekday Mass** Mon-Fri 9.15, Sat 10; **Confession** Sat 5.15-5.45pm

Canon Gerard King
60 Highbury Park N5 2XH Tel: 020 7226 0257
Email: highbury@rcdow.org.uk Web: www.stjoanofarcparish.co.uk
Islington Deanery (1920; 1962; cons 14 June 2001)

• Our Lady of Mercy Sisters, 40 Aberdeen Road N5 2XD Tel: 020 7359 3897
Srs Dolores Hyland, Roisin Kelly, Patricia Mockler
• Sisters of St Paul de Chartres, 30 Aberdeen Park N5 2BL Tel: 020 7359 1712
Email: spc_london11@yahoo.fr Web: stpaulrome.com
Srs Anna Song (Superior), Paul Marie Cushnan, Veronica Pak, June Ralph

HIGHGATE + ST JOSEPH

Sunday Mass (Sat 7pm), 8, 10, 12noon, 1.30pm (Polish), 7pm; **Holy Day Mass** (Vigil 6.30pm), 9.30, 6.30pm; **Weekday Mass** Mon-Fri 9.30, 6.30pm, Sat & Bank Holidays 9.30; **Confession** Sat 10-10.30, 6.30-6.45pm

Passionists (CP) Fr Patrick Fitzgerald, Fr George Koloth
St Joseph's Retreat, Highgate Hill N19 5NE Tel: 020 7272 2320
Email: highgate@rcdow.org.uk Web: www.stjosephshighgate.org.uk
Corner Dartmouth Park Hill; Archway Stn (TfL)
Islington Deanery (1858; 1888; cons 28 April 1932)
Community: Frs Tiernan Doherty (Rector), Patrick Fitzgerald, (Parish Priest), George Koloth, Benedict Lodge, Thomas Rockey
St Joseph's Parish Centre, Highgate Hill N19 5NE Tel: 020 7272 4571

• Whittington Hospital & Hornsey Central Hospital
Chaplain Fr Oliver Ugwu Tel: 020 7288 5337

HILLINGDON + ST BERNADETTE

Sunday Mass (Sat 6pm), 9, 11 (with Children's Liturgy), 5.30pm; **Holy Day Mass** 10, 7pm; **Weekday Mass** Mon, Wed-Sat 10; **Exposition** with **Benediction** Fri after Mass, also Fri 7.30pm; **Rosary** after weekday Mass; **Confession** Sat 10.30-11 & on request

Fr Matthew J Heslin, Rev Reg Abrahams (Deacon)
160 Long Lane, Hillingdon UB10 0EH Tel: 01895 234577
Email: hillingdon@rcdow.org.uk Web: parish.rcdow.org.uk/hillingdon
South Long Lane (half mile up from Uxbridge Road)
Hillingdon Deanery (1937; 1961; cons 7 October 1978)

• Sisters of Mercy, St Raphael's Convent, Court Drive, Hillingdon UB10 0BW
Tel: 01895 233771
• Hillingdon Hospital
Sunday and Holy Day Mass 4pm

HITCHIN + OUR LADY IMMACULATE AND ST ANDREW

Sunday Mass (Sat 6pm) 8.30, 10.30, 5pm; **Holy Day Mass** 7.30, 10, 7.30pm; **Weekday Mass** 10; **Confession** (French available) with **Exposition** and **Benediction** Sat 10.30-11.15

Assumptionists (a.a.) Fr Tom O'Brien, Fr Euloge Katsuva Kasine, Fr Michael Lambert, Fr Andrew O'Dell (in residence)
16 Nightingale Road, Hitchin SG5 1QS Tel: 01462 459126
Email: hitchin@rcdow.org.uk Web: parish.rcdow.org.uk/hitchin
Junction with Grove Road, opposite Bancroft Recreation Ground
Stevenage Deanery (1890; 1902; cons 18 December 1977)
Assistants Trish Bonnett (Pastoral), Susanna Hawksley (Sacraments)
Email: hitchinpastoral@rcdow.org.uk
Administrators Cheryl Saunders **(Mon-Thu)**, Antoinette Fernandes **(Fri)**

• Cheshire Home

HODDESDON + ST AUGUSTINE

Sunday Mass (Sat 4pm (Italian), 6.30pm), 9.15 (with Children's Liturgy), 11.15, ***First Sun only*** 5pm (Latin); **Holy Day Mass** 9.30, 12noon, 8pm; **Weekday Mass** Mon, Tue, Wed 9.15 (preceded by **Morning Prayer** 9), Fri 12noon, Sat 10; **Holy Hour *3rd Sun only*** 5pm; **Confession** Sat 10.30-11, 5.30-6.15pm, Sun 8.30-9

Fr Philip Miller, Fr Matthew Kattiyangal (in residence, Knanaya Chaplaincy)
The Presbytery, Esdaile Lane, Hoddesdon EN11 8DS
Tel: 01992 440986 Fax: 01992 440244
Email: hoddesdon@rcdow.org.uk Web: parish.rcdow.org.uk/hoddesdon
Junction of High Street with Charlton Way
Lea Valley Deanery (1932; 1962; cons 1971)

HOLBORN (CIRCUS), EC1: *SEE ELY PLACE*; (HIGH), WC1: *SEE LINCOLN'S INN FIELDS*

SECTION 3

HOLLOWAY + SACRED HEART OF JESUS A

Sunday Mass (Sat 6pm), 8.30, 11 (Sung, with choir); **Holy Day Mass** 10; **Weekday Mass** (**Morning Prayer** precedes by 15 mins) Mon, Wed, Thu, Fri 9.15, Public Holidays 10; **Confession** Sat 11-12noon & on request

Fr Gideon Wagay, Fr Henry Mobela (in residence, Zambian Chaplaincy, contact details below)
62 Eden Grove N7 8EN Tel: 020 7607 3594 Fax: 020 7607 1867
Email: holloway@rcdow.org.uk Web: www.sacredheartchurchholloway.org.uk
Off Holloway Road, opposite Metropolitan University and Emirates (Arsenal FC) Stadium
Islington Deanery (1855; 1870; cons 29 May 1928)
(Fr Henry Mobela Tel: 07495 866069 Email: kalusamobela@gmail.com)
Parish Administrator Elizabeth Ocampo
Catechetical Co-ordinator Nalini Nathan

- Sisters of La Sainte Union, 51 Freegrove Road N7 9RG Tel: 020 7609 7160
- Pentonville Prison Chaplains Valentine Ambe, Mary Ebbasi (See HM Prison Service)

HOMERTON + IMMACULATE HEART OF MARY AND ST DOMINIC

Sunday Mass (Sat 6.30pm), 9, 11; **Holy Day Mass** 9.30, 7pm; **Weekday Mass** 9.30; **Exposition** for Priests / Vocations Tue 10-10.30; **Confession** Sat 5.30-6pm

Fr Patrick Allsop, Fr Christian de Lisle
Presbytery, Ballance Road E9 5SS Tel: 020 8985 1495
Email: homerton@rcdow.org.uk Web: www.immaculatehearthomerton.org
Kenworthy Road
Hackney Deanery (1873; cons 30 June 1884)

HOUNSLOW + SS MICHAEL AND MARTIN

Sunday Mass (Sat 6.15pm), 9, 10.30, 12noon, 6pm; **Holy Day Mass** (Vigil 6pm), 7.30, 9, 6pm 7.30pm; **Weekday Mass** Mon-Wed 9, Thu 6pm, Fri 7pm; **Exposition**, followed by **Benediction** Sat 4.30-5.30pm; **Confession** Fri 6-6.30pm, Sat 9.30-10.15, 4.30-5.15pm **Ethnic Chaplaincy Masses** 3.30pm Syro-Malabar Mass *1st Sun only*, 4pm Sinhalese Mass *2nd Sun only*, 4pm Goan Mass *3rd Sun only*

Spiritans (CSSp) Fr Augustine Nwosu, Fr David Sandambongo, Fr Daniel Adayi (also Chaplain, Heathrow Airport Tel: 020 8570 1693 ext 6)
94 Bath Road, Hounslow TW3 3EH Tel: 020 8570 1693
Email: hounslow@rcdow.org.uk Web: parish.rcdow.org.uk/hounslow
Hounslow Deanery (1884; 1929; cons 12 October 1938)
Administrator Lavina Fernandes
Parish Catechists Colette Joyce, Jane Lowe
Youth Worker Ivan Cižmárik

HOXTON + ST MONICA'S PRIORY A

Sunday Mass (Sat 6.30pm), 9, 11, 7pm; **Holy Day Mass** (Vigil 7pm), 9.30, 12.30pm; **Weekday Mass** 9.30; **Exposition** Sat 5-6pm; **Confession** Sat 5-6pm

Augustinians (OSA) Fr Gabriel Hassan
19 Hoxton Square N1 6NT Tel: 020 7739 5006
Email: hoxton@rcdow.org.uk Web: parish.rcdow.org.uk/hoxton
Off Old Street, at Shoreditch Town Hall
Hackney Deanery (1864)
Parish Administrator Ingrid Bowie
Community Frs Barry Clifford (Prior), George Donaghy (Hospital Chaplain), Gabriel Hassan (Parish Priest); David Tan (Student)

• Little Sisters of Jesus, 148 Fellows Court, Weymouth Terrace E2 8LW
Tel: 020 7729 3605 Email: lsj.hackney@virgin.net Web: www.jesuscaritas.info/lsj
• Shalom Catholic Community 150 Kingsland Road E2 8EB Tel: 07432 501250
Email: london@comshalom.org Web: http://www.comshalom.org/en
Missionaries Emanuela Cardoso, Francisca de Fatima de Oliveira
• Ashwell House, Shepherdess Walk N1 7NA Tel: 020 7490 3296
Hall of residence for women university students
Pastoral care entrusted to Prelature of Opus Dei
• Mildmay Mission Hospital

SECTION 3

ISLE OF DOGS: *SEE MILLWALL*

ISLEWORTH + OUR LADY OF SORROWS AND ST BRIDGET OF SWEDEN

Sunday Mass (Sat 6pm), 8, 10, 12noon; **Holy Day Mass** (Vigil 7pm), 9, 7pm; **Weekday Mass** Mon-Thu 9, Mon, Fri 7pm, Sat 10; **Exposition** Mon-Thu half hour before Mass, Fri, Sat half hour after Mass, with **Benediction** Fri; **Confession** Sat 10.30-11, 5-5.30pm

Divine Word Missionaries (SVD) Fr Nicodemus Lobo Ratu, Fr Kieran Fitzharris
Memorial Square, 112 Twickenham Road, Isleworth TW7 6DL Tel/Fax: 020 8560 1431
Email: isleworth@rcdow.org.uk Web: parish.rcdow.org.uk/isleworth
Corner of South Street (traffic lights); opposite Gumley House
Hounslow Deanery (1675; 1910; cons 6 October 1910)

• Faithful Companions of Jesus, Gumley House Convent, 251 Twickenham Road, Isleworth TW7 6DN Tel: 020 8232 9570
Email: generalsecretary@fcjgeneralate.org Web: www.fcjsisters.org
The Generalate, central administration of the Community, is based here.
Srs Claire Sykes (General Superior), Patricia Binchy, Barbara Brown-Graham, Mary T Fitzpatrick, Seraphina Kimball, Mary Philomena Lyons, Alice Rimmer, Joanna Walsh

ISLINGTON + ST JOHN THE EVANGELIST

Sunday Mass (Sat 6pm), 9, 10.30 (Sung, with Children's Liturgy), 12noon (Sung), 6pm; **Holy Day Mass** 10, 12.30pm, 7.30pm; **Weekday Mass** 10; **Exposition** Sat 10.30-11.30; **Confession** Sat 10.30-11, 5.15-5.45pm

Mgr Séamus O'Boyle, Fr Allan Alvarado Gil, Fr Lawrence Milby (in residence)
(clergy also serve Copenhagen Street)
39 Duncan Terrace N1 8AL Tel: 020 7226 3277 Fax: 020 7704 8988
Email: islington@rcdow.org.uk Web: www.st-johns-islington-org
2 mins from Angel TfL Stn, via Islington High Street, right into Duncan Street, left into Duncan Terrace Islington Deanery (1839; 1843; cons 26 June 1873)

- **Sisters of the Cross and Passion, 40 Duncan Terrace N1 8AL Tel: 020 7359 8719**
Srs Kathleen Doran, Martin Joseph Taylor, Marcellina Cooney

ITALIAN CHURCH + ST PETER'S

Sunday Mass (Sat 7pm), 9.30, 11 (Sung), 12.30pm, 7pm; **Holy Day Mass** 10, 12.15pm, 7.30pm; **Weekday Mass** Mon-Fri 12.15pm; **Confession** (Italian, English, Sunday during Mass & on request)

Pallottine Fathers (SAC) Fr Andrea Fulco, Fr Giuseppe De Caro, Fr Ryszard Wrobel
St Peter's Italian Church, 136 Clerkenwell Road EC1R 5DL
(Correspondence etc. to 4 Back Hill EC1R 5EN)
Tel: 020 7837 1528 Fax: 020 7837 9071
Email: italianchurch@rcdow.org.uk Web: www.italianchurch.org.uk
Opposite the top end of Hatton Garden
Westminster Deanery (1863)

KENSAL NEW TOWN + OUR LADY OF THE HOLY SOULS ♿

Sunday Mass (Sat 6pm), 9, 11 (Family); **Holy Day Mass** 9.30, 7.30pm; **Weekday Mass** as announced; **Confession** Sat 5.15-5.45pm & on request

Fr Philip Baptiste
68 Hazlewood Crescent W10 5DJ Tel: 020 8969 2660
Email: kensalnewtown@rcdow.org.uk Web: parish.rcdow.org.uk/kensalnewtown
In Bosworth Road, off Kensal Road (near Halfpenny Bridge)
North Kensington Deanery (1862; 1882; cons 10 Nov 2012)
Parish Sister Sr Margarita RSM **Parish Administrator** Stephanie Mackay

- **Missionaries of Charity, 177 Bravington Road W9 3AR Tel: 020 8960 2644**
- **Sisters of Mercy, 76 Fifth Avenue W10 4DP Tel: 020 8960 2505**

KENSAL RISE + CHURCH OF THE TRANSFIGURATION A

Sunday Mass (Sat 6pm), 9, 11, 12.30pm (Italian); **Holy Day Mass** 10, 7pm; **Weekday Mass** Mon, Fri 7pm, Tues, Wed, Thurs, Sat 10 with **Exposition** one hour before each Mass; **Holy Hour** and **Benediction** Fri 6 pm; **Confession** Sat 10.30-11.15, 5-5.45pm

Fr Sean Thornton
Presbytery, 1 Wrentham Avenue NW10 3HT Tel: 020 8964 4040
Email: kensalrise@rcdow.org.uk Web: www.transfigparishkensalrise.org.uk
Corner of Wrentham Avenue and Chamberlayne Road, near Kensal Rise BR Stn
Brent Deanery (1977)

Parish Administrator Chelsea Bottomley (9:30 - 2:30pm, Mon-Wed, Fri)

• Daughters of Charity (SVP), 58 Wrentham Avenue NW10 3HG Tel: 020 8964 9796
• Sisters of Jesus and Mary, 200 Chamberlayne Road NW10 3JX
Tel: 020 8451 1957
• Stigmatine Fathers (CSS), 2 Leigh Gardens NW10 5HP
Tel/Fax: 020 8969 1414 Email: donnatalino@btinternet.com Fr Natalino Mignolli
• St Mary's Cemetery, 679-681 Harrow Road NW10 5NU Tel: 020 8969 1145

KENSINGTON 1 + OUR LADY OF VICTORIES

Sunday Mass (Sat 6.30pm), 9, 10.30, 12noon, 6.30pm; **Holy Day Mass** 7.30, 10, 7pm; **Weekday Mass** Mon-Fri 7.30, 10, Sat 10; **Exposition** Wed 10.30-12noon, ***First Sat only*** 10.30-12noon; **Confession** Sat 10.35-11.30, 5.30-6.25pm & on request

Mgr Jim Curry, Fr Daniel Herrero Peña, Fr Frederick Jackson, Rev Stéphane Joiris de Caussin (Deacon)
The Clergy House, 16 Abingdon Road W8 6AF Tel: 020 7937 4778 Fax: 020 7937 4221
Email: kensington1@rcdow.org.uk Web: parish.rcdow.org.uk/kensington1
235a High Street; south side of High Street, between Abingdon Road & Earls Court Road; not far from Kensington High Street Stn (TfL)
Kensington & Chelsea Deanery (1794; 1812; 1869; 1958)
Co-ordinator for Sacramental Programmes Sr Maureen McNamara RSM

• Daughters of St Paul, Pauline Books & Media, 199 Kensington High Street W8 6BA
Tel: 020 7937 4890 (Community), 020 7937 9591 (Book Centre)
Email: london@pauline-uk.org Web: www.paulineuk.org
• Augustinian Recollects (OAR), 18 Cheniston Gardens W8 6TQ Tel: 020 7937 7681
Frs Mark Powell, Robert Riezu

KENSINGTON 2 + OUR LADY OF MOUNT CARMEL & ST SIMON STOCK

Sunday Mass (Sat 6pm), 8.30, 10 (Family), 11 (Sung Latin), 12.15pm, 6pm (Folk); **Holy Day Mass** (Vigil 6pm), 8, 12.15pm, 6pm; **Weekday Mass** 8, 12.15pm, 6pm; **Confession** Mon-Fri 5.40-6pm, Sat 10.30-11.30, 5-6pm

Discalced Carmelites (OCD) Fr John Williamson
Carmelite Priory, 41 Kensington Church Street W8 4BB
Tel: 020 7937 9866 Fax 020 7938 1470
Email: kensington2@rcdow.org.uk Web: www.carmelitechurch.org
500 yards north of Kensington High Street
Kensington & Chelsea Deanery (1862; 1959)
Community: Frs Christopher Clarke (Prior), Fabian McCormick, John McGowan, Luke Dominic Onwe, Paul Vincent, John Williamson (Parish Priest), Tijo Xavior

• Adoratrices, Handmaids of the Blessed Sacrament and of Charity, 38/39 Kensington Square W8 5HP Tel: 020 7937 5237 Email: adorlonuk@hotmail.com
Web: www.adoratrices.com Hostel for Working Women & Students Tel: 020 7937 5237

SECTION 3

• Religious of the Assumption, Convent of the Assumption, 20 Kensington Square W8 5HH Tel: 020 7361 4720 Email: enquiries@assumptionreligious.org
Web: www.assumptionreligious.org
Srs Patricia Mitchell (Sister in charge), Catherine Cowley, Maureen Dempsey, Carolyn Morrison, Asterie Mukampore
Lay Volunteer Co-ordinator Helen Granger
Email: vc@assumptionvolunteers.org.uk Web: www.assumptionvolunteers.org.uk
Milleret House Retreat centre
Administrator Amy Holland Tel: 020 7361 4756
Email: enquiries@assumptionreligious.org
Web: www.assumptionreligious.org/Milleret-House
• Religious of Mary Immaculate, 15-16 Southwell Gardens SW7 4RN
Tel: 020 7373 2738 Email: rmilondon@btconnect.com
Srs Ruby (Superior), Matilde, Margaret, Lucia, Amparo, Valentina, Angeles, Bernadette
Hostel for working girls and students of all nationalities
Email: book@rmilondonhostel.org Web: www.rmilondonhostel.org Contact Sr Ruby;
Social services for *au pairs*
Tel: 020 7373 3869 Email: socialservices@rmilondonhostel.org
Spanish Social Centre Tel: 020 7373 3869
• Cromwell Hospital

KENTISH TOWN + OUR LADY HELP OF CHRISTIANS

Sunday Mass (Sat 6pm), 9 (Sung), 11 (Family), 6pm; **Holy Day Mass** 10, 7pm; **Weekday Mass** 10; **Divine Office** 9.35, 12noon, 6pm; **Rosary** 10.35; **Confession** Sat 10.30-11

Fr John Deehan, Fr Jabulani Cletus Magugu (in residence, Zimbabwean Chaplaincy)
4 Lady Margaret Road NW5 2XT Tel: 020 7485 4023
Email: kentishtown@rcdow.org.uk Web: parish.rcdow.org.uk/kentishtown
Corner of Falkland Road; 3 mins from Kentish Town Stn (TfL)
Camden Deanery (1859; cons 2 June 1925; new church 1970; cons 20 September 1979)
Parish Welfare Project Co-ordinator Richard Mallon Tel: 07951 600451

• Sisters of La Sainte Union, Croft Lodge, Highgate Road NW5 1RP Tel: 020 7485 6169
LSU Provincialate, 53 Croftdown Road NW5 1EL Tel: 020 7482 7225

KENTON + ALL SAINTS

Sunday Mass (Sat 6.30pm), 9, 11; **Holy Day Mass** as announced; **Weekday Mass** 9.15; **Confession** Sat 5.30-6pm

Fr Dermot O'Neill
The Presbytery, 2a Salehurst Close, Harrow HA3 0UG Tel: 020 8204 3550
Email: kenton@rcdow.org.uk Web: parish.rcdow.org.uk/kenton
Church at 531 Kenton Road HA3 0UL, corner of Claremont Avenue; 600 yards west of Kingsbury Circus/Kingsbury Stn (TfL); bus183
Harrow Deanery (1932; 1963)
Secretary Elizabeth Galea

RE Co-ordinator Pat Edwards **Email: patedwards@rcdow.org.uk**

KILBURN + SACRED HEART OF JESUS

Sunday Mass (Sat 6pm), 10, 12.30pm, 7pm; **Holy Day Mass** (Vigil 7pm), 10, 12.15pm, 7pm; **Weekday Mass** Mon-Fri 10, 12.15pm, Sat 12noon; **Filipino Mass *3rd Sun*** 3pm; **Adoration** Fri 1-4pm; **Confession** Sat 10.30-12noon, 5-6pm

Oblates of Mary Immaculate (OMI) Fr Michael O'Connor, Fr Thomas Devereux, Fr Terry Murray
New Priory, Sacred Heart Church, Quex Road NW6 4PS
Tel: 020 7624 1701 Fax 020 7328 8176
Email: kilburn@rcdow.org.uk Web: www.oblateskilburn.com
Camden Deanery (1864; 1879; cons 18 June 1909)
Community: Frs Michael O'Connor, Michael Phelan, Terence Murray, Thomas Devereux, Paschal Dillon, Lorcan O'Reilly

• The Missionary Association of Mary Immaculate (MAMI), 237 Goldhurst Terrace NW6 3EP Fr Paschal Dillon OMI **Tel: 020 7328 8610**
Catechetical Co-ordinator Awaiting appointment
Mazenod Centre Manager Anna Redmond **Tel: 020 7624 5517**
• Oblate Partners in Mission Office, Denis Hurley House, 14 Quex Road NW6 4PL Tel: 020 7624 7296 Fr Lorcan O'Reilly
• Oblate Vocations Director Fr John McFadden New Priory, Sacred Heart Church, Quex Road NW6 4PS Tel: 020 7624 1701 Email: j.mcfadden@oblates.co.uk
• Oblate Youth Service, Denis Hurley House, 14 Quex Road NW6 4PL Tel: 020 7624 7296
• Sisters of the Holy Family of Bordeaux, 2 Aberdare Gardens NW6 3PX Tel: 020 7624 7573
• Jesuits (SJ) Copleston House, 221 Goldhurst Terrace NW6 3EP Tel: 020 7604 5860
Community: Frs Michael Holman (Superior), Peter Gallagher, Joseph Munitiz, Aneesh Joseph Manivelil, Philip Moller, Pedro McDade, Patrick Vance Nogoy, Richard Salmi, Raymond Tangonyire, Chester Yacub

KILBURN WEST + IMMACULATE HEART OF MARY

Sunday Mass 9, 11.30; **Holy Day Mass** 9; **Weekday Mass** Tue, Fri 9; **Exposition** Sat 9.30-10.30; **Confession** Sat 9.45 & before & after each Mass

Oblates of Mary Immaculate (OMI) Fr Michael O'Connor
Immaculate Heart of Mary Presbytery, 1 Stafford Road NW6 5RS Tel: 020 7624 2188
Email: kilburnwest@rcdow.org.uk Web: parish.rcdow.org.uk/kilburnwest
Off Kilburn Park Road
Camden Deanery (1948)
Community: Fr John McFadden, Br Michael Moore
Marian Parish Centre Caretaker Francis Philip Bangura **Tel: 020 3665 9697 / 07737 470350**

SECTION 3

KINGSBURY GREEN + ST SEBASTIAN AND ST PANCRAS A

Sunday Mass (Sat 6pm), 8, 9.30 (Family), 11 (Parish), 12.30 (Romanian, with **Confession** available 11-12 noon); **Holy Day Mass** 9.15, 7.30pm; **Weekday Mass** Mon-Wed 9.15, Thu 7.30pm, Fri-Sat 9.15; **Confession** Sat 12-1pm

Fr Stewart Keeley, Fr Marcelin Blaj (in residence, Romanian Chaplain, contact details below)
The Presbytery, 22 Hay Lane NW9 0NG Tel: 020 8204 2834/2117 Fax: 020 8204 5842
Email: kingsburygreen@rcdow.org.uk Web: parish.rcdow.org.uk/kingsburygreen
Off Edgware Road, Colindale
Brent Deanery (1926; 2001)
(Fr Blaj Tel: 020 8204 4392 Email: romanianchaplaincy@gmail.com)

KING'S CROSS, EAST: *SEE COPENHAGEN STREET*; WEST: *SEE SOMERS TOWN*

KINGSLAND + OUR LADY AND ST JOSEPH A

Sunday Mass (Sat 6.30pm), 8, 9.30 (Family), 11 (Sung), 12.30pm, 6.30pm; **Holy Day Mass** (Vigil 7pm), 9, 12noon, 7pm; **Weekday Mass** Mon-Fri 9, 6pm, Sat 12noon followed by **Novena** & **Benediction**; **Exposition** Sat 5.30-6.15pm, Sun 5.15-6.15pm with **Benediction**; **Confession** Sat 11-11.45, 5.30-6.15pm

Fr Derek Hyett, Fr Nigel Woollen, Fr Dermot Power (in residence)
Presbytery, 100a Balls Pond Road N1 4AG Tel: 020 7254 4378
Email: kingsland@rcdow.org.uk Web: www.olsj.org
Off Kingsland High Street; at top end of Essex Road
Hackney Deanery (1854; 1964)
Parish Administrator Mrs Ann-Marie Burnett-Charles
Email: amburnettcharles@rcdow.org.uk
Parish Sister Sr Winifred Quinlan UJ

- Ursulines of Jesus (UJ), Pax, 6 King Henry's Walk N1 4PB Tel: 020 7254 3319
- Nigerian National Chaplaincy, 8 King Henry's Walk N1 4PB Tel: 07710 512244

Chaplains Fr Peter Babangida Audu, Fr Matthew 'Gbenga Madewa, Fr Peter Tochukwu Egboo

- St Martin of Tours House, 162 New North Road N1 7BH

Rehabilitation Centre Tel: 020 7226 7516

- St Vincent's (SVP shop and counselling centre) 484/486 Kingsland Road E8 4AE

Tel: 020 7272 1263

KNEBWORTH + ST THOMAS MORE A

Sunday Mass (Sat 6pm), 8, 10 (Sung); **Holy Day Mass** 9.30, 8pm; **Weekday Mass** Mon 7.15 pm, Tue-Fri 9.30, Sat 10; **Exposition** Fri after Mass-12noon; **Confession** Sat 5.15-5.45pm

Canon Daniel Cronin
72 London Road, Knebworth SG3 6HB Tel: 01438 813303
Email: knebworth@rcdow.org.uk Web: www.knebworthcatholicchurch.org
Stevenage Deanery (1929; 1936)
Office Manager / PA to Parish Priest Theresa Taylor-Brookes

LEBANESE MARONITE CHURCH + OUR LADY OF LEBANON

Sunday Mass (Maronite Rite) (Sat 7pm), 12.30pm, 7pm; **Weekday Mass** Wed, Fri 7pm. All Masses celebrated at Our Lady of Sorrows, Paddington

Lebanese Maronite Order (LMO) Fr Johnny Saba, Fr Aziz Azzi, Fr Charbel Trad
6 Dobson Close NW6 4RS Tel: 020 7586 1801
Email: lebanesechurch@rcdow.org.uk Web: www.maronitechurch.org.uk

LEICESTER SQUARE, WC2: *SEE FRENCH CHURCH*

LETCHWORTH GARDEN CITY+ ST HUGH OF LINCOLN

Sunday Mass (Sat 7pm), 8, 9.30, 11.30, 1pm (Polish); **Holy Day Mass** 9.30, 7.30pm; **Weekday Mass** Mon-Thu 9.30, **Liturgy of the Word** with **Holy Communion** Fri 9.30; **Confession** Sat 10-10.30, 6.15-6.45pm

Fr James Garvey
84 Pixmore Way, Letchworth Garden City SG6 3TP Tel: 01462 510015
Email: letchworth@rcdow.org.uk Web: parish.rcdow.org.uk/letchworth
Stevenage Deanery (1907; 1963; cons 2007)
Parish Administrator Aimee Barnes

- Sisters of Charity of Jesus and Mary, Provincial House, 108 Spring Road, Letchworth Garden City SG6 3SL Tel: 01462 682153 Email: elizabeth@scjm.org Web: www. scjmangloirishprovince.co.uk
- Garden House Hospice

LIMEHOUSE + OUR LADY IMMACULATE AND ST FREDERICK A S

Sunday Mass 12 noon; **Mass in Word and Sign** *2nd Sun only* 6pm *(not August)*; **Holy Day Mass** 7.15; **Confession** on request

Fr Keith Stoakes (also serves Poplar and resident at Clergy House, 9 Pekin Street E14 6EZ Tel: 020 7987 4523)
Island Row, 636 Commercial Road E14 7HS
Email: limehouse@rcdow.org.uk Web: parish.rcdow.org.uk/limehouse
(A13), between Limehouse DLR Stn and Burdett Road
Tower Hamlets Deanery (1881; 1934; cons 17 October 1945)

LINCOLN'S INN FIELDS + ST ANSELM AND ST CECILIA

Sunday Mass (Sat 6pm), 10 (Family), 12noon (Sung Latin), 4pm (Filipino, *2nd Sun only*), 6pm; **Holy Day Mass** (Vigil 6pm), 12.30pm, 6pm (Sung Latin); **Weekday Mass** Mon, Wed, Fri 12.30pm, 6pm, Tue, Thu 6pm; **Exposition** Mon-Sat 4-6pm; **Confession** Mon, Wed, Fri 12-12.20pm, Mon-Fri 5.30-5.50pm, Sat 5-5.40pm

Fr David Barnes, Mgr John Conneely (in residence)
70 Lincoln's Inn Fields WC2A 3JA Tel: 020 7405 0376
Email: lincolnsinnfields@rcdow.org.uk Web: parish.rcdow.org.uk/lincolnsinnfields
On east side of Kingsway, a few steps south of Holborn Stn (TfL)

SECTION 3

Westminster Deanery (1687; 1909; cons November 1959)
Parish Administrator / Bookkeeper Mrs Mandy O'Sullivan-Whiting
Parish Sister Sr M Lucina SPR **Apartment 4, 145 Drury Lane WC2B 5TA**
Tel: 07470 236999 Email: sistermarylucina@btinternet.com

- **Hospital for Sick Children, Great Ormond Street**
Chaplain Anne Marie O'Riordan **Tel: 020 7813 8232**
- **National Hospital for Neurology & Neurosurgery Tel: 020 3456 7890, Royal London Hospital for Integrated Medicine Tel: 0845 155 5000**
Chaplain Fr Peter Harries OP **Tel: 020 3447 3007**

LITHUANIAN CHURCH + ST CASIMIR A

Sunday Mass 10 (Lithuanian/English), 12noon (Lithuanian), 6pm (Lithuanian); **Holy Day Mass** 7pm; **Weekday Mass** 7pm; **Confession** (Lithuanian, Russian) daily before Mass & on request

Fr Petras Tverijonas, Fr Petras Gucevicius
21 The Oval, Hackney Road E2 9DT Tel: 020 7739 8735
Email: lithuanianchurch@rcdow.org.uk Web: www.londonas.co.uk
Tower Hamlets Deanery (1901; 1912)

LONDON COLNEY + OUR LADY, ST MARY OF WALSINGHAM A

Sunday Mass 11.30; **Holy Day Mass** as announced; **Weekday Mass** Mon, ***Monthly*** Wed evening as announced (in Shenley, see newsletter), Thu 10 ; **Prayer Group** Fri 8-9pm; **Filipino Adorers *4th Fri only*** 9pm-midnight; **Confession** Sun 11.10-11.25

Radlett: **Sunday Mass** 10; **Holy Day Mass** as announced; **Weekday Mass** Tue 10; **Confession** Sun 9.30-9.50

Shenley: **Sunday Mass** (Sat 5pm); **Holy Day Mass** as announced; **Weekday Mass** Wed 9.30, Monthly evening Mass as announced (see newsletter); **Exposition** Sat 4.15pm, with **Benediction** 4.50pm; **Confession** Sat 4.15-4.45pm

Fr Kevin Moule, Rev Tony Barter (Deacon), Rev Anthony Curran (Deacon) (clergy also serve Radlett and Shenley, Parish Priest resident at **22 The Crosspath, Radlett WD7 8HN Tel: 01923 635541**)
Haseldine Road, London Colney AL2 1RR
Email: radlett@rcdow.org.uk Web: parish.rcdow.org.uk/londoncolney
At junction of Hazeldine Road and High Street, London Colney AL2 1RP
St Albans Deanery (1959)
Parish Administrator Mrs Catherine King **Tel: 01923 635541**

MAIDEN LANE: *SEE COVENT GARDEN*

MANOR HOUSE + ST THOMAS MORE

Sunday Mass (Sat 6pm), 10 (Sung), 12noon (Sung), 5pm (Portuguese); **Holy Day Mass** 12.30pm; **Weekday Mass** Mon 9, Thu 12.30pm, Fri 9; **Confession** On request

Fr Clive Lee, Rev Kassa Tsegaye (Deacon, contact details below)
9 Henry Road N4 2LH Tel: 020 8802 9910
Email: manorhouse@rcdow.org.uk Web: parish.rcdow.org.uk/manorhouse
Off Portland Rise, south of Finsbury Park (near Manor House TfL Stn)
Hackney Deanery (1969; 1975)
(Rev Kassa Tsegaye **Tel: 07930 416927**)
Parish Administrator Ingrid Bowie

• **Ursulines of Jesus** Administration **Flat 14 Kimpton Court, 2 Murrain Road N4 2BN**
Tel: 020 8442 8800 Web: www.ursulinesjesus.org
Community **Flat 15 Kimpton Court, 2 Murrain Road,N4 2BN Tel: 020 8800 4486**

MARYLEBONE + OUR LADY OF THE ROSARY A

Sunday Mass (Sat 6pm), 8.30, 11 (Family), 6pm (Folk); **Holy Day Mass** 12.30pm, 6pm; **Weekday Mass** Mon-Sat 12.30pm; **Exposition** and **Benediction** Sat 5-5.30pm; **Confession** Sat 11-11.30, 5-5.30pm

Fr Michael Johnston
211 Old Marylebone Road NW1 5QT Tel: 020 7723 5101
Email: marylebone@rcdow.org.uk Web: parish.rcdow.org.uk/marylebone
South side of Old Marylebone Road, by junction with Marylebone Road
Marylebone Deanery (1855; 1963; cons 18 February 2006)
Parish Administrator Mrs Marion Egan

• **Tyburn Convent (Adorers of the Sacred Heart OSB), 8 Hyde Park Place W2 2LJ**
Tel: 020 7723 7262 Email: admin@tyburnconvent.org.uk
Web: www.tyburnconvent.org.uk
Perpetual Exposition of the Blessed Sacrament; chapel open daily 6.15(am)-8.30 pm
Sunday Mass 10, **Weekday Mass** Mon-Fri 7.30, Sat 10, Bank Holidays 10; **Vespers** 4.30pm
Chaplain Fr Brendan Carmody SJ
• **St Mary's (Praed Street), Western Eye Hospital**
Sunday Mass 11; **Weekday Mass** Thu 12.30pm
Chaplains Fr Giles Pinnock, Fr Gerard O'Brien **Tel 020 3312 1508**
• **Charter Nightingale Hospital**

MILE END + THE GUARDIAN ANGELS

Sunday Mass (Sat 7.30pm), 9, 11, 6pm; **Holy Day Mass** (Vigil as announced), as on weekdays; **Weekday Mass** Mon, Wed 9.30, Tue, Thu 9, Fri 7pm, Sat 12.30pm; **Confession** Sat 11.30-12.15pm & on request

Fr John D A Elliott, Fr Bryan Jones (in residence), Rev Jeremy Yates (Deacon)
377 Mile End Road E3 4QS Tel: 020 8980 1845
Email: mileend@rcdow.org.uk Web: parish.rcdow.org.uk/mileend
Near Grove Road/Burdett Road junction; 2 mins from Mile End Stn (TfL)
Tower Hamlets Deanery (1868; 1901; cons 20 October 1927)

SECTION 3

- Neo-Catechumenate Communities Paul Dennis **Tel: 07855 826086**
- Mile End Hospital & The Bancroft Unit, Pat Shaw House

MILL END (& MAPLE CROSS) + ST JOHN THE EVANGELIST

Sunday Mass (Sat 6pm), 10.30; **Holy Day Mass** as announced; **Weekday Mass** Mon, Wed 9.30; **Exposition** Sat 5.30-5.55pm; **Confession** on request & by appointment

Chorleywood: **Sunday Mass** (Sat 6pm), 9; **Holy Day Mass** as announced; **Weekday Mass** Tue, Fri 9.30; **Exposition** 1st Sat 5.30-5.55pm; **Confession** on request & by appointment

Rickmansworth: **Sunday Mass** 8.30, 11, 6pm; **Holy Day Mass** 9.30, 8pm; **Weekday Mass** Mon, Tue, Thu, Fri 9.30, Sat 10; **Exposition** and **Confession** Sat 10.30-11.30

Fr Shaun Church, Fr Damian Ryan (clergy also serve Chorleywood and Rickmansworth and are resident at 5 Park Road, Rickmansworth WD3 1HU Tel: 01923 773387)
Berry Lane, Rickmansworth WD3 7HG
Email: rickmansworth@rcdow.org.uk Web: parish.rcdow.org.uk/millend
Watford Deanery (1969; cons 30 April 2016))

MILL HILL + SACRED HEART AND MARY IMMACULATE

Sunday Mass (Sat 6pm), 8.30, 10 (Family), 11.30, 6pm; **Holy Day Mass** 10, 12.15pm, 7.30pm; **Weekday Mass** daily 10, also Mon 7.30pm; **Exposition** Mon 8-9pm, Wed, Thu 10.30-12noon, Sat 10.30-11.30; **Confession** Sat 10.30-11.30

Vincentians (CM) Fr Michael McCullagh
2 Flower Lane NW7 2JB Tel: 020 8959 1021
Email: millhill@rcdow.org.uk Web: www.shmi.info
The Broadway, just off Watford Way (A4) at Mill Hill Circus
Barnet Deanery (1889; 1922; cons 6 December 1923; 1995; cons 25 September 1996)
Community: Frs Michael McCullagh (Superior), Raymond Armstrong, Eamon Raftery, Noel Travers
Parish Administrator Melanie Gibbons

- Daughters of Charity, Provincial House, The Ridgeway NW7 1RE Tel: 020 8906 3777
Email: secretariat@dcmillhill.org Web: www.daughtersofcharity.org.uk
St Vincent's House (Provincialate), The Ridgeway, Mill Hill NW7 1RG Tel: 020 8906 7646
Chaplain to DC Provincial House Fr Raymond Armstrong
- Franciscan Sisters of Mill Hill, St Mary's Convent, 118 Chalet Estate, Hammers Lane NW7 4DN Tel: 020 8959 1364 Email: osfsistersmillhill@gmail.com

MILLWALL + ST EDMUND

Sunday Mass (Sat 6pm), 9, 11; **Holy Day Mass** 9.15, 8pm; **Weekday Mass** Mon-Wed, Fri 9.15; **Holy Hour** with **Exposition** Sat 5pm; **Confession** Sat 5-5.45pm.

Priest in Charge Fr Christopher Silva
297 Westferry Road E14 3RS Tel: 020 7987 4114
Email: millwall@rcdow.org.uk Web: parish.rcdow.org.uk/millwall
Westferry Road
Tower Hamlets Deanery (1846; 1874; 2000; cons 22 September 2000)
Parish Secretary Katherine Woznicka

• Canary Wharf Catholic Chaplaincy, The Prayer Room, Unit 11, 2 Churchill Place E14 5RB Correspondence to 1 St Catherine's Apartments, 179a Bow Road E3 2SH
Web: www. cwcc.org.uk
Chaplain Mgr Vladimir Felzmann Tel: 020 7477 1073 / 07810 116508
Mass Tue 12.30pm

MOORFIELDS + ST MARY MOORFIELDS

Sunday Mass 10; **Holy Day Mass** (Vigil 7pm) 8.05, 12noon, 12.30 pm, 1.05pm, 5.30pm; **Weekday Mass** Mon-Fri 8.05, 1.05pm; **Exposition** as announced; **Confession** Mon-Fri 12.30-12.50pm, 1.30-1.50pm

Fr Christopher Vipers, Fr Andrew Jaxa-Chamiec (clergy also serve Bunhill Row)
4/5 Eldon Street EC2M 7LS Tel: 020 7247 8390
Email: moorfields@rcdow.org.uk Web: www.stmarymoorfields.net
100 yards west of Liverpool Street Stn (BR/TfL); just before the Red Lion
Westminster Deanery (1710; 1903)

• St Bartholomew's Hospital Tel: 020 3416 5000
Chaplains Fr Rory Murphy IVD, Fr Andrew Jaxa-Chamiec Tel: 020 3465 7220
Emails: Rory.Murphy@bartshealth.nhs.uk, Andrew.Chamiec@bartshealth.nhs.uk
Hospital Church of St Bartholomew the Less
Weekday Mass Thu 12.30pm

MUCH HADHAM: *SEE BISHOP'S STORTFORD*

MUSWELL HILL + OUR LADY OF MUSWELL A

Sunday Mass (Sat 6.30pm), 8.30, 10, 11.45; **Holy Day Mass** 10, 7.30pm; **Weekday Mass** Mon-Thu, Sat 10, Fri 7.30pm; **Exposition** Sat 10.45-11.45; **Confession** Sat 10.45-11.45

Fr Mark Anwyll
1 Colney Hatch Lane N10 1PN Tel: 020 8883 5607 Fax: 020 8444 3464
Email: muswellhill@rcdow.org.uk Web: parish.rcdow.org.uk/muswellhill
Haringey Deanery (1917; 1938; cons 23 September 1959)

• Sisters of Marie Auxiliatrice, 20 Elgin Road N22 7UE Tel: 020 8881 8547
Srs Frances Mary Crowe, Eilis Mary Donohue, Sylvia Mary McCarthy, Elizabeth O'Brien,
The Paddock, Meadow Drive N10 1PL
Flat 8 Sr Pauline Mary Clarke, Flat 15 Sr Carmel M Ring
• St Luke's Woodside Hospital

NEASDEN + ST PATRICK A

Sunday Mass (Sat 6.30pm), 9.30, 11.30; **Holy Day Mass** 9.30, 7.30pm; **Weekday Mass** 9.30; **Confession** Sat 5.45-6.15pm

Fr Patrick McLoughlin
The Presbytery, Hardie Close NW10 0UH Tel: 020 8451 0367 Fax: 020 8830 3022
Email: neasden@rcdow.org.uk Web: parish.rcdow.org.uk/neasden

SECTION 3

Just off North Circular Road (A406), west side, adjacent to IKEA main entrance off Drury Way
Brent Deanery (1981)

• Abracadabra Nursery Tel: 020 8451 2544

NEW BARNET + MARY IMMACULATE AND ST PETER

Sunday Mass (Sat 6pm), 9.30, 11, 6pm; **Holy Day Mass** as announced; **Weekday Mass** Mon-Sat 9.30, preceded by **Morning Prayer** 9.10 & followed by **Rosary**; **Exposition** Fri 7-7.30pm; **Confession** Sat 10-10.30 & on request

Spiritans (CSSp) Fr James Ademola Fasakin, Fr Terkura Igbe (in residence, School Chaplain)
63 Somerset Road, New Barnet EN5 1RF Tel: 020 8449 1961
Email: newbarnet@rcdow.org.uk Web: www.stpetersnewbarnet.org.uk
Barnet Deanery (1912; 1938)
Parish Secretary Paula Lefevre
Parish Catechetical Co-ordinator Carol Ward

NEW SOUTHGATE + OUR LADY OF LOURDES A

Sunday Mass (Sat 6.30pm), 8.30, 9.45 (Choir), 11.15 (Family), 12.30pm, 6.30pm; **Holy Day Mass** 8, 10, 7.30pm; **Weekday Mass** Mon-Fri 8, 10, Sat 10; **Exposition** Fri 10.30-11, 7-8pm; **Confession** Sat 10.30-11, 5.30-6pm

Fr David Reilly, Fr Johnson Alexander (in residence, Keralan Chaplaincy), Mgr Thomas Parayadyil (in residence, Syro-Malabar Chaplaincy)
373 Bowes Road N11 1AA Tel: 020 8368 1638
Email: newsouthgate@rcdow.org.uk Web: www.ourladynewsouthgate.org.uk
200 yards right from Arnos Grove Stn (TfL)
Enfield Deanery (1923; 1935; 1990)

• Sisters of Our Lady of the Missions, 2 Brookdale N11 1BL
Tel: 020 8361 6848 Srs Anne, Margaret, Mary
• Sisters of St Louis, 16 Chaucer Close N11 1AU
Tel: 020 8617 0529 Email: philomenamorris@talktalk.net Sr Philomena Morris

NORTHFIELDS (WEST EALING) + SS PETER AND PAUL A

Sunday Mass (Sat 6.30pm), 8.30, 10 (Family/Children's Liturgy), 11.30 (Sung), 6.30pm; **Holy Day Mass** 9.30, 8pm; **Weekday Mass** Mon-Wed, Fri, Sat 9.30, with **Rosary**; **Weekday Morning Prayer** *(Advent & Lent only)* 9.15; **Holy Hour** Tue 10-11; **Divine Mercy Devotions** *First Sun only* 2.45pm; **Confession** Sat 10-10.30, 6-6.30pm

Fr Jim Duffy, Fr John Tabor
38 Camborne Avenue W13 9QZ Tel: 020 8567 5421
Email: northfields@rcdow.org.uk Web: parish.rcdow.org.uk/northfields
Off Northfield Avenue, 1/4 mile north of Northfields Stn
Ealing Deanery (1926; 1931; cons 29 October 1959)
Parish Administrator Rosa Bambury
Pastoral Assistant Anna Dupelycz Email: northfieldscat@rcdow.org.uk

• Medical Mission Sisters, 109 Clitherow Avenue W7 2BL Tel: 020 8567 1504
Email: unit.uk.office@gmail.com Web: www.medicalmissionsisters-uk.org
• Religious of the Sacred Heart of Mary, Provincial House, 54 Grange Road W5 5BX
Tel: 020 8567 7228 Web: www.rshm-nep.org
also 44 The Park W5 5NP Tel: 020 8567 4722

NORTHOLT: *SEE HARROW SOUTH*

NORTHWOOD + ST MATTHEW A

Sunday Mass (Sat 6pm), 9, 11.15 (Sung), 6pm; **Holy Day Mass** 10 and as announced; **Weekday Mass** 10, preceded by **Morning Prayer** 9.45; **Exposition** Tue, Sat 10.30, with **Benediction** Tue 11.15; **Confession** Sat 10.30-11.15, 5-5.45pm & by appointment

Fr Timothy Hutton
32 Hallowell Road, Northwood HA6 1DW Tel: 01923 825639 Fax: 01923 840736
Email: northwood@rcdow.org.uk Web: www.northwoodcatholics.org.uk
Off Green Lane (shopping centre); near Northwood Stn
Hillingdon Deanery (1924; cons 12 October 1954)
RE Co-ordinator Awaiting appointment

• Daughters of Charity, Rendu House, 32 Norwich Road, Northwood HA6 1NB
Tel: 01923 835330 Email: renduhouse@yahoo.co.uk
• Society of African Missions (SMA) White House, Watford Road, Northwood HA6 3PW
Tel: 01923 828015
Frs Peter Burrows (Plymouth Diocese), Anthony Cussen, Anthony Dampson, Dermot McCaul
• Joint Support Unit, Northwood HQ, Mount Vernon Hospital, Bishops Wood Hospital, Michael Sobell House

NOTTING HILL + ST FRANCIS OF ASSISI

Sunday Mass (Sat 6pm), 10, 11.30, 6pm; **Holy Day Mass** 9.30, 7pm; **Weekday Mass** Mon, Tue, Thu-Sat 9.30; **Rosary** Tue, Sat after Mass; **Exposition** Mon, Thu, Fri 10-11; **Confession** Sat 10-10.30

Fr Gerard Skinner
The Presbytery, Pottery Lane W11 4NQ Tel: 020 7727 7968
Email: nottinghill@rcdow.org.uk Web: www.stfrancisnottinghill.org.uk
North Kensington Deanery (1860)
Parish Administrator Paula Lopes McDermid Tel: 020 7727 7968

• Sisters of Jesus in the Temple, 28 Penzance Street W11 4QX Tel: 020 7603 3329

OGLE STREET + ST CHARLES BORROMEO

Sunday Mass (Sat 6pm, 8.15pm with Neo-Catechumenate), 9, 11; **Holy Day Mass** as weekday Mass; **Weekday Mass** Mon-Wed 12.30pm, Thu, Fri 6pm, for Bank Holidays see newsletter; **Confession** Daily after Mass & on request

SECTION 3

Fr David Barrow, Fr Gary Walsh (in residence, Albanian Chaplaincy)
8 Ogle Street W1W 6HS Tel: 020 7636 2883
Email: oglestreet@rcdow.org.uk Web: oglestreetblog.wordpress.com
Off New Cavendish Street, near BT Tower
Marylebone Deanery (1862; cons 4 October 1921)
Parish Assistant Sr Pauline Forde DC
Neo-Catechumenate Communities Michael Anderson Tel: 020 7584 2579

- University Chaplaincy: *see University* entry in this section
- Portland Hospital for Women & Children Tel: 020 7580 4400

Chaplains Fr Giles Pinnock, Fr Gerard O'Brien Tel 020 3312 1508

- University College Hospital Tel: 0845 155 5000

Sunday Mass 9.45; **Holy Day Mass** 1.30pm; **Weekday Mass** Mon-Thu 1.30pm, Fri 12.30pm
Chaplains Fr Peter Harries OP, Sr Pauline Forde DC

OLD HALL GREEN & PUCKERIDGE + ST EDMUND OF CANTERBURY & ENGLISH MARTYRS

Sunday Mass (Sat 6pm, Puckeridge); 11.15 (Old Hall Green); **Holy Day Mass** 10.30 (Puckeridge); **Weekday Mass** Wed 10.30 (Puckeridge); **Confession** Sat 5.15-5.45pm (Puckeridge)

Buntingford: **Sunday Mass** 9.15 (with term time Children's Liturgy, *2nd & 4th Sun only*) ; **Holy Day Mass** 7pm; **Weekday Mass** Tue, Thu 9.30, Fri 10.30, with **Exposition** and **Benediction** 11-11.30, Sat 9.30; **Confession** Sat 10.30-11

Fr Cyril Chiaha (also serves Buntingford and is resident at 3 Station Road, Buntingford SG9 9HT Tel: 01763 271471)
Email: oldhallgreen@rcdow.org.uk Web: parish.rcdow.org.uk/oldhallgreen
Old Hall Green + St Edmund and the English Martyrs
To rear of St Edmund's College (off A10 as signposted)
Lea Valley Deanery (1769; 1818; new church cons 2 December 1911)

Puckeridge + St Thomas of Canterbury
Off the A10, at end of Puckeridge High Street (opposite school)
Lea Valley Deanery (1926)

- St Edmund's College, Old Hall Green, Ware SG11 1DS (1793; 1853)

Tel: 01920 821504
Priest-in-Residence Fr Peter Lyness Tel: 01920 821504
Lay Chaplain Paula Pierce Tel: 01920 821334

ORATORY + IMMACULATE HEART OF MARY

Sunday Mass (Sat 6pm), 8, 9 (Extraordinary Form), 10 (Sung English), 11 (Solemn Latin), 12.30pm, 4.30pm, 7pm; **Holy Day Mass** (Vigil 6.30pm), 7, 8 (Extraordinary Form), 10, 12.30pm, 5.30pm, 6.30pm (Solemn Latin); **Weekday Mass** Mon-Fri 7, 8 (Extraordinary Form), 12.30pm, 6pm (Latin), Sat 7, 8 (Extraordinary Form), 10; **Sunday Vespers** and **Benediction** 3.30pm; **Holy Day Vespers** and **Benediction** (Vigil 5.30pm); **Benediction** Tue 6.30pm; **Holy Hour** Thu 6.30pm; **Confession** (French, German, Italian, Spanish) Sat 10-

12.55pm, 3-6pm, Sun after each morning Mass, 6-6.50pm, Mon-Fri at all times except 12.30-3pm & 6-7.45pm

Fathers of the Oratory of St Philip Neri (Oratorians) Fr Michael Lang
The Oratory SW7 2RP Tel: 020 7808 0900 Fax 020 7584 1095
Email: oratory@rcdow.org.uk Web: www.bromptonoratory.co.uk
Beside V&A Museum at convergence of Cromwell Road & Brompton Road; near South Kensington Stn (TfL)
Kensington & Chelsea Deanery (1854; 1884; cons 16 April 1884)
Community: Frs Julian Large (Provost), Edward van den Bergh, George Bowen, Ronald Creighton-Jobe, Charles Dilke, Patrick Doyle, John Fordham, Michael Lang, Rupert McHardy
The Little Oratory: Exercises of the Brotherhood Sun 4.30pm

• Congregation of Our Lady (Canonesses of St Augustine), More House, 53 Cromwell Road SW7 2EH Tel: 020 7581 8327 (Community) 020 7584 2040 (Hostel)
Email: mgabrielrobin@outlook.com (Community)
Srs Nicole Lien Duval, Gabriel Robin, Marie Claude Teer
• University Chaplaincy, More House: *see University* entry in this section
• Brompton Hospital

OSTERLEY + ST VINCENT DE PAUL

Sunday Mass 9.30 (with term time Children's Liturgy), 11.30, 6pm; **Holy Day Mass** 9.30, 7.30pm; **Weekday Mass** Mon, Wed-Sat 9.30, Tue 7.30pm; **Morning Prayer** Mon, Wed-Sat 9.10; **Rosary** Mon, Wed, Thu, Fri after Mass, Tue 7pm before Mass; **Exposition** Sat 10-11 followed by **Benediction** at 11; **Confession** Sat 10-10.30 & on request

Fr Mark Leenane
2 Witham Road, Osterley, Isleworth TW7 4AJ Tel: 020 8560 4737
Email: osterley@rcdow.org.uk Web: parish.rcdow.org.uk/osterley
Between Eversley Crescent & Spring Grove Road
Hounslow Deanery (1934; cons 1936; 2004; cons 24 September 2005)

PADDINGTON + OUR LADY OF SORROWS A

Sunday Mass 9.30 **Holy Day Mass** as Weekday Mass (Mon, Fri at Harrow Road); **Weekday Mass** Tue, Thu, Sat 10; **Exposition** and **Benediction** Tue, Thu, Sat 9-10; **Confession** Sat 9-10 or on request

Fr Michael Jarmulowicz (also serves Harrow Road, resident at Presbytery, 337 Harrow Road W9 3RB Tel: 020 7286 2170)
17 Cirencester Street W2 5SR Tel: 020 7286 2672
Email: paddington@rcdow.org.uk Web: parish.rcdow.org.uk/paddington
Off Harrow Road, near Royal Oak Stn (TfL)
North Kensington Deanery (1912; cons 1998)
Parish Administrator Mrs Mandy O'Sullivan-Whiting **Tue 10-2pm**
Maronite Rite: **Sunday Mass** (Sat 7pm), 12.30pm, 7pm; **Weekday Mass** Wed, Fri 7pm (see *Lebanese Church* entry in this section)

SECTION 3

PALMERS GREEN + ST MONICA

Sunday Mass (Sat 6pm), 7.45, 9, 10.30 (with Children's Liturgy), 12noon, 3.30pm (Polish), 5.30pm; **Holy Day Mass** 7, 9.35, 7.30pm; **Weekday Mass** 9.35 daily, preceded by **Morning Prayer** Mon-Fri 9.10, see weekly newsletter for other times; **Exposition** Sat 10-10.50, Mon, Wed 4-5pm, ***First Fri only*** 10-6.30pm; **Rosary Hour** Thu 7pm; **Confession** Sat 10-10.50, 5.15-5.45pm

Fr Mehall Lowry, Fr John Warnaby
(for Polish Chaplain, see details below)
The Presbytery, 1 Stonard Road N13 4DJ Tel: 020 8886 9568 Fax: 020 8886 5143
Email: palmersgreen@rcdow.org.uk Web: www.stmonica.co.uk
Enfield Deanery (1910; 1914; cons 6 October 1985)
Parish Sister Sr Joyce Dionne, Daughters of Providence (St Brieuc) c/o The Presbytery
Youth Programme Co-ordinator Anna McMullan
Parish Centre, Cannon House, Cannon Hill N14 7HG

• Polish Chaplain Fr Krzysztof Chaim, resident at Holy Family of Nazareth Convent, 52 London Road, Enfield EN2 6EN Tel: 07902 432343
• Grovelands Priory Psychiatric Hospital

PARSONS GREEN + HOLY CROSS

Sunday Mass (Sat 6.30pm), 9.30 (Family), 11.30 (**Sunday Mass in August** (Sat 6.30pm), 10.30); **Holy Day Mass** as announced; **Weekday Mass** 9.30 (except Wed), with **Morning Prayer** 9.15, *1st Sat only* 9.30, then **Exposition** and **Benediction**; **Confession** Sat 5.45-6.15pm & on request

Fr Michael Daley, Fr Tibor Borovsky (in residence, Slovak and Czech Chaplaincy)
22 Cortayne Road SW6 3QA Tel: 020 7736 1068
Email: parsonsgreen@rcdow.org.uk
Web: http://www.holycrosschurchparsonsgreen.org.uk
Ashington Road off New Kings Road, opposite Munster Road; between Parsons Green & Putney Bridge Stns (TfL)
Hammersmith & Fulham Deanery (1843; 1884; 1924; cons 11 October 1928)
Parish Administrator Mrs Annie D'Souza Mon-Fri 9-1pm
Catechetical Co-ordinator / Pastoral Assistant Mrs Alexandra Fisher

PERIVALE + ST JOHN FISHER

Sunday Mass (Sat 6.30pm), 9.30 (Family), 11.30, 6.30pm; **Holy Day Mass** (Vigil 7.30pm), 10; **Weekday Mass** Mon, Tue, Thu, Fri 10; **Holy Hour** Mon 10.30, Sat 5-6pm; **Confession** Sat 5.15-5.45pm & on request

Fr Agustin Conesa
41/42 Langdale Gardens, Perivale, Greenford UB6 8DQ Tel/Fax: 020 8997 3164
Email: perivale@rcdow.org.uk Web: parish.rcdow.org.uk/perivale

On north side of Western Avenue (A40), just past the Hoover building
Ealing Deanery (1936; 1970)

PIMLICO + HOLY APOSTLES A

Sunday Mass (Sat 6pm), 9, 10.30 (Family), 12.30pm (Spanish) **Albanian Sunday Mass** 3 pm, *every 2 weeks*; **Holy Day Mass** (Vigil 7pm), 10, 7pm; **Weekday Mass** 9.30 (10 if a funeral); **Exposition** Wed 10-11, Sat 5-5.45pm; **Confession** Sat 5-5.30pm & by appointment

Canon Pat Browne, Fr Charles Soyombo (in residence)
47 Cumberland Street SW1V 4LY Tel: 020 7834 6965 Fax: 020 7821 8609
Email: pimlico@rcdow.org.uk Web: www.holyapostlespimlico.org
Winchester Street off Lupus Street, near Pimlico Stn (TfL)
Westminster Deanery (1917; 1957; cons 10 May 1974)
Parish Sister Sr Louise Callan DC

• Franciscan Sisters of the Heart of Jesus, 9-11 St George's Drive SW1V 4DJ
Tel: 020 7834 4020 (Convent) 020 7834 5356 (Hostel) Fax: 020 7976 6862
Email: fransisuk09@gmail.com
• Sisters of Notre Dame, Bella Best House, 5B Westmoreland Terrace SW1V 4AW
Web: sndden.org Sr Margaret Foley **Flat 6**, Sr Rachel Mary Harrington **Flat 4 Tel: 020 7834 3299**, Sr Myra Poole **Flat 7 Tel: 020 7233 5136**, Sr Margaret Helen Wears **Flat 9**
• Apostleship of the Sea, 39 Eccleston Square SW1V 1PX Tel: 020 7901 1931
Email: info@apostleshipofthesea.org.uk Web: www.apostleshipofthesea.org.uk
• Catholic Bishops' Conference of England and Wales, 39 Eccleston Square SW1V 1BX
Tel: 020 7630 8220 Fax: 020 7901 4820 Email: secretariat@cbcew.org.uk
• Missio (APF), 23 Eccleston Square SW1V 1NU Tel: 020 7821 9755
Fax: 020 7630 8466 Email: director@missio.org.uk

PINNER + ST LUKE

Sunday Mass (Sat 6pm), 9, 11; **Holy Day Mass** (Vigil 7.30pm), 10; **Weekday Mass** Mon-Fri 10; **Exposition** Tue 9.30-10; **Confession** Sat 11-11.30, 4.30-5pm

Canon Robert Plourde
28 Love Lane, Pinner HA5 3EX Tel: 020 8866 0098
Email: pinner@rcdow.org.uk Web: parish.rcdow.org.uk/pinner
In town centre, 3 mins from Pinner Stn (TfL), off Bridge Street
Harrow Deanery (1914; 1957)
Parish Secretary Mrs Pat Williams (Mon-Fri 8.30-1pm)
Pastoral Assistant (Catechetics) Norah O'Hare **Tel: 020 8868 4175**
Pastoral Outreach Worker Mariola Griffiths **Tel: 020 8866 0098**

• Daughters of Charity, 43 High Street, Pinner HA5 5PJ
Tel: 020 8866 4442 Email: pinnerdcs@hotmail.com
• Diocesan Centre for Youth Ministry, 125 Waxwell Lane, Pinner HA5 3EP
Tel: 020 3757 2516 Email: youth@rcdow.org.uk Web: http;//dowym.com
(see under *Westminster Youth Ministry*, Section 2)

SECTION 3

• SPEC, Waxwell House, 125 Waxwell Lane, Pinner HA5 3EP
Tel: 020 3757 2500 Email: spec@rcdow.org.uk
Diocesan Retreat Centre for Young People (see under *Westminster Youth Ministry*, Section 2)

POLISH CHURCH 1 + OUR LADY OF CZESTOCHOWA AND ST CASIMIR A

Sunday Mass (Sat 6pm), 9, 11, 12.30pm, 3.30pm, 7pm; **Holy Day Mass** 10.30, 7pm
Weekday Mass Mon-Fri 10.30, 7pm, Sat 7.30; **Confession** 30 min before Mass

Fr Bogdan Kołodziej, Fr Leszek Buba
2 Devonia Road N1 8JJ Tel: 020 7226 9944 Fax: 020 7359 8042
Email: polishchurch1@rcdow.org.uk Web: www.parafia-devonia.org.uk
Near Angel TfL Station
Islington Deanery (1905; 1930)
Parish Office Tue-Fri 5-6pm
• Polish Catholic Mission, 4 Devonia Road N1 8JJ
Tel: 020 7226 3439 Fax 020 7226 7677
Mgr Stefan Wylezek (Vicar Delegate), Canon Krzysztof Tyliszczak (Chancellor), Mgr Janusz Tworek ((Financial Administrator)

POLISH CHURCH 2 + ST ANDREW BOBOLA

Sunday Mass (Sat 6pm), 8.30, 10, 12noon, 6pm; **Holy Day Mass** 10, 12noon, 7pm;
Weekday Mass 10, 7pm; **Confession** Mon-Fri 9.30-10, 6.30-7pm, Thu 7.30-9pm, Sat 5-6pm

Fr Marek Reczek, Fr Maciej Michalek
1 Leysfield Rd W12 9JF Tel: 020 8743 8848
Email: polishchurch2@rcdow.org.uk Web: www.bobola.church
Hammersmith & Fulham Deanery (1961)

POLISH CHURCH 3 + OUR LADY MOTHER OF THE CHURCH

Sunday Mass (Sat 7pm), 8.30, 10 (Family), 11.30, 1pm, 2.30pm (*Seasonal from Sep-Jun*) 5.15pm, 7pm (Youth), 8.30pm; **Weekday Mass** 8 (Latin), 10, 3.30pm *English on 1st Fri*, 7pm

Marian Fathers (MIC) Fr Michał Kozak, Fr Jakub Biernacki, Fr Wiktor Gumienny, Fr Grzegorz Leszczyk, Fr Dariusz Mazewski
2 Windsor Road W5 5PD Tel: 020 8567 1746
Email: polishchurch3@rcdow.org.uk Web: www.parafiaealing.co.uk
Ealing Deanery (1986)

• Sisters of the Holy Name of Jesus, 57 Mount Park Road W5 2PU Tel: 020 8997 2030
Sunday Mass (Sat 5pm, Polish)
• Sisters of the Resurrection, 84 Gordon Road W5 2AR Tel: 020 8998 8954
Weekday Mass Mon-Fri 7.30
• Divine Mercy Apostolate: see *Ealing* parish entry
• Kolbe House (Nursing Home) 18 Hanger Lane W5 3HH Tel: 020 8992 4978
Sunday Mass (Sat 4.30pm)

PONDERS END + CHURCH OF MARY, MOTHER OF GOD A

Sunday Mass (Sat 6pm), 8, 9.30 (Family), 11 (Sung), 12.30pm (Italian), 6pm; **Holy Day Mass** 9.30, 12.30pm, 8pm; **Weekday Mass** Mon, Tue, Wed, Thu, Sat 9.30, Fri 7.30pm; **Confession** Sat 10-11

Fr John B. Shewring
192 Nags Head Road, Enfield EN3 7AR
Tel: 020 8804 2149 / 07973 539907 Fax: 020 8804 2749
Email: pondersend@rcdow.org.uk Web: www.marymotherofgod.church
Enfield Deanery (1912; 1921; cons 8 September 1985)
Catechetical Co-ordinator Muriel Akahi Tel: 020 8443 4069 / 07514 225506
Email: murialakahi@rcdow.org.uk

• Italian Catholic Centre
Fr Antonio Serra 197 Durants Road, Enfield EN3 7DE Tel: 020 8804 2307

POPLAR + SS MARY AND JOSEPH S

Sunday Mass (Sat 6pm), 10; **Holy Day Mass** (Vigil 7pm), 10; **Weekday Mass** Mon-Fri 9.30 (may vary); **Confession** Sat 5.15pm

Fr Keith Stoakes (also serves Limehouse)
Clergy House, 9 Pekin Street E14 6EZ Tel: 020 7987 4523
Email: poplar@rcdow.org.uk Web: parish.rcdow.org.uk/poplar
Church at junction of Upper North Street and Canton Street
Tower Hamlets Deanery (1816; 1856; 1954; new church cons 12 October 1960)
• Faithful Companions of Jesus, The Lodge, Hale Street E14 0BS
Tel: 020 7517 9599 Email: nip65@msn.com Web: www.fcjsisters.org
Srs Christine Frost, Katherine Mary O'Flynn, Bernadette O'Malley, Anouska Robinson-Biggin, Elizabeth Ryan

POTTERS BAR + OUR LADY & ST VINCENT

Sunday Mass (Sat 6pm), 9, 11 (with Children's Liturgy) (**Sunday Mass August** (Sat 6pm), 10); **Holy Day Mass** (Vigil 7.30pm), 7, 10; **Weekday Mass** 10 as announced; **Confession** Sat 5.15– 5.45pm, Advent & Lent 10.30 – 11.30 (with **Exposition**)

Canon Shaun Lennard, Rev Donal Hopkins (Deacon)
243 Mutton Lane, Potters Bar EN6 2AT Tel: 01707 654359
Email: pottersbar@rcdow.org.uk Web: www.olasv.org.uk
Enfield Deanery (2006; 2006)
Catechetical Co-ordinator Mrs Francesca Khaliq Email: pottersbarcat@rcdow.org.uk
Parish Safeguarding Representative Michael Sibley

• Sisters of Charity of St Jeanne Antide, 1a The Avenue, Potters Bar EN6 1EG
Tel: 01707 645901 Email: paxirene@live.co.uk
Srs Irene Brogan, Christina O'Dwyer
• Potters Bar District Hospital

SECTION 3

QUEENSWAY + OUR LADY, QUEEN OF HEAVEN

Sunday Mass (Sat 5.30pm), 10, 11.30, 1pm (Ethiopian, Gheez rite); **Holy Day Mass** 9.30, 6pm; **Weekday Mass** Mon 6pm, Tue, Wed 9.30, Fri 6pm and 7.30pm **Brazilian Mass**; **Holy Hour** Sat 4.15-5.15pm; **Confession** Sat 4.15-5.15pm & on request

Fr Saviour Grech
4a Inverness Place W2 3JF Tel: 020 7229 8153
Email: queensway@rcdow.org.uk Web: parish.rcdow.org.uk/queensway
Queensway, opposite Bayswater Stn (TfL); close to Queensway Stn (TfL)
North Kensington Deanery (1954; 1973; cons 21 April 2002)

• Prelature of Opus Dei, 4 Orme Court W2 4RL Tel: 020 7229 7574
Mgr Nicholas Morrish (Regional Vicar), Frs Peter Bristow, Paul Hayward, Bernard Marsh, Gerard Sheehan, Andrew Soane

RADLETT + ST ANTHONY OF PADUA, AND SHENLEY + THE GOOD SHEPHERD

Radlett: **Sunday Mass** 10; **Holy Day Mass** as announced; **Weekday Mass** Tue 10; *Monthly* Wed evening as announced (in Shenley, see newsletter); **Confession** Sun 9.30-9.50

Shenley: **Sunday Mass** (Sat 5pm); **Holy Day Mass** as announced; **Weekday Mass** Wed 9.30; Monthly evening as announced (see newsletter); **Exposition** Sat 4.15pm, with **Benediction** 4.50pm; **Confession** Sat 4.15-4.45pm

London Colney: **Sunday Mass** 11.30; **Holy Day Mass** as announced; **Weekday Mass** Mon, *Monthly* Wed evening as announced (in Shenley, see newsletter), Thu 10; **Prayer Group** Fri 8-9pm; **Filipino Adorers** ***4th Fri only*** 9pm-midnight; **Confession** Sun 11.10-11.25

Fr Kevin Moule, Rev Tony Barter (Deacon), Rev Anthony Curran (Deacon) (clergy also serve London Colney)
22 The Crosspath, Radlett WD7 8HN Tel: 01923 635541

+ St Anthony of Padua
Email: radlett@rcdow.org.uk Web: parish.rcdow.org.uk/radlett
St Albans Deanery (1905; new church 1910)
+ The Good Shepherd, Black Lion Hill, Shenley WD7 9DH
Email: radlett@rcdow.org.uk Web: parish.rcdow.org.uk/shenley
St Albans Deanery (1969; 1976)
Parish Administrator Mrs Catherine King Tel: 01923 635541

REDBOURN (FLAMSTEAD AND MARKYATE) + ST JOHN FISHER

Sunday Mass (Sat 5.30pm), 9; **Holy Day Mass** as announced; **Weekday Mass** as announced; **Confession** Sat 9.45-10.15, 5.45-6.15pm

Fr Michael Mannion (also serves Wheathampstead)
1 Peppard Close, Redbourn, St Albans AL3 7EB Tel: 01582 792270
Email: redbourn@rcdow.org.uk Web: parish.rcdow.org.uk/redbourn
Dunstable Road, north of the village on the old A5
St Albans Deanery (1936; 1967; cons 22 June 2003)

RICKMANSWORTH + OUR LADY HELP OF CHRISTIANS

Sunday Mass 8.30, 11, 6pm; **Holy Day Mass** 9.30, 8pm; **Weekday Mass** Mon, Tue, Thu, Fri 9.30, Sat 10; **Exposition** and **Confession** Sat 10.30-11.30

Chorleywood: **Sunday Mass** (Sat 6pm), 9; **Holy Day Mass** as announced; **Weekday Mass** Tue, Fri 9.30; **Exposition** 1st Sat 5.30-5.55pm; **Confession** on request & by appointment

Mill End: **Sunday Mass** (Sat 6pm), 10.30; **Holy Day Mass** as announced; **Weekday Mass** Mon, Wed 9.30; **Exposition** Sat 5.30-5.55pm; **Confession** on request & by appointment

Fr Shaun Church, Fr Damian Ryan (clergy also serve Chorleywood and Mill End)
5 Park Road, Rickmansworth WD3 1HU Tel: 01923 773387
Email: rickmansworth@rcdow.org.uk Web: parish.rcdow.org.uk/rickmansworth
On main road beside roundabout at bottom of Scots Hill (east end of High Street)
Watford Deanery (1886; 1909)

ROYSTON + ST THOMAS OF CANTERBURY AND THE ENGLISH MARTYRS A

Sunday Mass (Sat 6.30pm), 9, 10.30; **Holy Day Mass** 9.15, 7.30pm; **Weekday Mass** Tue 7.30pm Wed-Fri 9.15; **Confession** Sat 5.45pm & by appointment, with **Exposition** from 5.30pm

Fr Philip Knights
6 Melbourn Road, Royston SG8 7DB Tel: 01763 243117
Email: royston@rcdow.org.uk Web: www.roystoncatholicchurch.co.uk
Left side of A10 just beyond central roundabout, towards Cambridge
Stevenage Deanery (1911; 1917)

SECTION 3

• Sisters of Providence (of the Immaculate Conception), Providence House, 4 Melbourn Road, Royston SG8 7DB Tel: 01763 250956 Email: providencemarian@yahoo.co.uk

RUISLIP + MOST SACRED HEART

Sunday Mass (Sat 6pm), 8.30, 10 (Family), 11.30 (Sung), 6pm; **Holy Day Mass** (Vigil 8pm), 8, 10, 8pm; **Weekday Mass** 10 and as announced; **Exposition** Mon-Fri 10.30-11, Sat 10.30-12noon; **Confession** Sat 10.30-11.30, 5.15-5.30pm

Fr Duncan Adamson, Fr Sebastian Joseph
73 Pembroke Road, Ruislip HA4 8NN Tel: 01895 632739
Email: ruislip@rcdow.org.uk Web: parish.rcdow.org.uk/ruislip
Ruislip Manor, near traffic lights; near Ruislip Manor Stn; 1/3 mile Ruislip Stn
Hillingdon Deanery (1921; new church cons 15 June 1939)
Administrator Mrs Anne O'Connor
Catechetical Co-ordinator Mrs Jo Marsh Tel: 01895 673983
Parish Youth Worker Siobhan Denny

RUISLIP SOUTH + ST GREGORY THE GREAT A

Sunday Mass (Sat 5.30pm), 10 (Sung), 6pm; **Holy Day Mass** 10, 8pm; **Weekday Mass** 10 (except Thu); **Exposition** Sat 10.30-11; **Confession** Sat 10.30-11, 6.30-7pm

Mgr Canon Paul McGinn
447 Victoria Road, South Ruislip HA4 0EG Tel: 020 8845 2186
Email: ruislipsouth@rcdow.org.uk Web: www.st-gregory.org.uk
Corner of Angus Drive, near South Ruislip shops/Stn
Hillingdon Deanery (1958; 1967; cons 1 November 1975)
Pastoral Assistant Sr Joanna Whooley RSHM
Parish Administrator Gillian Harrington

ST ALBANS + SS ALBAN AND STEPHEN A

Sunday Mass (Sat 6pm), 8, 9.30, 11.30, 7pm; **Holy Day Mass** (Vigil 7pm) 10, 7pm; **Weekday Mass** Mon-Fri 10, Mon, Wed, Fri 7pm; **Confession** Sat 10.30-11.30, 6.45-7pm
Mass at St Albans Abbey, in the Lady Chapel Fri 12noon

Missionaries of the Sacred Heart (MSC) Fr Tom Plower, Fr Jimmy Stubbs, Fr Alan Neville; Rev Steve Pickard (Deacon)
14 Beaconsfield Road, St Albans AL1 3RB Tel: 01727 853585
Email: stalbans@rcdow.org.uk Web: www.albanstephen.com
Close to St Albans City Stn
St Albans Deanery (1840; 1904; cons 1977)
Mass Centre, Marshalswick (St John Fisher School)
Sunday Mass 9

ST ALBANS SOUTH + ST BARTHOLOMEW

Sunday Mass (Sat 6pm), 8.30, 10.30; **Holy Day Mass** as announced; **Weekday Mass** Mon 12noon, Tue, Wed 9, Fri 9.30, Sat 9; **Exposition** Sat 9.30-10; **Confession** Sat 9.30-10, 5.15-5.45pm & by appointment
Mass at St Albans Abbey, in the Lady Chapel Fri 12noon

Fr Francis Antwi-Darkwah, Rev Justin Cross (Deacon)
47 Vesta Avenue, St Albans AL1 2PE Tel: 01727 850066
Email: stalbanssouth@rcdow.org.uk Web: parish.rcdow.org.uk/stalbanssouth
On Watling Street (A5183), just above the North Orbital Road/A414 roundabout
St Albans Deanery (1959; cons 9 November 1985)

• Brothers of the Sacred Heart, Watling House, 8 King Harry Lane, St Albans AL3 4AW Tel: 01727 861969
Brs Nelson Dionne, Clement Pelletier, Daniel St Jacques, Paul Vaillancourt (Superior)

ST CHARLES SQUARE (NORTH KENSINGTON) + ST PIUS X

Sunday Mass (Sat 6pm), 9, 11; **Holy Day Mass** 8.20, 12.30pm; **Weekday Mass** Mon-Fri 8.20, preceded by **Morning Prayer** 8.05; **Confession** Sat 5.15-5.45pm

Fr Peter Wilson, Fr Brian Creak (in residence, University Chaplain, contact details below)
79 St Charles Square W10 6EB Tel: 020 8969 6844 Fax: 020 8960 6589
Email: stcharlessquare@rcdow.org.uk Web: parish.rcdow.org.uk/stcharlessquare
West of Ladbroke Grove, just north of Stn (TfL) & motorway bridge
North Kensington Deanery (1937; 1955)

(Fr Brian Creak **Tel: 020 8968 3373**)
Fr Peter-Michael Scott in residence at **81 St Charles Square W10 6EB Tel: 020 8960 2609**

• Carmelite Nuns, Monastery of the Most Holy Trinity, 87 St Charles Square W10 6EA
Tel: 020 8969 8702 Email: carmelnottinghill@talktalk.net
Web: carmelitesnottinghill.org.uk Chaplain Fr Marcus Winter Tel: 020 3673 9540
Daily Mass 8.15
• Little Sisters of Jesus, 41 Bonchurch Road W10 5NN Tel: 020 8960 0440
• Princess Louise Home
• St Charles Square Centre for Health and Wellbeing (Mental Health Units)
Tel: 020 8969 2488
• St Charles Square Palliative Care, Pembridge Hospice

ST JOHN'S WOOD + OUR LADY A

Sunday Mass (Sat 6pm), 9, 10.30 (Latin Polyphony), 12noon, 6pm; **Holy Day Mass** 7.30pm; **Weekday Mass** Mon-Wed 10, Thu 7pm, Fri-Sat 10; **Exposition** Mon-Sat 6(am)-Midnight; **Confession** Sat 10.30-11, 5.15-5.45pm & by arrangement
Our Lady Queen of the World: see below

Fr Jeffrey Steel
54 Lodge Road NW8 8LA Tel: 020 7286 3214
Email: stjohnswood@rcdow.org.uk Web: www.rcsjw.org.uk
Top of Lisson Grove, close to junction with St John's Wood Road (by Lords Cricket Ground)
Marylebone Deanery (1833; 1836; cons 14 May 1925)
Parish Sister Sr Brigid

• Handmaids of the Sacred Heart of Jesus, 25 St Edmund's Terrace NW8 7PY
Tel: 020 7722 2756 Email: provincialsec@aol.com Web: http://aciengland.org
Chapel of Our Lady, Queen of the World: **Holy Day Mass** as announced; **Weekday Mass** Mon-Fri 8; **Exposition** daily 8.30-12noon
• Carmelite Missionaries, 189 Gloucester Place NW1 6BU Tel: 020 7262 4737
Email: ukcm91@gmail.com Web: www.carmelitasmisioneras.org or www.carmiseuropa.org
Srs Teresa Fernandez, Vivien Gavan, Ciciliamma Jose, Margarita Marques
• Mercy Union Generalate, 11 Harewood Avenue NW1 6LD Tel: 020 7723 2527
9 Wimborne House, Harewood Avenue NW1 6NU Tel: 020 7723 4794
39 Alma Square NW8 9PY Tel: 020 7289 3657
91 Ashmill Street NW1 6RA
• Redemptoris Mater House of Formation, St Edward's Convent, 11 Harewood Avenue NW1 6LD Tel: 020 7723 9364 Fax: 020 7258 3914 Email: rmhf.london@gmail.com
Fr Lorenzo Andreini
• Hospital of St John & St Elizabeth, 60 Grove End Road NW8 9NH Tel: 020 7806 4000
Chaplain Fr Hugh MacKenzie
Hospital chapel (Church of St John of Jerusalem)
Sunday Mass 11; **Weekday Mass** Tue 11

SECTION 3

• Wellington Hospital Tel: 020 7586 5959
Chaplains Fr Giles Pinnock, Fr Gerard O'Brien Tel 020 3312 1508

ST MARGARETS-ON-THAMES + ST MARGARET OF SCOTLAND

Sunday Mass (Sat 6.30pm), 8.30, 10.30, 6.30pm; **Holy Day Mass** 7.15, 10, 8pm; **Weekday Mass** Mon, Tue 10, Wed 7.15 (term time only), Thu-Sat 10; **Confession** Sat 10.30-11, Sun 10-10.20

Canon Peter Newby
130 St Margarets Road, Twickenham TW1 1RL Tel: 020 8892 3902
Email: stmargaretsonthames@rcdow.org.uk Web: www. stmargarets-church.co.uk
Opposite St Margarets Stn (BR); close to Chertsey Road (A316) and Richmond Road (A305)
Upper Thames Deanery (1930; 1969)
Parish Administrator Jean McGinley
Parish Youth Worker Molly Bayliss-Conway

SAWBRIDGEWORTH: *SEE BISHOP'S STORTFORD*

SHENLEY + THE GOOD SHEPHERD: *SEE RADLETT*

SHEPHERDS BUSH + THE HOLY GHOST AND ST STEPHEN A

Sunday Mass (Sat 6pm), 9.15, 11 (Family), 12.30pm; **Holy Day Mass** 9.30, 8pm; **Weekday Mass** Mon, Tue 9.30, Wed 7, Thu 7pm; Fri, Sat 9.30; **Exposition** Sat 10-10.45, with **Benediction**; **Confession** Sat 10.15-10.45, 5.15-5.45pm

Fr Mark Vickers
44 Ashchurch Grove W12 9BU Tel: 020 8743 5196
Email: shepherdsbush@rcdow.org.uk Web: www.rcshepherdsbush.org
Off Askew Road, near junction with Goldhawk Road; nearest Stn Stamford Brook (TfL)
Hammersmith & Fulham Deanery (1889; 1904; cons 24 April 1936)

• Franciscan Missionaries of Mary (Provincialate), 5 Vaughan Avenue W6 0XS
Tel: 020 8748 4077 Email: provsecuk@aol.com Web: www.fmmii.org

SHEPPERTON + ST JOHN FISHER

Sunday Mass (Sat 6pm), 8.30, 10.30 (Children's 1st Sun); **Holy Day Mass** as announced; **Weekday Mass** as announced; **Exposition** Mon 7-7.30pm; **Confession** Sat 5.30pm

Awaiting appointment
15 Wood Road, Shepperton TW17 0DH Tel: 01932 563116
Email: shepperton@rcdow.org.uk Web: www.sjfchurch.org.uk
In Shepperton Green (sign on Shepperton-Staines road)
Upper Thames Deanery (1936; 1965)
Parish Secretary Traci Blundell (Thu 9-1pm) Email: shepperton@rcdow.org.uk

SOHO SQUARE + ST PATRICK

Sunday Mass (Sat 4pm (Portuguese), 6pm), 11, 5pm, 6pm (Spanish); **Holy Day Mass** 8, 12.30pm, 1.05pm, 6pm; **Weekday Mass** Mon-Fri 12.45pm; **Exposition** Mon-Fri 1.30-6pm, Sat 7-9pm; **Confession** Mon-Fri 12.15-12.40pm, Sat 5.30-6pm

Canon Alexander Sherbrooke
21a Soho Square W1D 4NR Tel: 020 7437 2010
Email: sohosquare@rcdow.org.uk Web: www.stpatricksoho.org
Near junction of Oxford Street and Charing Cross Road, south of Tottenham Court Road TfL Stn
Westminster Deanery (1792; 1893)
Parish Sister Sr Mary Kenefick SMG

- Latin American Chaplaincy Fr Carlos Abajos Eguileta Tel: 020 7820 1697
- Shalom Catholic Community at St Patrick's

Missionaries Emanuela Cardoso, Francisca de Fatima de Oliveira
Tel: 07432 501250 Email: london@comshalom.org Web: http://www.comshalom.org/en
- SOS Prayer Line Tel: 020 7434 9211
- St Patrick's School of Evangelisation (SPES) 21a Soho Square W1D 4NR

Tel: 020 7434 9965 Email: spes@stpatricksoho.org Web: www.stpatricksoho.org

SECTION 3

SOMERS TOWN + ST ALOYSIUS A

Sunday Mass (Sat 6pm), 9.30, 11.30, 6pm; **Holy Day Mass** 7.30, 9.30, 12.30pm, 6pm; **Weekday Mass** Mon, Tue, Thu, Fri 9.30; **Confession** Sat 5pm & by appointment

Fr Jeremy Trood, Fr Mark Walker (in residence, Diocesan Youth Chaplain)
20 Phoenix Road NW1 1TA Tel: 020 7387 1971
Email: somerstown@rcdow.org.uk Web: parish.rcdow.org.uk/somerstown
Off Eversholt Street, east of Euston Stn
Camden Deanery (1798; 1808; 1968; cons 24 May 1992)

- Faithful Companions of Jesus, FCJ Spirituality Centre, 32 Phoenix Road NW1 1TA

Email: fcjspiritualitycentre@gmail.com Web: fcjsisters.org
Srs Margarita Byron, Bernadette Coughlin, Ellen McCarthy, Rita McLoughlin, Brenda Wallace
- Poor Servants of the Mother of God, 70-71 Euston Square NW1 1DJ

Tel: 020 7387 5855 Email: st.philomenas@psmgs.org.uk Web: www.poorservants.com
- St Pancras Hospital

SOUTHALL + ST ANSELM

Sunday Mass (Sat 6.30pm), 8, 9.45, 11.30, 6.30pm; **Holy Day Mass** 9.15, 12.15pm, 7.30pm; **Weekday Mass** Mon-Fri 9.15; **Holy Hour** Sun 4.30pm; **Novena** Sun 5.30pm; **Confession** Sat 11-12noon
Ethnic Chaplaincy Masses: Sri Lankan (Tamil) *1st Sun* 2pm; **Konkani (Goan)** *3rd Sat* 4pm; **Malayalam** *3rd Sun* 3pm; **Urdu** *last Sun* 3pm

Jesuits (SJ) Fr Gerard Mitchell, Fr George Stephen Thayriam;
Rev Stephen Khokhar (Deacon)
St Anselm's Rectory, The Green, Southall UB2 4BE
Tel: 020 8574 3300 Fax: 020 8813 8784
Email: southall@rcdow.org.uk Web: stanselmchurchsouthall.com
To the south of Southall Stn (BR), opposite Osterley Park Road
Ealing Deanery (1906; 1930; 1968)
Parish Evanglisation Co-ordinator Susan Cawley Email susancawley@rcdow.org.uk

• Missionaries of Charity, 41 Villiers Road, Southall UB1 3BS Tel: 020 8574 1892

SPANISH PLACE + ST JAMES A

Sunday Mass (Sat 6pm), 8.30, 9.30 (Extraordinary Form), 10.30 (Sung Latin), 12noon, 4pm, 7pm; **Holy Day Mass** 7.15, 11 (Extraordinary Form), 12.30pm, 6pm, 7pm; **Weekday Mass** Mon-Fri 7.15, 12.30pm, 6pm, Sat 10; **Holy Hour** Sat 4.45pm; **Confession** Mon-Fri 12-1pm; Sat 10.30-12noon, 5-5.45pm & on request

Fr Christopher Colven, Fr David Irwin (in residence, Episcopal Vicar and Co-ordinator for Ethnic Chaplaincies, contact details below), Fr Hugh MacKenzie (in residence)
22 George Street W1U 3QY Tel: 020 7935 0943
Email: spanishplace@rcdow.org.uk Web: www.sjrcc.org.uk
Bottom of Marylebone High Street; Baker Street or Bond Street TfL Stns
Marylebone Deanery (1791; 1890; cons 28 April 1949)
(Fr David Irwin **Tel: 020 7935 4420**)

• Heart Hospital Tel: 020 3456 7890
Chaplain Fr Peter Harries OP Tel: 020 3447 3007
• London Clinic, King Edward VII Hospital for Officers
• Harley Street Clinic
Chaplains Fr Giles Pinnock, Fr Gerard O'Brien Tel 020 3312 1508
• Princess Grace Hospital
Chaplains Fr Giles Pinnock, Fr Gerard O'Brien Tel 020 3312 1508

SPITALFIELDS, E1: *SEE UNDERWOOD ROAD*

STAINES-UPON-THAMES + OUR LADY OF THE ROSARY

Sunday Mass (Sat 6.30pm) 9, 11; **Holy Day Mass** 7, mid-morning as announced, 7pm; **Weekday Mass** Tue-Thu 9.15, Fri as announced; **Exposition** Tue 9.35-9.50; **Confession** Sat 5.30-6pm

Fr Philip Dyer-Perry
The Presbytery, 59 Gresham Road, Staines TW18 2BD Tel: 01784 452381
Email: staines@rcdow.org.uk Web: parish.rcdow.org.uk/staines
Near Staines Stn (BR), opposite footbridge
Upper Thames Deanery (1890; 1932)

STAMFORD HILL + ST IGNATIUS S

Sunday Mass (Sat 7pm), 8.30, 10 (Family), 11.30 (Sung), 1.30pm (Polish), 4.30pm (Latin American), 6pm, 7.30pm (Polish); **Holy Day Mass** 10, 7.30pm; **Weekday Mass** 10, 6.30pm; **Confession** Sat 10.30-11.15, 6-6.45pm

Jesuits (SJ) Fr Andrew Cameron-Mowat
27 High Road N15 6ND Tel: 020 8800 2121 Fax: 020 8802 8102
Email: stamfordhill@rcdow.org.uk Web: parish.rcdow.org.uk/stamfordhill
Corner of High Road (A10) & St Ann's Road near Seven Sisters Stn (TfL)
Haringey Deanery (1894;1903)
Community: Frs Edward Bermingham, Michael Bossy, Mateusz Konopinski, Bogdan Lesniak, Paul O'Reilly (Superior); David Stewart
Catechetical Co-ordinator Elwira Pniewski

- Servite Sisters, St Mary's Convent, 90 Suffolk Road N15 5RH Tel: 020 8800 2940
- Ursulines of Jesus, 149 Bethune Road N16 5DY Tel: 020 8800 4623
- Pope's Worldwide Prayer Network 27 High Road N15 6ND

National Promoter Fr David Stewart SJ Tel: 020 8442 5232
Email: prayernetwork@jesuit.org.uk Office hours Mon, Tue only

SECTION 3

STANMORE + ST WILLIAM OF YORK

Sunday Mass (Sat 5.30pm), 8, 10 (Sung); **Holy Day Mass** 9.30, 7pm; **Weekday Mass** Mon-Wed, Sat 9.30, Fri 7pm; **Confession** Sat 10-10.30

Canon Michael Munnelly
1 Du Cros Drive, Stanmore HA7 4TJ Tel: 020 8954 1299
Email: stanmore@rcdow.org.uk Web: parish.rcdow.org.uk/stanmore
Off Marsh Lane, 1/4 mile south of The Broadway
Harrow Deanery (1938; 1960)
Parish Secretary Frances Bright

- Royal National Orthopaedic Hospital, Woodland Hall Home

STANWELL + ST DAVID

Sunday Mass (Sat 6pm), 10, 6pm; **Holy Day Mass** 9.30, 7.30pm; **Weekday Mass** Mon, Tue, Thu, Fri 9.30; **Rosary** Fri 6.45pm; **Exposition** Fri 7.15-8pm; **Confession** Sat 5.15-5.45pm

Fr Voytek Przyjalkowski
St David's, Everest Road, Stanwell, Staines TW19 7EE Tel/Fax: 01784 255973
Email: stanwellparish@rcdow.org.uk Web: parish.rcdow.org.uk/stanwell
Upper Thames Deanery (1964; 1967)

- Ashford Hospital

STEVENAGE PARISHES A

Bedwell, St Joseph: **Sunday Mass** (Sat 6pm), 12.15 **Holy Day Mass** 9.15; **Weekday Mass** Wed 7pm, Thu, Fri 9.15; **Rosary** Wed, Thu after Mass; **Adoration**, then **Benediction** Fri 6-7pm; **Confession** Wed 7.30-8pm, Fri 6-6.40 pm, Sat 5.15-5.30pm and on request

Old Town, Transfiguration: **Sunday** (Sat 5pm), 9; **Holy Day Mass** 9.30; **Weekday Mass** Mon, Fri 9.30; **Confession** Sat 4.30-4.45pm

Shephall, St Hilda: **Sunday Mass** (Sat 6.30pm), 9.30 (Sung), 11 (with Children's Liturgy); **Holy Day Mass** 9.30; **Weekday Mass** Mon, Tue, Sat 9.30; **Exposition** and **Benediction** Thu 7-8pm, Fri 10-11; **Confession** Sat 10, 6pm

Fr Michael Doherty SDS (resident at **9 Breakspear, Stevenage SG2 9SQ Tel: 01438 352182**), Fr Brian McMahon (resident at **St Joseph's Presbytery, Bedwell Crescent, Stevenage SG1 1NJ Tel: 01438 351243**)

+ St Joseph (Stevenage Bedwell)
St Joseph's Presbytery, Bedwell Crescent, Stevenage SG1 1NJ
Email: stevenagebedwell@rcdow.org.uk Web: parish.rcdow.org.uk/stevenage
Off roundabout linking Bedwell Crescent and Fairlands Way
Stevenage Deanery

+ Transfiguration of Our Lord
Grove Road, Stevenage SG1 3PX (Stevenage Old Town)
Email: stevenageoldtown@rcdow.org.uk Web: www.stevenage-rc.org.uk
Off Church Lane, east of High Street
Stevenage Deanery (1912)

• Sisters of Charity of Jesus and Mary, 3 Hitchin Road, Stevenage SG1 3BJ
Tel: 01438 354247 Sr Mary Catherine Callaghan
• Lister Hospital
Tel: 01438 314333

+ St Hilda (Stevenage Shephall)
9 Breakspear, Stevenage SG2 9SQ
Email: stevenageshephall@rcdow.org.uk Web: parish.rcdow.org.uk/stevenageshephall
Stevenage Deanery (1958; cons 1986)

STOKE NEWINGTON + OUR LADY OF GOOD COUNSEL

Sunday Mass (Sat 6.30pm), 9, 11; **Holy Day Mass** 10, 7pm; **Weekday Mass** Mon-Fri 10 (followed by Marian devotions); **Zimbabwean Mass** *First Sat only* 2pm; **Holy Hour** *First Sat only* 11; **Confession** Sat 11.30-12noon, 5.30-6pm & on request

Fr Martin Tate, Fr John Rufaro Mudereri (in residence, Zimbabwean Chaplaincy)
24 Bouverie Road N16 0AJ Tel: 020 8800 5250
Email: stokenewington@rcdow.org.uk Web: parish.rcdow.org.uk/stokenewington
Hackney Deanery (1882; 1936; 1976)

• Little Sisters of the Poor, St Anne's Home, 77 Manor Road N16 5BL
Tel: 020 8826 2500 Email: ms.stanne@lsplondon.co.uk Web: www.lsplondon.co.uk
Chaplain Fr Daniel Magnier

STONEBRIDGE + THE FIVE PRECIOUS WOUNDS A

Sunday Mass (Sat 6pm), 10 (Sung), 12noon (Family); **Holy Day Mass** 10, 7pm; **Weekday Mass** Mon-Fri 10; **Confession** Fri 10.30-11, Sat 5.15-5.45pm

Fr Antonio Ritaccio
The Presbytery, Brentfield Road NW10 8ER Tel: 020 8965 3313
Email: stonebridge@rcdow.org.uk Web: parish.rcdow.org.uk/stonebridge
Off Harrow Road (A404), 1/4 mile east of junction with North Circular Road
Brent Deanery (1926; 1957; cons 14 May 1967)

STROUD GREEN + ST PETER-IN-CHAINS A

Sunday Mass (Sat 6.30pm), 9.45 (Sung), 11.15 (Family), 7pm; **Holy Day Mass** 9, 7.30pm; **Weekday Mass** Mon-Sat 9; **Morning Prayer** 15 mins before weekday Mass; **Holy Hour** Fri 7.30-8.30pm; **Exposition** Sat 9.30-10; **Confession** Sat 9.30-10, 6-6.20pm

Fr Sean Carroll
12 Womersley Road N8 9AE Tel: 020 8340 3394
Email: stroudgreen@rcdow.org.uk Web: www.stpeterinchains.com
Haringey Deanery (1894; 1896)

• Sisters of Christian Instruction (St Gildas), 36 Dickenson Road N8 9ET
Tel: 020 8340 7203 Web: http://soeurs-de-stgildas-nantes.cef.fr
• Sisters of Providence, 78 Oakfield Road N4 4LB Tel: 020 8340 1088
also 78a Oakfield Road N4 4LB Tel: 020 8341 1788
Email: prov.london@yahoo.com Web: www.providenceruillesurloir.com

SUDBURY + ST GEORGE

Sunday Mass (Sat 6.15pm), 8.30, 9.45 (Family), 11.15 (Solemn), 5.30pm (Sung); **Holy Day Mass** 9.30, 8pm; **Weekday Mass** 9.30; **Confession** Sat 5.15-6pm

Mgr Jeremy Fairhead, Fr Tony Thomas
970 Harrow Road, Sudbury, Wembley HA0 2QE
Tel: 020 8904 2552 Fax: 020 8904 0744
Email: sudbury@rcdow.org.uk Web: parish.rcdow.org.uk/sudbury
On corner of St Andrew's Avenue, east of Greenford Road / Sudbury Court Drive junction
Harrow Deanery (1924; 1926; cons 18 April 1928)
Parish Team Mgr Jeremy Fairhead, Fr Tony Thomas, Mr Peter Kingsley (Pastoral Assistant and Catechetical Co-ordinator), Mrs Toni Miles (Parish Secretary)

• Northwick Park Hospital
• Wembley Hospital, Clementine Churchill Hospital

SECTION 3

SUNBURY-ON-THAMES + ST IGNATIUS OF LOYOLA

Sunday Mass (Sat 6pm), 9.30, 11.30; **Holy Day Mass** 9, 11.30, 7pm; **Weekday Mass** 9.30; **Confession** Sat 9.30

Fr Michael Tuck
The Rectory, Green Street, Sunbury-on-Thames TW16 6QB Tel: 01932 783507
Email: sunburyonthames@rcdow.org.uk Web: parish.rcdow.org.uk/sunburyonthames
Main road, South Sunbury Stn (BR) / M3 interchange
Upper Thames Deanery (1862; 1869; cons 22 May 1884)
Parish Sister Sr Liza Randall
The Loyola Centre (opposite church, *Hall available for hire*) Tel: 07725 023811

• Sunbury Nursing Home, Ashton Lodge, Beechwood Court

SWISS COTTAGE + ST THOMAS MORE A

Sunday Mass 10, 12noon (Sung), 6.30pm; **Holy Day Mass** 7,10, 7pm; **Weekday Mass** Mon-Fri 7,10, Sat 10; **Exposition** Sun 5.15-6.15pm, Fri 10.30-4pm; **Confession** daily, before & after Mass

Fr Stefan Hnylycia, Fr Paul Diaper
Presbytery, Maresfield Gardens NW3 5SU Tel: 020 7435 1388
Email: swisscottage@rcdow.org.uk Web: parish.rcdow.org.uk/swisscottage
Off Fitzjohn's Avenue, near Finchley Road and Swiss Cottage TfL Stns
Camden Deanery (1938; 1968; cons 8 May 1977)

• Lakefield, Maresfield Gardens NW3 5RY Tel: 020 7794 5669
Web: www.lakefield.org.uk Catering and education centre
Pastoral Care entrusted to the Prelature of Opus Dei
• Netherhall House, Nutley Terrace NW3 5SA Tel: 020 7435 8888
Web: www.nh.netherhall.org.uk Hall of Residence for male University students
Pastoral Care entrusted to the Prelature of Opus Dei
Fr Dancho Azagra, Mgr Richard Stork
• Eden Hall (Marie Curie) Hospice

TEDDINGTON (& HAMPTON WICK) + THE SACRED HEART

Sunday Mass (Sat 6.30pm), 9.30 (Family), 11.15 (Sung); **Holy Day Mass** 9.30, 7.30pm; **Weekday Mass** Mon-Thu 9.30; **Confession** Sat 6-6.30 & by appointment

Fr Reg Dunkling
262 Kingston Road, Teddington TW11 9JQ Tel: 020 8977 2986
Email: teddington@rcdow.org.uk Web: www.loguk.com/sacredheart
Upper Thames Deanery (1882; 1893; cons 14 June 1944)

• Sons of Divine Providence (FDP), 25 Lower Teddington Road, Hampton Wick KT1 4HB
Tel: 020 8977 5130 Email: info@orionecare.org Web: sonsofdivineprovidence.org
Sunday Mass 9.30 (English), 11 (Polish); **Weekday Mass** Mon-Fri 6.45pm
Community: Frs John C Perrotta (Superior), Henryk Halman, Carlo Mazzotta, Sidon Sagar
Orione Care Main Office 13 Lower Teddington Road, Hampton Wick KT1 4EU

Email: info@orionecare.org Web: orione care.org
Colombo House, 1 Ferry Road, Teddington TW11 9NN Supported living flats for people with learning disabilities
St John's, 1 Ferry Road, Teddington TW11 9NN Tel: 020 8977 7574 Residential Care for people with learning disabilities
Orione House, 12 Station Road, Hampton Wick, Kingston-upon-Thames KT1 4HG
Tel: 020 8977 0754 Residential Care Home for older people, including Dementia Care
Mass Tue, Sat 12noon

TOLLINGTON PARK + ST MELLITUS

Sunday Mass (Sat 6.30pm), 10.30, 6.30pm; **Holy Day Mass** 7.30, 9.15, 6.30pm; **Weekday Mass** Mon, Tue, Thu, Fri 9, Wed 9 (9.15 in School Term), Sat 10; **Confession** Sat 10.30-11, 6-6.20pm, Sun 10-10.20, 6-6.20pm

Canon John O'Leary
The Presbytery, St Mellitus Church, Tollington Park N4 3AG
Tel: 020 7272 3415 Fax: 020 7263 2211
Email: tollingtonpark@rcdow.org.uk Web: https://sites.google.com.sites/tollingtonpark
Off Stroud Green Road; north end of Fonthill Road, 5 mins from Finsbury Park Stn (BR/TfL)
Islington Deanery (1925; 1959)

TOTTENHAM + ST FRANCIS DE SALES

Sunday Mass (Sat 7pm), 8.30, 10.30, 12.15pm; **Holy Day Mass** 9.30, 7pm; **Weekday Mass** Mon-Thu 9.30, Fri 7pm, Sat 10 with **Rosary** and **Exposition**; **Confession** Sat 10.30-11.15, 6-6.45pm

Fr Hector Rouco Gutierrez
729 High Road N17 8AG Tel: 020 8808 3554
Email: tottenham@rcdow.org.uk Web: parish.rcdow.org.uk/tottenham
Main road, opposite Tottenham Hotspur FC Ground
Haringey Deanery (1793; 1895)

TOTTENHAM (SOUTH): *SEE STAMFORD HILL*

TOTTENHAM (WEST): *SEE WEST GREEN*

TOWER HILL + THE ENGLISH MARTYRS

Sunday Mass (Sat 6.30pm), 9, 11; **Holy Day Mass** 9.30, 12noon, 1pm; **Weekday Mass** Tue-Fri 1pm

Oblates of Mary Immaculate (OMI) Fr Angodage Don Joseph Alex
30 Prescot Street E1 8BB Tel: 020 7488 4654 Fax: 020 7488 1418
Email: towerhill@rcdow.org.uk Web: parish.rcdow.org.uk/towerhill
Close to junction with Mansell Street
Tower Hamlets Deanery (1865;1876)

• DeMazenod House, Spirituality Centre, 62 Chamber Street E1 8BL
Tel: 020 7702 3544 Email: demazenodhouse@oblates.co.uk

SECTION 3

TRING + CORPUS CHRISTI

Sunday Mass (Sat 6pm), 12.15pm; **Holy Day Mass** as announced; **Weekday Mass** Mon, Thu 10; **Confession** Sat 5.15-5.45pm

Fr David Burke (also serves Berkhamsted, and resident at **Sacred Heart Church, Park Street, Berkhamsted HP4 1HX Tel: 01442 863845**)

Corpus Christi Church, Langdon Street, Tring HP23 6BA Tel: 01442 823161

Email: tring@rcdow.org.uk Web: parish.rcdow.org.uk/tring

St Albans Deanery (1910; 1913; cons 16 February 2001)

TWICKENHAM + ST JAMES A

Sunday Mass (Sat 6pm) 8, 10.30, 12.15pm; **Holy Day Mass** 9, 7.30pm; **Weekday Mass** Mon, Tue, Thu-Sat 9, **Eucharistic Service** Wed 9; **Confession** Sat 9.45-10.45

Fr Ulick Loring

61 Pope's Grove, Twickenham TW1 4JZ Tel: 020 8892 4578

Email: twickenham@rcdow.org.uk Web: www. stjamestwickenham.org.uk

Upper Thames Deanery (1883; 1885; cons 23 July 1887)

- **Religious of the Assumption, 259 Waldegrave Road, Twickenham TW1 4SY Tel: 020 8744 1642 Email: christinercharlwood@gmail.com Web: www.assumptionreligious.org**
Srs Christine Charlwood (Superior), Jessica Gatty, Cathy Jones, Mary Ann Tyler
- **Sisters of Mercy, 88 Pope's Grove, Twickenham TW1 4JX Tel: 020 8744 2812**
- **St Mary's University, Waldegrave Road, Strawberry Hill, Twickenham TW1 4SX**
See entry below for *Universities and Institutes of Higher Education Chaplaincy*

TWICKENHAM (EAST): *SEE ST MARGARETS-ON-THAMES*

UKRAINIAN CATHEDRAL + THE HOLY FAMILY

The Cathedral belongs to the Eparchy of the Holy Family of London
(see ***Other Jurisdictions***, page 148)

Sunday Liturgy 8, 10, 12noon, 6.15pm; **Holy Day Liturgy** as weekdays, also 10.30; **Weekday Liturgy** 7, 6.15pm (Mon 6.15pm only), ***2nd Sat only*** 4pm (English); **Confession** Daily before Divine Liturgy

Very Rev Andrew B Choma (Pastor & Protosyncellus), Very Rev Mykola Matwijiwskyj, Fr Irineu Kraiczyi OSBM, Fr Carlos Mekekiuk, Fr Mark Woodruff (English Liturgy)

Duke Street W1K 5BQ Tel: 020 7629 1534 / 07561 473888

(Correspondence etc. to 22 Binney Street W1K 5BQ)

Email: cathedral@ukrainianchurch.org.uk Web: www.ucc-gb.com

UNDERWOOD ROAD + ST ANNE

Sunday Mass 10.30 **Holy Day Mass** as announced; **Confession** by appointment.
See entry for ***Brazilian Chaplaincy*** under Ethnic Chaplaincies

Fr Paulo Bagini
St Anne's Church, Underwood Road E1 5AW Tel: 020 7247 7833
Email: braziliancp@rcdow.org.uk Web: parish.rcdow.org.uk/underwoodroad *and* www.ccblondres.com
Off Vallance Road
Tower Hamlets Deanery (1850; 1855; cons 27 September 1905)
Parish and Chaplaincy Administrator Telma Melo
• **Brazilian Chaplaincy** Fr Paulo Bagini (Principal Chaplain), Fr Patrick Longo Francischini mps (Lead Chaplain), Fr Jose Flavio Gomes mps; Sr Denilde dos Santos Oliveira mps, Sr Valdineia Bernadina da Silva mps

UNIVERSITIES AND INSTITUTES OF HIGHER EDUCATION CHAPLAINCY

Sunday Mass 10.30 (all year). ***All other services termtime only:* Sunday** 7.30pm; **Holy Day Mass** as announced; **Weekday Mass** Mon-Fri 5.30pm; **Exposition** Sun 6.15-7.15pm, Tue 6-9pm, then **Benediction**; **Confession** Sun 6.15-7.15pm, Wed 4.15-5.15pm & on request

Newman House, 111 Gower Street WC1E 6AR Tel: 020 7387 6370
Email: enquiries@universitycatholic.net Web: www.universitycatholic.net

Particular Pastoral Responsibility Bishop John Sherrington

Senior Chaplain and Chaplain to LSE Fr Stephen Wang
Email: swang@universitycatholic.net
Domestic Bursar Alison Reilly
Email: alison@universitycatholic.net
Receptionist Team Elizabeth Elive, Ann Molloy, Louise Nicholson
Email: reception@universitycatholic.net
Pastoral Associate Chris Castell
Email: chris@universitycatholic.net
In residence Fr Elijah Owens OSB
Email: frelijahosb@gmail.com

Chaplains
Fr Andrew Connick **(Queen Mary University of London)**
Email: a.connick@qmul.ac.uk (Wapping)
Sr Catherine Cruz FMVD **(University of Westminster, City University)**
Email: cruzc@westminster.ac.uk
Fr Brian Creak **(Goodenough College)**
Email: bcreak@mac.com (St Charles Square)
Fr Oliver Keenan OP **(Imperial College)**
Email: oliver.keenan@english.op.org
Sr Mary Kenefick SMG **(Brunel University, University College London)**
Email: mary.kenefick@brunel.ac.uk, m.kenefick@ucl.ac.uk
Fr John McFadden OMI **(King's College London)**
Email: j.mcfadden@oblates.co.uk (Kilburn)

SECTION 3

Sr Carolyn Morrison RA **(Social Outreach Chaplain, based in Newman House)**
Email: carolyn@universitycatholic.net
Olivia Raw **(SOAS)**
Email: or5@soas.ac.uk

- **Goodenough College, Mecklenburgh Square WC1 2AB**

  Sunday Mass 10

Fr Brian Creak (contact details above)

- **More House, 53 Cromwell Road SW7 2EH Tel: 020 7584 2040**

(Imperial College, Royal College of Art, Royal College of Music)

  Sunday Mass 11 (all year). *All other services termtime only:* **Sunday** 6pm; **Weekday Mass** Mon-Fri 7.30

- **St Mary's University, Waldegrave Road, Strawberry Hill, Twickenham TW1 4SX**
Email: chaplaincy@stmarys.ac.uk Web: stmarys.ac.uk/chaplaincy

  Sunday Mass 11 (all year), 6pm (*term only*); **Holy Day Mass** 1.05pm; **Weekday Mass** Mon-Fri 1.05pm (chapel); **Confession** Mon-Fri 12.30-1pm

Chaplain Canon Peter Newby **Tel: 020 8240 4006**
Email: peter.newby@stmarys.ac.uk
Deputy Chaplain (Pastoral) Caroline Stanton **Tel: 020 8240 4002**
Email: caroline.stanton@stmarys.ac.uk
Deputy Chaplain (Events) Louise Gordon **Tel: 020 8240 4331**
Email: louise.gordon@stmarys.ac.uk
Chaplaincy Administrator Grazia Hazell **Tel: 020 8240 2327**
Email: grazia.hazell@stmarys.ac.uk
Choral Director Martin Foster **Tel: 020 8240 2327**
Email: martin.foster@stmarys.ac.uk
Benedict XVI House (for students) 7 Waldegrave Road, Twickenham TW1 4JZ

- **University of Hertfordshire**

  Student Mass Sun 6pm at St Peter's, Hatfield South (see ***Hatfield South*** parish entry for other times)

Fr Julius Otoaye MSP **(Hatfield South) St Peter's Presbytery, Bishop's Rise, Hatfield AL10 9HN Tel: 01707 262121 Email: juliusotoaye@rcdow.org.uk**

UPPER HOLLOWAY: *SEE ARCHWAY*

UXBRIDGE + OUR LADY OF LOURDES AND ST MICHAEL

Sunday Mass (Sat 6.30pm) 8.30, 10.30 (Solemn), 5pm; **Holy Day Mass** 9.30, 7pm; **Weekday Mass** Mon-Wed, Fri 9.30, Sat 10; **Holy Hour** Sun 3.45-4.45pm; **Confession** Sat 10.30-11

Fr Nicholas Schofield
Presbytery, Osborn Road, Uxbridge UB8 1UE Tel: 01895 233193
Email: uxbridge@rcdow.org.uk Web: www.catholicchurchuxbridge.org.uk
Beside Oxford Road, at junction with Harefield Road
Hillingdon Deanery (1891; 1931; cons 14 May 1936)
Pastoral Assistant Angela Atkins

• Sisters of the Sacred Hearts of Jesus and Mary, Pield Heath House, Pield Heath Road, Hillingdon UB8 3NW Tel: 01895 233092 Email: convent@pieldheathschool.org.uk
Srs Rosemary Clerkin, Mary Janet Finnegan, Catherine P Lehane, Mary Rooney, Julie Rose
Special School Tel: 01895 258507
also Marian House Care Home, 100 Kingston Lane, Uxbridge UB8 3PW
Tel: 01895 253299
• Clare House Nursing Home

WALTHAM CROSS + OUR LADY OF THE IMMACULATE CONCEPTION AND ST JOSEPH

Sunday Mass (Sat 6.30pm, 8pm Polish), 8.30, 9.30 (Polish), 11, 12.30pm, 5pm (Italian), 6.30pm; **Holy Day Mass** 10, 8pm; **Weekday Mass** 10; **Ukrainian Rite Liturgy** as announced; **Exposition** Fri 9.15-9.45; **Confession** Sat 10.30-11, 5.45-6.15pm

Fr John Cunningham
204 High Street, Waltham Cross EN8 7DP Tel: 01992 623156
Email: walthamcross@rcdow.org.uk Web: parish.rcdow.org.uk/walthamcross
Lea Valley Deanery (1859; 1931; cons 3 July 1971)
Parish Secretary Jacqueline Farley

WAPPING + ST PATRICK

Sunday Mass (Sat 6.30pm), 10, 6.30pm; **Holy Day Mass** 9, 7.30pm; **Weekday Mass** Mon-Wed 10, Thu, Fri 6.30pm, Sat 10; **Exposition** Sun 5.45-6.15pm, Mon 10.30-11; **Confession** Sat, Sun 6pm

Fr Andrew Connick
The Presbytery, Dundee Street E1W 2PH Tel: 020 7481 2202
(St Patrick's Church is on Green Bank)
Email: wapping@rcdow.org.uk Web: parish.rcdow.org.uk/wapping
Off Wapping Lane; close to Wapping Stn (Overground)
Tower Hamlets Deanery (1871; 1892; cons 22 May 1902)
Parish Secretary Lucy Knights Email: lucyknights@rcdow.org.uk
Events Co-ordinator Joann Condon Email: joanncondon@rcdow.org.uk

• Hurtado Jesuit Centre, 2 Chandler Street E1W 2QT Tel: 020 7488 7325
Director Br Stephen Power SJ Administrator Rebecca Gormally Tel: 020 7488 7325
• Jesuit Refugee Service [JRS-UK] Director Sarah Teather Tel: 020 7488 7310
• Jesuit Community (SJ): Frs Michael Smith (Superior), Harry Elias, Brian McClorry, Keith McMillan, John Moffatt; Br Stephen Power Tel: 020 3217 6922

SECTION 3

WARE + SACRED HEART OF JESUS AND ST JOSEPH A

Sunday Mass (Sat 6.30pm), 8.30, 10.30 (Sung & Family); **Holy Day Mass** 10, 7.30pm; **Weekday Mass** as announced; **Confession** Sat 11-11.30, 5.30-6pm ***on first Sat of month*** & on request

Fr Charles Cahill, Rev Adrian Cullen (Deacon)
1 King Edward's Road, Ware SG12 7EJ Tel: 01920 462140
Email: ware@rcdow.org.uk Web: www.sacredheartware.com
Junction of New Road (off High Street)
Lea Valley Deanery (1870; 1921; 1939)

• Carmelite Monastery, Ware Park SG12 0DT Tel: 01920 462154
Email: prioress@warecarmel.com Web: www.warecarmel.com
Chaplain Fr Anthony Baxter The Lodge, Ware Park, Ware SG12 0DS Tel: 01920 487287
Sunday Mass 11; Weekday Mass Mon-Sat 8
• Ashview, Ashwood, Highfield, Hillview, Nightingale, Riverside Place, Snowdrop House, Westgate, Willowthorpe Care Homes

WARWICK STREET + OUR LADY OF THE ASSUMPTION AND ST GREGORY

Sunday Mass (Sat 6pm), 10.30 (Solemn), 5pm; **Holy Day Mass** 8, 12.45pm; **Weekday Mass** Tue-Fri 8, Mon-Fri 12.45pm, Sat 12 noon (Extraordinary Form); **Exposition** Sat 5.15-5.45pm; **Confession** Mon-Fri 12.15-12.35pm & after Mass, Sat 5.15-5.45pm

in care of the Personal Ordinariate of Our Lady of Walsingham
Priest in Charge Fr Mark Elliott Smith (Tel: 020 7284 0033), Mgr Keith Newton (in residence, contact details below)
Presbytery address: 24 Golden Square W1F 9JR
(Church & Communication address: Warwick Street W1B 5LZ Tel: 020 7734 9313)
Email: warwickstreet@rcdow.org.uk Web: parish.rcdow.org.uk/warwickstreet
Between Beak Street/Glasshouse Street; off Regent Street, close to Piccadilly Circus
Westminster Deanery (1730; 1790; cons 24 July 1928)
(Mgr Newton Tel: 020 7440 5750)

WATFORD + HOLY ROOD

Sunday Mass (Sat 6pm), 8, 9.30 (Sung), 11 (Folk), 2.15pm (Polish), 5pm; **Holy Day Mass** 8.30, 12noon, 7pm; **Weekday Mass** 8.30, 12noon followed by **Rosary**, Sat 11; **Malayalam Mass** ***4th Sat*** 3pm; **Exposition** Sat 4.30-5.30pm; **Confession** Sat 11.30, 5pm

Fr Derek McGuire, Fr Joseph Okoro, Rev Neville Dyckhoff (Deacon)
Holy Rood Rectory, Exchange Road, Watford WD18 0PJ Tel: 01923 224085
Email: watford@rcdow.org.uk Web: www.holyroodrc.com/
In town centre, corner of Market Street
Watford Deanery (1883; 1890; cons 5 July 1900)
Parish Secretary Deirdre Edwards Tel: 01923 224085 Mon 10-1pm, Tue 1-4pm, Wed 10-4pm, Thu 10-1pm, Fri 1-4pm

• Watford General Hospital Tel: 01923 244366
Chaplain Colette Lennon Tel: 01923 217994

WATFORD NORTH + ST HELEN A

Sunday Mass 9, 11, 6pm; **Holy Day Mass** 10, 7.30pm; **Weekday Mass** Mon-Thu 10, Fri 6pm, Sat 10; **Confession** Sat 11.30-12.30pm

Fr Patrick Foley, Rev Liam Lynch (Deacon)
Church of St Helen, The Harebreaks, Watford WD24 6NJ Tel: 01923 223175
Email: watfordnorth@rcdow.org.uk Web: parish.rcdow.org.uk/watfordnorth
Watford Deanery (1925; 1935)
Parish Secretary Annette Nugent Mon-Wed 9-3pm Tel: 01923 223175

WEALDSTONE (& HARROW WEALD) + ST JOSEPH

Sunday Mass (Sat 6pm), 8.15, 9.30 (Family), 11 (Sung), 12.30pm, 6pm; **Holy Day Mass** 7.30, 10, 7.15pm; **Weekday Mass** 7.30 (not Sat), 10; ***First Fri only* Exposition** and **Confessions** 6.15-6.45pm, **Mass** 7pm; **Baptism** Sun 3pm; **Confession** Sat 10.30-11, 7-7.30pm

Salvatorians (SDS) Fr Paul Harris, Fr Fortunatus Bansi, Fr Frank Waters
St Joseph's Presbytery, 191 High Road, Harrow Weald HA3 5EE
Tel: 020 8427 1955
Email: wealdstone@rcdow.org.uk Web: www.catholicwealdstone.org
On main road, half mile north of Harrow & Wealdstone Stn (BR)
Harrow Deanery (1898; 1901; 1931)Parish Secretaries Terri Cousins Mon/Tue 9-5pm, Julie Conneely Wed/Thu/Fri 9-4pm
Salvatorians (SDS), Salvatorian Community House, 189 High Street, Wealdstone, Harrow HA3 5DY Tel: 020 8427 2808

• Sisters of Our Lady of the Missions, 108 Spencer Road, Wealdstone, Harrow HA3 7AR Tel: 020 8427 5783 Provincial House. Provincial Sr Margo Murphy
Email: margorndm@hotmail.co.uk Web: www.rndm.org
also 192 High Street, Wealdstone, Harrow HA3 7UA Tel: 020 8427 1541
Email: hartiganliz8@gmail.com
also 176 High Street, Wealdstone, Harrow HA3 7AX Tel: 020 8861 1148

WELWYN GARDEN CITY PARISHES A

St Bonaventure: **Sunday Mass** 8, 10.30; **Holy Day Mass** as announced; **Weekday Mass** Tue, Fri 9.30, Sat 10; **Confession** Sat 10.30-11

Digswell, Holy Family: **Sunday Mass** 9.30, 6pm; **Holy Day Mass** as announced; **Weekday Mass** Wed, Thu 9.30; **Confession** Thu 10-10.30

East, Our Lady Queen of Apostles: **Sunday Mass** (Sat 6pm), 11.30; **Holy Day Mass** as announced; **Weekday Mass** Mon 9.30, Tue, Fri 7 pm; **Confession** Sat 5-5.30pm

SECTION 3

Fr Norbert Fernandes (resident at Our Lady, Queen of Apostles **Tel: 01707 323234**), Fr Tom Montgomery (resident at Holy Family Church **Tel: 01707 327434**)
Parish Secretary Kathryn Hubbard **Tel: 01707 322579**

+ St Bonaventure (Welwyn Garden City)
(in residence, Bishop Paul McAleenan)
81 Parkway, Welwyn Garden City AL8 6JF
Email: welwyngdncity@rcdow.org.uk Web: www.wgc-catholics.org.uk
Stevenage Deanery (1925; 1926; cons 14 September 1974)

+ Holy Family (Welwyn Garden City Digswell)
194 Knightsfield, Shoplands, Welwyn Garden City AL8 7RQ
Email: welwyngdncitydigs@rcdow.org.uk
Web: www.wgc-catholics.org.uk
Stevenage Deanery (1967; cons 13 May 2007)

+ Our Lady Queen of Apostles (Welwyn Garden City East)
141 Woodhall Lane, Welwyn Garden City AL7 3TP
Email: welwyngdncityeast@rcdow.org.uk Web: www.wgc-catholics.org.uk
Stevenage Deanery (1961; cons 18 December 1973)

• Focolare Movement (Residential Conference Centre) 69 Parkway, Welwyn Garden City AL8 6HH **Tel: 01707 323620** Fr Francis Johnson (in residence)
• Queen Elizabeth II Hospital
Tel: 01438 314333
• Queen Victoria Memorial Hospital, Danesbury Hospital, Isabel Hospice

WEMBLEY 1 + ST JOSEPH A

Sunday Mass (Sat 6.30pm), 9, 12noon, 7.30pm; **Holy Day Mass** (Vigil 7.30pm) 9.30, 12noon; **Weekday Mass** Mon-Thu 7, 9.30, Fri 7, 12noon, Sat 9.30; **Confession** (also **Exposition**) Sat 10-10.45

Carmelites of Mary Immaculate (CMI) Fr John Menonkari, Fr Joseph Kaduthanam, Fr Tebin Puthenpurackal
St Joseph's Presbytery, 339 High Road, Wembley HA9 6AG **Tel: 020 8902 0081**
Email: wembley1@rcdow.org.uk Web: parish.rcdow.org.uk/wembley
At 'The Triangle' (junction of High Road, Harrow Road & Wembley Hill Road)
Brent Deanery (1901; 1957)

WEMBLEY 2 + ENGLISH MARTYRS

Sunday Mass (Sat 6pm), 9, 11 (Family/with Children's Liturgy), 6pm; **Holy Day Mass** 9.30, 7pm; **Weekday Mass** Mon, Tue, Thu-Sat 9.30, preceded by **Morning Prayer** 9.15, also Wed 7pm; **Filipino Mass *2nd Sun only*** 2pm; **Exposition** Thu after Mass until 11, Sun 5-5.45pm; **Novena to Our Lady of Perpetual Help** Sat after morning Mass; **First Friday Devotion** 7-8pm; **Confession** Sat 10-10.30, 5.15-5.45pm & on request

Fr Albert Ofere
The Presbytery, Chalkhill Road, Wembley Park HA9 9EW Tel: 020 8904 2306
Email: wembley2@rcdow.org.uk Web: parish.rcdow.org.uk/wembleypark
Blackbird Hill, corner of Chalkhill Road, below Blackbird Cross
Brent Deanery (1930; 1970)

WEMBLEY 3 + ST ERCONWALD (PRESTON ROAD)

Sunday Mass (Sat 5.30pm), 9, 11.30; **Holy Day Mass** (Vigil 7pm) 9.30, 7pm; **Weekday Mass** Mon-Wed, Fri 9.30; **Confession** Sat 4.30-5pm & after Mass

Fr Anthony Psaila
112 Carlton Avenue East, Wembley HA9 8NB Tel: 020 8904 6031
Email: wembley3@rcdow.org.uk Web: www.erconwald.org.uk
Off Preston Road, 400 yds east
Brent Deanery (1932; 1970)
Parish Hall Manager Elizabeth Patten Email: wembley3@rcdow.org.uk

• Sisters of La Sainte Union, 128 Elmstead Avenue, Wembley HA9 8NZ
Tel: 020 8908 3715
• Kenbrook, Birchwood Grange, Brook House, Preston Lodge

WEST DRAYTON AND YIEWSLEY + ST CATHERINE OF ALEXANDRIA

Sunday Mass (Sat 7pm), 9, 11 (Sung/with Children's Liturgy), 6pm; **Holy Day Mass** 9, 11, 7.30pm, (*School holidays* 9.30, 7.30pm); **Weekday Mass** Mon-Fri 9.30 as announced, Sat 10; **Confession** Sat 10.30, 6.30pm

Fr Brian Smith, Rev Nick Agule (Deacon)
20 The Green, West Drayton UB7 7PJ Tel: 01895 442777
Email: westdrayton@rcdow.org.uk Web: parish.rcdow.org.uk/westdrayton
Hillingdon Deanery (1867; 1869; cons 29 September 1893)

WEST GREEN + ST JOHN VIANNEY A

Sunday Mass (Sat 6pm), 9, 11; **Holy Day Mass** 9.15, 10 (*when school attending*), 7.30pm; **Weekday Mass** 9.15; **Confession** Sat 9.45-10.15

Fr Joe Ryan (Tel: 020 8888 9036)
4 Vincent Road N15 3QH Tel: 020 8888 5518 (Parish Office)
Email: westgreen@rcdow.org.uk Web: stjohnvianneywestgreen.co.uk
Haringey Deanery (1927; 1959; cons 20 June 1964)
Parish Sister Sr Devy Pranadjaja Tel: 07455 544065

• Sisters of St John of God, 103 Black Boy Lane N15 3AS Tel: 020 8374 1693
• Sisters of Verbum Dei Missionary Fraternity, 4a Vincent Road N15 3QH
Tel: 020 8351 4986 Email: verbumdei.lon@gmail.com Web: uk.verbumdei.org
Srs Monica Cardona, Catherine Cruz, Ann Marie D'Souza, Jeanette Kong, Devy Pranadjaja
• Justice and Peace Commission Office, 4 Vincent Road N15 3QH
Tel: 020 8888 4222 Email: justice@rcdow.org.uk

• London Catholic Worker, Giuseppe Conlon House, 49 Mattison Road N4 1BG
Tel: 020 8348 8212
• Haringey Migrant Support Centre, 386 West Green Road N15 3QL Tel: 07544 078332
Email: info@haringeymsc.org Web: www.haringeymsc.org
Assessment sessions on Mondays (not Bank Holidays), registration 11-1pm.

WHEATHAMPSTEAD + ST THOMAS MORE ♿ 🦻

Sunday Mass 11 (with Children's Liturgy), 5pm; **Holy Day Mass** as announced; **Weekday Mass** as announced; **Confession** as announced

Redbourn: **Sunday Mass** (Sat 5.30pm), 9; **Holy Day Mass** as announced; **Weekday Mass** as announced; **Confession** Sat 9.45-10.15, 5.45-6.15pm

Fr Michael Mannion (also serves Redbourn, resident at 1 Peppard Close, Redbourn, St Albans AL3 7EB Tel: 01582 792270)
7 Marford Road, Wheathampstead AL4 8AY Tel: 01582 832114
Email: wheathampstead@rcdow.org.uk Web: parish.rcdow.org.uk/wheathampstead
St Albans Deanery (1936; 1938; 1978)

WHETSTONE + ST MARY MAGDALEN ♿ 🦻

Sunday Mass (Sat 6pm), 9 (with Children's Liturgy), 11 (Solemn and with Children's Liturgy), 4pm (Polish); **Holy Day Mass** 9.30, 7pm; **Weekday Mass** 9.30, preceded by **Morning Prayer**; **Exposition** Sat 4.45-5.45pm (replaced in Lent by **Stations of the Cross**); **Confession** Sat 10-10.30, 4.45-5.45pm

Fr Gladstone Liddle
6 Athenaeum Road N20 9AE Tel: 020 8445 0838
Email: whetstone@rcdow.org.uk Web: www.stmarymagdalens.com
Off High Road (A1000), Totteridge Lane/Oakleigh Road intersection
Barnet Deanery (1926; 1958; cons 1979)
Catechist Co-ordinator Winnie Brady Tel: 07702 094650

• Sisters of the Sacred Heart of Jesus (St Jacut), 6 Oakleigh Park South N20 9JU
Tel: 020 8445 4655 Email: dbissonnette@fsmail.net
Web: www.soeursdusacrecoeurdeJesus.com

WHITECHAPEL, E1: *SEE COMMERCIAL ROAD, GERMAN CHURCH AND UNDERWOOD ROAD*

WHITE CITY + OUR LADY OF FATIMA ♿ 🦻 S

Sunday Mass (Sat 6pm, *Sign interpreted on 3rd Sat*), 9, 11, 6pm; **Holy Day Mass** 9.15, 7.30pm; **Weekday Mass** 9.15, preceded by **Morning Prayer** 9; **Exposition** *First Fri only* 10-11, *First Sat only* 10-11, Sat 6-6.45pm; **Confession** Sat 10-10.30, 6-6.30pm

Fr Richard Nesbitt, Fr Ephrem Andom (in residence, Eritrean Chaplaincy)
The Catholic Presbytery, Commonwealth Avenue, White City W12 7QR
Tel: 020 8743 8334 (Fr Ephrem Andom Tel: 020 8743 8315)
Email: whitecity@rcdow.org.uk Web: www.ourladyoffatima.biz
Off Bloemfontein Road, between Western Avenue/Uxbridge Road

Hammersmith & Fulham Deanery (1951; 1965; cons 17 May 1980)
Parish Office Mon, Wed, Fri, 10-4pm)

• Marist Sisters, 22 Bloemfontein Road W12 7BX Tel: 020 8749 4850
Email: maristsisters@btinternet.com

WHITTON + ST EDMUND OF CANTERBURY A S

Sunday Mass (Sat 6.30pm), 9.30 (Family), 11.15 (Sung), 6pm; **Holy Day Mass** 9.30, 7.30pm; **Weekday Mass** Mon-Fri 9.15, Sat 10.30; **Exposition** *First Fri* 24 hours from 10; **Confession** Sat 11-11.30

Fr Nigel Griffin
Presbytery, St Edmund's Lane, 213 Nelson Road, Whitton TW2 7BB Tel: 020 8894 9923
Email: whitton@rcdow.org.uk Web: parish.rcdow.org.uk/whitton
Right at Whitton BR Stn, left at Nelson Pub; presbytery behind the church
Upper Thames Deanery (1934; 1935; cons 1972)
Administrator Paul Hampartsoumian
Co-ordinator of Lay Ministry Chiara Aletti

WILLESDEN + OUR LADY OF WILLESDEN

Sunday Mass (Sat 6pm), 9, 11 (Sung), 5.30pm (Extraordinary Form); **Holy Day Mass** (Vigil 7pm), 7, 10, 7.30pm (Sung); **Weekday Mass** 10, 7pm; **Exposition** Tue 10.30-6.50pm, Sat 10.30-5.50pm; **Shrine Prayers** Tue 7.30pm (*see* Catholic Societies and Organisation, Section 6, ***Guild of Our Lady of Willesden***); **Confession** Tue 6.30-7pm, Sat 10.30-11.30, 5-5.45pm

Fr Stephen Willis
The Presbytery, 1 Nicoll Road NW10 9AX Tel: 020 8965 4935
Email: willesden@rcdow.org.uk Web: parish.rcdow.org.uk/willesden
At junction of Acton Lane, near Jubilee Clock, Harlesden
Brent Deanery (1886; 1931)
Shrine of Our Lady of Willesden
Catechetical Co-ordinator AnneMarie Sylvester-Charles

• Brazilian Sunday Mass (Sat 7.30pm), 2pm; Weekday Mass Wed, Fri 7.30pm

WILLESDEN GREEN + ST MARY MAGDALEN A

Sunday Mass (Sat 6.30pm), 9, 10.30 (Sung), 12noon (Sung), 6.30pm; **Holy Day Mass** 9.30, 7pm; **Weekday Mass** Mon-Sat 9.30, Fri 6.30pm; **Holy Hour** ***(first Fri only)*** 7-8pm; **Exposition** Mon-Sat 8.30-9.30, Sat 5.30-6.15pm; **Confession** Sat 10-10.30, 5.30-6.15pm

Fr Kevin Jordan, Fr Sudham Maharage Perera (in residence, Sri-Lankan (Sinhalese) Chaplaincy)
Clergy House, Peter Avenue NW10 2DD Tel: 020 8451 4677
Email: willesdengreen@rcdow.org.uk Web: parish.rcdow.org.uk/willesdengreen
Harlesden Road, south side of High Road, via St Andrew's Road; not far from Willesden Green Stn (TfL)
Brent Deanery (1901; 1939; cons 1958)

SECTION 3

Parish Administrator Kathleen Reddington

• **Congregation of Jesus (CJ), 244 Willesden Lane NW2 5RE**
Tel: 020 8459 5378 Web: www.cjengland.org, www.congregatiojesu.org
• **Daughters of Wisdom (La Sagesse), 9 The Oaks, 25 Brondesbury Park NW6 7BY**
Tel: 020 8830 2530 Sr Monica Tywang
• **Missionary Sisters of Christ the King (MChR) 180 Walm Lane NW2 3AX**
Tel: 020 3638 4753 Email: michalik.mchr@op.pl Web: www.mchr.pl
Srs Małgorzata Michalik (Superior), Justyna Rafalska, Katarzyna Kosidłowska
• **Sisters of the Holy Family of Bordeaux, 83 St Gabriel's Road NW2 4DU**
Tel: 020 8452 3844 Email: stgabriels@holyfamilybordeaux.org
Web: www.holyfamilybordeaux.org
• **St Boniface Secular Institute (English Region), 44 Exeter Road NW2 4SB**
Tel: 020 8438 9628 Email: info.house42@yahoo.com Web: www.hostel-lioba-house.de
(see also ***German Church*** entry) Barbara von Alten, Christa von Gleichenstein, Maria Lohre, Dr Eva Roettgers
• **Divine Word Missionaries (SVD), 8 Teignmouth Road NW2 4HN**
Tel: 020 8452 8430 Email: svdlondon@gmail.com
Frs Albert Escoto (Praeses), Eamonn Donnelly, Krzysztof Krzyskow, John McCarthy, Martin McPake
• **Hospitaller Order of St John of God (OH), 52 Kenneth Crescent NW2 4PN**
Tel: 020 8452 8879 Email: johnoneill@sjog.org.uk Web: www.hospitaller.org.uk
Brs Malachy Brannigan (Prior), Bonaventure Gerrard, John O'Neill, Andrzej Zach
• **Jesuits (SJ), Our Lady of Mercy, 182 Walm Lane NW2 3AX Tel: 020 8452 4304**
Email: londyn@jezuici.pl Web: polishjesuits.co.uk
Frs Adam Baczewski, Leszek Szuta, Adam Tomaszewski (Superior)
Sunday Mass (Polish) 10.30, Noon; Mon-Sat 7.30 (English), Wed 7.30pm (Polish)
St Francis of Assisi, Fleetwood Road NW10 1NQ
Sunday Mass (Polish) 9, 10.30, Noon, 7 pm; Weekday Mass (Polish) Mon, Tue, Thu, Fri 7pm;
Exposition, with Confession Thu 7.30-8pm;
Lectio Divina: lectio.divinaOLM@gmail.com; Men of St Joseph: london.msj@gmail.com
• **Montfort Missionaries, 27 St Gabriel's Road NW2 4DS Tel: 020 8450 4291**
Frs John K Flynn, John Mary Ahimbisibwe, Oscar Sagwanti
• **De Paul Trust, 247 Willesden Lane NW2 5RY Tel: 020 8830 1093**
• **Willesden General Hospital Tel: 020 8438 7000**

WOOD GREEN + ST PAUL THE APOSTLE

Sunday Mass (Sat 6.30pm), 8, 10 (Family), 12noon (Sung); **Holy Day Mass** 9.30, 7.30pm; **Weekday Mass** Mon-Fri 9.30, Sat 10.30; **Holy Hour** Sat 11-12noon; **Confession** Sat 11-12noon, 5.30-6pm

Fr Perry Sykes, Fr Jonathan Stogdon
Presbytery & Communication Address: 22 Bradley Road N22 7SZ Tel: 020 8888 2390
(Church address: Station Road N22 7SY)
Email: woodgreen@rcdow.org.uk Web: parish.rcdow.org.uk/woodgreen

Wood Green TfL Stn (Piccadilly line), near junction with Mayes Road
Haringey Deanery (1882; 1904; 1970)
Parish Administrator Rose Mary Correia

• Daughters of Divine Love, 82/84 Sylvan Avenue N22 5HY Tel: 020 8888 1898
Email: divinelovedaughters@yahoo.co.uk Web: www.ddlenglishregion.org

YEADING + ST RAPHAEL

Sunday Mass (Sat 7pm), 9, 10.30 (Sung), 12noon; **Holy Day Mass** 9.30, 7.30pm; **Weekday Mass** (incorporates **Morning Prayer**) Mon-Thu 9.30, Fri, Sat 12noon; **Rosary** 30 mins before Weekday Mass; **Exposition** ***First Fri only*** 7pm; **Confession** Sat 11.30, 6.30pm

Fr John Welsh
St Raphael's House, Morrison Road, Yeading UB4 9JP Tel: 020 8845 1919
Email: yeading@rcdow.org.uk Web: parish.rcdow.org.uk/yeading
In Ayles Road, off Kingshill Avenue (west of Yeading Lane)
Hillingdon Deanery (1957; 1961; cons 4 May 1975)
Catechetical Co-ordinator Jane Foskett
Parish Administrator Paulina Louison

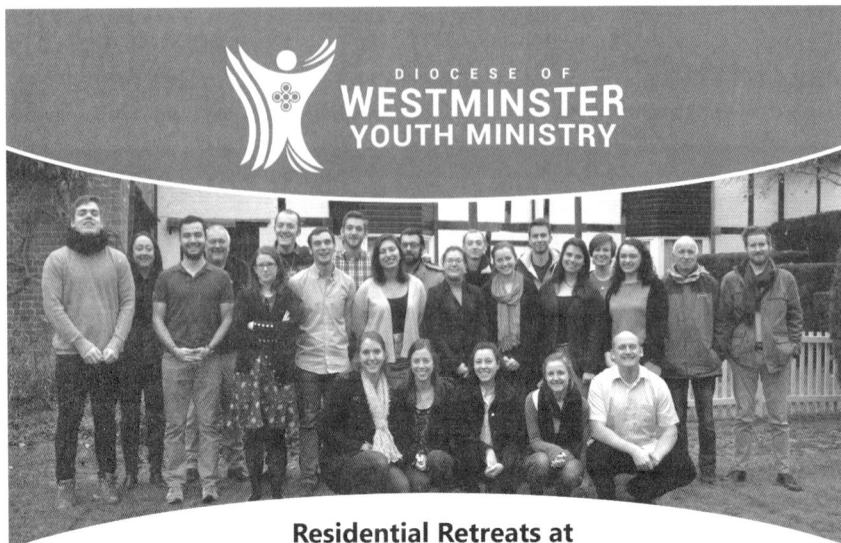

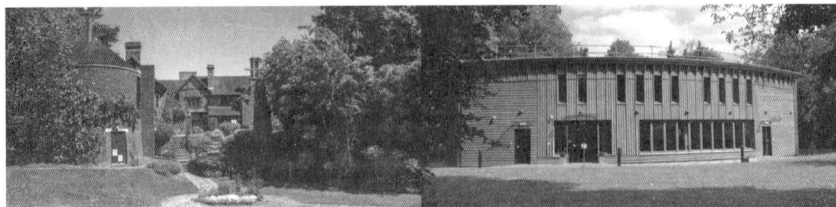

MASS IN THE EXTRAORDINARY FORM

Masses regularly celebrated in the Extraordinary Form of the Roman Rite are as follows:

Westminster Cathedral, Most Precious Blood	**2nd Saturday 4pm** Low Mass (Lady Chapel)
Baldock, Holy Trinity	**1st Sunday 3pm** Low Mass
Covent Garden, Corpus Christi	**Monday 6.30pm** Sung Mass **2nd Friday 6.30pm** Low Mass
Ely Place, St Etheldreda	**1st Friday 6pm** Low Mass
Hackney, St John the Baptist	**1st Friday 6pm** Low Mass
Moorfields, St Mary Moorfields	**Dates as publicised** Sung Mass
Old Hall Green, St Edmund of Canterbury & English Martyrs	**3rd Sunday 3pm** Low Mass
Oratory, Immaculate Heart of Mary	**Sunday 9** Low Mass **Monday - Sat 8** Low Mass (St Philip's Altar) **Saturday 12.15pm** Low Mass (usually St Wilfrid's Chapel) **Holy Days 8** Low Mass
Spanish Place, St James	**Sunday 9.30** Low Mass **Holy Days 11** Low Mass
Uxbridge, Our Lady of Lourdes and St Michael	**1st Friday 7pm** Sung Mass
Warwick Street, Our Lady of the Assumption and St Gregory	**Wednesday 7pm** Sung Mass **Saturday Noon** Low Mass
Willesden, Our Lady of Willesden	**Sunday 5.30pm** Low Mass

By decision of the Bishops' Conference, ratified by the Holy See, the Solemnity of the Ascension of the Lord will henceforth by celebrated on its traditional day. The Solemnity of Corpus Christi may be celebrated in the Extraordinary Form on the traditional day (in 2019 this will be Thursday 20 June), but the obligation to attend Mass is transferred to the following Sunday. The Solemnity of the Epiphany (which in 2019 falls on Sunday 6 January) is kept on its proper date, unless it falls on a Saturday or Monday, in which case it is observed on the Sunday.

Anyone wishing to attend any of the Masses listed above is advised to check that it is taking place; for further details, see the Latin Mass Society entry in Section 6, Catholic Societies and Organisations

For listings of Ordinary Form Masses in Latin in the diocese visit the website of the Association for Latin Liturgy, also in Section 6, Catholic Societies and Organisations.

CHAPLAINCIES

Information about Chaplaincies can be found at **www.rcdow.org.uk/chaplaincies**

AIRPORT CHAPELS

GATWICK AIRPORT (Diocese of Arundel & Brighton) Chapels in North and South Terminals (Diocese of Arundel & Brighton); for times of services **Tel: 01293 503851**
Web: www.gatwickairportchapel.org

HEATHROW AIRPORT St George's Chapel
See page 83 in Parish Directory.

ARMED FORCES, PRINCIPAL CHAPLAINCIES

ARMY Fr Michael Fava QHC,DCG **MOD Chaplains (Army), Army Headquarters, Blenheim Building, Marlborough Lines, Andover SP11 8HJ Tel: 01980 618744**
Email: Michael.fava553@mod.gov.uk

ROYAL AIR FORCE Fr (Wg Cdr) James E Caulfield **Chaplain's Office, Defence Academy of the United Kingdom, Shrivenham, Swindon SN6 8LA Tel: 01793 314488**
Email: JCaulfield.hq@da.mod.uk

ROYAL NAVY Mgr Andrew McFadden QHC PhB STL VG RN **Chaplaincy PDC (RC), NW Admiralty House, PP13, HM Naval Base, Portsmouth PO1 3LR Tel: 023 9272 24232**
Email: andrew.mcfadden375@mod.uk

EASTERN CATHOLIC CHURCHES

Episcopal Vicar for Eastern Catholic Churches Mgr John Conneely

BELARUSIAN CATHOLIC CHURCH

Chaplain:	Fr Serge Stasievich
Address:	Church of St Cyril of Turau and All the Patron Saints of the Belarusian People, adjacent to Marian House, Holden Avenue N12 8HY
Tel:	020 8446 3378
Email:	belarusmission@gmail.com
Mass times:	Sunday 10 (Slovak), 11.30 (Belarusian)

CHALDEAN CATHOLIC CHURCH

Chaplain:	Fr Nadheer Dako
Address:	38-40 Cavendish Avenue W13 0JQ
Tel:	020 8997 6370
Email:	nadheer.dako@chaldeans.uk
Web:	www.chaldeans.uk
Mass times:	*Acton West,* Sunday 12.45pm

GHEEZ RITE (Eritrea)

Chaplain:	Fr Ephrem Andom
Address:	The Catholic Presbytery, Commonwealth Avenue W12 7QR (*White City*)
Tel:	020 8743 8315

Email: abbaephrem@yahoo.co.uk
Mass times: *Acton East,* Sunday 1pm

GHEEZ RITE (Ethiopia)

Chaplain: Fr Ufayissa Dea Madalcho CM
Address: 1 Waller Road SE14 5LE
Tel: 07498 328188
Email: ufiyeedm@gmail.com
Mass times: *Queensway,* Sunday 1pm

KNANAYA

Chaplain: Fr Mathew Kattiyangal
Address: The Presbytery, Esdaile Lane Hoddesdon EN11 8DS *(Hoddesdon)*
Tel: 01992 440986 / 07491 623832
Email: mkattiyangal@yahoo.com
Mass times: *St Alban, Hornchurch RM12 5JX (Brentwood),* 1st and 3rd Sunday 2.30pm
Our Lady of Gillingham, Gillingham ME7 1YL (Southwark) 2nd Sunday 3pm

MARONITE CATHOLIC CHURCH

Chaplains: Fr Aziz Azzi, Fr Johnny Saba (Superior), Fr Charbel Trad
Address: 6 Dobson Close NW6 4RS
Tel: 020 7586 1801 (10.30-1.30pm)
Email: admin@maronitechurch.org.uk
Web: www.maronitechurch.org.uk
Mass times: (for Lebanese) *Paddington,* Saturday 7pm; Sunday 12.30, 7pm; Wednesday, Friday 7pm
(for Cypriots) *Holy Family Convent, 52 London Road, Enfield EN2 6EN* Sunday 10.30

MELKITE CATHOLIC CHURCH

Chaplain: Archmandrite Shafiq Abouzayd
Address: 46 Sunderland Avenue, Oxford OX2 8DU
Tel: 01865 514041 / 07977 495150
Email: melkitelondon@gmail.com
Web: www.melkite.uk

Chaplain: Fr Robert (Robin) Gibbons
Address: St John's Skete, 40 Nethercote Road, Tackley, Oxford OX5 3AT
Tel: 01869 331186
Email: melkitelondon@gmail.com
Mass times: *St Barnabas C of E Church, Pimlico Road SW1W 8PF* Sunday 12noon

SYRIAC CATHOLIC CHURCH

Chaplain: Mgr Nizar Semaan
Address: 41 Brook Green W6 7BL *(Brook Green)*
Tel: 020 7602 2834 / 07769 352525
Email: nizarsemaan@hotmail.com
Mass times: *Brook Green,* Sunday 1pm

SECTION 3

SYRO-MALABAR CHURCH (see *Other Jurisdictions*, page 149)

Chaplain: Mgr Thomas Parayadyil MST
Address: 373 Bowes Road N11 1AA (New Southgate)
Tel: 020 8368 3016 / 07523 100870
Email: parayadyt@gmail.com

Chaplain: Fr Joseph Anthiamkulam MCBS (in charge of 9 Centres in Brentwood Diocese)
Address: 132 Shernhall Street E17 9HU
Tel: 020 8520 5877
Email: joseajmcbs@gmail.com

Chaplain: Fr Sebastian Chamakala John
Address: 165 Arlington Road NW1 7EX *(Our Lady of Hal)*
Tel: 07429 307307
Email: sebchamakala@yahoo.com

Mass times: *Edmonton,* 4th Sunday 4 pm (2.30-3.30pm Catechism; 3.30-4pm Rosary & Confessions, BVM Novena)
Enfield, OLW and English Martyrs Chapel of Ease, 1st Saturday 5 pm; 3rd Sunday 4 pm (2.30-3.30pm Catechism; 3.30-4pm Rosary & Confessions, BVM Novena)
Harefield, 2nd Sunday 5 pm (4pm-5pm Catechism & Confessions, Rosary, BVM Novena)
Hayes, 2nd Sunday 2.30pm-3pm Confessions & Rosary, BVM Novena; 4th Friday 5pm
Hounslow, 1st Sunday 3 pm (2pm-3pm Catechism, Rosary & Confessions)
Stevenage Bedwell 3rd Saturday 10 (11.30-12.30pm Adoration, Catechism & Confessions)
Ware, 3rd Wednesday 5pm
Watford, 2nd Friday 4.30pm
4th Saturday 4 pm (followed by BVM Novena)
Wembley 1, 4th Sunday 4pm

SYRO-MALANKARA CHURCH

Chaplain: Fr Thomas Madukkamoottil
Address: St John the Baptist, 349 Wanstead Park Road, Cranbrook, Ilford IG1 3TS
St John the Baptist, Ilford (Brentwood)
Tel: 020 8554 3763

UKRAINIAN CATHOLIC CHURCH (see *Other Jurisdictions*, page 148, also *Ukrainian Cathedral, Feltham* and *Waltham Cross* parish entries)

ETHNIC CHAPLAINCIES

Particular Pastoral Responsibility — Bishop Paul McAleenan

Episcopal Vicar for Ethnic Chaplaincies — Fr David Irwin

Where a Chaplaincy is based at a parish, the name of the parish is given in italics after the address. Parish names are also in italics in the list of Mass times - please refer to the Parish Directory for the parish address.

AFRICAN CATHOLIC MISSION IN BRITAIN

Chaplain: Rev Joseph Baffour-Awuah (Deacon)
Address: St George's Presbytery, 132 Shernhall Street E17 9HU
Tel: 020 8521 2359 / 07786 501371
Email: africath@clara.co.uk
Mass times: Pan-Africa Annual Mass on 3rd Sunday in September

ALBANIAN – KOSOVAN

Chaplain: Fr Gary Walsh
Address: 8 Ogle Street W1W 6HS *(Ogle Street)*
Tel: 07791 054137
Email: garywalsh2001@yahoo.com
Mass times: *Pimlico*, 2nd and 4th Sunday 3pm
Wood Green, 1st and 3rd Sunday 1.30pm

BRAZILIAN

Principal Chaplain:
Fr Paulo Bagini
Lead Chaplain:
Fr Patrick Longo Francischini mps
Assistant: Fr Jose Flavio Gomes mps
Religious: Sr Valdinea Bernadina da Silva mps, Sr Denilde dos Santos Oliveira mps
Address: St Anne's Church, Underwood Road E1 5AW *(Underwood Road)*
Tel: 020 7247 7833
Email: braziliancp@rcdow.org.uk
Web: www.ccblondres.com
Mass times: (Brazilian Masses)
Brixton (Southwark), Sunday 7pm
Crystal Palace (Southwark), Sunday 9
Manor House, Sunday 5pm
Queensway, Friday 7.30pm
Underwood Road, Thursday 7.30pm, Saturday 7pm; Sunday 12.30pm
Willesden, Wednesday 7.30pm, Saturday 7.30pm, Sunday 2pm

CARIBBEAN

Chaplain: Rev Jon Dal Din (Deacon)
Address: 112 Kelmscott Road SW11 6PT
Tel: 07527 758729 / 07889 536957
Email: jondaldin@rcdow.org.uk
President: Lloyd Booker
Address: 17a Cambray Road SW12 0DX
Tel: 020 8675 0607

SECTION 3

CHINESE

Chaplain: Fr Joseph Liang
Address: Assumption Priory, Victoria Park Square E2 9PB *(Bethnal Green)*
Tel: 020 8709 5281 / 07753 471611
Email: josephliang1998@gmail.com
Web: http://londonccc.wordpress.com
Mass times: *Bethnal Green,* (Chinese) Sunday 2.15pm

CONGOLESE

Chaplain: Fr Julien Matondo Mboko
Address: 2 Lukin Street E1 0AA *(Commercial Road)*
Tel: 020 7790 2211/ 07452 772111
Email: julienmboko@hotmail.fr / julienmboko@rcdow.org.uk
Mass times: *Highbury,* (Lingala) Sunday 2pm

CROATIAN

Chaplain: Fr Ljubomir Šimunović OFM
Address: 17 Boutflower Road SW11 1RE
Tel: 020 7223 3530
Email: hkmlondon@gmail.com
Web: www.hkmlondon.org
Mass times: *Sacred Heart Church (Cathedral Chapel of Ease), Horseferry Road SW1P 2EF,* Sunday 4pm

CZECH

Please contact the Slovak Chaplaincy

FILIPINO

Chaplain: Fr Cirino Potrido CM (Co-ordinator)
Address: 1 Waller Road SE14 5LE
Tel: 07857 709545
Email: cgpotrido@yahoo.com

Chaplain: Fr Agustin Paunon (based at London North West Healthcare NHS Trust HA1 3UJ)
Address: Rm 235, Block 4 Hodgson Court, Nightingale Avenue, Harrow HA1 3GH
Tel: (Office) 020 8869 2112; (Pager) 07659 136452; (Mobile) 07880 558225
Email: agustinpaunon@rcdow.org.uk, agustinpaunon@nhs.net

Chaplain: Fr Ronan Ayag CS (Southwark)
Address: 20 Brixton Road SW9 6BU
Tel: 020 7735 8235

Bible Study: *Mill Hill,* 3rd Friday 8pm
Palace Court, 3rd Saturday 1pm
Mass times: *Behtnal Green,* 4th Sunday 5pm
Feltham, 4th Saturday 3pm
Kilburn, 3rd Sunday 3pm

Lincoln's Inn Fields, 2nd Sunday 4pm
Mill Hill, 2nd Saturday 7pm
Stonebridge, 1st Sunday 3pm

FRENCH

Chaplains: Fr Pascal Boidin sm, Fr Hubert Bonnet-Eymard sm, Fr Damien Diouf sm, Fr Kevin Duffy sm (from Jan 2019), Br Ivan Vodopivec sm
Address: Notre Dame de France, 5 Leicester Place WC2H 7BX *(French Church)*
Tel: 020 7437 9363
Mass times: See *French Church* in Parish Directory

GERMAN

Chaplain: Fr Andreas Blum
Address: St Boniface, 47 Adler Street E1 1EE *(German Church)*
Tel: 020 7247 9529
Email: pfarrer@dkg-london.org
Mass times: See *German Church* in Parish Directory

GHANAIAN

Chaplain: Fr Dominic Yaw Assuahene
Address: St Mary Magdalen Church, 71 Comerford Road SE4 2BA
Tel: 020 8305 8004 / 07393 613906
Email: dyassuahene@gmail.com

GOAN

Chaplain: Fr Patrick D'Souza SFX
Address: (Office) St Thomas of Canterbury School, Commonside East, Mitcham, CR4 1YG
Tel: 020 8665 2176
Email: goanchaplaincy@gmail.com
Address: (Home) Sts Peter and Paul Church, 1 Cranmer Road, Mitcham CR4 4LD
Mass times: *Cranford,* (Konkani) 4th Sunday 5pm
Hounslow, (Konkani) 3rd Sunday 4pm
Mitcham (Southwark), (Konkani) 2nd Sunday 3pm
Heathrow Airport, (Konkani) 2nd Saturday 5pm
Southall, (Konkani) 3rd Saturday 4pm
Wembley 1, (Konkani) 1st Sunday 4 pm

HUNGARIAN

Chaplain: Fr János Csicsó
Address: 62 Little Ealing Lane W5 4EA
Tel: 020 8566 0271
Email: hungarian.chaplaincy@btinternet.com
Web: www.magyarkatolikusok.co.uk
Mass times: *62 Little Ealing Lane,* 1st & 3rd Sunday 11.30

SECTION 3

IRISH

CEO: Eddie Gilmore
Address: 52 Camden Square NW1 9XB
Tel: 020 7482 5528
Email: info@irishchaplaincy.org.uk
Web: www.irishchaplaincy.org.uk
Mass times: 12noon *(First Friday only)*

ITALIAN CHURCH

Chaplains: Fr Andrea Fulco SAC, Fr Giuseppe De Caro SAC
Fr Ryszard Wrobel SAC
Address: St Peter's Italian Church, 4 Back Hill EC1R 5EN *(Italian Church)*
Tel: 020 7837 1528
Email: italianchurchlondon@gmail.com
Mass times: See *Italian Church* in Parish Directory

ITALIAN MISSION

Chaplain: Fr Antonio Serra
Address: 197 Durants Road, Enfield EN3 7DE *(Ponders End)*
Tel: 020 8804 2307
Email: mci.london@hotmail.com
Web: www.mcilondon.org
Mass times: *Italian Centre* Sunday 9.30, Tue, Fri 7.30pm; Adoration Fri 6.30pm
Hoddesdon, Saturday 4pm
Ponders End, Sunday 12.30pm
Waltham Cross, Sunday 5pm
Confessions: 30 min before each Mass.

JAPANESE

There is no Japanese Chaplaincy at present.

KERALAN / MALAYALAM (Latin Rite)

Chaplains: Fr Johnson Alexander, Fr Sebastian Joseph *(resident at Ruislip)*
Address: 373 Bowes Road N11 1AA *(New Southgate)*
Tel: 07438 182888 / 07958376955
Email: fr.johnsonalexander@gmail.com
Mass times: *East Ham (Brentwood)*, 2nd & 4th Sunday 4pm, preceded by Catechism 3pm and Rosary 3.30pm, 1st Saturday 7pm Rosary & Charismatic Prayer
Forest Gate (Brentwood), 2nd Tuesday 7.10pm & Novena to St Anthony 7pm
New Southgate, 2nd Sunday 3.30pm & Perpetual Help Novena 3pm
Pollards Hill (Southwark), 1st Sunday 3.30pm & Perpetual Help Novena 3pm
Ruislip, 1st Sunday 4pm
Southall, 3rd Sunday 3pm, preceded by Adoration and Confession 2pm

KOREAN

Chaplain: Fr Joong Hee Kwon
Address: Korean Catholic Community, 104-106 Benhill Wood Road, Sutton SM1 3SR
Tel: 020 8644 1223
Email: londoncatholic@gmail.com
Web: www.londoncatholic.net
Mass times: (Saturday 7pm), Sunday 11

LATIN AMERICAN

Chaplains: Fr Carlos Abajos OAR, Fr Gerardo Cortes OAR
Address: 363 Kennington Lane SE11 5QY
Tel: 020 7820 1697
Email: capellanialatinoamericana@gmail.com
Mass times: *St George's Cathedral (Southwark)*, Sunday 1pm
St Anthony, Forest Gate (Brentwood), Sunday 3pm
St Anne, Vauxhall (Southwark), Sunday 1.30pm
Stamford Hill, Sunday 4.30pm
Soho Square, Sunday 6pm

LITHUANIAN

Chaplains: Fr Petras Tverijonas, Fr Petras Gucevicius
Address: 21 The Oval, Hackney Road E2 9DT (*Lithuanian Church*)
Tel: 020 7739 8735
Email: parish@londonas.co.uk
Mass times: See *Lithuanian Church* in Parish Directory

MALTESE

Chaplain: Fr Victor Camilleri OFM
Address: 47 Adler Street E1 1EE *(German Church)*
Tel: 07930 198251
Email: victor-camilleri@hotmail.com

NIGERIAN

Chaplains: Fr Peter Babangida Audu, Fr Matthew 'Gbenga Madewa, Fr Peter Tochukwu Egboo
Address: 8 King Henry's Walk N1 4PB *(Kingsland)*
Tel: 07710 512244 (Fr Peter A); 07399 434762 (Fr Matthew); 07440 653821 (Fr Peter E)
Email: ncchaplaincy@ncchapeng.org
Web: www.ncchapeng.org
Mass times: *Dagenham (Brentwood)*, 1st Sunday 2pm
Feltham, 4th Sunday 2.30pm
Kingsland, 3rd Sunday 2pm
Mill Hill, 4th Sunday 2pm
Peckham (Southwark), 1st Sunday 2pm

SECTION 3

Tottenham, 1st Sunday in third month of the quarter 2pm
Language Masses 2nd Sundays 2pm
Night Vigil 3rd Fridays *Walworth (Southwark)*

POLISH

Vicar Delegate: Mgr Stefan Wylezek
Address: 2-4 Devonia Road N1 8JJ
Tel: 020 7226 3439
Email: biuro@pcmew.org
Mass times: See *Polish Church 1, 2 & 3* in Parish Directory

PORTUGUESE

Chaplain: Fr Carlos Gabriel
Address: Portuguese Catholic Mission, 6 Minerva Close SW9 6NZ
Tel: 020 7587 0881 / 07443 885815
Email: carlosgabriel@rcdow.org.uk, ukportuguesechaplain@gmail.com
Web: www.mcportuguesa.wix.com/portugal
Mass times: *Bayswater,* Sunday 11
Camden Town, Sunday 5pm
Clapham Common (Southwark), Sunday 5pm
Fulham 1, Sunday 3pm
Northwood, dates as announced 7.30pm

ROMANIAN

Chaplains: Fr Marcelin Blaj
Address: Presbytery, 22 Hay Lane NW9 0NG *(Kingsbury Green)*
Tel: 020 8204 4392 / 07424 372813
Email: romanianchaplaincy@gmail.com
Mass times: *Kingsbury Green,* Sunday 11

SLOVAK (see also CZECH)

Chaplains: Fr Tibor Borovsky
Address: 14 Melior Street SE1 3QP *(Bermondsey-Melior Street, Southwark)*
Tel: 07597 637411
Email: info@scmlondon.org, secretary@scmlondon.org
Website: www.scmlondon.org
Mass times: Sunday 1pm, *1Oct-30 Jun* 7.30pm
Monday 7.30pm, *1st Friday* 7.30pm
Confession Sunday 12.30-12.50pm, 2.45-3.30pm, 7-7.20pm
Monday 6.30-7.20pm
1st Friday 6.30-7.20pm
Exposition *1st Friday* 8-8.30pm
3rd Monday 6.30-7.20
Rosary 30 minutes before each Mass

SLOVENE

Chaplain: Fr Stanislav Cikanek
Address: 62 Offley Road SW9 0LS *(Kennington Park, Southwark)*
Tel: 020 7735 6655
Email: cikanek@msn.com
Mass times: *62 Offley Road,* Sunday 11, 2nd Sunday 4pm

SPANISH

Please contact the Latin American Chaplaincy

SRI-LANKAN (SINHALESE-SPEAKING)

Chaplain: Fr Sudham Maharage Perera
Address: Clergy House, Peter Avenue NW10 2DD *(Willesden Green)*
Tel: 020 8451 4677
Email: sudhamperera@rcdow.org.uk
Mass times: *Hounslow,* 2nd Sunday 4pm
Willesden Green, Last Sunday of the month 4.30pm
Woolwich (Southwark), 3rd Sunday 3pm

SRI-LANKAN (TAMIL-SPEAKING)

Chaplains: Fr Elmo Arulnesan Jeyarasa
Address: 304 Garratt Lane SW18 4EH
Tel: 020 8870 6257
Email: elmojeyarasa@rcdow.org.uk
Web: www.tamil-rcchaplaincy.org.uk
Mass times: *Earlsfield (Southwark),* 3rd Sunday 4.30pm
Forest Gate (Brentwood), 4th Sunday 4.30pm
Kenton, 1st Sunday 4pm
Lewisham (Southwark), 2nd Sunday 3.45pm
Southall, 1st Sunday 1.30pm
Wembley 1, 3rd Sunday 3.30pm

TRAVELLER, GYPSY AND ROMA COMMUNITIES

National
Chaplain: Fr Dan Mason
Address: 21 Laindon Road, Billericay CM12 9LL *(Brentwood)*
Tel: 01277 624891
Email: frdanmason@gmail.com
Pastoral
Co-ordinator: Sr Petronia Williams
Address: 12 Clevelys Road E5 9JN
Tel: 020 8880 0257
Email: petroniawilliams@rcdow.org.uk / petroniaosm@yahoo.co.uk

UGANDAN

There is no Ugandan Chaplaincy, but communities meet for Mass
Co-ordinator: Rev Alfred Joseph Banya (Deacon)

SECTION 3

Tel: 020 7252 6401 / 07429 124369
Email: alfred.banya@gmail.com
Mass times: Blessed Jildo Irwa & Daudi Okello Uganda Catholic Community
Kingsland, 2nd Sunday 3pm
Uganda Martyrs Catholic Community
Archway, Last Sunday of the month 3pm
Ugandan Croydon Catholic Community
South Norwood (Southwark), 2nd Sunday 2pm

VIETNAMESE

Chaplains: Fr Simon Thang Duc Nguyen, Fr Tam Huu Nguyen, Fr Van Dien Nguyen
Rev Paul Song Trong Ly (Deacon)
Address: 117 Bow Common Lane E3 4AU *(Bow Common)*
Tel: 020 7987 3477 / 07920 044275
Email: Simon_hue@yahoo.co.uk
Mass times: *130 Poplar High Street E14 0AG*, Catechesis School for Vietnamese Catholic Children Tel: 020 7536 2844
Sunday Mass 1pm (except school holidays)
Bow Common, Sunday 12noon, Monday, Tuesday 10, Thursday, Friday 8pm, Saturday 10

ZAMBIAN

Chaplain: Fr Henry Mobela
Address: 62 Eden Grove N7 8EN *(Holloway)*
Tel: 020 7607 3594 / 07495 866069
Email: kalusamobela@gmail.com
Mass times: *Clerkenwell*, 4th Saturday 3pm

ZIMBABWEAN

Chaplains: Fr John Rufaro Mudereri, Fr Jabulani Cletus Magugu
Address: 24 Bouverie Road N16 0AJ *(Stoke Newington, Fr Mudereri)*;
4 Lady Margaret Road NW5 2XT *(Kentish Town, Fr Magugu)*
Tel: 020 3624 5989 / 07943 875189 *(Fr Mudereri)*; 020 7485 4023 *(Fr Magugu)*
Email: zimbabweanchaplaincy@rcdow.org.uk; rufarojm@gmail.com *(Fr Mudereri)*;
maguguj2002@yahoo.com *(Fr Magugu)*
Mass times: *Stoke Newington*, 1st Saturday 2pm

HM PRISON SERVICE

Particular Pastoral Responsibility Bishop Paul McAleenan, assisted by Mgr Martin Hayes

National Catholic Chaplain for Prisons, HMPPS / NOMS Roman Catholic Faith Advisor
Fr Paul Douthwaite
CBCEW, 39 Eccleston Square SW1V 1BX. Tel: 07930 855056
Email: Prisons.Chaplain@CBCEW.org.uk

Adviser and Co-ordinator for the Diocese Awaiting appointment

Bovingdon: HM Prison The Mount, Molyneaux Avenue, Hemel Hempstead HP3 0NE
Chaplain Kim Davey **Tel: 01442 836300 Email: kim.davey@hmps.gsi.gov.uk**
Bronzefield: HM Prison, Woodthorpe Road, Ashford TW15 3JZ
Chaplain Karen Connaughton **Tel: 01784 425690**
Email: Karen.Connaughton@hmps.gsi.gov.uk
Feltham: HM Young Offenders Institution and Remand Centre, Bedfont Road, Feltham TW13 4ND
Chaplains Barry Phillips-Devaney, Bridget Brinkley **Tel: 020 8844 5326**
Email: barry.devaney@hmps.gsi.gov.uk, bridget.brinkley@hmps.gsi.gov.uk
Pentonville: HM Prison, Caledonian Road N7 8TT
Chaplains Valentine Ambe, Mary Ebbasi **Tel: 020 7023 7217**
Email: Valentine.Ambe@hmps.gsi.gov.uk, Mary.Ebbasi@hmps.gsi.gov.uk
Wormwood Scrubs: HM Prison, PO Box 757, London W12 0AE
Chaplain Fr Chima Ibekwe **Tel: 020 8588 3200 Email: chima.ibekwe@hmps.gsi.gov.uk**

SECTION 3

HOSPITAL AND HOSPICE CHAPLAINS

Particular Pastoral Responsibility Bishop Paul McAleenan, assisted by Mgr Martin Hayes

RC Chaplain at St Joseph's Hospice, Cardinal's Advisor for Healthcare Chaplaincy and Programme Consultant at St Mary's University Fr Peter-Michael Scott
Assistant Co-ordinators of Healthcare Chaplains Fr Giles Pinnock, Rev Anthony Clark (Deacon)
Healthcare Chaplaincy Office is at **81 St Charles Square W10 6EB**
Email: peterscott@rcdow.org.uk
For further information please see **www.rcdow.org.uk/healthcare**
In light of the Data Protection Act 1998, please indicate on entering hospital that your details may be passed to the RC Chaplain. Also state that you would like the RC Chaplain to visit you.

Hospital telephone numbers are listed after the name of the hospital, followed by the name and telephone number of the specially appointed Hospital Chaplain, where there is one, or the name in italics of the parish from which the hospital is served and the parish's telephone number.

Ashford Hospital Tel: 01784 884488 Chaplain: Frances Castledine Tel: 01784 884488

Barnet Hospital Tel: 0845 111 4000 Chaplain: Fr Arnel Tadeo Tel: 07405 960391
Bishops Wood Tel: 01923 835814 ***Northwood*** Tel: 01923 825639
Bushey BUPA Tel: 020 8950 9090 ***Bushey*** Tel: 020 8950 2077

Capio Nightingale Tel: 020 7535 7700 ***Marylebone*** Tel: 020 7723 5101
Central Middlesex Tel: 020 8965 5733 Chaplain: Fr Agustin Paunon Tel: 020 8869 2112; Pager: 07659 136452
Charing Cross Tel: 020 3311 1056 Chaplains: Fr Giles Pinnock, Fr Gerard O'Brien
Chase Farm Tel: 0845 111 4000 Chaplain: Fr Arnel Tadeo Tel: 07405 960391
Chelsea & Westminster Tel: 020 8746 8000 Chaplain: Awaiting appointment
Clayponds Tel: 020 8560 4011 ***Brentford*** Tel: 020 8560 1671
Clementine Churchill Tel: 020 8872 3872 ***Sudbury*** Tel: 020 8904 2552

Colindale Tel: 020 8952 2381 ***Kingsbury Green*** Tel: 020 8204 2834 / 2117
Cromwell Tel: 020 7460 2000 ***Kensington 2*** Tel: 020 7937 9866

Ealing Tel: 020 8746 8000 Chaplain: Awaiting appointment
East London & The City Mental Health NHS Trust Tel: 0845 155 5000 Chaplain: Raphael Zennoff Tel: 020 7794 0500
Edenhall Marie Curie Centre Tel: 020 7794 0066 ***Swiss Cottage*** Tel: 020 7435 1388
Edgware Community Tel: 020 8952 2381 Chaplain: Awaiting appointment
Elizabeth Garrett Anderson Wing Tel: 0845 155 5000 or **020 3456 7890** Chaplain: Fr Peter Harries OP Tel: 020 3447 3007

Finchley Memorial Tel: 020 8349 3121 ***Finchley Church End*** Tel: 020 8346 2459
Fitzroy Nuffield Tel: 020 7723 1288 ***Spanish Place*** Tel: 020 7935 0943

Garden House Tel: 01462 679540 ***Letchworth*** Tel: 01462 683504
Gordon (The) Tel: 020 8746 8733 Chaplains: Fr Giles Pinnock, Fr Gerard O'Brien Tel: 020 3312 1508
Great Ormond Street Tel: 020 7405 9200 Chaplain: Anne-Marie O'Riordan

Hammersmith, Queen Charlotte's & Chelsea Tel: 020 3313 4574 Chaplains: Fr Giles Pinnock, Fr Gerard O'Brien
Harefield Tel: 01895 823737 ***Harefield*** Tel: 01895 822365
Harley Street Clinic Tel: 020 7935 7700 Chaplains: Fr Giles Pinnock, Fr Gerard O'Brien Tel: 020 3312 1508
Harpenden BUPA Tel: 01582 763191 ***Harpenden*** Tel: 01582 712245
Hendon Tel: 020 8457 4500 ***Hendon*** Tel: 020 8202 0560
Hertfordshire Partnership Foundation Trust Tel: 01727 804814
Hillingdon Tel: 01895 238282 Lead Chaplain: Fr Jack Creagh Tel: 01895 279433
Homerton Tel: 020 8510 5555 Chaplain: Fr George Donaghy Tel: 020 8510 5555 / 020 7739 5006
Hospital for Tropical Diseases Tel: 0845 155 5000 or **020 3456 7890** Chaplain: Fr Peter Harries OP Tel: 020 3447 3007

King Edward VII Tel: 020 7486 4411 ***Spanish Place*** Tel: 020 7935 0943

Lister (The) Tel: 020 7730 3417 ***Chelsea 1*** Tel: 020 7589 5487
Lister Stevenage (The) Tel: 01438 314333 Chaplain: John O'Neil Tel: 01438 314333
London Clinic Tel: 020 7935 4444 ***Spanish Place*** Tel: 020 7935 0943

Meadow House Hospice Tel: 020 8746 8000
Mildmay Mission Hospital Tel: 020 7613 6300 Lead Chaplain: Sr Bernie Devine SP Tel: 020 7613 6307
Mile End Tel: 020 7377 7000 ***Mile End*** Tel: 020 8980 1845
Moorfields Eye Tel: 020 7253 3411 ***Moorfields*** Tel: 020 7247 8390
Mount Vernon Tel: 01923 826111 Chaplain Tel: 01438 314333

National Hospital for Neurology & Neurosurgery Tel: 020 3456 7890 or **0845 155 5000** Chaplain: Fr Peter Harries OP Tel: 020 3447 3007
North London Hospice Tel: 020 8343 8841 ***Finchley North*** Tel: 020 8446 0224
North London Nuffield Tel: 020 8366 2122 ***Enfield*** Tel: 020 8363 2569

North Middlesex Tel: 020 8887 2000 ***Edmonton*** Tel: 020 8803 6631
Northwick Park Tel: 020 8864 3232 Chaplain: Fr Agustin Paunon Tel: 020 8869 2112; Pager: 07659 136452

Peace Hospice (The) Tel: 01923 330330 ***Watford*** Tel: 01923 224085
Portland Hospital for Women & Children Tel: 020 7580 4400 Chaplains: Fr Giles Pinnock, Fr Gerard O'Brien Tel: 020 3312 1508
Potters Bar Tel: 01707 653286 ***Potters Bar*** Tel: 01707 654359
Princess Grace Tel: 020 7486 1234 Chaplains: Fr Giles Pinnock, Fr Gerard O'Brien Tel: 020 3312 1508

Queen Elizabeth II Tel: 01438 314333 Chaplain: John O'Neil Tel: 01438 314333
Queen Victoria Memorial Tel: 01707 365291 ***Welwyn Garden City (Digswell)*** Tel: 01707 327 434

Royal Brompton Tel: 020 7352 8121 Chaplain: Fr Edward van den Bergh Tel: 020 7808 0900
Royal Free Tel: 020 7794 0500 Chaplain: Fr John McCarthy Tel: 020 7830 2742
Royal London Hospital for Integrated Medicine (formerly Royal London Homoeopathic Hospital) Tel: 0845 155 5000 or **020 3456 7890** Chaplain: Fr Peter Harries OP Tel: 020 3447 3007
Royal London (Whitechapel) Tel: 020 3416 5000 Chaplains: Fr Rory Murphy IVD, Fr Andrew Jaxa-Chamiec Tel: 020 3594 2070, Sr Andrena Mulligan SM, Sr Frances Rowe RSM
Royal Marsden Tel: 020 7352 8171 Chaplain: Fr Joseph McCullough Tel: 07881 464236
Royal National Orthopaedic Tel: 020 8954 2300 ***Stanmore*** Tel: 020 8954 1299
Royal National Throat, Nose & Ear Tel: 020 7915 1300 See National Hospital for Neurology and Neurosurgery

St Alban's City Tel: 01727 866122 Chaplain: Colette Lennon Tel: 01923 217994
St Andrew's Tel: 020 7476 4000 ***Bow*** Tel: 020 8980 3961
St Andrew's at Harrow Bowden House Clinic Tel: 020 8966 7000 ***Harrow-on-the-Hill*** Tel: 020 8422 2513
St Bartholomew's Tel: 020 3416 5000 Chaplains: Fr Rory Murphy IVD, Fr Andrew Jaxa-Chamiec Tel: 020 3465 7220
St Bernard's Tel: 020 8967 5000 Chaplain: Awaiting appointment
St Charles Square Centre for Health and Wellbeing (Mental Health Units) Tel: 020 8969 2488
St Charles Square Palliative Care, Pembridge Hospice ***St Charles Square*** Tel: 020 8969 6844
St John and St Elizabeth & St John's Hospice Tel: 020 7806 4000
Chaplain: Fr Hugh MacKenzie Tel: 020 7806 4040
St Joseph's Hospice Tel: 020 8525 6000 Chaplain: Fr Peter-Michael Scott Tel: 020 8525 3032
St Luke's Kenton Grange Hospice Tel: 020 8382 8000 ***Kenton*** Tel: 020 8204 3550
St Luke's Woodside Tel: 020 8219 1800 ***Muswell Hill*** Tel: 020 8883 5607
St Mark's (Northwick Park) Tel: 020 8864 3232 Chaplain: Fr Agustin Paunon Tel: 020 8869 2112; Pager: 07659 136452
St Mary's Tel: 020 3312 1508 Chaplains: Fr Giles Pinnock, Fr Gerard O'Brien
St Pancras Hospital Tel: 020 7530 3500 Chaplain: Awaiting appointment

St Pancras Hospital (Jubilee, Rochester & Oakwood Wards) Tel: 0845 155 5000 or **020 3456 7890** Chaplain: Fr Peter Harries OP Tel: 020 3447 3007

University College (UCLH) Tel: 0845 155 5000 or **020 3456 7890** Chaplains: Fr Peter Harries OP, Sr Pauline Forde Tel: 020 3447 3007

University College at Westmoreland Street Tel: 020 3456 7898 Chaplains Fr Peter Harries OP Tel: 020 3447 3007

Watford General Tel: 01923 244 366 Chaplain: Colette Lennon Tel: 01923 217994

Wellington (The) Tel: 020 7586 5959 Chaplains: Fr Giles Pinnock, Fr Gerard O'Brien Tel: 020 3312 1508

West Middlesex Tel: 020 8321 5447 Chaplain: Sr Clementina Nasimiyu

Western Eye Tel: 020 3312 1508 Chaplains: Fr Giles Pinnock, Fr Gerard O'Brien

Whittington Tel: 020 7272 3070 Chaplain: Fr Oliver Ugwu Tel: 020 7288 5337

Willesden Community Tel: 020 8459 1292 *Willesden Green* Tel: 020 8451 4677

SPORT

Chaplain Mgr Vladimir Felzmann **Vaughan House, 46 Francis Street SW1P 1QN Tel: 07810 116508 Email: Info@jp2f4s.org**

UNIVERSITIES AND INSTITUTES OF HIGHER EDUCATION

See page 121 in Parish Directory

OTHER JURISDICTIONS

BISHOPRIC OF THE FORCES

Wellington House, St Omer Barracks, Thornhill Road, Aldershot GU11 2BG
Tel: 01252 348234
Bishop of the Forces Paul Mason (2016; 2018) **Email: Paul.mason111@mod.gov.uk**
Wellington House, St Omer Barracks, Thornhill Road, Aldershot, Hants GU11 2BG
Chancellor Fr Stephen Sharkey RAChD **Email: Stephen.sharkey941@mod.gov.uk**
Secretary Diane Restall **Email: Diane.restall654@mod.gov.uk**

EPARCHY OF THE HOLY FAMILY OF LONDON

The Eparchy serves Ukrainian and Belarusian Catholics, and also Slovakian Greek Catholics
Chancery, 22 Binney Street W1K 5BQ Tel: 020 7629 1073
Eparch Bishop Hlib Lonchyna MSU
Protosyncellus Very Rev Andrew B Choma **Chancellor** Very Rev Mykola Matwijiwskyj
See *Ukrainian Cathedral* entry in Parish Directory section and *Belarusian Catholic Church* in the Eastern Catholic Churches listing under the Chaplaincies listed above.

ORDINARIATE OF OUR LADY OF WALSINGHAM

On 15 January 2011 the Congregation for the Doctrine of the Faith published a Decree which formally established a 'Personal Ordinariate' in England and Wales for groups of Anglican faithful and their clergy who wish to enter into full communion with the Catholic Church.

The Ordinariate of OLW, c/o Catholic Bishops' Conference of England and Wales, 39 Eccleston Square SW1V 1BX

Email: enquiries@ordinariate.org.uk Web: www.ordinariate.org.uk

Ordinariate Clergy in the Diocese: Mgr Keith Newton (Ordinary), Frs Simon Chinery, Mark Elliott-Smith, Alan Griffin, Antony Homer, Anthony Watkins (see Other Priests in the Diocese, Section 4, for contact details)

Warwick Street Parish is in the care of the Ordinariate; and a Sunday Mass is also celebrated at **Hemel Hempstead West Parish.**

PERSONAL PRELATURE OF THE HOLY CROSS AND OPUS DEI

Prelate (resident in Rome) Mgr Fernando Ocáriz

Regional Vicar for Great Britain Mgr Nicholas Morrish MA STD

(1) 4 Orme Court W2 4RL Tel: 020 7229 7574 (Queensway)

Other centres in the diocese:

(2) Pembridge House, 29 Pembridge Square W2 4DS Tel: 020 7221 0588 (Bayswater)

(3) Dawliffe Hall, 1/2 Chelsea Embankment SW3 4LG Tel: 020 7351 0719 (Chelsea 1)

(4) Lakefield, 41a Maresfield Gardens NW3 5RY Tel: 020 7794 5669 (Swiss Cottage)

(5) Netherhall House, Nutley Terrace NW3 5SA Tel: 020 7435 8888 (Swiss Cottage)

(6) Westpark, 1 Leopold Road W5 3PB Tel: 020 8992 3954 (Gunnersbury)

(7) Woodlands, 12 Gunnersbury Avenue W5 3NJ Tel: 020 8992 4025 (Gunnersbury)

(8) Ashwell House, Shepherdess Walk N1 7NA Tel: 020 7490 3296 (Hoxton)

(9) Elmore, 8 Orme Court W2 4RL Tel: 020 7243 9411 (Queensway)

Priests: Azagra, Dancho (5), Bristow, Peter (9), Diaper, Paul (5), Hayward, Paul (1), Hnylycia, Stefan (5), Marsh, Bernard (9), Morrish, Mgr Nicholas (1), Pereiro, James (6), Sheehan, Gerard (9), Soane, Andrew (1), Stork, Mgr Richard (5)

Opus Dei Information Office, 6 Orme Court W2 4RL Tel: 020 7221 9176

Fax: 020 7243 9400 Email: info.uk@opusdei.org Web: www.opusdei.org.uk

SYRO-MALABAR EPARCHY OF GREAT BRITAIN

Pope Francis established the Syro-Malabar Eparchy of Great Britain on 28 July 2016 for members of the Syro-Malabar community in England, Scotland and Wales.

Eparch Bishop Joseph Srampickal (2016)

Eparchial Curia, St Alphonsa Cathedral, St Ignatius Square, Preston PR1 1TT

Tel: 01722 396065 Email: smcuria@gmail.com Web: www.eparchyofgreatbritain.org

Protosyncellus Mgr Thomas Parayadyil

373 Bowes Road N11 1AA Tel: 07523 100870 Email: parayadyt@gmail.com

SECTION 3

LISTED BUILDINGS

in order of Parish, Building, Address, Local Authority and Grade

Cathedral, Most Precious Blood Victoria Street SW1P 1QW City of Westminster I

Allen Hall Seminary Chapel Beaufort Street SW3 5AA Kensington & Chelsea II
Ashford, St Michael Clarendon Road TW15 2QD Spelthorne II

Bayswater, St Mary of the Angels Church and Presbytery Moorhouse Road W2 5DJ, City of Westminster II*,
Bethnal Green, Our Lady of the Assumption Victoria Park Square E2 9PB Tower Hamlets II
Bishops Stortford, St Joseph & the English Martyrs Windhill CM23 2ND East Herts II
Bow, Our Lady Refuge of Sinners and St Catherine of Siena 177 Bow Road E3 2SG Tower Hamlets II
Brentford, St John the Evangelist Boston Park Road TW8 9JF Hounslow II
Brook Green, Holy Trinity Brook Green W6 7BL Hammersmith & Fulham II*
Buntingford, St Richard of Chichester Station Road SG9 9HT East Herts II

Chelsea, St Mary Cadogan Street SW3 2QR Kensington & Chelsea II*
Chelsea, Most Holy Redeemer & St Thomas More Cheyne Row SW3 5HS Kensington & Chelsea II
Chiswick, Our Lady of Grace & St Edward High Road W4 4PU Hounslow II
Chorleywood, St John Fisher Shire Lane WD3 5NH Three Rivers II
Clerkenwell, Sts Peter & Paul Amwell Street EC1R 1UL Islington II
Commercial Road, St Mary & St Michael Lukin Street E1 0AA Tower Hamlets II
Covent Garden, Corpus Christi Maiden Lane WC2E 7NB City of Westminster II

Ealing, Abbey Church of St Benedict Charlbury Grove W5 2DY Ealing II
Ely Place, St Etheldreda Holborn Circus EC1N 6RY Camden I

Farm Street, The Immaculate Conception Farm Street W1K 3AH City of Westminster II*
French Church, Notre Dame de France Leicester Place WC2H 7BX City of Westminster II*
Fulham, St Thomas of Canterbury Rylston Road SW6 7HW Hammersmith & Fulham **Church** II*, **Presbytery** II, **War Memorial & Adjacent Tomb** II
Fulham Road, Our Lady of Dolours Fulham Road SW10 9EL Kensington & Chelsea II

Golders Green, St Edward the Confessor Finchley Road NW11 7NE Barnet II

Hammersmith, Sacred Heart School Hammersmith Road W6 7DG Hammersmith & Fulham II*
Hampstead, St Mary Holly Place NW3 6QU Camden II*
Harpenden, Our Lady of Lourdes Kirkwick Avenue, Harpenden AL5 2QH St Albans II
Harrow on the Hill, Our Lady & St Thomas of Canterbury Roxborough Park HA1 3BE Harrow II
Hatfield, Marychurch, Salisbury Square, Old Hatfield AL9 5JD Welwyn Hatfield II
Haverstock Hill, St Dominic Southampton Road NW5 4LB Camden II*
Hertford, Immaculate Conception & St Joseph St John's Street SG14 1RX East Herts II
Highgate, St Joseph Highgate Hill N19 5NE Islington II*

Holloway, Sacred Heart of Jesus Eden Grove N7 8EN Islington II
Hoxton, St Monica Hoxton Square N1 6NT Hackney II

Islington, St John the Evangelist Duncan Terrace N1 8AL Islington II
Italian Church, St Peter Clerkenwell Road EC1R 5DL Camden II*

Kensal New Town, Our Lady of the Holy Souls Bosworth Road W10 5DJ Kensington & Chelsea II
Kensington 1, Our Lady of Victories Kensington High Street W8 6AF Kensington & Chelsea II
Kensington 2, Our Lady of Mt. Carmel & St Simon Stock Kensington Church Street W8 4BB Kensington & Chelsea II
Kensington 2, Assumption Convent Kensington Square W8 5HH Kensington & Chelsea II
Kentish Town, Our Lady Help of Christians Lady Margaret Road NW5 2XT Camden II

Lincoln's Inn Fields, Sts Anselm & Cecilia Kingsway WC2A 3JA Camden II

Marylebone, Our Lady of the Rosary Old Marylebone Road NW1 5QT City of Westminster II
Mile End, Guardian Angels Mile End Road E3 4QS Tower Hamlets II
Moorfields, St Mary Eldon Street EC2M 7LS City of London II

Notting Hill, St Francis of Assisi Pottery Lane W11 4NQ Kensington & Chelsea II*

Ogle Street, St Charles Borromeo Ogle Street W1W 6HS City of Westminster II
Oratory, Immaculate Heart of Mary Brompton Road SW7 2RP Kensington & Chelsea II*

Pinner, St Luke Love Lane HA5 3EX Harrow II
Polish Church, Our Lady of Czestochowa Devonia Road N1 8JJ Islington II
Poplar, St Mary & St Joseph Pekin Street E14 6EZ Tower Hamlets II

Queensway, Our Lady Queen of Heaven Inverness Place W2 3JF City of Westminster II

Ruislip South, St Gregory the Great (Church and Hall) Victoria Road HA4 0EG Hillingdon II

St John's Wood, Chapel of the Hospital of St John and St Elizabeth Grove End Road NW8 9NH City of Westminster II
St John's Wood, Our Lady Lisson Grove NW8 8LA City of Westminster II
St John's Wood, St Edward's Convent Harewood Avenue NW1 6LD City of Westminster II*
St Margarets-on-Thames, St Margaret St Margaret's Road TW1 1RL Richmond II
Shepherds Bush, The Holy Ghost and St Stephen (Church and Presbytery) Ashchurch Grove W12 9BU Hammersmith & Fulham II
Soho Square, St Patrick Soho Square W1D 4NR City of Westminster II *
Spanish Place, St James George Street W1U 3QY City of Westminster (Church II*, Presbytery II)
Stamford Hill, St Ignatius High Road N15 6ND Haringey II
Stanmore, St William of York Du Cros Drive HA7 4TJ Harrow II
Sudbury, St George Harrow Road HA0 2QE Brent II
Swiss Cottage, St Thomas More Maresfield Gardens NW3 5SU Camden II

Tollington Park, St Mellitus Tollington Park N4 3AG Islington II
Tower Hill, English Martyrs Prescot Street E1 8BB Tower Hamlets II

SECTION 3

Twickenham, St Mary's University Waldegrave Road TW1 4ST Richmond I
Ukrainian Cathedral, Holy Family Duke Street W1K 5BQ City of Westminster II
Underwood Road, St Anne Underwood Road E1 5AW Tower Hamlets II*
University Chaplaincy 111 Gower Street WC1E 6AR Camden II

Wapping, St Patrick Dundee Street E1W 2PH Tower Hamlets II
Ware, Chapel of St Edmund's College Old Hall Green SG11 1DS East Herts I
Warwick Street, Our Lady of the Assumption & St Gregory Golden Square W1F 9JR City of Westminster II*
Watford, Holy Rood Market Street WD18 0PJ Watford I
Wealdstone, St Joseph Wealdstone High Road HA3 5EE Harrow II
Wembley I, St Joseph High Road, Wembley HA9 6AG Brent II
West Drayton, St Catherine's The Green, West Drayton UB7 7PJ Hillingdon II
Willesden, Our Lady of Willesden Acton Lane NW10 9AX Brent II

CENTRAL LONDON CHURCHES

CHURCHES NEAR RAILWAY TERMINALS

CANNON STREET; FENCHURCH STREET; LONDON BRIDGE: The English Martyrs, 26 Prescot Street E1 8BB *(Tower Hill)*
CHARING CROSS: Corpus Christi, 1 Maiden Lane WC2E 7NB *(Covent Garden)*
EUSTON; KING'S CROSS (West side); ST PANCRAS & EUROSTAR TERMINAL: St Aloysius, Phoenix Road NW1 1TA *off Eversholt Street (Somers Town)*
KING'S CROSS (East side): The Blessed Sacrament, 165 Copenhagen Street N1 0SR *off York Way (Copenhagen Street)*
LIVERPOOL STREET: St Mary Moorfields, 4-5 Eldon Street EC2M 7LS *(Moorfields)*
LONDON BRIDGE: Our Lady of La Salette & St Joseph, 14 Melior Street SE1 3QP Tel: 020 7407 1948 *(Southwark)*
MARYLEBONE; PADDINGTON: Our Lady of the Rosary, 211 Old Marylebone Road NW1 5QT *(Marylebone)*
VICTORIA: Westminster Cathedral, Victoria Street SW1P 1QW *(Cathedral)*
WATERLOO: St Patrick's, 26 Cornwall Road SE1 8TW Tel: 020 7928 4818 *(Southwark)*

CENTRAL LOCATIONS

Services in the Churches listed will be found in the Parish Directory section, under the entry indicated here in bold and italic.

CITY (I) St Mary Moorfields, Eldon Street EC2M 7LS *north of Finsbury Circus, near Liverpool Street Stn & Moorgate TfL Stn* Tel: 020 7247 8390 *(Moorfields)*
CITY (II) The English Martyrs, 26 Prescot Street E1 8BB *off Mansell Street, near Tower of London* Tel: 020 7488 4654 *(Tower Hill)*
CITY (III) St Joseph, Lamb's Buildings EC1Y 8LE *off Bunhill Row, near Barbican Centre* Tel: 020 7628 0326 *(Bunhill Row)*

HOLBORN CIRCUS St Etheldreda, Ely Place EC1N 6RY *off Charterhouse Street, beside Holborn Circus* Tel: 020 7405 1061 *(Ely Place)*

HOLBORN KINGSWAY St Anselm and St Cecilia, Kingsway WC2A 3JA *east side just south of Holborn TfL Stn*
Tel: 020 7405 0376 *(Lincoln's Inn Fields)*

LEICESTER SQUARE Notre Dame de France, Leicester Place WC2H 7BX *north side of Leicester Square* Tel: 020 7437 9363 *(French Church)*

MAYFAIR Immaculate Conception, Farm Street W1K 3AH *entrance also in Mount Street, between South Audley Street and Berkeley Square* Tel: 020 7493 7811 *(Farm Street)*

PICCADILLY CIRCUS The Assumption, Warwick Street W1R 3PA *close to Piccadilly Circus* Tel: 020 7437 1525 *(Warwick Street)*

SOHO St Patrick, Soho Square W1D 4NR *in angle between Oxford Street and Charing Cross Road; near Tottenham Court Road TfL Stn* Tel: 020 7437 2010 *(Soho Square)*
STRAND Corpus Christi, 1 Maiden Lane WC2E 7NB *off Southampton Street on north side of the Strand; near Covent Garden* Tel: 020 7836 4700 *(Covent Garden)*
VICTORIA Westminster Cathedral, Ashley Place SW1P 1QW *south side of Victoria Street, close to Victoria Stn* Tel: 020 7798 9097 *(Cathedral)*
WEST END (I) St Charles Borromeo, Ogle Street W1W 6HS *off eastern end of New Cavendish Street* Tel: 020 7636 2883 *(Ogle Street)*
WEST END (II) St James, George Street W1U 3QY *eastern end, near junction with Marylebone High Street* Tel: 020 7935 0943 *(Spanish Place)*
WEST END (III) Our Lady of the Rosary, Old Marylebone Road NW1 5QT *south side of Old Marylebone Road, by junction with Marylebone Road* Tel: 020 7723 5101 *(Marylebone)*
WEST END (IV) Tyburn Convent, 8 Hyde Park Place W2 2LJ *in Bayswater Road, close to Marble Arch* Perpetual Exposition of the Blessed Sacrament Tel: 020 7723 7262 *(Marylebone)*

SECTION 3

PARISHES AND LONDON POSTAL DISTRICTS

Parishes are listed according to the postal address of the church or presbytery; postal district numbers following the name of a parish indicate that parts of those districts are also within the parish. Districts south of the Thames (Southwark Diocese) or east of the Lea (Brentwood) are not included.

E1	Commercial Road
E1	German Church
E1	Tower Hill EC3
E1	Underwood Road E2
E1	Wapping
E2	Bethnal Green E1
E2	Lithuanian Church
E3	Bow
E3	Bow Common E14
E3	Mile End E1
E5	Clapton E8, N16
E5	Clapton Park E9
E9	Hackney E8
E9	Homerton E5
E14	Limehouse
E14	Millwall
E14	Poplar
EC1	Bunhill Row
EC1	Clerkenwell WC1, N1
EC1	Ely Place EC4
EC1	Italian Church
EC2	Moorfields EC1, EC3, EC4, E1
N1	Copenhagen Street
N1	Hoxton E2, EC2, EC1
N1	Islington EC1
N1	Kingsland N5, N16, E8
N1	Polish Church 1
N2	Finchley (East) N3, N6, N12, NW11
N3	Finchley (Church End) N12, NW11, NW7
N4	Manor House
N4	Tollington Park N7, N19
N5	Highbury N4
N7	Holloway N5, N19
N8	Stroud Green N4, N19
N9	Edmonton N13, N18, N21

N10	Muswell Hill N2
N11	New Southgate N13, N14, N20, N22
N12	Finchley (North) N3, N20
N13	Palmers Green N14, N21
N14	Cockfosters N21
N15	Stamford Hill N16, E5
N15	West Green N8, N17, N22
N16	Stoke Newington N4
N17	Tottenham
N19	Highgate N6, N8, NW5
N19	Archway
N20	Whetstone N12
N22	Wood Green N8, N11, N17
NW1	Somers Town WC1
NW1	Marylebone W1, W2
NW1	Camden Town N1, N7
NW2	Cricklewood NW3, NW11, NW6
NW2	Dollis Hill NW10
NW3	Hampstead
NW3	Swiss Cottage NW6, NW8
NW4	Hendon NW7, NW9
NW5	Haverstock Hill NW3, NW1
NW5	Kentish Town NW1, N7, N19
NW6	Kilburn NW2, NW8
NW6	Kilburn West
NW7	Mill Hill
NW8	St John's Wood NW1, W2, W9
NW9	Grahame Park
NW9	Hendon (West) NW4
NW9	Kingsbury Green
NW10	Kensal Rise NW6
NW10	Neasden
NW10	Stonebridge
NW10	Willesden
NW10	Willesden Green NW2, NW6
NW11	Golders Green NW3, N2

SW1	Westminster Cathedral
SW1	Pimlico
SW3	Chelsea 1 SW1
SW3	Chelsea 2 SW10
SW6	Fulham
SW6	Parsons Green
SW6	Stephendale Road
SW7	Oratory SW1, SW3, W2, W8
SW10	Fulham Road SW3, SW5, SW7
W1	Farm Street SW1
W1	Ogle Street WC1
W1	Soho Square EC1, WC2
W1	Spanish Place
W1	Ukrainian Cathedral
W1	Warwick Street SW1
W2	Bayswater W11
W2	Paddington
W2	Queensway
W3	Acton
W3	East Acton NW10, W10, W12
W3	West Acton W5
W3	Gunnersbury W5
W4	Chiswick
W4	Grove Park
W5	Ealing W13
W5	Polish Church 3
W6	Brook Green W12, W14
W6	Hammersmith SW6
W7	Hanwell W13
W8	Kensington 1 SW5, W11, W14
W8	Kensington 2 SW5, SW7, W11
W9	Harrow Road
W10	Kensal New Town W9
W10	St Charles Square
W11	Notting Hill W10
W12	Polish Church 2
W12	Shepherd's Bush W3, W6
W12	White City
W13	Northfields W5, W7
WC2	French Church
WC2	Lincoln's Inn Fields EC4, WC1
WC2	Covent Garden SW1

DIOCESAN STATISTICS

Priests of the Diocese	
Working in the Diocese	183
Chaplains / Teaching	18
Further Studies	3
Others working outside the Diocese	26
Sabbatical	2
Retired / Supply	95
Total (includes Bishops)	**333**

Priests of other Dioceses	
From England & Wales	6
From Ireland & Scotland	1
From other countries (includes Poland)	22
Eastern Catholic (20, not resident in diocese 5, Diocesan Priest 1; Religious 8)	15
Ethnic Chaplains (excludes Deacons, Religious)	42
Ethnic Chaplains resident in diocese (also excludes those otherwise counted, e.g. Religious)	20
Ordinariate OLW (6, not resident in diocese 1)	5
Prelature of Opus Dei	11
Total working in the diocese	**102**
Total resident in the diocese	**71**

Priests of Religious Congregations & Societies of Apostolic Life, including Chaplains

African Missions Society 3; Assumptionists: 7; Augustinians: 9; Augustinian Recollects: 1; Benedictines (English): 14; Benedictines (Olivetan): 1; Benedictines (Other): 1; Carmelites (Discalced): 7; Carmelites of Mary Immaculate: 3; Chemin Neuf Community: 2; Claretians: 5; Columban Fathers: 5; Comboni Missionaries 5; Congregation of the Sacred Hearts: 7; Consolata Fathers: 2; Divine Providence, Sons of: 4; Divine Word Missionaries: 7; Dominicans: 8; Franciscans: 2; Institute of Charity: 1; Jesuits: 37; Lebanese Maronite: 3; Marian Fathers: 6; Marist Fathers: 4; Mill Hill Missionaries: 1; Missionaries of Africa: 19; Missionary Community of Divine Providence: 2; Missionaries of St Paul: 3; Missionary Society of St Thomas the Apostle: 1; Monaci Studiti Ucraini: 2; Montfort Missionaries: 3; Oblates of Mary Immaculate: 8; Oratorians: 9; Pallottine Fathers: 7; Passionists: 7; Redemptorist: 1; Sacred Heart, Missionaries of the: 3; Salvatorians: 9; Scalabrini Fathers: 1; Servites: 5; Society of Christ: 1; Society of Divine Vocations: 2; Spiritans 7; Stigmatines: 1; Vincentians: 4

Total (includes Bishops)	240
Total for Other & Religious Priests	342
Other & Religious Priests resident in the diocese	311

Permanent Deacons	26
Parishes	214

SECTION 3

PARISH STATISTICS 2017

In the Parish Directory each parish has its deanery noted thus: *Westminster Deanery*.
The following tables are compiled from the parish returns; where no figures are given, returns have not been received.
Mass attendance was counted over four Sundays during October 2017.
Mass attendance for 2018 has been counted over the last two Sundays in September and the first two Sundays of October, following a decision of the Bishops' Conference.

Parish	Sunday Mass	Baptisms	Receptions	Marriages
Barnet Deanery				
Barnet	918	25	2	5
Burnt Oak	682	63	4	3
Cricklewood	1018	73	0	4
Edgware	768	35	8	1
Finchley Church End	702	25	3	3
Finchley East	538	30	2	1
Finchley North	677	32	1	0
Golders Green	693	22	0	4
Grahame Park	311	24	1	0
Hendon	484	8	5	1
Hendon West	333	10	0	0
Mill Hill	865	52	4	4
New Barnet	385	23	1	0
Whetstone	671	43	1	3
Brent Deanery				
Dollis Hill	860	18	0	3
Kensal Rise	562	37	0	2
Kingsbury Green	765	159	0	38
Neasden	241	13	0	4
Romanian Chaplaincy	584	132	1	4
Stonebridge	421	21	0	0
Wembley 1	2129	84	0	1
Wembley 2	921	41	1	0
Wembley 3	461	11	0	0
Willesden	1407	49	1	1
Willesden Green	1033	93	0	3

Parish	Sunday Mass	Baptisms	Receptions	Marriages
Camden Deanery				
Camden Town	500	34	0	3
Hampstead	701	38	0	12
Haverstock Hill	557	51	2	3
Kentish Town	559	17	0	1
Kilburn	1509	128	0	5
Kilburn West	170	9	2	0
Somers Town	408	32	3	2
Swiss Cottage	404	22	1	1
Ealing Deanery				
Acton	900	66	5	2
Acton East	368	72	6	0
Acton West	294	14	3	3
Ealing	1477	89	1	13
Greenford	2024	98	0	7
Hanwell	916	10	0	2
Northfields	888	41	0	0
Perivale	500	8	1	1
Polish Church 3	4390	185	1	9
Southall	2082	90	3	9
Enfield Deanery				
Cockfosters	458	8	1	10
Cuffley	151	5	0	5
Edmonton	1153	45	1	13
Enfield	2239	138	1	4
New Southgate	1367	42	2	12
Palmers Green	1641	110	4	7
Ponders End	1225	26	3	0
Potters Bar	583	33	0	0
Hackney Deanery				
Clapton	470	19	0	7
Clapton Park	301	20	0	0
Hackney	497	10	0	1
Homerton	596	44	7	6
Hoxton	440	33	4	6
Kingsland	940	61	3	5
Manor House	238	13	3	0
Stoke Newington	223	22	0	1

Parish	Sunday Mass	Baptisms	Receptions	Marriages
Hammersmith & Fulham Deanery				
Brook Green	1126	63	2	5
Fulham 1	783	35	1	3
Fulham 2 (Stephendale Road)	248	30	0	0
Hammersmith	1043	64	2	1
Parsons Green	585	65	2	0
Polish Church 2		32	0	2
Shepherds Bush	651	33	2	2
White City	581	26	2	0
Haringey Deanery				
Muswell Hill	867	34	0	6
Stamford Hill	1732	139	4	5
Stroud Green	577	37	4	2
Tottenham	915	104	4	7
West Green	687	33	4	3
Wood Green	1085	33	0	1
Harrow Deanery				
Harrow-on-the-Hill	1052	41	3	7
Harrow North	895	34	1	2
Harrow South and Northolt	943	13	0	3
Headstone Lane	485	27	4	2
Kenton	824	38	5	8
Pinner	728	13	11	5
Stanmore	358	16	0	0
Sudbury	1585	56	6	10
Wealdstone & Harrow Weald	1383	62	0	4
Hillingdon Deanery				
Eastcote	356	8	0	2
Harefield	263	16	0	2
Hayes	1682	55	1	13
Heathrow Airport	127	3	0	0
Hillingdon	692	24	4	3
Northwood	509	15	0	2
Ruislip	1118	65	2	5
Ruislip South	556	41	2	2
Uxbridge	771	50	1	5
West Drayton	656	18	1	2
Yeading	852	47	47	3

Parish	Sunday Mass	Baptisms	Receptions	Marriages
Hounslow Deanery				
Brentford	480	32	0	1
Chiswick	1408	72	4	4
Cranford	523	34	0	2
Feltham	1928	100	0	10
Grove Park	102	4	0	0
Gunnersbury	70	0	0	0
Heston	604	41	5	3
Hounslow	3656	103	1	10
Isleworth	832	62	2	4
Osterley	490	18	0	1
Islington Deanery				
Archway	400	10	5	0
Bunhill Row	70	1	0	0
Clerkenwell	252	8	1	0
Copenhagen Street	209	8	0	0
Highbury	628	34	0	8
Highgate	743	73	0	4
Holloway	545	26	1	1
Islington	524	69	2	8
Polish Church 1	1330	54	0	9
Tollington Park	346	36	2	1
Kensington and Chelsea Deanery				
Chelsea 1	655	46	5	4
Chelsea 2	1193	27	3	3
Fulham Road	835	42	2	4
Kensington 1	1501	52	2	8
Kensington 2	856	26	0	3
Oratory	2223	157	5	37
Lea Valley Deanery				
Bishop's Stortford	953	62	0	13
Buntingford	77	6	0	1
Cheshunt	283	10	3	0
Hertford	489	40	1	12
Hoddesdon	587	46	0	3
Old Hall Green and Puckeridge	59	0	0	1
Waltham Cross	1466	69	1	8
Ware	463	31	3	6

SECTION 3

Parish	Sunday Mass	Baptisms	Receptions	Marriages
Marylebone Deanery				
Farm Street	692	74	1	35
Marylebone	560	22	4	0
Ogle Street	289	12	0	3
St John's Wood	1078	40	4	5
Spanish Place	1341	76	7	15
University	329	5	0	0
North Kensington Deanery				
Bayswater	736	48	1	8
Harrow Road	254	7	2	0
Kensal New Town	436	15	0	1
Notting Hill	664	33	0	5
Paddington	109	5	0	0
Queensway	315	10	0	0
St Charles Square	403	23	0	0
St Albans Deanery				
Berkhamsted	330	11	0	0
Borehamwood	455	62	1	2
Borehamwood North	281	3	0	2
Harpenden	748	47	2	7
Hemel Hempstead Boxmoor	499	42	1	2
Hemel Hempstead East	669	46	0	4
Hemel Hempstead North	110	0	0	0
Hemel Hempstead West	120	7	0	1
London Colney	305	6	0	0
Radlett	162	5	0	1
Redbourn	167	5	0	0
St Albans	1215	117	6	10
St Albans South	510	23	1	2
Shenley	108	1	0	0
Tring	187	4	0	0
Wheathampstead	164	8	0	4

Parish	Sunday Mass	Baptisms	Receptions	Marriages
Stevenage Deanery				
Baldock	348	17	2	2
Hatfield	227	7	0	2
Hatfield South	488	28	0	1
Hitchin	430	34	1	1
Knebworth	301	19	0	3
Letchworth	626	22	0	1
Royston	363	18	2	3
Stevenage Bedwell	702	44	3	1
Stevenage Old Town	286	14	0	0
Stevenage Shephall	553	39	3	0
Welwyn Garden City	209	16	0	4
Welwyn Garden City Digswell	333	7	0	0
Welwyn Garden City East	427	47	3	21
Tower Hamlets Deanery				
Bethnal Green	269	35	1	6
Bow	498	32	0	3
Bow Common	587	73	0	6
Commercial Road	387	42	5	7
German Church	50	3	0	0
Limehouse	146	6	2	2
Lithuanian Church	370	212	1	10
Mile End	341	24	0	3
Millwall	431	26	4	1
Poplar	367	31	9	3
Tower Hill	178	10	0	3
Underwood Road	109	54	0	8
Wapping	352	13	1	3
Upper Thames Deanery				
Ashford	620	54	0	7
Hampton Hill	436	34	0	1
Hampton-on-Thames	268	28	0	0
St Margarets-on-Thames	411	27	0	2
Shepperton	178	20	1	1
Staines-upon-Thames	612	33	2	0
Stanwell	106	5	1	2
Sunbury-on-Thames	384	19	1	4
Teddington	400	15	4	5
Twickenham	575	69	5	5
Whitton	884	49	4	3

SECTION 3

Parish	Sunday Mass	Baptisms	Receptions	Marriages
Watford Deanery				
Abbots Langley	483	25	0	3
Bushey & Oxhey	870	54	8	6
Carpenders Park	185	39	0	2
Chipperfield	152	9	0	0
Chorleywood	95	1	1	0
Croxley Green	208	13	0	0
Garston	558	44	8	5
Mill End and Maple Cross	256	8	2	1
Rickmansworth	357	30	2	7
Watford	1577	80	3	9
Watford North	504	33	1	4
Westminster Deanery				
Cathedral	3632	93	12	5
Covent Garden	258	2	0	0
Ely Place	127	38	0	44
French Church	650	37	0	2
Italian Church	1000	132	5	19
Lincoln's Inn Fields	525	21	2	4
Moorfields	94	8	0	3
Pimlico	556	24	1	1
Soho Square	597	21	1	6
Warwick Street	116	1	2	3
TOTAL FOR DIOCESE	**144,223**	**8,293**	**394**	**874**

Note to the Statistics: These figures do not include those which are reported separately to Rome, e.g. those for the Eastern Catholic Churches and chaplaincies. Baptisms, Marriages and Receptions undertaken by Ethnic Chaplaincies and recorded in parish registers are included in the above statistics. However, Sunday Mass attendances for the majority of the Ethnic Chaplaincies are not included.

JUSTICE AND PEACE CONTACTS

Here are listed the Justice and Peace contacts for each parish. If the parish is not noted below, then please contact the Parish Priest with regard to Justice and Peace matters. Please contact **justiceandpeace@rcdow.org.uk** if the details below need updating.

Cathedral Mary Wogar

Archway Rachel McGonigal

Berkhamsted David & Lesley Brinsden
Bishop's Stortford Astrid Davies
Bow Sr Maria Fay
Bunhill Row Martin Pendergast
Burnt Oak Joey Flores & Dominic Roberts
Bushey Sue Schmitt

Chelsea I John Wilson
Chiswick Hugh Caldin
Cockfosters Frances Halliday
Copenhagen Street Sr Miriam Bruder

Ealing Abbey Martha Rumian
Edmonton Lauri Clarke
Enfield Tony Sheen

Finchley Church End Anne Godwin
Finchley East Daniel Servini
Fulham I Kevin Lawler
Fulham Road Henry Stovell

Garston Deacon Paul Quinn
Greenford Teresa Byrne

Hackney Tigger Cullinan
Hammersmith Social Justice Forum Manager
Hampstead Santana Luis
Hampton Hill Bernie McKay
Hanwell Angie Harris
Harpenden Graham & Liz Ryan
Harrow North Elspeth Everitt
Harrow Road Patricia McAllister
Harrow-on-the-Hill Angela Gannon
Hatfield Angela Madden
Haverstock Hill Keiran Proffer
Hayes Ann Mullaney
Headstone Lane Dominic Rodriguez
Hemel Hempstead Boxmoor Richard Dodd
Hemel Hempstead East David Toorawa
Hemel Hempstead West Camille Fidgett
Heston Martin Birdseye
Highgate Edmund Tierney
Hillingdon Jill Rhodes
Hitchin One World Group
Hoddesdon Tony Barrell
Holloway Edmund Dean
Hounslow Corrine Lynch

Kensal Rise Oonagh O'Toole
Kentish Town Margaret Harvey
Kenton Colette Lennon
Kilburn Fr Lylie Fernando
Kilburn West Benedict Ogbolu
Kingsbury Green Ann Wade
Kingsland Henrietta Cullinan

Letchworth Garden City Mary Ryan

Manor House Barbara Kentish
Mill End Sue Schmitt

New Barnet Sheila Gallagher & Fausta Valentine
New Southgate John Donnelly
Northfields Anna Maria Dupelycz

Osterley Nicolette Robson

Pimlico Fleur Brennan
Pinner Ian & Belinda Brandon
Potters Bar Rosaleen Pinto

Queensway Evelyn Lopez

Radlett Deacon Tony Barter
Redbourn Mark Yate
Rickmansworth Judy Gordon
Ruislip Robert Nunn

St Albans Anne Romain
St Albans South Adelheid Smith

SECTION 3

St Charles Square Vanessa Davies
St John's Wood Priscilla Sharp
St Margarets-on-Thames Judith Burman
Sawbridgeworth Eugene Keddy
Shepperton Daphne Argent
St Albans South Adelheid Smith
St Charles Square Vanessa Davies
St John's Wood Priscilla Sharp
St Margarets-on-Thames Judith Burman
Stamford Hill Fr David Ardagh-Walter
Stevenage Bedwell Sr Geraldine
Stevenage Transfiguration Hannah Wright
Stroud Green Sr Anne Hogan
Sudbury Anne Nemeth
Sunbury-on-Thames Colin Bennet

Tollington Park Jo Bownas
Tottenham Innocent Uworibhor
Tring Michael Demidecki

University Chaplaincy Sr Carolyn Morrison
Uxbridge Ken Lobo

Ware Deacon Adrian Cullen
Wealdstone Ellen Teague
Welwyn Garden City East John Fogarty
Welwyn Garden City Kathryn Hubbard
Welwyn Garden City Digswell CAFOD Group
Wembley I Rebecca Chatelier
West Green Mariantha Fomenky
Wheathampstead Marie Rose Law
White City Hilda McCafferty
Willesden Bernadette Ogombu
Willesden Green Brigid Hegarty

Section 4

ARCHBISHOPS OF WESTMINSTER SINCE THE RESTORATION OF THE HIERARCHY

Cardinal Nicholas Patrick Stephen Wiseman

Born Seville, Spain, 3 August 1802; ordained Priest 11 March 1825; ordained as Vicar Apostolic Coadjutor for the Midland District 8 June 1840; translated to the newly-erected Diocese of Westminster 29 September 1850; created Cardinal 30 September 1850; died 1 February 1865.

Cardinal Henry Edward Manning

Born Totteridge House, London 15 July 1808; ordained Priest 16 June 1851; ordained as Archbishop of Westminster 8 June 1865; created Cardinal 15 March 1875; died 14 January 1892.

Cardinal Herbert Vaughan

Born Gloucester 15 April 1832; ordained Priest 28 October 1854; ordained as Bishop of Salford 28 October 1872; translated to Westminster 8 April 1892; created Cardinal 16 January 1893; died 19 June 1903.

Cardinal Francis Alphonsus Bourne

Born Clapham, London 23 March 1861; ordained Priest 11 June 1884; ordained as Bishop Coadjutor of Southwark 1 May 1896; succeeded as Bishop 9 April 1897; translated to Westminster 11 September 1903; created Cardinal 27 November 1911; died 1 January 1935.

Cardinal Arthur Hinsley

Born Selby, Yorkshire 25 August 1865; ordained Priest 23 December 1893; ordained Bishop of the titular see of Sebastopolis in Armenia 30 November 1926; translated to the titular see of Sardis 9 January 1930; translated to Westminster 25 March 1935; created Cardinal 13 December 1937; died 17 March 1943.

Cardinal Bernard William Griffin

Born Birmingham 21 February 1899; ordained Priest 1 November 1924; ordained as Auxiliary Bishop of Birmingham 30 June 1938; translated to Westminster 18 December 1943; created Cardinal 18 February 1946; died 20 August 1956.

Cardinal William Godfrey

Born Liverpool 25 September 1889; ordained Priest 1916; ordained Bishop as Apostolic Delegate 21 December 1938; translated to Liverpool 14 November 1953; translated to Westminster 3 December 1956; created Cardinal 15 December 1958; died 22 January 1963.

Cardinal John Carmel Heenan

Born Ilford, Essex 26 January 1905; ordained Priest 6 July 1930; ordained as Bishop of Leeds 12 March 1951; translated to Liverpool 17 May 1957; translated to Westminster 2 September 1963; created Cardinal 22 February 1965; died 7 November 1975.

Cardinal George Basil Hume OSB OM

Born Newcastle-upon-Tyne 2 March 1923; ordained Priest 23 July 1950; ordained as Archbishop of Westminster 25 March 1976; created Cardinal 24 May 1976; died 17 June 1999.

Cardinal Cormac Murphy-O'Connor

Born Reading 24 August 1932; ordained Priest 28 October 1956; ordained as Bishop of Arundel and Brighton 21 December 1977; translated to Westminster 22 March 2000; created Cardinal 21 February 2001; retired 3 April 2009; died 1 September 2017.

Cardinal Vincent Nichols

Born Crosby, Liverpool 8 November 1945; ordained Priest 21 December 1969; ordained as Auxiliary Bishop of Westminster 24 January 1992; translated to Birmingham 29 March 2000; translated to Westminster 21 May 2009; created Cardinal 22 February 2014.

PRIESTS OF THE DIOCESE

Seniority by year of ordination; **r** indicates a priest who is retired.

1950

r Miles, Mgr Canon Frederick

1951

r Garvey, Charles A

1953

r Miller, John M

1955

r Crowe, Bernard

1956

r Stark, Mgr Anthony

1957

r Dwyer, Peter
r Noctor, James
r O'Halloran, John
r Young, Henry

1960

r Burke, Canon Gerard T
r Scholes, Canon Bernard
r Stanley, Cedric
r Walker, Adrian

1961

r Coghlan, Mgr John
r Fullam, Seamus
r Ward, Brian

1962

r Berry, Canon Vincent
r Ffrench, Barry F
r Helm, John
r Matthews, Canon Edward
r Reynolds, Brian
r Seeldrayers, Anthony

1963

r Crewe, Hilary
Tuck, Michael

1964

r Brunning, Antony
r Wilby, William

1965

r Crowley, Bishop John
Delany, Stephen
Garnett, Michael
Sharratt, Aidan
r Wahle, Francis

1966

r Egan, Patrick
r Turner, Mgr Canon Henry

1967

Boylan, Bernard
r Brockie, Canon Michael
r Duffy, James
r Egan, Mgr Canon Thomas

1968

r Gawecki, Christopher
r Murphy, Seamus

1969

r Baker, Desmond
r Crewe, Vincent
Felzmann, Mgr Vladimir
r McDevitt, Kevin
r McGeoghan, Seamus
Nichols, Cardinal Vincent
r Whatling, Colin

1970

r Ardagh-Walter, David
r Maher, Peter
r Sharp, Peter
r Wilson, David

1971

Convery, Antony
Foley, Patrick
Leonard, Francis
r McCumiskey, Bernard
Ryan, Joseph

1972

McGinn, Mgr Canon Paul
r O'Brien, Eamonn
Watters, Denis

1973

r Doyle, Anthony
Munnelly, Canon Michael
r O'Connor, Timothy
Overton, Mgr James

1974

Browne, Canon Patrick
Carroll, Patrick
r Cross, Canon Philip
Davies, Jeremy
Ponsonby Meredyth
McNicholas, James
Magnier, Daniel
Sawyer, Guy

1975

r Carroll, Edward
Connor, Christopher
Deehan, John
Lebasi, Kidane
r Mallon, James
Plourde, Canon Robert
r Quinn, Thomas
Rowland, Mgr Phelim
Wiley, John
r Williamson, David
Zsidi, Gabriel

1976

Barltrop, Mgr Keith
Barnes, David
r Barry, Robert
Byrne, John
Seabrook, John
Shewring, John

1977

Azzopardi, Frans
Buckley, John
Cronin, Canon Daniel
Cunningham, John
r Forde, Thomas
Kelly, David
Law, Philip
Psaila, Anthony

1978

Baxter, Anthony
r Kirinich, Roger
Price, Richard
Winter, Marcus

1979

Conlon, Antony
Doyle, Michael
Power, Dermot

1980

Brady, Mgr Vincent
Creak, Brian
Gullan-Steel, Stuart
Kennedy, Jim
Liddle, Gladstone
McGuckin, Terence
Ryan, Canon Paschal

1981
Doe, Anthony
Donaghy, Michael
Johnston, Michael
r McLean, Colin
O'Boyle, Mgr Seamus
Press, Francis
Scurlock, Anthony
1982
O'Neill, Dermot
r Stewart, Michael
r Whooley, John
1983
Anwyll, Mark
Duffy, James
Paris, Anthony
Phipps, Canon Terence
Stoakes, Keith
Stokes, John
Webb, Christopher
1984
Dwyer, Canon Anthony
r Gray, John
Hayes, Mgr Martin
King, Canon Gerard
McPartlan, Mgr Paul
Quinn, Gerard
Smith, Brian
r White, John
1985
Healy, Bruno
Leathem, Michael
Letellier, Robert
McAleenan, Bishop Paul
Skehan, William
Sykes, Perry
1986
r Boland, John
Cahill, Charles
r Carter, Joseph
Curry, Mgr James
Dunkling, Reginald
Hudson, Bishop Nicholas
McLoughlin, Patrick
Mannion, Michael
1987
Davies, Canon Colin
Loring, Ulick
Sherrington, Bishop John
1988
Carroll, Sean
Conneely, Mgr John
Fernandes, Norbert
Hannigan, Neil
r Harrington, Thomas
Hutton, Timothy
Poole, Robert
Sherbrooke, Canon Alexander
r Stevens, Michael
1989
Adamson, Duncan
Booth, Michael
Middleton, Shaun
r Stevens, Peter
Thornton, Sean

1990

Andom, Ephrem
Grech, Saviour
Langham, Mgr Mark
Newby, Canon Peter
Piccolomini, Charis
Seasman, Terence
Wadsworth, Mgr Andrew
1991
Byrne, Dominic
Garvey, James
James, Howard
Lowry, Mehall
Morris, Allen
Przyjalkowski, Voytek
Scott, Peter-Michael
1992
r Dean, Timothy
Dermody, John
O'Doherty, Michael
O'Leary, Canon John
Salvans, Albert
1993
O'Connell, Andrew
Tastard, Terry
Wagay, Gideon
Whitmore, Mgr Philip
1994
Antwi-Darkwah, Francis
Campbell, David
r de Lord, Richard
Harris, Peter
Lennard, Canon Shaun
McKenna, Dominic
Welsh, John
1995
Andrew, Richard
Cullinan, Michael
Evans, David
Fairhead, Mgr Jeremy
Graham, Donald
Irwin, David
Lyness, Peter
MacKenzie, Hugh
McGuire, Derek
r Marriott, Canon Richard
Reader, Mgr Roger
Reynolds, Neil
Touw Tempelmans-Plat, Dennis F P
Tuckwell, Canon Christopher
Wilson, Bishop John
Woodruff, Mark
1996
r Burgess, Robin
Coker, Stephen
Colven, Christopher
Edgar, Timothy
Hasker, Stewart
r Klyberg, Mgr John
r Palmer, David
Willis, Stephen
Wilson, Canon Stuart
1997
Griffin, Nigel
Griffiths, Brian
Jackson, Frederick
Robinson, Alan
Silva, Christopher
Vipers, Christopher
Wilson, Peter
1998
Arnold, Paul
Baptiste, Philip
Gosnell, Nicholas
Lee, Clive,
Leenane, Mark
Parsons, Richard
r Rimini, Kenneth
Wang, Stephen
1999
Heslin, Matthew
Jordan, Kevin
Miller, Philip
Nguyen, Simon
Ritaccio, Antonio
r Sammarco, Anthony

2000

r Ablewhite, John
Everson, Simon
McDermott, Paul
O'Boy, Michael
Pham, John Hai
Taylor, Canon Roger

r Usher, Thomas

2001

Barrow, David

r Burton, Edward

Church, Shaun

r Horan, Danny

Shekelton, Peter

Trood, Jeremy

2002

Eastell, Kevin

Knights, Philip

Sarsfield, Denis

Skinner, Gerard

2003

Pachuta, Robert

Schofield, Nicholas

Vickers, Mark

2004

Braz, Cristiano

Dunne, Michael

Dyer-Perry, Philip

Master, Alexander

r Pellegrini, Anthony

Ruiz-Ortiz, F Javier

2005

Daley, Michael

Mulligan, Jim

Rouco Gutierrez, Hector

Witoń Sławomir

2006

Conesa, Agustin

McKenna, John

2007

Elliott, John D A

Nesbitt, Richard

2008

Arulananthem, Thevakingsley

Moule, Kevin

Neal, James

Reilly, David

2009

Nicol, William

2010

O'Brien, Gerard

Seaton, Stuart

2011

Bagini, Paulo

Connick, Andrew

Gallagher, Andrew

Richardson, Paul

Stokes, Graham

2012

Addison, Kim

Andreini, Lorenzo

Millico, Ivano

2013

Ardila, Oscar

Downie, Jeffrey

Pantisano, Fortunato

Pinnock, Giles

Plunkett, Martin

Steel, Jeffrey

Tate, Martin

Walker, Mark

2014

Hyett, Derek

Jaxa-Chamiec, Andrew

O'Mahony, Brian

Richards, Shaun

2015

Bowder, Bill

Burke, David

Chiaha, Cyril

Humphreys, Daniel

Lucuy Claros, David

2016

de Lisle, Christian

Montgomery, Tom

Ryan, Damian

Scott, John

Thomas, Tony

Udo, Chinedu

2017

Albornoz Bolivar, Julio

Bowden, Andrew J

Jarmulowicz, Michael

McMahon, Brian

Maguire, Michael

Okoro, Joseph

Quito, Carlos

Warnaby, John

2018

Allsop, Patrick

Alvarado Gil, Allan

Dunglinson, Mark

Herrero Peña, Daniel

Michael, Rajiv

Pineda, Antonio

Stogdon, Jonathan

Tabor, John

CLERGY OF THE DIOCESE

In alphabetical order, figures following each surname indicate year of birth and of ordination to the priesthood, a place name in brackets refers to an entry in the Parish Directory section. Unless stated otherwise, all email addresses are formed: **first name+surname@rcdow.org.uk**

ARCHBISHOP

Nichols (1945; 1969) PhL, MA, MEd, STL, His Eminence Cardinal Vincent; **Archbishop's House, Ambrosden Avenue SW1P 1QJ**

AUXILIARY BISHOPS

Hudson (1959; 1986) MA, PhB, STB, STL, Right Rev Nicholas; **Archbishop's House, Ambrosden Avenue SW1P 1QJ Tel: 020 7931 6061**
McAleenan (1951; 1985) Right Rev Paul; **Archbishop's House, Ambrosden Avenue SW1P 1QJ Tel: 020 7931 6062**
Sherrington (1958; 1987) MA, STL, Right Rev John; **Archbishop's House, Ambrosden Avenue SW1P 1QJ Tel: 020 7798 9060**
Wilson (1968; 1995) BA, STB, STL, PhD, Right Rev John; **Archbishop's House, Ambrosden Avenue SW1P 1QJ Tel: 020 7798 9043**

RETIRED BISHOP

Crowley (1941; 1965) Right Rev John; **Flat 2,, Francis Court, Caddington Road NW2 1RP Tel: 020 8452 6200 (Bishop Emeritus of Middlesborough)**

PRIESTS

Ablewhite (1943; 2000) John; **46 Tower Court, Ely CB7 4XS Tel: 01353 968056**
Adamson (1948; 1989) Duncan; **73 Pembroke Road, Ruislip HA4 8NN Tel: 01895 632739 (Ruislip)**
Addison (1975; 2012) Kim; **The Presbytery, Rant Meadow, Hemel Hempstead HP3 8PG Tel: 01442 210610 (Hemel Hempstead East and North)**
Albornoz Bolivar (1981; 2017) Julio; **Cathedral Clergy House, 42 Francis Street SW1P 1QW Tel: 020 7931 6097 (Cathedral)**
Allsop, Patrick (1952; 2018); **The Presbytery, Ballance Road E9 5SS Tel: 020 8985 1495 (Homerton)**
Alvarado Gil (1982; 2018) Allan; **39 Duncan Terrace N1 8AL Tel: 020 7226 3277 (Islington, Copenhagen Street)**
Andom (1960; 1990) STB, STL, MTh Ephrem; **The Catholic Presbytery, Commonwealth Avenue W12 7QR Tel: 020 8743 8315 (White City, Eritrean Chaplaincy)**
Andreini (1977; 2012) Lorenzo; **11 Harewood Avenue NW1 6LD (Superior, Redemptoris Mater House of Formation)**
Andrew (1953; 1995) MA, Richard; **41 Brook Green W6 7BL Tel: 020 7603 3832 (Brook Green)**
Antwi-Darkwah (1957; 1994) STB, DIP. COUNS, Francis A; **47 Vesta Avenue, St Albans AL1 2PE Tel: 01727 850066 (St Albans South)**

SECTION 4

Anwyll (1957; 1983) Mark; **1 Colney Hatch Lane N10 1PN Tel: 020 8883 5607 (Muswell Hill)**
Ardagh-Walter (1941; 1970) BA, David; **17 St Ann's Road N15 6NG**
Tel: 020 8800 8374 / 07399 881072
Ardila (1976; 2013) Oscar; **(on loan, Diocese of Plymouth)**
Arnold (1953; 1998) MA, Paul; **St Elizabeth's Centre, South End, Much Hadham SG10 6EW**
Tel: 01279 842145 (Bishop's Stortford)
Arulananthem (1973; 2008) BA, STB, MA, Thevakingsley; **17 Kenninghall Road E5 8BS**
Tel 020 8985 2178 (Clapton)
Azzopardi (1951; 1977) Frans; **Flat 3 Copper Beeches, 6 Witham Road, Isleworth TW7 4AW**
Tel: 020 8568 6581

Bagini (1980; 2011) Paulo; **St Anne's Church, Underwood Road E1 5AW**
Tel: 020 7247 7833 (Underwood Road, Brazilian Chaplaincy)
Baker (1940; 1969) Desmond; **75 Fern Road, St Leonards-on-Sea TN38 0UP**
Tel: 01424 423769 / 07986 785429
Baptiste (1971; 1998) Eugene Philip; **68 Hazlewood Crescent W10 5DJ (Kensal New Town)**
Barltrop (1947; 1976) MA, STL, Mgr Keith; **The Presbytery, Moorhouse Road W2 5DJ**
Tel: 020 7229 0487 (Bayswater)
Barnes (1944; 1976) BA, LicPsych, David; **70 Lincoln's Inn Fields WC2A 3JA**
Tel: 020 7405 0376 (Lincoln's Inn Fields)
Barrow (1963; 2001) BSc, MSc, STB, David; **8 Ogle Street W1W 6HS**
Tel: 020 7636 2883 (Ogle Street)
Barry (1945; 1976) Robert; **St Vincent's Nursing Home, Wiltshire Lane, Pinner HA5 2NB**
Baxter (1944; 1978) MA, BD, MPhil, PhD, Anthony; **The Lodge, Ware Park, Ware SG12 0DS**
Tel: 01920 487287 (Chaplain, Ware Carmel)
Berry (1937; 1962) Canon Vincent; **14 The Hyde, Weston Turville, Bucks HP22 5RP**
Tel: 01296 615976
Boland (1947; 1986) John; **Nazareth House, 162 East End Road N2 0RU (Chaplain)**
Booth (1954; 1989) STL, MFT, KHS, Michael; **Scripps Mercy Catholic Hospital, Behavioral Health Outpatient Program, 4077 Fifth Avenue, San Diego, CA 92103, USA**
Tel: 619 260 7066 Email: booth.michael@scrippshealth.org
Bowder (1946; 2015) Bill; **Parish House, 2 Tynemouth Street SW6 2QT**
Tel: 020 7736 4864 (Fulham 2 Stephendale Road)
Bowden (1971; 2017) BD, PgDL, STB, Andrew; **Cathedral Clergy House, 42 Francis Street SW1P 1QW Tel: 020 7798 9373 (Cathedral)**
Boylan (1942; 1967) Bernard; **110 Station Road, Hampton-on-Thames TW12 2AS**
Tel: 020 8979 3596 (Hampton-on-Thames)
Brady (1956; 1980) Mgr Vincent G; **54 Parkside SW19 5NE Tel: 020 8944 7189 (Nunciature)**
Braz (1974; 2004) STB, Cristiano; **52 Uxbridge Road W7 3SU (Hanwell)**
Brockie (1942; 1967) JCL, Canon Michael; **7 St Joseph's Cottages, 38 Cadogan Street SW3 2QU Tel: 020 7581 0868**
Browne (1948; 1974) Canon Patrick; **47 Cumberland Street SW1V 4LY**
Tel: 020 7834 6965 (Pimlico)

Brunning (1940; 1964) Antony; **Flat 19, St Joseph's House, 42 Brook Green W6 7BL**
Buckley (1950; 1977) John; **35 Cricklewood Lane NW2 1HR**
Tel: 020 8452 2475 (Cricklewood)
Burgess (1949; 1996) MA, Robin; **20 Willowmead Close W5 1PT Tel: 020 8998 4710**
Burke (1975; 2015) MA, STB, David; **Sacred Heart Church, Park Street, Berkhamsted HP4 1HX Tel: 01442 863845 (Berkhamsted, Tring)**
Burke (1935; 1960) Gerard T; **13 Mill Way, Feltham TW14 0JX**
Tel: 020 8582 8642 / 07919 284373
Burton (1940; 2001) AKC, Edward; **20 Wilbury Grange, Wilbury Road, Hove BN3 3GN**
Tel: 01273 774271
Byrne (1955; 1991) MA, JCD, STL, Dominic; **c/o Archbishop's House SW1P 1QJ (Sabbatical)**
Byrne (1951; 1976) John; **St Lawrence's Presbytery, The Green, Feltham TW13 4AF**
Tel: 020 8890 2367 / 07879 058732 (Feltham)

Cahill (1955; 1986) Charles; **1 King Edward's Road, Ware SG12 7EJ**
Tel: 01920 462140 (Ware)
Campbell (1955; 1994) David; **c/o Archbishop's House SW1P 1QJ**
Carroll (1933; 1975) Edward; **2 Delmer Court, Aycliffe Road, Borehamwood WD6 4HS**
Tel: 020 8236 9565
Carroll (1947;1974) Patrick; **4 Church Close, Cuffley, Herts EN6 4LS**
Tel: 01707 873308 (Cuffley)
Carroll (1956; 1988) Sean; **12 Womersley Road N8 9AE Tel: 020 8340 3394 (Stroud Green)**
Carter (1936; 1986) Joseph; **10 Stevenson Park, Lurgan, Craigavon, Co. Armagh BT67 9DR**
Chiaha (1981; 2015) BA, BPhil, MBA, BD, STB, Cyril; **3 Station Road, Buntingford SG9 9HT**
Tel: 01763 271471 (Buntingford, Old Hall Green and Puckeridge)
Church (1964; 2001) STB, BA, Shaun; **5 Park Road, Rickmansworth WD3 1HU**
Tel: 01923 773387 (Rickmansworth. Chorleywood and Mill End)
Coghlan (1934;1961) Mgr John; **c/o Archbishop's House SW1P 1QJ**
Coker (1953; 1996) Stephen P; **3 Wissen Drive, Letchworth Garden City SG6 1FT**
Tel: 07976 400954
Colven (1945; 1996) BA, Christopher G; **22 George Street W1U 3QY**
Tel: 020 7935 0943 (Spanish Place)
Conesa (1973; 2006) STB Agustin; **42 Langdale Gardens, Perivale, Greenford UB6 8DQ**
Tel: 020 8997 3164 (Perivale)
Conlon (1949; 1979) HEL, PhD, Antony; **R.C. Rectory, Ferry Lane, Goring-on-Thames RG8 9DX Tel: 01491 872181 (On loan, Archdiocese of Birmingham)**
Conneely (1956; 1988) JCL, Mgr John; **70 Lincoln's Inn Fields WC2A 3JA**
Tel: 020 7405 0376 (Lincoln's Inn Fields, Judicial Vicar, Episcopal Vicar for Eastern Catholic Churches)
Connick (1982; 2011) Andrew; **The Presbytery, Dundee Street E1W 2PH**
Tel: 020 7481 2202 (Wapping, University Chaplaincy)
Connor (1947; 1975) MA, Christopher; **165 Arlington Road NW1 7EX**
Tel: 07947 561414 (Camden Town, School Chaplain)

Convery (1947; 1971) Antony; **700 Finchley Road NW11 7NE**
Tel: 020 8455 1300 (Golders Green)
Creak (1940; 1980) MA, PhD, Brian; **79 St Charles Square W10 6EB**
Tel: 020 8968 3373 (St Charles Square, University Chaplaincy)
Crewe (1933; 1963) Hilary; **Bramley House, Half Acre, Brentford TW8 8BH**
Tel: 020 8847 4550 (Chaplain)
Crewe (1930; 1969) Vincent; **c/o Archbishop's House SW1P 1QJ**
Cronin (1952; 1977) LLM, KCHS, Canon Daniel; **72 London Road, Knebworth SG3 6HB**
Tel: 01438 813303 (Knebworth)
Cross (1936; 1974) Canon Philip; **St Anne's Home, 77 Manor Road N16 5BL**
Tel: 020 8826 2500
Crowe (1930; 1955) Bernard; **Franciscan Residential Home, 2 Broad Road, Bocking, Braintree CM7 9RS Tel: 01376 345503**
Cullinan (1957; 1995) MA, MASt, PhD, STD, Michael; **36 Chiswick Court, Moss Lane, Pinner HA5 3AP Tel: 020 8429 3349 (Director of Maryvale Higher Institute of Religious Sciences, Director of BDiv Programme, and Reader in Moral Theology, Maryvale Institute, Birmingham)**
Cunningham (1952; 1977) John; **204 High Street, Waltham Cross EN8 7DP**
Tel: 01992 623156 (Waltham Cross)
Curry (1960; 1986) KCHS, STB, Mgr James; **The Clergy House, 16 Abingdon Road W8 6AF**
Tel: 020 7937 4778 (Kensington 1)

de Lisle (1988; 2016) MA, STB, Christian; **The Presbytery, Ballance Road E9 5SS**
Tel: 020 8985 1495 (Homerton)
de Lord (1946; 1994) STB, Richard; **18 Rannoch Court, Adelaide Road, Surbiton, Surrey KT6 4TE Tel: 020 8251 2036**
Daley (1959; 2005) BA, BSc, (Hons) STB, MA, RGN, Cert.Ed, Michael; **22 Cortayne Road SW6 3QA Tel: 020 7736 1068 (Parsons Green)**
Davies (1948; 1987) Canon Colin; **4 Thirleby Road, Burnt Oak, Edgware HA8 0HQ**
Tel: 020 8959 1971 (Burnt Oak)
Davies (1935; 1974) Jeremy Ponsonby Meredyth ; **52 Castle Street, Luton LU1 3AG**
Dean (1942;1992) Timothy; **7 Hutchings Lodge, High Street, Rickmansworth WD3 1EY**
Tel 07812 248234
Deehan (1949; 1975) MA, STB, LSS, John; **4 Lady Margaret Road NW5 2XT**
Tel: 020 7485 4023 (Kentish Town)
Delany (1940; 1965) Stephen; **c/o Archbishop's House SW1P 1QJ**
Dermody (1955; 1992) BA, John P; **Priests House, Gravel Hill N3 3RJ**
Tel: 020 8346 2459 (Finchley Church End)
Doe (1950; 1981) BA, MA, STL, PhD, Anthony; **Via di Monserrato 45, 00186 Rome, Italy**
Tel: 00390 6686 8546 (Venerable English College)
Donaghy (1956; 1981) BD, PGCE, Michael; **Cathedral Clergy House, 42 Francis Street SW1P 1QW Tel: 020 7798 9048 (Cathedral)**

Downie 1970; 2013) Jeffrey; **St Luke's, 14 Sellers Grange, Orton Goldhay, Peterborough PE2 5XX Tel: 01733 370877 Email: saintlukesparish@yahoo.co.uk (on loan, Diocese of East Anglia)**

Doyle (1948; 1973) Anthony; **Paraíso de la Bahia, Bloque 10-2J, 29690, Casares Costa, Provincia de Málaga, Spain**

Doyle (1948; 1979) Michael; **Allen Hall, 28 Beaufort Street SW3 5AA Tel: 020 7349 5610 (Seminary)**

Duffy (1938; 1967) MEd, James A; **4 Merry Hill Road, Bushey WD23 1DY Tel: 020 8950 8985 / 07885 670483 Email: jimduffy@rcdow.org.uk**

Duffy (1956; 1983) James; **38 Camborne Avenue W13 9QZ Tel: 020 8567 5421 (Northfields)**

Dunglinson (1959; 2018) Mark; **41 Brook Green W6 7BL Tel: 020 7603 3832 (Brook Green)**

Dunkling (1962; 1986) Reginald; **262 Kingston Road, Teddington TW11 9JQ Tel: 020 8977 2986 (Teddington)**

Dunne (1964; 2004) BA, Michael; **247 High Road W4 4PU Tel: 020 8994 2877 (Chiswick)**

Dwyer (1952; 1984) Canon Anthony; **1 Kirkwick Avenue, Harpenden AL5 2QH Tel: 01582 712245 (Harpenden)**

Dwyer (1933; 1957) BA, MA, Peter; **31 Monks Horton Way, St Albans AL1 4HA Tel: 01727 761183**

Dyer-Perry (1976; 2004) STB, Philip; **The Presbytery, 59 Gresham Road, Staines TW18 2BD Tel: 01784 452381 (Staines)**

Eastell (1942; 2002) BA, STh, MEd, PhD, Kevin; **7 rue de la Breche, Les Verchers sur Layon, 49700 France Tel: 0033 241 599750 (Chaplain to English-speaking community in Diocese of Angers)**

Edgar (1956; 1996) MA, BD, AKC, Timothy; **4 Egerton Gardens NW4 4BA Tel: 020 8202 0560 (Hendon)**

Egan (1937; 1966) MA, MSc, Patrick; **Domino's Chapel, 24 Frank Lloyd Wright Drive, PO Box 466, Ann Arbor, Michigan 48106-0466 USA Email: fatheregan@gmail.com**

Egan (1942; 1967) BEd, Mgr Canon Thomas; **Flat 2, 90 Station Road N22 7SY Tel: 07803 891545**

Elliott (1962; 2007) John D A; **377 Mile End Road E3 4QS Tel: 020 8980 1845 (Mile End)**

Evans (1959; 1995) BSc, BTh, David; **3 King Edward's Road E9 7SF Tel: 020 8985 2496 (Hackney)**

Everson (1958; 2000) BA, Simon; **Farleigh School, Red Rice, Andover SP11 7PW Tel: 01264 710747 (Headmaster/Chaplain)**

Fairhead (1960; 1995) MA, BTh, Mgr Jeremy; **970 Harrow Road, Sudbury, Wembley HA0 2QE Tel: 020 8904 2552 (Sudbury)**

Felzmann (1939; 1969) KCHS, DD, MSc(Eng), Mgr Vladimir; **1 St Catherine's Apartments, 179a Bow Road E3 2SH Tel: 07810 116508 (Canary Wharf Chaplaincy, Catholic Chaplain for Sport)**

SECTION 4

Fernandes (1964; 1988) BD, Norbert; **141 Woodhall Lane, Welwyn Garden City AL7 3TP Tel: 01707 323234 (Welwyn Garden City Parishes)**
Ffrench (1936; 1962) Barry; **Ballymoney, Gorey, Co Wexford, Ireland**
Foley (1944; 1971) Patrick; **Church of St Helen, The Harebreaks, Watford WD2 5NJ Tel: 01923 223175 (Watford North)**
Forde (1943, 1977) Thomas; **6 Leighton Close NW5 2QY**
Fullam (1932; 1961) Seamus; **Abbeylara Road, Granard, County Longford, Ireland Tel: 0035 34366 86141 / 0035 38636 65448**

Gallagher (1981; 2011) Andrew; **Cathedral Clergy House, 42 Francis Street SW1P 1QW Tel: 020 7798 9098 (Cathedral)**
Garnett (1935; 1965) MA, PhL, Michael; **Santa Apolonia 146, Apartado 319, Cajamarca, Peru Tel: 0051 7636 3517 Email: miguelgarnett@yahoo.es (On loan)**
Garvey (1926; 1951) MA, Charles Austin; **Nazareth House, 162 East End Road N2 ORU Tel: 020 8883 1104**
Garvey (1962; 1991) James P; **84 Pixmore Way, Letchworth Garden City SG6 3TP Tel: 01462 683504 (Letchworth)**
Gawecki (1939; 1968) Christopher; **9 White Court, 200 Westhill SW15 3JB Tel: 07967 341259**
Gosnell (1958; 1998) SRN, BTh, MA(Ed), MA, Nicholas; **Administrator, St Michael and St George, The Cathedral Church of the Bishopric of the Forces, Queens Avenue, Aldershot GU11 2BY Tel: 01252 315042 (Army Chaplain)**
Graham (1952; 1995) STB, Donald; **167 West Hendon Broadway NW9 7EB Tel: 020 8202 5143 (Hendon West)**
Gray (1944; 1984) John; **11 St Mary's Close, Longridge, Preston. PR3 3NW Tel: 07739 904456**
Grech (1965; 1990) MTh, MA, Saviour; **4a Inverness Place W2 3JF Tel: 020 7229 8153 (Queensway)**
Griffin (1948; 1997) MA, BSc, Dip Th, FRSA, Nigel; **The Presbytery, St Edmund's Lane, 213 Nelson Road, Whitton TW2 7BB Tel: 020 8894 9923 (Whitton)**
Griffiths (1960; 1997) Brian; **The Presbytery, Everglade Strand NW9 5PX Tel: 020 8205 6830 (Grahame Park)**
Gullan-Steel (1943; 1980) BD, Stuart; **c/o Archbishop's House SW1P 1QJ (On loan)**

Hannigan (1947; 1988) Neil; **131 Glenarm Road E5 0NB Tel: 020 8525 1929 (Clapton Park)**
Harrington (1935; 1988) Thomas; **St Joseph's, Carrowmore Meadows 32, Knock, Co Mayo, Ireland**
Harris (1951; 1994) BEd, MTh, Peter; **St Joseph's, 3 Windhill, Bishop's Stortford CM23 2ND Tel: 01279 654063 (Bishop's Stortford)**
Hasker (1961; 1996) BA, CQSW, Stewart P; **c/o Archbishop's House SW1P 1QJ**
Hayes (1956; 1984) VG, BA, BD, KHS, Mgr Martin; **St Mary's Rectory, Draycott Terrace SW3 2BG Tel: 020 7589 5487 (Vicar General)**
Healy (1952; 1985) Bruno J; **Tan Y Cefn, Garnfadryn, Pwllheli, Gwynedd LL53 8TG (Eremitical Life)**

Helm (1936; 1962) John; **41 Parkside, Welwyn AL6 9DQ**
Tel: 01438 718524
Herrero Peña (1989; 2018) Daniel; **The Clergy House, 16 Abingdon Road W8 6AF**
Tel: 020 7937 4778 (Kensington 1)
Heslin (1960; 1999) BA, HDipEd, STB, Matthew; **160 Long Lane, Hillingdon UB10 0EH**
Tel: 01895 234577 (Hillingdon)
Horan (1934; 2001) Danny; **1 Nettleden Avenue, Wembley HA9 6DP**
Tel: 07973 913989
Humphreys (1974; 2015) Daniel; **Cathedral Clergy House, 42 Francis Street SW1P 1QW**
Tel: 020 7798 9180 (Cathedral)
Hutton (1944; 1988) TD, FCII, Timothy CR; **32 Hallowell Road, Northwood HA6 1DW**
Tel: 01923 825639 (Northwood)
Hyett (1979; 2014) BA (Hons), STB, Derek; **The Presbytery, 100a Balls Pond Road N1 4AG**
Tel: 020 7254 4378 (Kingsland)

Irwin (1944; 1995) AKC, David; **22 George Street W1U 3QY**
Tel: 020 7935 4420 / 07786 769392 (Spanish Place, Episcopal Vicar for Ethnic Chaplaincies)

Jackson (1943; 1997) BA, Frederick; **The Clergy House, 16 Abingdon Road W8 6AF**
Tel: 020 7937 4778 (Kensington 1)
James (1959;1991) MA, BSc, STB, Howard; **(On loan, West Indies)**
Jarmulowicz (1950; 2017) BSc, MB.BS, BDiv, FRCPath, KSG Michael; **Presbytery, 337 Harrow Road W9 3RB Tel: 020 7286 2170 (Harrow Road, Paddington)**
Jaxa-Chamiec (1976; 2014) Andrew; **4/5 Eldon St EC2M 7LS Tel: 020 7247 8390 (Bunhill Row, Moorfields, Hospital Chaplaincy)**
Johnston (1946; 1981) MTh, MA, BD, Dip Ed, Michael; **211 Old Marylebone Road NW1 5QT (Marylebone)**
Jordan (1968;1999) BVetMed, STB, Kevin; **Clergy House, Peter Avenue NW10 2DD**
Tel: 020 8451 4677 (Willesden Green)

Kelly (1953; 1977) David; **c/o Archbishop's House SW1P 1QJ**
Kennedy (1943; 1980) Jim; **c/o Archbishop's House SW1P 1QJ (On loan)**
Kennedy (1950; 1977) Michael; **c/o Archbishop's House SW1P 1QJ (On loan)**
King (1960; 1984) Canon Gerard; **60 Highbury Park N5 2XH**
Tel: 020 7226 0257 (Highbury)
Kirinich (1953; 1978) MA, STL, Roger; **c/o Archbishop's House SW1P 1QJ**
Klyberg (1931; 1996), Mgr Charles John; **44 Naildown Road, Hythe, Kent CT21 5TB**
Tel: 01303 239445
Knights (1960; 2002) MA, BA, PhD, Philip; **6 Melbourn Road, Royston SG8 7DB (Royston)**

Langham (1960; 1990) MA, STL, STD, Mgr Mark; **Fisher House, Guildhall Street, Cambridge CB2 3NH Tel: 01223 742192 (Cambridge University Catholic Chaplaincy)**
Law (1950; 1977) Philip; **19 Deanscroft, Knebworth SG3 6BD Tel: 01438 816444**
Leathem (1960; 1985) Michael; **c/o Archbishop's House SW1P 1QJ**

Lebasi (1946; 1975) STL, Kidane; St Joseph's House, 42 Brook Green W6 7BW
Lee (1959; 1998) Clive; 9 Henry Road N4 2LH Tel: 020 8802 9910 (Manor House)
Leenane (1964; 1998) BSc (Surv), BA, Mark; 2 Witham Road, Osterley, Isleworth TW7 4AJ Tel: 020 8560 4737 (Osterley)
Lennard (1957; 1994) Canon Shaun; 243 Mutton Lane, Potters Bar EN6 2AT Tel: 01707 654359 (Potters Bar)
Leonard (1936; 1971) Francis; 4 Basils Road, Stevenage SG1 3PX Tel: 01438 364165
Letellier (1953; 1985) MA, MLitt, PhD, SSL, STD, Robert Ignatius; 7 Parker Street, Cambridge CB1 1JL (Further Studies)
Liddle (1948; 1980) BA, Gladstone; 6 Athenaeum Road N20 9AE Tel: 020 8445 0838 (Whetstone)
Loring (1946; 1987) MA, BD, BACP, Ulick; 61 Pope's Grove, Twickenham TW1 4JZ Tel: 020 8892 4578 (Twickenham)
Lowry (1961; 1991) Mehall; 1 Stonard Road N13 4DJ Tel: 020 8886 9568 (Palmers Green)
Lucuy Claros (1975; 2015) David; 390b Northolt Road, South Harrow HA2 8EX (Harrow South and Northolt)
Lyness (1948; 1995) MA, Peter; St Edmund's College, Old Hall Green, Ware SG11 1DS Tel: 01920 821504 (Priest-in-Residence)

MacKenzie (1962; 1995) MSc, PhL, Hugh; 22 George Street W1U 3QY Tel: 020 7935 0943 Email: hughm1@aol.com (Spanish Place, Further Studies, Hospital Chaplain)
McCumiskey (1938; 1971) MA, BSc(Psy), STL, JCL, Bernard; 53 Village Court, Whitley Bay, Tyne and Wear NE26 3QA Tel: 0191 670 4858 / 07712 328218
McDermott (1970; 2000) Paul; 186 St John's Road, Boxmoor HP1 1NR Tel: 01442 391759 (Hemel Hempstead Boxmoor and West)
McDevitt (1943; 1969) Kevin; Blackwater, Enniscorthy, Co. Wexford, Ireland Tel: 0035 3539 129288
McGeoghan (1945; 1969) Seamus; St Vincent's Nursing Home, Wiltshire Lane, Eastcote, Pinner HA5 2NB
McGinn (1947; 1972) Mgr Canon Paul; 447 Victoria Road, South Ruislip HA4 0EG Tel: 020 8845 2186 (Ruislip South)
McGuckin (1950; 1980) BA, STL, MA, MLitt, BD, DD, Terence; c/o Archbishop's House SW1P 1QJ
McGuire (1967; 1995) Derek; Holy Rood House, Exchange Road, Watford WD18 0PJ Tel: 01923 224085 (Watford)
McKenna (1950;1994) Dominic; 291 Shenley Road, Borehamwood WD6 1TG Tel: 020 8953 1294 (Borehamwood & Borehamwood North)
McKenna (1966; 2006) BA, STB, MTh, John; 82 Union Street, Barnet EN5 4HZ Tel: 020 8449 3338 (Barnet)
McLean (1934; 1981) Colin; Flat 2, 165 Arlington Road NW1 7EX Tel: 020 7267 0214
McLoughlin (1947; 1986) BD, CertSp, MBTI, MA(Sp), Patrick; The Presbytery, Hardie Close NW10 0UH Tel: 020 8451 0367 (Neasden)

McMahon (1958; 2017) MSc, BA, FdA, Brian; St Joseph's Presbytery, Bedwell Crescent, Stevenage SG1 1NJ Tel: 01438 351243 (Stevenage Parishes)

McNicholas (1944; 1974) BD, MTh, James; Sacred Heart Presbytery, London Road, Bushey WD23 1BA Tel: 020 8950 2077 (Bushey and Oxhey)

McPartlan (1955; 1984) MA, STL, DPhil, Mgr Paul; Carl J Peter Professor of Systematic Theology and Ecumenism, School of Theology and Religious Studies, The Catholic University of America, Washington DC 20064 USA Tel: 001 202 319 6515 Email: mcpartlan@cua.edu

Magnier (1949; 1974) Daniel J; St Anne's Home, 77 Manor Road N16 5BL Tel: 020 8802 0362 (Chaplain)

Maguire (1978; 2017) BSc, BD, STB, PGDip, Michael; 247 High Road W4 4PU Tel: 020 8994 2877 (Chiswick)

Maher (1944; 1970) Peter; 90 Evelyn Road Dunstable Beds LU5 4NQ Tel: 01582 528178

Mallon (1940; 1975) James; Flat 2, 8 Morpeth Terrace, SW1P 1QE Tel: 07850 640179

Mannion (1952; 1986) Michael; 7 Marford Road, Wheathampstead AL4 8AY (Redbourn and Wheathampstead)

Marriott (1938; 1995) MA, Canon Richard; c/o Archbishop's House SW1P 1QJ

Master (1976; 2004) Alexander; Archbishop's House, Ambrosden Avenue SW1P 1QJ Tel: 020 7798 9041 (Private Secretary to the Cardinal Archbishop)

Matthews (1937; 1962) LTL, Canon Edward; 16 Halls Drive, Faygate, Horsham, West Sussex RH12 4QN Tel: 01293 851503

Michael (1978; 2018) Rajiv; Cathedral Clergy House, 42 Francis Street SW1P 1QW Tel: 020 7798 9055 (Cathedral)

Middleton (1962; 1989) STB, MA, Shaun; St Mary's Rectory, Draycott Terrace SW3 2BG Tel: 020 7589 5487 (Chelsea I)

Miles (1925; 1950) ProtAp, MA, Mgr Canon Frederick A; 2a Meadow Road SW8 1QH Tel: 020 7793 1338

Miller (1923; 1953) John M; 13 Highlands, 131 Oakleigh Road North N20 9HA Tel: 020 8445 8896

Miller (1966; 1999) MA, PhD, STL, Philip; The Presbytery, Esdaile Lane, Hoddesdon EN11 8DS Tel: 01992 440986 (Hoddesdon)

Millico (1972; 2012) MA, MSc, BD (Hons), STB, Ivano; 5 Amwell Street EC1R 1UL (Clerkenwell)

Montgomery (1973; 2016) B.Th, Tom; 194 Knightfield, Shoplands, Welwyn Garden City AL8 7RQ Tel: 01707 327434 (Welwyn Garden City)

Morris (1956;1991) MA, BA, BD, Allen; 243 Jockey Road, Sutton Coldfield B73 5US Tel: 0121 354 1763 (on loan, Archdiocese of Birmingham)

Moule (1954; 2008) Kevin; 22 The Crosspath, Radlett WD7 8HN Tel: 01923 635541 (Radlett and Shenley, London Colney)

Mulligan (1946; 2005) MA, BTh, James; St Paul's House, 2 Merle Avenue, Harefield UB9 6DG Tel: 01895 822365 (Harefield)

Munnelly (1949; 1973) BD, MA, Canon Michael; 1 Du Cros Drive, Stanmore HA7 4TJ Tel: 020 8954 1299 (Stanmore)

SECTION 4

Murphy (1937; 1968) Seamus; 3 Luii Na Greine, opp. St Michael's Church, Creeslough, Co. Donegal, Ireland

Neal (1962; 2008) MA, STL, James; The Presbytery, 17 Mandeville Road, Northolt UB5 5HE Tel: 080 8864 5455 (Harrow South and Northolt)
Nesbitt (1966; 2007) Richard; The Catholic Presbytery, Commonwealth Avenue, White City W12 7QR Tel 020 8743 8334 (White City)
Newby (1958; 1990) MA, PhL, Canon Peter; 130 St Margarets Road, Twickenham TW1 1RL Tel: 020 8892 3902 (St Margarets-on-Thames, Chaplain, St Mary's University)
Nguyen (1958; 1999) MA, STB, Simon Thang Duc; 117 Bow Common Lane E3 4AU Tel: 020 7987 3477 / 07920 044275 Email: Simon_hue@yahoo.co.uk (Bow Common, Vietnamese Chaplaincy)
Nicol (1952; 2009) William; Allen Hall, 28 Beaufort Street SW3 5AA (Seminary)
Noctor (1928; 1957) Seamus; Glenashling Nursing Home, Old Town Road, Celbridge, Co. Kildare, Ireland Tel: 00353 1627 2694

O'Boy (1968; 2000) BA, PhD, STB, MTh, STL, Michael; Allen Hall, 28 Beaufort Street SW3 5AA Tel: 020 7349 5608 (Seminary)
O'Boyle (1957; 1981) STL, Mgr Seamus; 39 Duncan Terrace N1 8AL Tel: 020 7226 3277 (Islington, Copenhagen Street, Episcopal Vicar for Safeguarding)
O'Brien (1948; 1972) Dip RE, Eamonn; 11 Elm Park Drive, Croom, Co. Limerick, Ireland Tel: 00353 61 397 213 / 00353 86 076 7521
O'Brien (1963; 2010) Gerard; Flat 5, 8 Morpeth Terrace SW1P 1EQ Tel: 07500 101413 (Imperial College Trust Hospitals Chaplaincy)
O'Connell (1963; 1993) Andrew; 45B Pemberton Gardens N19 5RR Email: andrewoconnell@rcdow.org.uk
O'Connor (1949; 1973) BA, Dip Rel Ed, Timothy; Abbeyville, Croom, Co Limerick, Ireland V35 AK 10
O'Doherty (1964; 1992) Michael; 216 Dollis Hill Lane NW2 6HE Tel: 020 8452 6158 (Dollis Hill)
O'Halloran (1924; 1957) MA, John; Nazareth House, 162 East End Road N2 0RU
O'Leary (1967; 1992) STB, PhL, PhD, Canon John; The Presbytery, St Mellitus Church, Tollington Park N4 3AG Tel: 020 7272 3415 (Tollington Park, Vocations Director)
O'Mahony (1978; 2014) BA (Hons), BD, STB, Brian; Via di Monserrato 45, 00186 Rome, Italy (Further Studies)
O'Neill (1959; 1982) Dermot; The Presbytery, 2a Salehurst Close, Kenton HA3 0UG Tel 020 8204 3550 (Kenton)
Okoro (1977; 2017) Joseph; Holy Rood House, Exchange Road, Watford WD18 0PJ Tel: 01923 224085 (Watford)
Overton (1941; 1973) MA, STL, BD, Mgr James; 112 Clarendon Road, Ashford TW15 2QD Tel: 01784 252230 (Ashford)

Pachuta (1977; 2003) Robert; 5 Garratt Road, Edgware HA8 9AN Tel: 020 8952 0663 (Edgware)

Palmer (1933; 1996) BA, David; **29 Manor House Way, Isleworth TW7 6BJ**
Tel: 020 8847 4632
Pantisano (1979; 2013) Fortunato; **Our Lady and St Michael Catholic Church, Crown Rise, Garston WD25 0NE Tel: 01923 673239 (Garston)**
Paris (1956; 1983) Anthony B; **The Presbytery, 4 Lord's Croft, Amesbury, Wiltshire SP4 7EP Tel: 01980 622177 (on loan, Diocese of Clifton)**
Parsons (1946; 1998) BD, MTh, MPhil, STL, DProf, AKC, Richard; **22 Boniface Walk, Harrow HA3 6PU Tel: 020 8428 3260 / 020 8864 8021 (Headstone Lane)**
Pellegrini (1940; 2004) KSG, KMCO, BA, BTh, ARCO, Anthony; **16 Elm Close, North Harrow HA2 7BT Email: asjp@btopenworld.com**
Pham (1966; 2000) STB, John Hai; **165 Arlington Road NW1 7EX**
Tel: 020 7485 2727 (Camden Town)
Phipps (1950; 1983) MA, STL, Canon Terence; **23 St John's Street, Hertford SG14 1RX**
Tel: 01992 582109 (Hertford)
Piccolomini (1955; 1990) Charis; **c/o Archbishop's House SW1P 1QJ**
Pineda (1970; 2018) STL, STB, MA, BSc, Antonio; **291 Shenley Road, Borehamwood WD6 1TG Tel: 020 8953 1294 (Borehamwood & Borehamwood North)**
Pinnock (1967; 2013) Giles; **31 Finstock Road W10 6LU**
Tel: 020 8960 0923 / 07792 971375 (Imperial College Trust Hospitals Chaplaincy)
Plourde (1944; 1975) Canon Robert; **28 Love Lane, Pinner HA5 3EX**
Tel: 020 8866 0098 (Pinner)
Plunkett (1968; 2013) Martin; **32 Field End Road, Eastcote, Pinner HA5 2QT**
Tel: 020 8866 6581(Eastcote)
Poole (1955; 1988) Robert; **PO Box 7111, Ottawa, Ontario K1L 8E2, Canada**
Power (1952; 1979) BA, BD, STL,STD, Dermot; **The Presbytery, 100a Balls Pond Road N1 4AG Tel: 020 7254 4378**
Press (1955; 1981) Francis; **32 High Street, Cranford, Hounslow TW5 9RG**
Tel: 020 8759 9136 (Cranford)
Price (1947; 1978) Richard; **The Presbytery, Moorhouse Road W2 5DJ Tel: 020 7229 0487 (Bayswater)**
Przyjalkowski (1955; 1991) BD MTh, Voytek; **St David's, Everest Road, Stanwell, Staines TW19 7EE (Stanwell)**
Psaila (1952; 1977) Anthony; **112 Carlton Avenue East, Wembley HA9 8NB**
Tel: 020 8904 6031 (Wembley 3)

Quinn (1955; 1984) BA, STL, Gerard; **44 Boston Park Road, Brentford TW8 9JF**
Tel: 020 8560 1671 (Brentford)
Quinn (1943; 1975) Thomas; **Nazareth House, 162 East End Road N2 0RU**
Quito (1990; 2017) Carlos; **St Joseph's, 3 Windhill, Bishop's Stortford CM23 2ND**
Tel: 01279 654063 (Bishop's Stortford)

Reader (1958; 1995) KHS, BA, Mgr Roger; **c/o Archbishop's House SW1P 1QJ (Awaiting appointment)**

SECTION 4

Reilly (1978; 2008) MA, David; 373 Bowes Road N11 1AA
Tel: 020 8368 1638 (New Southgate)
Reynolds (1938; 1962) Brian; 186a St John's Road, Boxmoor HP1 1NR
Tel: 01442 382118
Reynolds (1959; 1995) BEd Hons, Neil Francis; The Presbytery, Vale Lane W3 0DY
Tel: 020 8992 1308 (Acton West)
Richards (1962; 2014) BTh, Shaun; c/o Archbishop's House SW1P 1QJ (Sabbatical)
Richardson (1947; 2011) Paul; 86 Fitzalan Street SE11 6QU Tel: 020 7091 4299
Rimini (1942; 1998) MISM, AIM, Kenneth; c/o Archbishop's House SW1P 1QJ
Ritaccio (1970;1999) STB, Antonio; The Presbytery, Brentfield Road NW10 8ER
Tel: 020 8965 3313 (Stonebridge)
Robinson (1953; 1997) KHS, MA, Alan Ian P; Corpus Christi Presbytery, Maiden Lane WC2E 7NB Tel: 020 7836 4700 (Covent Garden)
Rouco Gutierrez (1972; 2005) BA, BATS, Hector; 729 High Road N17 8AG
Tel: 020 8808 3554 (Tottenham)
Rowland (1949; 1975) Mgr Phelim; 4 Holly Place NW3 6QU
Tel: 020 7435 6678 (Hampstead)
Ruiz-Ortiz (1976; 2004) STB, SSL, STD, F Javier; 177 Bow Road E3 2SG
Tel: 020 8980 3961 (Bow)
Ryan (1981; 2016) Damian; 5 Park Road, Rickmansworth WD3 1HU
Tel: 01923 773387 (Rickmansworth, Chorleywood and Mill End)
Ryan (1946; 1971) Joseph; 4 Vincent Road N15 3QH Tel: 020 8888 5518 (West Green)
Ryan (1955; 1980) Canon Paschal; 7 Cheyne Row SW3 5HS
Tel: 020 7352 0777 (Chelsea 2)

Salvans (1959; 1992) MTh, Albert; c/o Archbishop's House SW1P 1QJ (Missions)
Sammarco (1940: 1999) Anthony; Flat 1, Croft Court, Brickwall Lane, Ruislip HA4 8JT
Tel: 01895 638771
Sarsfield (1962; 2002) STB, Denis; Holy Trinity Church, London Road, Baldock SG7 6LQ
Tel: 01462 893127 (Baldock)
Sawyer (1946; 1974) Guy; 22 Roxborough Park, Harrow-on-the-Hill HA1 3BE
Tel: 020 8422 2513 (Harrow-on-the-Hill)
Schofield (1975; 2003) MA, STB, FSA, FRHistS, Nicholas; The Presbytery, Osborn Road, Uxbridge UB8 1UE Tel: 01895 233193 (Uxbridge, Archivist Tel: 020 7938 3580)
Scholes (1936; 1960) MA, Canon Bernard; 186b St John's Road, Boxmoor HP1 1NR
Tel: 01442 385118
Scott (1952; 2016) John; Cathedral Clergy House, 42 Francis Street SW1P 1QW
Tel: 020 7931 6041 (Cathedral)
Scott (1970; 1991) STB, Peter-Michael; 81 St Charles Square W10 6EB Tel: 020 8960 2609 (St Charles Square, Cardinal's Advisor for Healthcare Chaplaincy, St Joseph's Hospice Chaplain)
Scurlock (1951;1981) Anthony John; c/o Archbishop's House SW1P 1QJ

Seabrook (1947; 1976) BD, MA, John; 1 Bolton Road W4 3TE
Tel: 020 8994 6861 (Grove Park)
Seasman (1990) MA, BACP, Terence; 20 Government Row, Enfield Island Village, Enfield EN3 6JN (Ponders End)
Seaton (1975; 2010) BA, MA, Stuart; 9 Meadow View, Harrow-on-the-Hill HA1 3DN
Tel: 020 8422 1862 (Harrow-on-the-Hill, Catholic Chaplain, Harrow School)
Seeldrayers (1937; 1962) Anthony; 8 Burroughs Gardens NW4 4TY
Tel: 07811 221787
Sharp (1938; 1970) Peter; 25 Albert Street, Lytham, Lancs FY8 5EB
Tel: 01253 732524
Sharratt (1940; 1965) BA, STL, Aidan; 2 Lukin Street E1 0AA
Tel: 020 7790 5911 (Commercial Road)
Shekelton (1970; 2001) Peter; St Lawrence's Presbytery, The Green, Feltham TW13 4AF
Tel: 020 8890 2367 (Feltham)
Sherbrooke (1957; 1988) Canon Alexander; 21a Soho Square W1D 4NR
Tel: 020 7437 2010 (Soho Square)
Shewring (1941; 1976) John; 192 Nags Head Road, Enfield EN3 7AR
Tel: 020 8804 2149 (Ponders End)
Silva (1949; 1997) BSc, Christopher; 297 Westferry Road E14 3RS
Tel: 020 7987 5187 (Millwall)
Skehan (1960;1985) William; 2 Lukin Street E1 0AA
Tel: 020 7790 5911 (Commercial Road)
Skinner (1970; 2002) GRSM, LRAM, PhB, STL, FRSA, Gerard; The Presbytery, Pottery Lane W11 4NQ Tel: 020 7727 7968 (Notting Hill)
Smith (1958; 1984) SLitDip, Brian; 20 The Green, West Drayton UB7 7PJ
Tel: 01895 442777 (West Drayton)
Stanley (1935; 1960) MBE, Cedric; 1 Dunster Close, Harefield UB9 6BS
Tel: 01895 824229
Stark (1932; 1956) Prot. Ap. KCHS, Mgr Anthony G; 31 Southdown Road SW20 8QJ
Tel: 020 8947 2598
Steel (1969; 2013) BA, MDiv, Lit Cert, STB, PhD Jeffrey; 54 Lodge Road NW8 8LA
Tel: 020 7286 3214 Fax: 020 7266 5859 (St John's Wood)
Stevens (1935; 1988) Michael; 5 Layfield Road, Newcastle-upon-Tyne NE3 5AA
Tel: 01912 368101 Email: micste68@msn.com
Stevens (1931; 1989) Peter Francis; St Anne's Home, Manor Road N16 5BL
Tel: 07979 822520 Email: peter@stevens75.orangehome.co.uk
Stewart (1935; 1982) Michael; 50 Bull Stag Green, Hatfield AL9 5DE
Tel: 01707 264213
Stoakes (1958; 1983) Keith; Clergy House, 9 Pekin Street E14 6EZ
Tel: 020 7987 4523 (Poplar, Limehouse)
Stogdon (1988; 2018) Jonathan; 22 Bradley Road N22 7SZ
Tel: 020 8888 2390 (Wood Green)
Stokes (1972; 2011) Graham; 80 Imperial Close, North Harrow HA2 7LW
Tel: 020 8868 7531 (Harrow North)

SECTION 4

Stokes (1945; 1983) John; 12 Chapel Street, Newport, Isle of Wight PO30 1PY
Tel: 01983 525039 (Chaplain, HMP Isle of Wight)
Sykes (1959; 1985) Perry; 22 Bradley Road N22 7SZ Tel: 020 8888 2390 (Wood Green)

Tabor (1973; 2018) BD, John; 38 Camborne Avenue W13 9QZ
Tel: 020 8567 5421 (Northfields)
Tastard (1947; 1993) MA, PhD, Terry; 279 High Road N2 8HG
Tel: 020 8883 4234 (Finchley East)
Tate (1954; 2013) Martin; 24 Bouverie Road N16 0AJ
Tel: 020 8800 5250 (Stoke Newington)
Taylor (1957; 2000) MA, STB, MA, Canon Roger; Allen Hall, 28 Beaufort Street SW3 5AA
Tel: 020 7349 5600 (Seminary)
Thomas (1972; 2016) Tony; 970 Harrow Road, Sudbury, Wembley HA0 2QE
Tel: 020 8904 2552 (Sudbury)
Thornton (1964; 1989) Sean; Presbytery, 1 Wrentham Avenue NW10 3HT
Tel: 020 8964 4040 (Kensal Rise)
Touw Tempelmans-Plat (1949; 1995) MA, Dennis F P; 60 Rylston Road SW6 7HW
Tel: 020 7385 4040 (Fulham 1)
Trood (1961; 2001) MA, STB, MCL, JCL, ACA Jeremy; 20 Phoenix Road NW1 1TA
Tel: 020 7387 1971 (Somers Town, Chancellor)
Tuck (1939; 1963) Michael; The Rectory, Green Street, Sunbury-on-Thames TW16 6QB
Tel: 01932 783507 (Sunbury-on-Thames)
Tuckwell (1945; 1995) Canon Christopher; Cathedral Clergy House, 42 Francis Street SW1P 1QW Tel: 020 7798 9374 (Cathedral)
Turner (1941; 1966) Mgr Canon Henry; 8 Rothamsted Court, Harpenden AL5 2BZ
Tel: 01582 965207 (Ecumenical Chaplaincy at St Albans Abbey)

Udo (1982; 2016) BD, STB, Chinedu; 45 London Road, Enfield EN2 6DS
Tel: 020 8363 2569 (Enfield)
Usher (1942; 2000) BA, Thomas; c/o Archbishop's House SW1P 1QJ

Vickers (1966; 2003) BA, STB, Mark; 44 Ashchurch Grove W12 9BU
Tel: 020 8743 5196 (Shepherds Bush)
Vipers (1963; 1997) BA, Christopher J; 4/5 Eldon St EC2M 7LS Tel: 020 7247 8390 (Bunhill Row, Moorfields, Director of Agency for Evangelisation)

Wadsworth (1961; 1990) MA, GTCL, LTCL, LRAM, Mgr Andrew; ICEL Secretariat, 1100 Connecticut Avenue, NW, Suite 710, Washington DC 20036-4101, USA
(Executive Director, ICEL)
Wagay (1953; 1993) BA, MA, STB, Gideon; 62 Eden Grove N7 8EN
Tel: 020 7607 3594 (Holloway)
Wahle (1929; 1965) STL, BSc, Francis; 17 Chiltern Court, Baker Street NW1 5TD
Tel: 020 7487 5956 Email: francis@wahle.plus.com

Walker (1931; 1960) Adrian; 42 Bell Street, Maidenhead SL6 1BR
Tel: 01628 637796
Walker (1985; 2013) Mark; 20 Phoenix Road NW1 1TA
Tel: 020 7387 1971 (Somers Town, Diocesan Youth Chaplain)
Wang (1966; 1998) MA, PhL, STL, PhD, Stephen; Newman House, 111 Gower Street WC1E 6AR Tel: 020 7387 6370 (University Chaplaincy)
Ward (1937; 1961) Brian; 2 Evergreen Park, Tanderagee, Binion, Clonmany, Co Donegal, Ireland Tel: 0035 37493 78887
Warnaby (1960; 2017) MA, BD, John; 1 Stonard Road N13 4DJ
Tel: 020 8886 9568 (Palmers Green)
Watters (1947; 1972) Denis; Oaken Holt Care Home, Eynsham Road, Cumnor, Oxford OX2 9NL
Webb (1953; 1983) Christopher; 311 Norbreck Road, Thornton Cleveleys, Blackpool FY5 1PB
Tel: 01253 853535 (On loan)
Welsh (1946; 1994) John; St Raphael's House, Morrison Road, Yeading UB4 9JP
Tel: 020 8845 1919 (Yeading)
Whatling (1929; 1969) Colin; 2B Eton Avenue, Heston TW5 0HB
Tel: 020 8606 9544
White (1952; 1984) John; 32 Old Brewery Close, Aylesbury HP21 7SH
Tel: 01296 841776
Whitmore (1959; 1993) MA, DPhil, STL, Mgr Philip; Via di Monserrato 45, 00186 Rome, Italy
Tel: 00390 6686 8546 Email: philipjwhitmore@gmail.com (Venerable English College)
Whooley (1942; 1982) John; 24 The Crosspath, Radlett WD7 8HN
Wilby (1939; 1964) William; St Wilfred's Convent, 29 Tite Street SW3 4JX
Tel: 020 7351 5339 (Chaplain)
Wiley (1947; 1975) KJSJ, MA, BD, John; 185 Baldwins Lane, Croxley Green, Rickmansworth WD3 3LL Tel: 01923 231969 (Croxley Green)
Williamson (1945; 1975) STD, David; Nazareth House, 162 East End Road N2 0RU
Willis (1965; 1996) BA, Stephen A; The Presbytery, 1 Nicoll Road NW10 9AX
Tel: 020 8965 4935 (Willesden)
Wilson (1938; 1970) David; Le Figuier, 1 ter rue du Presbytère, Ambleteuse 62164, France
Tel: 03 61 87 70 52 Email: davgilwil@sfr.fr
Wilson (1965; 1997) BA, HDipEd, Peter J; 79 St Charles Square W10 6EB
Tel: 020 8969 6844 (St Charles Square)
Wilson (1947; 1996) MA, BSc, Canon Stuart M P; Allen Hall, 28 Beaufort Street SW3 5AA
Tel: 020 7349 5620 (Seminary, Spiritual Director, also Vocations Promoter)
Winter (1948; 1978) Marcus; The Lodge, 87 St Charles Square W10 6EA
Tel: 020 3673 9540 (Notting Hill Carmel Chaplain)
Witoń (1975; 2005) STB, Sławomir; 45 London Road, Enfield EN2 6DS
Tel: 020 8363 2569 (Enfield)
Woodruff (1959; 1995) BA, Mark; c/o Sainsbury Family Charitable Trusts, The Peak, 5 Wilton Road SW1V 1AP Tel: 020 7410 0330 (English Liturgy Chaplain and Co-ordinator, Ukrainian Cathedral)

Young (1932; 1957) MA, Henry; 63 Heathfield Court, Heathfield Terrace W4 4LS

Zsidi (1951; 1975) Gabriel; c/o Archbishop's House SW1P 1QJ

PERMANENT DEACONS

Abrahams (1960; 2017) Reginald; 126 Midhurst Gardens, Hillingdon UB10 9DW Tel: 01885 270989 / 07841617438 Email: rega25@virginmedia.com (Hillingdon)

Agule (1966; 2012) BSc (Acct), BA (Theol), MBA, FCA, Nick; 11 Admiralty Close, West Drayton UB7 9NG Tel: 020 8150 9222 (West Drayton and Yiewsley)

Barter (1956; 2017) Tony; 22 The Crosspath, Radlett WD7 8HN Tel: 01923 635541 (Radlett, Shenley and London Colney)

Burke (1953; 2018) MTh, BD (Hons), PGCE, NPQH, FdA, QTS, Alex; Ealing Abbey Parish Office, 2 Marchwood Crescent W5 2DX Tel: 020 8862 2162 / 07834 150480 Email: jamesalexburke1@btinternet.com (Ealing)

Clark (1945; 2008) BA, BD, LicPhil, Anthony; 6a Rodborough Road NW11 8RY Tel: 020 8455 9822 (Golders Green)

Cross (1975; 2014) FdA, BSc(Econ), MA, ACIS, Justin; 17 Cape Road, St Albans AL1 5DJ Tel: 01727 893192 Email: justincross@rcdow.org.uk (St Albans South)

Cullen (1957; 2009) MBA, BSc (Hons), Adrian; 1 King Edward's Road, Ware SG12 7EJ Tel: 01920 462140 (Ware)

Curran (1971; 2012) MA, BA (Hons), PhB, Dip Coun, Anthony; 22 The Crosspath, Radlett WD7 8HN Tel: 01923 635541 (Radlett and Shenley, London Colney)

Dyckhoff (1941; 2006) OBE, FIH, FRSPH, Neville; Holy Rood House, Exchange Road, Watford WD18 0PJ Tel: 01923 224085 (Watford)

Edwards (1965; 2014) FdA, BEng, PgDip, CEng, MIET, Ian; Ealing Abbey Parish Office, 2 Marchwood Crescent, Ealing, London W5 2DX Tel: 020 8862 2162 Email: ianedwards@rcdow.org.uk (Ealing)

Hemming (1962; 1997) BA, MA, MPhil, PhD, Laurence; 5 Westmoreland Place SW1V 4AB Tel: 020 7828 2737 Email: l.p.hemming@lancaster.ac.uk

Hopkins (1950; 2011) FD, BA (Hons), Donal; 47 Ladbrooke Drive, Potters Bar EN6 1QR Tel: 01707 855255 (Potters Bar)

Izundu (1952; 2018) BA, BSc (Hons), MSC, PhD, MRTPI, Kingsley; 38 Sach Road E5 9LJ Tel: 020 8880 0695 Email: kingsleyizundu@rcdow.org.uk (Clapton)

Joiris de Caussin (1971; 2017) Stéphane; Our Lady of Victories, 16 Abingdon Road W8 6AF Tel: 020 7937 4778 Email: sjc@live.be (Kensington I)

Khokhar (1968; 2014) FD (Telecom Engineer) Stephen; 35 Palgrave Avenue, Southall UB1 2LY (Southall)

Levett (; 2005) Robert; St George's Chapel, Heathrow Airport, Hounslow TW6 1BP Tel: 020 8745 4261 (Heathrow Airport)

Lynch (1980; 2017) BSc (Hons), MA, PGdip, PGcert (Edu), QTS, Liam; Church of St Helen, The Harebreaks, Watford WD24 6NJ Tel: 01923 223175 Email: liamlynch@rcdow.org.uk (Watford North)

MacPherson (1940; 1992) MA, DMin, KHS, Duncan; 16 Ormond Drive, Hampton TW12 2TN Tel: 020 8274 0210 Email: duncan@deaconduncan.com

Macken (1962; 2018) FD (Pastoral Ministry), Colin; c/o St Lawrence's, 9 The Green, Feltham TW13 4AF Tel: 020 8890 2367 Email: colinmacken@rcdow.org.uk (Feltham)

Nunn (1956; 2008) Gordon; Ealing Abbey Parish Office, 2 Marchwood Crescent W5 2DX Tel: 020 8862 2162 (Ealing)

Pereira (1963; 2007) BA (Hons) QTS, FCoT, Tito; Our Lady of Lourdes, 5 Berrymead Gardens W3 8AA Tel: 020 8992 2014 Email: titopereira@rcdow.org.uk (Acton)

Pickard (1945; 2009) Steve; 17 Kimberley Road, St Albans AL3 5PX Tel: 01727 863925 (St Albans)

Quinn (1972; 2017) FdA, Paul; Our Lady & St Michael, Crown Rise, Garston, Watford WD25 0NE Tel: 01923 673239 Email: paulquinn@rcdow.org.uk (Garston)

Tsegaye (1943; 2007) BA, MSc, MCILIP, Kassa; St Thomas More, 9 Henry Road N4 2LH Tel: 020 8802 9910 / 07930 416927 (Manor House)

Wright (1953; 2008) BSc, PhD, Simon; 186 St John's Road, Boxmoor HP1 1NR Tel: 01442 391759 (Hemel Hempstead Parishes)

Yates (1967; 2017), FdA, MA, MSC, PhD, Jeremy; 377 Mile End Road E3 4QS Tel: 020 8980 1845 Email: jeremyyates@rcdow.org.uk (Mile End)

DEACONS IN FORMATION FOR PRIESTHOOD IN WESTMINSTER

Amari (1980; 2015) Guido

Seery (1960; 2017) Ronald (Enfield)

Woodley (1973: 2018) Benjamin (Venerable English College, Rome)

SECTION 4

SEMINARIANS IN FORMATION FOR PRIESTHOOD IN WESTMINSTER

Allen Hall Seminary

***Redemptoris Mater* House of Formation**

Thomas Blackburn
Matteo Di Giuseppe
Julio Flores
Paolo Gambardella
José Miguel Hernandez
Jakub Joszko
David Knight
Kiril Kovatchev
Tim Mangatal
Marco Salvagnini
Robert Smialek
Axcel Soriano
Piotr Staniszewski
Francis Thomas
Pietro Trevisan

Extended Pastoral Placement & Itinerancy:
Daniel Daley
Julian Davies
Adam Dora
Michael Guthrie
William Johnstone
Marco Lazzaron
Domagoj Matokovic
Marcin Nadolski
Michael Oxenford
Michał Pastuszka
Dominic Quirke
Juan Sola Garcia

Venerable English College, Rome

Alexander Balzanella

OBITUARIES

Fr Thomas Burke RIP

Born in Cragga, Bala in County Mayo in the west of Ireland on 5 May 1923, one of six children born to John and Mary Burke, the young Thomas was educated locally until the age of 16. Having been accepted as a student for priesthood in the diocese of Westminster, he studied from 1952-4 at Campion House, Osterley before going to seminary at St Edmund's College, Ware. Before acceptance as a student, Thomas had worked in Ireland as a clerk in the New Ireland Assurance Company, and in London as a clerk with British Railways. Thoughts about offering himself for the priesthood came at a young age, but Thomas remained in Mayo due to his father's ill-health and declared his intention to apply to the diocese in 1951, at the age of 28. The Superior at Campion House commented on his assiduity at study, his zeal to help others, his devotion to prayer and to duty. Similar reports were given by the President of St Edmund's College. Fellow seminarians found Thomas to be likeable, and somewhat reserved. He was ordained to the priesthood in Westminster Cathedral on 11 June 1960 by Cardinal Godfrey.

Fr Tom served in the parish of St Thomas of Canterbury, Fulham. In 1967 illness necessitated his return to Ireland for treatment and rest. He had thoughts of offering himself for missionary work overseas, but recognised that his age and poor health were obstacles. In the winter of 1968, after a holiday in Uganda, he returned to Westminster where he served as Assistant Priest in Willesden Green and then Northfields. In 1970 he requested, and was given, permission to have time away from the diocese due to illness. His testimonial letter, written by the Vicar General, described Fr Tom as 'a hard working priest and completely worthy of any trust which may be given to him'. He returned to Ireland for treatment and rest. Life and ministry in London no longer suited Fr Tom, and the diocese recognised this and supported his need and desire to remain in Ireland, benefitting from the relative tranquility. He had his own house in Athlone, with nine acres of land, and provided supply ministry both locally and in counties Westmeath and Offaly. In 1978 Fr Tom felt well enough to return to Westminster, and he was appointed to serve as Assistant Priest in East Acton. However, soon after taking up the appointment health issues continued to cause concern and on medical advice Fr Tom returned to Ireland for weekly treatment in Dublin while living in Mayo. He was apologetic that his personal situation meant that he had to be considered as retired from ministry in Westminster, and was supported in this by Cardinal Basil Hume. The Vicar General, Mgr Ralph Brown, kept in touch with Fr Tom and ensured that his material needs were supported by Westminster. Fr Tom was grateful for the understanding and assistance given to him.

He became involved in the work of the Shrine at Knock in County Mayo, serving as a Chaplain. When Pope St John Paul II visited Knock in September 1979 to mark the centenary of the apparitions, Fr Tom was there accompanying sick pilgrims, and was pleased to meet Cardinal Hume on that occasion. He lived at St Francis, Churchfield, Knock and continued to receive support from the diocese, and visits from Westminster bishops and

SECTION 4

priests when they were in the vicinity. Over the years he became a familiar figure at the Shrine, celebrating daily Mass in the Apparition Chapel and continuing to do so until just a few months before his death. He had a devoted following among parishioners and pilgrims. He was something of an expert on the history of Knock and the surrounding area, and he persuaded Mrs (later Dame) Judy Coyne – the founder of the Knock Shrine Society in the 1930s with Liam, her husband – to write her memoirs, which she did on the understanding that they would be published only after her death. She died in 2002, aged 97, and publication as a book followed, *Providence My Guide*, a mine of information on the development of Knock Shrine and the religious culture of the west of Ireland.

Faithful to his prayers and to the daily celebration of Mass, and attentive to the needs of parishioners and pilgrims, Fr Tom's own needs necessitated admission to the Ave Maria Nursing Home in Ballyhaunis, County Mayo, where he lived in recent months before dying peacefully on 10 September at the age of 95, having served as a priest, predominantly in Ireland, for 58 years.

May he rest in peace.

Fr Richard George Dangerfield RIP

Fr George, as he was known, devoted most of his ministry to the education of young people in various Catholic secondary schools in the diocese. He touched the lives of countless numbers of young people and of teachers, too. Writing to the Cardinal in 2001, a teacher at St George's School, Maida Vale was full of praise for Fr George: 'As a Muslim, I have always found Father George to be very open, welcoming and interested in my faith, belief and way of life ... I have noticed a great difference in the spiritual life of the school since Fr George has been with us. He is an inspiration to members of all faiths at St George's.' It was because he attended to his own spiritual life, including starting the day typically before dawn for personal prayer, and his devotion to daily Mass, that he was able to nurture the life of the spirit in others.

George was born in London on 26 April 1932, the sole child of Arthur and Margaret (formerly Weldon) Dangerfield. His father was not a Catholic, whilst his mother was, but non-practising. The young George was unaware that he was a Catholic, even though he attended the local Catholic school in Brook Green. He was a bright pupil, and went on to the Salesian College in Battersea when he was 14. He embraced the faith and became a regular altar server, developing a devotion to St John Bosco. When he was 17 years of age he was confirmed by Bishop Craven at Westminster Cathedral and made it known that he wanted to be a priest. His parents were supportive of his application to the diocese as a student. At St Edmund's College, Ware he was praised by the President of the Seminary for being 'a tremendously hard worker…I doubt whether there is another student who works so hard.' Whilst hard-working, George did not excel academically and struggled with Latin. He was ordained to the priesthood at Holy Trinity, Brook Green on 27 May 1956 by Cardinal Griffin.

Fr George's first appointment was to Swiss Cottage as Assistant Priest, 1956-58. He was then appointed as Assistant Priest to Isleworth until 1964. During these years he ministered in local hospitals, and also in Nazareth House and Gumley House. His next appointment was to Stoke Newington where he remained for a few months before being appointed Assistant Priest at Burnt Oak until 1970. By 1968 Fr George had become the Diocesan Director of Pueri Cantores, boys' choirs operating out of The Annunciation Centre at Burnt Oak. This appointment involved introducing the vernacular sung liturgical texts into diocesan schools. From 1970 to 1974 Fr George continued in this role while based in Hendon, involved with various schools and working with their choirs. He continued this ministry while based at Stonebridge until 1977. He then went to live at his parents' home in Uxbridge, where he was to remain until the summer of 2017. From 1977-78 Fr George studied at St Mary's College, Strawberry Hill, gaining a Certificate of Education. From 1972-79 he taught music at St Gregory's School, Kenton. This was followed by a year at Cardinal Hinsley School in Harlesden. With the support of Cardinal Hume, and encouraged by priest-friends, Fr George went to teach at the Cardinal Wiseman Secondary School in Greenford from 1980-91. He then moved to Douay Martyrs School, Ickenham where he taught from 1991-98. He went on to teach and minster at St George's School, Maida Vale in difficult circumstances. He and the Head Teacher, Marie, Lady Stubbs, did much, with others, to improve the school. Fr George was reluctant to retire from teaching, and carried on well beyond the usual retirement age. Throughout his career as a teacher he was faithful to the Prayer of the Church, the recitation of the Rosary, and to the Mass. His preference was for the Tridentine Mass, and the life of the Church pre-Vatican II, yet he had an understanding of, and empathy with, contemporary young people.

He served as Chaplain to the Bridgettine Sisters at Iver Heath from 1989-99 and made himself available to celebrate Masses in prison in west London He was a regular celebrant of Tridentine Masses at St James, Spanish Place on Sunday mornings and regularly took part in 'A Day with Mary' on Saturdays in churches around the diocese, being also the National Director for the World Apostolate of Fatima in England. Fr George was also involved with 'Mission Together' (Holy Childhood) in 1999, but after a few months he retired from this work due to difficulties with travelling around the diocese. In February 2000 he wrote of his love of supply ministry at Spanish Place, and of his longing to return to teaching, even at the age of 68! He let the new Archbishop know that he had 'just left teaching after 30 years and await something to do … I would like to be one of the first of your priests to find out what I could do in your Archdiocese to help you'. Devoted to his mother, who died in his arms in February 2002, Fr George returned to teach at Douay Martyrs School, but by the spring of 2012 there was concern for his failing health and conversations about retirement followed. Over the years he made annual visits to Archbishop's House to apprise the Archbishops of his activities, and regularly wrote letters to express his interests and concerns.

Fr George could be somewhat temperamental, a trait noticed while he was a seminarian. Priests and teaching colleagues who worked with him learnt to cope with this and perhaps he was far more suited to teaching than to parochial ministry. When appointed to a parish in North London, Fr George met with the Parish Council. He was made aware of the desire for the members to continue to share responsibility for the administration of the parish; this was not music to his ears and he resigned, leaving within a week of his arrival. A tall and energetic man until affected by the consequences of old age, who had been described as 'sartorially elegant' in his prime and beyond, he made a deep impression on those with whom he was involved – in parish ministry, various chaplaincies, as a teacher and as a gifted musician and singer.

Fr George arranged for the diocesan Pueri Cantores to travel to the Vatican and sing for Pope St Paul VI. With his love for the papacy, he made regular visits to Rome and took part in papal audiences, with his last visit being in February this year. With carers from the Whitby Dene Care home in Ruislip, where he had been living since the summer of 2017, Fr George attended the General Audience at the end of which he met and spoke with Pope Francis, arranged by Cardinal Vincent as a gift to a priest of the diocese of 62 years who had over those years touched and influenced the lives of countless children, parents, colleagues and parishioners. He died peacefully at Whitby Dene Care home on 6 October. May he rest in peace.

Fr Michael Durand RIP

Fr Michael Durand, who died peacefully at St Wilfrid's Care Home, Tite Street SW3 on Sunday 19 August 2018, attained the age of 93 and served as a priest for 28 years. The only child of Alan and Iris Durand, he was born in Weston-Super-Mare on 13 April 1925, although much of the first part of his life was to be spent in Wales. He attended King Henry VIII Grammar School in Abergavenny, where his senior years coincided with the outbreak of the Second World War. Having gained a place at New College, Oxford, he went up for a year in 1943 to read Greats, but his education was then disrupted until 1947 by military service in the Royal Signals, where he was a Cipher Sergeant, serving in part on the North-West frontier in India. Returning to Oxford, he completed his degree in 1950 and began his teaching career, offering Latin, Music and French. A series of posts followed as he moved between three small schools run by Religious, although it seems that he may briefly have tested his vocation with the Capuchin Friars after his first few years of teaching. Spiritual influences came to bear on him not only through the schools being run by Religious, but also through contact with the Carmelite community at Dolgellau, where a teaching colleague from Llanarth Court School became a Sister, and where Fr Michael was to celebrate Mass shortly after his ordination to the priesthood. Also influential was Fr Conrad Pepler OP, for whom, with Frs Henry St John OP and Alan Cheales OP, he records his thanks. Spode House, the former Dominican Conference Centre, had both an intellectual and social life all its own, and lives on in Spode Music Week, which Michael attended in the company of George Malcolm; he remained a Patron of the Music Week to the present time.

Michael's classical education, coupled with his linguistic awareness and artistic sensitivity, therefore found much beside his studies to occupy his attention when, in 1986, he entered the Beda College in Rome for formation. Ordained to the priesthood by Cardinal Hume in Westminster Cathedral on 30 June 1990, he was appointed as full-time Chaplain to the Royal London Hospital, where he served for six and a half years, moving in 1997 to the Cathedral as a member of the College of Chaplains and also, appropriately given his background, as Chaplain to the Choir School. He maintained a theological interest in the Early Church and in the life of the Orthodox Churches whilst, on his retirement from the Cathedral in May 2000, he took up the chaplaincy at the (former) St Anne's Home. Initially this was combined with co-ordinating HIV/Aids ministry, which he knew from his time at the Royal London, but developments in treatment and in those affected led him to suggest that the work would properly be done by a younger person.

The redevelopment of St Anne's led to a return to the Cathedral in 2002, a move anticipated to be temporary, but which lasted until 2014. Here Fr Michael took his full part in the work of the Chaplains, working with the Oblates and running a weekly scripture study group. The choristers had their own reason for naming him 'Fr Speedy Priest', as his homilies were not lengthy; but they were well-considered and valued by those who heard them. Towards the end of this period his mobility became more problematic and a circuitous route had to be developed to come down from the altar to give Holy Communion. Yet his voice remained as good as ever and even after his final move to St Wilfrid's he returned to act as Cantor for Chapter Vespers.

On holiday, usually dressed in clericals, the Divine Office would be recited and colleagues cajoled into concelebration, whilst churches would be visited and stained glass examined with binoculars and explicated before a carefully researched lunch or dinner was taken, with appropriate wine. His sense of European civilisation meant that France and Italy were his chosen destinations, lands of Romance language, which therefore precluded Germany, although the music of Mozart was appreciated, and a Bach Prelude or Fugue after Mass would bring him back to the sanctuary to hear it out.

Finally diagnosed with cancer in late 2017, his decision was to return to St Wilfrid's and receive palliative care, which kept him comfortable until death.

Colleagues and friends remember a priest of faithful devotion, with wide intellectual and artistic interests, and an abiding interest in and concern for other people, upheld by a spiced sense of humour and an appreciation of a good bottle of wine.

May he rest in peace.

SECTION 4

Fr Nicholas Kavanagh RIP

Fr Nicholas Kavanagh exercised ministry in the Church of England and in the Catholic Church. Many Christians will be united in their appreciation of his ministry, characterised by gentleness, kindness and patience, and are now united in prayer for the peaceful repose of his soul following his death at St Mary's Hospital, Paddington, on 20 March, the day after his 69th birthday.

Nicholas Kavanagh was born in Wanstead, Essex on 19 March 1949, the second son of Commander Charles Kavanagh RN, a Catholic, and Constance Joanne, who was an Anglican. He was educated at Douai Abbey School, Berkshire from 1962 to 1966. He then went to study at Exeter College, Oxford for three years and in 1970 he studied at the Middle Temple in London. In 1976 he went to King's College, London for three years and then proceeded to study for Anglican ministry at Westcott House, Cambridge. His studies resulted in a Master of Arts in Jurisprudence, a Bachelor of Divinity and the Cambridge

Theology Certificate. Between 1970 and 1976 he enjoyed a variety of work experience. The first sacraments received by Nicholas were as a Catholic, baptised in the year of his birth and confirmed in 1958. However, he seems to have lost all faith as he grew up. He then rediscovered his faith when at Oxford University. He embraced 'high' Anglicanism, leading to a sense of vocation to ministry and ordination as a deacon in the Church of England in 1980 and, the following year, as a priest. He served in the parish of Christ Church, Forest Hill from 1980 to 1984 and then went to Papua New Guinea for two years to teach. He returned to London in 1986 as Curate at St Mary's, Bourne Street in the Diocese of London until 1992. He was then appointed Vicar in Brighton, East Sussex before resigning from ministry in the Church of England in September 1994. With several other Anglican priests who had resigned over issues relating to authority in the Church, Nicholas had close contact with the Diocese of Westminster, experiencing empathy and generosity. He participated in seminars and courses on Canon Law and Moral Theology at Allen Hall Seminary, Chelsea. Then on 25 March 1995 Nicholas was received as a mature Catholic by the late Fr John Formby at St Bernadette's, Hillingdon. He sought ordination as a Catholic priest, but there were complications because of his baptism as a Catholic and subsequent embrace of Anglicanism. His cause was taken up by friends and colleagues, and the late Cardinal George Basil Hume petitioned the Vatican to make an exception to allow Nicholas to proceed to ordination. On a visit to Rome in 1997 the Cardinal hand-delivered a letter to Pope Saint John Paul II, requesting the necessary dispensation. The Congregation for the Doctrine of the Faith wrote to Cardinal Hume in February 1998 to let him know that his petition, 'having received the favourable decision of the Eminent Fathers of this Congregation, in derogation of its norms, was granted by the Holy Father on 16 January 1998'. This gave permission for Nicholas to be ordained deacon, then priest for service in the Diocese of Westminster. His ordination to the Diaconate was on 19 March 1998, his birthday, at Our Lady's, St John's Wood by Bishop Patrick O'Donoghue and on 29 May 1998 he was ordained to the Priesthood at Westminster Cathedral by Cardinal Hume. Fr Nicholas was appointed to serve as Assistant Priest at St John's Wood. Before and after ordination his legal training was put to effective use in the Metropolitan Tribunal, and he was encouraged to do further studies to enhance his contribution to this work. He was accepted on a two-year course to study for a Licence in Canon Law at the Angelicum in Rome. This began in the autumn of 1999. Fr Nicholas lived at the Pontifical North American College, with accommodation at the Casa Santa Maria. However, he suffered a life-threatening heart attack in November 2000 and was rushed to hospital. After treatment he returned to London for additional care. After being discharged he devoted more time to work with the Tribunal, while giving weekend assistance at the Sacred Heart of Jesus, Holloway Road, where he was living. The hope of resuming studies in Rome was not fulfilled. In 2002 Fr Nicholas moved to live in the rectory at St James', Spanish Place. In December 2007 he had further heart surgery, but suffered a stroke. Before being admitted to hospital he wrote: 'I am informed that this is a fairly routine procedure, but a degree of apprehension is not unjustified'. Prompt medical attention, and speech therapy, enabled him to return to his work. However, he remained rather frail and somewhat nervous. His health deteriorated over recent months, and hospital visits and admissions, and rehabilitation, enabled him to return home to Spanish Place before his final hospital admission.

The regularity of work with the Westminster Tribunal gave him satisfaction and he gave colleagues much support. Good and enduring friendships were formed. He served as a Judge, having been given permission by Rome because he had not obtained the usual academic qualifications. The decisions he wrote have been praised as outstanding in their juridic reasoning. He had a sharp intellect and could get to the heart of issues and address them with clarity and precision. Many of the decisions he wrote have been used to assist students who are learning, and others who are applying, Canon Law. He was an Ecclesiastical Knight Commander of the Equestrian Order of the Holy Sepulchre of Jerusalem, founded in 1099 and reconstituted in 1847 to support the work of the Latin Patriarchate of Jerusalem and the life and work of Christians in the Holy Land. He became Prior of the Westminster Section in 2010 until 2017, when failing health necessitated retirement from this role. In November 2016 he was awarded the Silver Palm of Jerusalem in recognition of his work.

The faith Nicholas had rediscovered at Oxford remained strong and sustained him in his ministry and during his illness. Although very unwell in recent months he remained resilient, uncomplaining but realistic. He continued to work at the Tribunal, a sign of his commitment and sense of responsibility and care for those with whom he was involved. In previous times he had a strong appetite for life, enjoying poetry recitation and gaining knowledge and ideas from history, archaeology, horticulture, cooking, travel, politics and more. He had fun, enjoying good food, wine and the company of friends and colleagues. He was an excellent raconteur and had a large repertoire of quotations, used to bring depth and humour to conversations, along with his dry sense of humour. He enjoyed driving his motorbike, and did so 'with flair'. Kind and sympathetic, Fr Nicholas was essentially a private person, and a good listener who treated people kindly. While not well-suited to the rough and tumble of parish ministry, Fr Nicholas' gifts were put at the service of the parishes where he lived. As a Priest he shared his faith through the quiet witness of his life and through his preaching, with homilies carefully prepared and written out word for word and delivered with care. His crisp and insightful homilies at the early Sunday Mass at Spanish Place were much admired.

Fr Nicholas is survived by his brothers Anthony and Jeremy. His journey through life took many turns. We pray that he will reach the destination he believed in, to share the fullness of life in Heaven.

May he rest in peace.

Fr Timothy McCarthy RIP

Timothy McCarthy came from Ireland to England and then, after several years of ministry as a priest of the Diocese of Westminster, he went to Canada to continue his priestly ministry in the Archdiocese of Vancouver until his death on 6 March 2018 at the age of 82. Born on 13 August 1935 in Rosscarbery, County Cork, to Denis and Katherine McCarthy, Timothy had seven brothers and five sisters. He was educated at Lisavaird National School from the age of six and then he went to study at St Mary's College, Clonakilty, 1952-1955.

He moved to live in London where he had siblings. Here he worked in retail, but was to experience God's call to service of the diocese as a priest and was accepted as a student, sent first to Campion House, Osterley in 1960 and then to St Edmund's College, Ware in Hertfordshire from 1963–1969. He was ordained on 6 April 1969 at the church of Our Lady of Grace and St Edward, Chiswick by Cardinal John Heenan. Fr Timothy was appointed Assistant Priest at St Catherine's, Bow until 1971, when he was appointed to St Bernadette's, Hillingdon. He was then appointed to St Joseph's, Hanwell where he served from 1975–1977. Fr Tim was committed to the work of the Handicapped Children's Pilgrimage Trust, and served as Chaplain to Group 32 during the Easter Week pilgrimage to Lourdes for some five years. He was gifted at recruiting both pilgrims and nurses, many of whom remained active with HCPT for many years. In 1974 Fr Tim visited Vancouver, Canada where one of his brothers had settled, and met Archbishop James Carney, a meeting that was to change the course of his life.

With the blessing of Cardinal George Basil Hume in 1977 Fr Tim went back to Vancouver for ministry. He intended staying a few years but, as he wrote to Cardinal Vincent Nichols in November 2016: 'The years passed so quickly that retirement caught up with me, so I decided to stay … My ministry here has been most enjoyable. British Columbia is, in many ways, still missionary territory with the growth of new churches and schools'. Fr Tim's ministry was not only enjoyable for him, but very fruitful. He spent most of his priestly life in the Lower Mainland of Vancouver. He served at St Paul's, Richmond. The Parish Priest with whom he ministered said, at Fr Tim's Silver Jubilee of Ordination in 1994, that he could be compared to the lovable protagonist of a popular musical: 'his approach to people has always reminded me of Mary Poppins, "a spoonful of medicine makes the medicine go down", only with Fr Tim it was a spoonful of gentleness and kindness and patience.' He went on to serve at Corpus Christi, St Mary's (Chilliwack) and St Anthony's. He was devoted to the care of people who were unwell, and those bereaved. He had a strong sense of the presence and activity of the Holy Spirit, and he loved God's creation in all aspects. When St Anthony's was split into two parishes, the new parish of Christ the Redeemer, West Vancouver was created with Fr Tim as the founding pastor. He oversaw the completion of the church and rectory, and remained there for nearly 20 years. The present parish priest looks back on his life and work with gratitude: 'A week didn't go by that I didn't thank the Lord for Fr Tim's tremendous stewardship. When I became pastor I inherited a parish and school without debt. Jesus was a carpenter by trade who identified himself as a shepherd, and Fr Tim McCarthy was both: a builder and a pastor.' Fr Tim wrote: 'My last posting was to build a new church, rectory and school, to create a new parish. It was a wonderful experience and with the help of great people, I did not have to go to the bank for money.' After 29 years of active ministry in Vancouver, he retired in August 2006 but remained active, generously providing supply ministry, and assisting as a Chaplain with the Apostleship of the Sea.

Fr Tim's Funeral Mass took place on 12 March at the church he founded. The homily was given by Bishop Gary Gordon, Bishop of Victoria, British Columbia. As a young priest, Bishop Gary worked with Fr Tim, his pastor and mentor. They became friends. Bishop Gary recalled Fr Tim's deep faith in God's presence with his people and his great way of affirming peoples' gifts. He challenged colleagues and the faithful to be the best version of themselves, inviting people to live up to who God saw them to be. For him every activity was an opportunity to evangelise, and he did this in ways that were always gracious and respectful of others.

He will be remembered as a committed and faithful priest with artistic flair and organisational ability. He was committed to parish life and to Catholic education, and maintained links with Westminster, returning for the installation of Vincent Nichols as Archbishop of Westminster in May 2009 and for the installation of George Stack, an Auxiliary Bishop in Westminster, as Archbishop of Cardiff in June 2011. He maintained a positive attitude, and praised the clergy and people of Vancouver, a Church 'very much alive…blessed with fine priests and Religious Congregations. Vancouver is very beautiful … Thank God we have great Catholic high schools to guide our youth towards a meaningful life', he wrote in 2016. Vancouver had touched him, deeply, and he touched the hearts and minds of so many people there. He, and his legacy, will be fondly remembered. He was a priest whose life was filled with faith and vision, which he generously shared.

May he rest in peace.

Fr Patrick Joseph Sammon RIP

'A man of God and of the people' is how many relatives and friends of Fr Pat Sammon will remember him, and want others to do so. As a man of God he was faithful to the Breviary, as used by priests, religious and many of the faithful to pray through the psalms and other scriptural readings, and writings of the Fathers of the Church. Devotion to Mass and the Blessed Sacrament, and to Our Lady, with pilgrimages to holy places, especially the Holy Land and Marian Shrines including Knock, Lourdes, Fatima and Medjugorje, were an important feature of his spiritual life. As a man of the people, he loved the diversity of life in the parishes where he served. He had an interest in people from different cultures and traditions, living simply and with a love for the poor and marginalised, at home and overseas. In the face of the human person, no matter whom or where, he saw something of the face of God. Faithful to God, and welcoming, kind and understanding, Fr Pat was a man and priest connected with God and God's people. He was, for many, a link between them and God. In him people saw, and responded to, a man and priest comfortable in his relationships with God, with people and with himself. His friendships with others were characterised by an interest in them and their families, and their concerns both spiritual and temporal. He was proud of his Irish roots and heritage, whilst loving to experience other cultures through the sharing of meals, music and stories, and the wearing of exotic shirts from distant lands!

Patrick Joseph Sammon was born in Quinn, Co. Clare in the west of Ireland on 19 April 1945. Both parents died when he was young. Educated at Quinn National School and by the Christian Brothers at their college in Ennis, Co. Clare from 1959 – 64, after finishing studies at school he worked for two years in the hospitality industry and then as a wages clerk. He felt called to the priesthood and was accepted for the diocese of Westminster and sent to Campion House, Osterley, a house of studies run by the Jesuits to help prepare men for seminary education and formation. After two years he moved on to Allen Hall, initially at St Edmund's College, Ware and then to its new location in Chelsea, from 1975. Pat found the studies somewhat challenging, especially essay-writing. On days off he undertook a Pitman's typing course and benefitted from this. He gained pastoral experience through involvement with St Joseph's Hospice in Hackney and with the homeless at St Mungo's. He enjoyed reading and also the social life of the seminary. He wanted to grow a beard, but the rules of those days prevented him doing so; once a deacon, he was free to grow a beard, and had one for the rest of his life.

Pat was ordained as a deacon at Westminster Cathedral in July 1977 and spent a very happy year in the parish of Ss Sebastian and Pancras, Kingsbury Green as formation for ordination to the priesthood continued. He became much loved in the parish, and decided to be ordained there. Cardinal Hume ordained him to the priesthood on 13 May 1978. His first appointment as an Assistant Priest was to the parish of St Anthony of Padua, Edgware where he remained until 1982. He was then appointed Assistant Priest at Our Lady of Lourdes, Acton until 1984, when he was appointed Parish Priest at St John Fisher, Perivale. Fr Pat requested and was given sabbatical leave to do biblical studies in Jerusalem in 1997 and then to spend time with family and friends in Ireland. On his return to the diocese he was appointed Parish Priest at Holy Trinity and St Augustine of Canterbury, Baldock, returning in 2000 to his beloved Edgware as Parish Priest in succession to Fr Tom Kiernan who retired to live in Dublin. The parishes in which he served were welcoming and inclusive of all under his gentle pastoral leadership, with a diverse range of people actively involved in parish life and liturgy. Unknown to many, he was a volunteer with the Samaritans for many years, responding to telephone calls from people who needed to share their burdens with a good listener who was able to give support and encouragement.

Within a few years as Parish Priest at Edgware Fr Pat became burdened by poor health, necessitating reliance on kind and loyal parishioners to give him the support needed. In 2011 more serious problems relating to his health prompted his request to step down as Parish Priest, and he was appointed Chaplain at Nazareth House care home in Hammersmith. However, declining health meant that Fr Pat himself became a resident, benefitting from the care given by the Sisters and staff and the new Chaplain. If in our prayer to God we can be, at times, upset and even angry with God, then it is understandable that we can be so with God's people. Perhaps in the years when Fr Pat had to bear the cross of illness and suffering, this aspect of his humanity was seen on more occasions that he would have wanted, but people showed to him the understanding and compassion that, over the years, he had shown to others in their distress. Nazareth House is helpfully located near hospitals in west London where he needed treatment on many occasions as his health deteriorated. His final hospital admission was to St Mary's Hospital in Paddington where he died peacefully on 15 May 2018.

May he rest in peace.

Canon Digby Samuels RIP

.Very soon after the sad news of the death, on March 17, of Canon Digby was circulated to the priests and parishes across the diocese a response was received from a priest: 'The diocese has lost a saint'. Canon Digby will be remembered with gratitude by many priests, religious and lay people for helping them to grow in sanctity. To be holy is to be close to God, the source of holiness, and Digby was close to God throughout his life. He was ready to go to God as he endured physical frailty in his final weeks, cared for in St Anne's Home by the sisters, staff and the friends who visited him and sent him messages of encouragement and assurances of prayer.

Born on 8 May 1948 in Bovington, Dorset, the son of Major Frederick and Anna Maria Samuels, Canon Digby wrote: 'My mother was Catholic, my father nominal Church of England. Not surprisingly, it was my mother who taught me my prayers and introduced me to Mass, sharing her own faith with me'. The young Digby was educated at Ampleforth College. Known as 'Dig', he enjoyed his school years while also experiencing what he described as 'the turbulent years of early teens and the transition from one boarding school to another'. He had a sense of the closeness of God and a one-to-one relationship with Jesus in prayer. The influence of the Benedictine monks, and their way of life, made a deep and lasting impression. Dig wrote home regularly, giving details of his studies, sporting and social activities. In 1967 he left Ampleforth to undertake studies in law at Aberdeen University and was awarded LLB in 1970. He applied for, and was accepted as, a student for the priesthood in the diocese of Westminster. He studied at Allen Hall in Ware and at the Venerable English College, Rome. As a student he was popular and very much liked. On 17 July 1976 Digby was ordained priest by Bishop Gerald Mahon MHM at the church of Our Most Holy Redeemer and St Thomas More, Chelsea.

Fr Digby served as Assistant Priest at Muswell Hill from 1976 to 1978, when he was appointed to Hertford. In 1980 he moved to the parish of St Francis of Assisi, Notting Hill as Assistant Priest and then on to More House as Chaplain from 1983 to 1989. This was followed by a time of sabbatical leave until he went to the Shrine at Walsingham to serve as Chaplain to Pilgrims from 1990 to 1993. He then spent two years at Potters Bar, doing retreat work, before returning to Ampleforth Abbey to explore the possibility of a monastic vocation. It was discerned that this was not to be. In 1997 he was appointed Assistant Priest at St Charles Square, where he served until 1999. He was then appointed Parish Priest at St Patrick's church, Wapping. There he found stability and purpose. He grew in his knowledge and love of the East End and the people there. He appreciated their faith and spirit. He was appointed Dean of Tower Hamlets in 2001 and in January 2006 he was appointed as a Canon of the Chapter of the Metropolitan Cathedral where he became the Canon Penitentiary. In 2012 Canon Digby moved from Wapping to have a few months sabbatical leave, spent with Carmelites and then Jesuits, until January 2013 when he took up his appointment as resident Chaplain at St Anne's Home in Stoke Newington. Failing health meant retirement from that role last year. He remained in residence, continuing his ministry of spiritual direction and accompaniment and as a confessor to priests, religious, seminarians and lay people.

Canon Digby was a man and priest committed to prayer. He described prayer as a deep listening to God, to discern God's purposes. He talked openly about the spiritual life, and helped others to deepen their relationship with God. He did so with sensitivity and wisdom. While characteristically gentle, he was able quietly to challenge others, with his sincerity and goodness helping others to grow closer to God and responsive to his will for them. His outwardly cheerful and breezy disposition allowed him access to the hearts and minds of many people, as he was able to endear himself to the strong and weak alike through the immediately imparted sensation that he was in touch with the inner self of the other. He remained a 'spiritual seeker' himself, at times intensely so, and sometimes experiencing periods of darkness and desolation but remaining faithful, trusting that the light of God would continue to shine on him. Through his ministry, marked by empathy and compassion, the light of God shone into the lives of others. His friends appreciated his loyalty and his kindness, and helped him to take himself less seriously than he might have been inclined, and moments of joy and laughter will remain memorable. To his family – his sister Jacqueline and her children – Digby was an uncle first and a priest second, sharing times of recreation including playing golf and tennis and watching sport, especially rugby, and country walks. For Digby, trekking for long distances could constitute 'some of life's best experiences', he wrote. Gifts at Christmas would come from the CAFOD catalogues, helping poor people and bringing joy to the recipients. His family were proud of him and were inspired by his generosity and his ability to relate to people young and old, rich and poor, seeing the person before anything else, and seeing something of God in them. He Digby was a priest through and through, and rather ascetic, but never 'clerical'. A close priest-friend described Canon Digby as having 'the heart of a child', a person of joy and innocence. He saw everyone as a child of a loving father, the God in whom he had profound and transparent trust.

May he rest in peace.

Canon Louis Russell Thomas RIP

On 9 July 2017 Canon Louis celebrated his 100th birthday at Nazareth House, East Finchley, where he was living, He did so with Cardinal Vincent Nichols, Bishop John Sherrington, other priests and Religious and with family, friends and fellow residents. It was a happy and memorable occasion, and Canon Louis was very grateful to everyone who came and to all who sent cards and message of congratulations and good wishes. Gratitude characterised his life. He never failed to acknowledge with thanks all the kindness shown to him over the years. He responded to all who sent him cards and good wishes on his birthdays and the anniversaries of ordination as a priest, as well as at Christmas and Easter. Gratitude and courtesy, good manners and good humour marked out Canon Louis as a man and priest who enjoyed life and people.

Born in London on 9 July 1917 to Norbert and Gertrude Thomas, Louis had one sister, Joy, who predeceased him. His father was not a Catholic, but was: 'a very good man, a perfect gentleman in every sense. I respected and admired him greatly', said Canon Louis at the time of his 70th anniversary of ordination. He described his mother as: 'a good Catholic and a very good woman who was keenly interested in my well-being and that I should always try to do the right thing.' Louis and Joy attended the Rosminian Sisters' preparatory school in Ely Place. He went on to The Vale School, St John's Wood and when he left school he worked for Oxford University Press for a couple of years, an experience he found very useful. He was then accepted as a student for the priesthood and went to study at St Edmund's College in Ware. Summer holidays were spent doing farm work, 'useful public service', as seminarians were exempt from military service. Louis enjoyed his years at the seminary.

Ordained to the priesthood in Westminster Cathedral by Bishop Myers on 19 June 1943, he was appointed to St Agnes, Cricklewood as Assistant Priest until 1945 when he went to Holy Redeemer, Chelsea. He then went to St Mary's, Cadogan Street, Chelsea. His next appointment was to St Mary Moorfields. In 1960 he was appointed to St Mary and St Joseph, Poplar as Assistant Priest, followed by his appointment as Parish Priest at St Philip the Apostle, Finchley where he served from 1964 until his retirement in 1993. In 1987 Cardinal Hume appointed him to the Metropolitan Chapter as a Canon.

He was very much a 'Vatican II priest', and the teachings of the Council endorsed his style of ministry and encouraged him greatly. He saw the Church's liturgy as the context for the worship of God by priest and people together, and this overflowed into the life and work of the Church bringing the Good News to all, by priests and people praying and working together. In 2013 he said: 'I thank God every moment of my life for Vatican II and everything that it means – indeed, I would see myself as a servant of Vatican II'. He was a zealous pastor and a committed ecumenist, seeing the good in other traditions. He trusted people and his gentle manner helped to make people feel welcomed and valued, with their part to play in the life and work of the Church. His pastoral concern was manifested by regular and extensive home visiting and care for people who were bereaved, sick or disabled. He participated on courses concerned with the liturgical renewal called for by the Council, and he shared his knowledge generously. He was faithful to attendance at deanery meetings and other gatherings of priests, and this remained true while living in retirement. Canon Louis paid attention to detail, and he organised himself, and others, well. He enjoyed arranging and participating in parish social events and pilgrimages. Banneux was his favourite shrine. With humour, he spoke of 'the theology of the coach outing'! He was thoughtful and meticulous, but not obsessive.

Alongside parish ministry Canon Louis served as chaplain to several hospitals. As a member of the Council of Priests, he was invited by Cardinal Hume to join a group to plan the organisation of the diocese, based on Pastoral Areas. The plan was published as 'Planning for the Spirit', with an introduction written by Canon Louis and signed by the Cardinal. His gentle manner and warmth made him accessible and popular among priests and parishioners alike. He was also humble, preferring the title 'Father' to 'Canon' ('don't call me Canon because cannons go off with a bang!'). In retirement he took on the chaplaincy at the North London Hospice for 10 years, and he continued to attend the meetings of 'Churches Together in Finchley'. It was a sadness to him that others did not share his commitment to ecumenism.

Throughout his long life Canon Louis maintained an interest in politics and current affairs, national and international. He read the newspapers and The Tablet regularly. He enjoyed watching television, especially Question Time and Newsnight, the Proms, Songs of Praise and anything about the Royal Family. He was a keen photographer who had built up a collection from his travels. Above all, he maintained a strong priestly persona, marked by cheerfulness and gratitude, faithfulness to prayer and to the Church. He loved the diocese and the clergy, Religious and lay people that he had met and had yet to meet. When asked what was his most special day of his long life, he answered with enthusiasm: 'the day I became a priest'; and as such he served for 74 years. Canon Louis died peacefully at Nazareth House, East Finchley on 20 November 2017.

May he rest in peace.

DIOCESAN CLERGY ANNIVERSARIES

JANUARY

1	Cardinal Francis Bourne (1935) Fr Brendan Soane (2000)
2	Fr Sidney Dommersen (1970) Fr Alexander Wells (1970) Fr Cyril Wilson (1988)
3	Fr Donald Campbell (1985) Fr Denis Cantwell (1995)
4	Fr Bernard Canham (1990) Fr William Brown (2001)
6	Fr Thomas Anderson (1974) Fr Thomas McNamara (1976) Mgr Graham Leonard (2010) Mgr Ralph Brown (2014)
7	Fr John T Carberry (1988)
8	Fr John Kearsey (2004)
10	Mgr Ernest T Bassett (1990) Fr William Kahle (1993) Fr Patrick Nolan (2014)
11	Mgr Eustace Bernard (1972) Fr Mark Coningsby (2014)
12	Fr Arthur P Mintern (1993)
14	Cardinal Henry Manning (1892) Fr Peter Lyons (1998)
15	Canon James Hathway (1976) Fr Anthony Busuttil (2013)
16	Fr Edward Hinsley (1976) Canon Frederick Smyth (2007)
17	Fr Edward Dering Leicester (1977) Fr George O'Connor (1989)
18	Fr Gerry Ennis (2000) Fr Robin Whitney (2012)
19	Fr Oldrich Trnka (2003)
20	Mgr George Leonard (1993) Fr Thomas Gardner (1995) Fr Stephen Bartlett (2012)
21	Preb Ronald Pilkington (1975)
22	Cardinal William Godfrey (1963)
23	Fr Derek Jennings (1995)
25	Fr Bernard Fisher (1990)
26	Bishop Patrick Casey (1999)
29	Fr Frederick Vincent (1973)
30	Fr Joseph Fehrenbach (1985) Fr Patrick Howard (2000) Fr Philip Dayer (2005)

FEBRUARY

1	Fr Harold Gadsden (1972) Mgr Edward Dunderdale (2001)
2	Fr Charles Lowe (1978) Bishop Philip Harvey (2003) Fr James McCormick (2009)
3	Fr Hugh Bishop (1984)
6	Fr Patrick McEvoy (1974) Canon William Ward (1993) Canon Daniel Kay (2003) Fr Kenneth McCabe (2013)
7	Fr Bernard Ferry (1970) Fr George Haines (2000) Fr Michael John Groarke (2008)
9	Canon George Groves (1997)
11	Fr Alan Body (1988)
12	Fr Joseph Francis (1984) Canon Edward Armitage (1987) Mgr Canon Francis Bartlett (1992)
13	Fr Patrick O'Callaghan (1970) Mgr Canon Maurice Kelleher (1994)
15	Cardinal Nicholas Wiseman (1865) Fr Richard Wakeling (1988) Fr Leo Straub (2000) Mgr Canon Adrian Arrowsmith (2014)
16	Mgr Bernard Chapman (1999) Fr John Kirwin (2003) Canon Patrick Davies (2010)
19	Fr Ronald Aylward (2010)
20	Fr Joseph Scholles (1983)
21	Fr Michael Hollings (1997) Canon Peter Bourne (2001) Fr Cathal McGonagle (2010)
22	Deacon James Richards (2014)
23	Canon John O'Callaghan (1981)
24	Canon Thomas FitzGerald (1968) Mgr Canon Arthur Rivers (1978)
25	Fr Charles McMenemy (1976) Fr Archibald Bardney (1985) Fr Andrew Clancy (1986)
26	Fr Brian Heaney (2013)
27	Fr Nicholas Lambert (1976) Canon Michael Richards (1997) Canon Charles McGowan (2006)

	Canon Peter Moore (2006)
28	Fr Joseph Gilligan (1990)
	Fr John Taylor (2005)
29	Fr Frank Rochla (1992)
	Fr John McCoy (2012)

MARCH

6	Mgr Frederick Row (1974)
	Mgr Canon Clement Parsons (1980)
	Fr Geoffrey Webb (2014)
	Fr Timothy McCarthy (2018)
7	Fr Henry Dodd (1992)
	Fr Harold Riley (2003)
8	Fr Thomas Nobbs (1977)
9	Fr Paul Lenihan (1992)
13	Fr Patrick English (1971)
14	Bishop David Cashman (1971)
	Canon Jeremiah Galvin (1973)
	Fr Reginald Watt (1975)
15	Bishop George Craven (1967)
	Fr Walter Donovan (1981)
17	Cardinal Arthur Hinsley (1943)
	Fr Michael Buckley (1993)
	Fr Lionel Keane (1997)
	Fr Charles Connor (2005)
	Canon Digby Samuels (2018)
18	Fr John Nelson-Turner (2015)
20	Canon Desmond Swan (1995)
	Fr Edward Bushey (1996)
21	Fr James de Felice (1978)
22	Fr Edward Higgs (1988)
23	Fr Peter Day (2006)
24	Fr John Gill (1985)
	Fr Pat Heekin (2006)
25	Mgr Richard Kenefeck (1982)
27	Fr Cormac Rigby (2007)
	Fr James Brand (2013)
30	Fr William Hutchinson (1984)

APRIL

3	Fr Francis Kenney (1987)
4	Fr Peter Dunn (1974)
	Fr Robert Holmes-Walker (2010)
5	Fr Albert Parisotti (1970)
	Fr David Evans (1989)
7	Fr John Keep (2002)
9	Fr Ronald Cox (1994)
	Fr Thomas Hookham (1998)
	Fr James Wooloughan (2003)
	Fr Gerard Meaney (2010)
10	Mgr Canon John M T Barton (1977)
	Fr Brian Laycock (2004)
11	Fr John Bebb (1975)
	Bishop James O'Brien (2007)
12	Fr John Mills (1975)
	Fr Anton Cowan (2016)
13	Fr Albert Davey (1987)
14	Fr Michael Hendry (1994)
16	Fr Clement Tigar (1976)
	Mgr Canon Lancelot Long (1978)
	Fr Bernard McGuinness (1978)
17	Canon Lionel Dove (1971)
19	Fr Joseph McEntee (1978)
	Canon Harold Winstone (1987)
20	Fr Patrick Smyth (1978)
21	Canon Reginald Fuller (2011)
22	Fr Herbert Crees (1974)
	Fr Robert Tollemach (1998)
	Fr John Robson (2000)
23	Canon Frank Martin (2002)
24	Canon Clement Rochford (1978)
	Fr Derek McClughen (1991)
25	Canon Francis Hegarty (2004)
27	Fr Stanley Harrison (1973)
	Mgr John F McDonald (1992)
28	Canon John Longstaff (1986)
29	Fr Michael Moriarty (1996)

MAY

2	Fr John Farrelly (1990)
	Fr John Coughlan (1997)
	Fr Francis Finnegan (1999)
	Fr Edward Bilsborrow (2007)
4	Fr Peter Lowry (1972)
	Fr Raymond Tomalin (1996)
5	Canon Herbert Welchman (1982)

	Fr Denys Lucas (1995)
6	Fr John Hathway (1995)
	Fr Anthony Potter (2003)
7	Fr Alastair Russell (1997)
9	Fr Bernard Lagrue (1995)
10	Fr Patrick Keegan (1992)
	Mgr Canon Oliver Kelly (1995)
	Canon Denis Britt-Compton (2002)
	Fr Charles Mercer (2005)
	Fr Frederick de L'Orme (2016)
11	Fr Thomas Kean (1981)
13	Mgr Stephen Shaw (1998)
14	Fr Dominic McEwan (1969)
	Fr Peter Boshell (1993)
15	Fr William O'Brien (2004)
	Fr Patrick Sammon (2018)
20	Fr Stanislaus Savage (1975)
	Fr Michael Markey (2014)
22	Fr Ronald Richardson (1999)
	Fr Charles MacMahon (2003)
23	Fr Bernard Bussy (1992)
	Fr Hugh McAleese (1994)
	Fr Matthew Burrows (2010)
24	Fr Denis Ward (1978)
	Fr Philip Rogers (1995)
	Fr Michael Garvey (2002)
	Fr Denis Nottingham (2002)
25	Mgr Canon John Bagshawe (1971)
	Mgr Denis McGuinness (1993)
	Fr John Oldland (1995)
26	Canon Patrick J Murphy (1974)
	Fr John Murray (1995)
30	Fr Albert Purdie (1976)
31	Canon Reginald Crook (1990)
	Fr John Luke (2003)
	Fr Kevin Greene (2004)

JUNE

1	Fr Philip Carpenter (1992)
	Bishop Victor Guazzelli (2004)
2	Fr Stephen Finnegan (1993)
	Fr Damien McManus (1997)
4	Fr Joseph Rees (2007)
	Fr William McConalogue (2009)
7	Fr John O'Connell (1970)
8	Fr Harold Hamill (2016)
9	Mgr David Norris (2010)
10	Fr John Harrington (2007)
11	Fr Vincent McCarthy (1974)
	Fr Francis Davis (2003)
13	Canon Alfonso de Zulueta (1980)
14	Fr George Lee (1987)
16	Fr Michael Pinot de Moira (2013)
17	Cardinal Basil Hume OSB (1999)
18	Fr Michael Connor (2007)
19	Cardinal Herbert Vaughan (1903)
20	Fr Thomas Kiernan (2013)
21	Fr J Brian Campbell (1983)
22	Fr Anthony Turbett (2000)
26	Fr John Moran (1988)
	Mgr Canon Roderick More O'Ferrall (1991)
27	Fr Raleigh Addington, (1980)
28	Fr Cuthbert Boddy (1970)
	Canon Denis Crowley (1980)
29	Fr Richard Fitzgibbon (2006)
30	Fr Edmund R J Henry (1971)
	Fr William Anderson (1972)
	Fr Christopher Bedford (2008)

JULY

1	Mgr Anthony Howe (2011)
3	Fr William M Brown (1989)
	Fr George Ennis (2007)
4	Fr Joseph Anthony Carr (1999)
6	Fr Terence Wardle (2010)
7	Canon Alfred Cuming (1978)
	Fr Frank Morrall (1995)
	Fr John Power (2002)
8	Fr Joseph Gardner (1992)
9	Fr Christopher Pemberton (1983)
	Fr John Norton (1989)
10	Fr Peter Harris (1976)
	Fr Thomas Kelly (1983)
12	Fr Daniel Higgins (1996)
14	Mgr Canon Joseph Williams (1991)

15	Fr Christopher McKenna (2003)
16	Fr Michael Giffney (1987)
	Canon John McKenzie (1988)
17	Fr Horatio Hosford (2014)
19	Fr Peter Pearson (1971)
	Canon Peter Gilburt (2017)
21	Canon Philip Moore (1976)
	Fr Anthony O'Sullivan (1997)
	Fr Norman Kersey (1999)
	Canon Herbert Veal (2005)
22	Fr Tom Allan (2007)
26	Fr George Fonseca (1998)
	Fr David Roderick (2005)
27	Fr Graham Feint (2000)
28	Fr Ralph Gardner (1976)
	Fr Patrick Whyte (1988)
	Deacon Sydney Adams (2005)
30	Fr Calum MacLean (1982)
	Fr Vincent Commerford (1997)
31	Fr Malachy Riddle (1969)
	Fr Albert Vaughan (1995)

AUGUST

1	Fr Richard Johnson (1992)
	Fr Ignatius Tonna (1993)
2	Fr Thomas Stack (1984)
	Fr Michael Archer (2014)
3	Mgr Canon John Mostyn (1981)
5	Fr William Lynagh (1977)
	Fr Alan Fudge (2011)
6	Fr Anthony Sacré (2015)
9	Fr John Greene (1980)
11	Fr Laurence Allan (1981)
	Fr Guy Martin Heal (2009)
12	Fr Roderick Cuming (1981)
	Fr Wilfrid Soggee (1990)
	Fr John Milne (2001)
	Fr Joseph Finnegan (2002)
	Fr John D'Arcy Dutton (2013)
14	Fr Philip Dwerryhouse (1986)
15	Fr John Adam (1979)
	Fr Bernard Mortimore (1980)
16	Canon Denis O'Sullivan (1983)
	Fr Peter Latham (2005)
17	Mgr Walter Drumm (2015)
19	Canon George Davey (1986)
	Fr Leslie Cole (1997)
	Fr Michael Durand (2018)
20	Cardinal Bernard Griffin (1956)
	Fr Joseph McVeigh (1977)
	Fr Desmond Mullin (1988)
21	Fr Percival Fielden (1990)
	Fr Edward Houghton (2009)
24	Fr Patrick Cassidy (2007)
25	Fr James Gunston (1972)
	Mgr Canon Herbert Haines (2004)
	Fr Raymond Legge (2015)
	Fr Sean McWeeny (2016)
26	Fr Thomas Kilcoyne (1972)
	Fr Peter Keenan (1984)
27	Mgr John Coonan (1979)
	Fr Norman Wrigley (2015)
29	Fr Edward Fowler (1973)
	Fr Michael Lynam (1984)
31	Fr William Rees (1984)
	Canon Maurice O'Leary (1997)

SEPTEMBER

1	Cardinal Cormac Murphy-O'Connor (2017)
2	Fr Gerard Strain (1980)
3	Deacon Timothy Marsh (2013)
4	Fr John O'Neil (1971)
6	Canon Michael Roberts (2004)
7	Canon John F Marriott (1977)
10	Fr Thomas Burke (2018)
11	Fr William Erby (1974)
	Mgr Canon Cuthbert Collingwood (1980)
	Fr James Whitehead (1983)
12	Fr Leslie Wood (1984)
14	Fr William Ruhman (1978)
	Fr Leonard Collingwood (1985)
15	Fr Brian Connaughton (1979)
	Fr Robert Gates (2014)
16	Canon Nicholas Kelly (1988)

	Fr Patrick David O'Driscoll (2016)
17	Fr Frederick Thomas (1986)
	Fr John Pakenham (1987)
18	Canon John L Wright (1978)
19	Fr Alan Ashton (2014)
	Fr Patrick Lyons (2015)
20	Fr Des O'Neill (2008)
	Fr Austin Hart (2013)
21	Fr George Ingram (1992)
23	Fr Godfrey Wilson (1998)
24	Mgr Peter Anglim (2016)
26	Fr James Loughnane (1993)
	Fr Bernard Lang (2005)
	Fr Lance Joseph Boward (2011)
	Mgr Augustine Hoey (2017)
28	Fr Robert Newbery (1981)
	Fr Gerard Barry (1998)
30	Fr Michael O'Dwyer (1977)
	Fr Joseph Murray (1989)
	Fr John B Elliott (2017)

OCTOBER

2	Canon Des Sheehan (2004)
5	Fr John Fleming (1974)
	Fr Walter Meyjes (1987)
6	Fr Denis Murphy (1999)
	Fr George Dangerfield (2018)
7	Fr Thomas Daniel (1984)
	Canon Peter Phillips (2014)
8	Fr Thomas Allan (1982)
10	Fr Norman Fergusson (1986)
	Fr Arthur Moraes (2008)
11	Fr Joseph Davey (1970)
12	Fr James Finn (1977)
	Canon John P Murphy (1989)
13	Fr Norman Brown (2017)
14	Fr Henry Bryant (1972)
	Fr John Woods (2002)
	Fr Barry Carpenter (2012)
16	Mgr Canon Terence Keenan (1984)
18	Fr John Eveleigh Woodruff (1976)
	Fr John Murphy (2005)
19	Fr John Farrell (1983)
21	Fr Richard Berry (1989)
22	Fr David Cullen (1974)
	Fr Herbert Keldany (1988)
	Fr Ben Morgan (2005)
23	Fr Joseph O'Hear (1970)
	Fr Joe Gibbons (2002)
	Fr Dermot McGrath (2012)
24	Fr John Halvey (1990)
	Fr Ken Dain (2010)
25	Fr Andrew Moore (1994)
	Fr John Kearney (2007)
26	Fr John Clayton (1992)
	Fr George Talbot (2004)
27	Fr Colin Kilby (1985)
29	Canon Leo Ward (1970)
	Fr Joseph Eldridge (1993)
30	Canon William Gordon (1976)
31	Fr William Dempsey (2008)

NOVEMBER

1	Fr Horace Tennant (2000)
2	Mgr Canon George Tomlinson (1985)
	Fr Terence Brady (1989)
5	Fr Eric Chadwick (1993)
6	Fr Peter Geraerts (1980)
7	Cardinal John Carmel Heenan (1975)
	Canon Charles Carr (1985)
	Fr Raymond Geraerts (1995)
8	Fr Jeremiah Ryan (2001)
9	Fr George Barringer (1978)
	Fr James Ethrington (1981)
10	Fr Richard M Sutherland (1974)
	Fr John Spencer (1980)
11	Fr Gerald Freely (2013)
12	Fr James R Coughlan (1974)
	Fr Peter Johnson (2000)
14	Fr Maurice Ryan (1983)
	Canon Louis Marteau (2002)
15	Fr James Stephenson (1970)
16	Fr Ian Dommerson (1996)
17	Fr Samuel Steer (1996)
20	Canon Louis Thomas (2017)

22	Mgr Reginald Butcher (1976) Fr Christopher Fullerton (1980)
24	Canon Edmund Hadfield (1982)
25	Fr Joseph Doyle (1978) Canon Joseph Geraerts (1979) Fr John Galvin (2010) Fr John Formby (2015)
26	Fr James Woodward (1976) Fr William Wood (1986) Fr Anthony John Cooke (2007)
27	Fr Joseph Scally (1995) Fr Peter O'Reilly (2005)
29	Fr Christopher Hamilton-Gray (2012) Fr Brian Nash (2014)
30	Canon Arthur Welland (1978)

DECEMBER

3	Fr Harold Purney (1983)
4	Fr John Simcox (1972) Fr Peter Allen (1978) Mgr Wilfrid Purney (1987) Fr Benedict Westbrook (1989)
6	Fr John Harper-Hill (1998) Mgr Alexander Groves (1998)
11	Fr Dalton Haughey (1991)
12	Fr Laurence Kingseller (1975)
13	Fr Jeremiah Daly (1974)
14	Deacon Michael Bykar (2008)
15	Fr Francis Donovan (1983)
16	Mgr George Tancred (2002) Fr John Donlan (2006)
18	Canon Bernard George (1980)
19	Canon John Shaw (1981) Fr Edward Gwilliams (1981) Fr Edward Scanlan (1992) Fr William Campling (1996) Canon John McDonald (2016)
21	Fr Clive Godwin (1974)
23	Fr Ian Dickie (2012)
24	Fr Manoel Gomes (1989)
25	Deacon Ron Saunders (2007) Canon Charles Acton (2016)
26	Fr Alan O'Connor (1992) Fr Bernard Lavin (1999)
27	Fr Andrew Morley (1993)
28	Mgr Canon Joseph Collings (1978) Fr Gerard Mulvaney (1996)
29	Fr Robert Bradley (1976)
30	Canon Alexander Stewart (1976)
31	Fr Wilfrid Trotman (1976) Fr Stephen Rigby (1978) Fr George Swanton (1979) Fr Dennis Skelly (1996) Fr Michael Ware (1998)

OTHER PRIESTS IN THE DIOCESE

The entry in brackets following each surname indicates the diocese, order, congregation or society to which the priest belongs. A place name in brackets refers to a parish entry where further details may be found.

a.a.	Assumptionist
CCN	Chemin Neuf Community
CM	Vincentian
CMF	Claretian Missionary
CMI	Carmelite of Mary Immaculate
CP	Passionist
CS	Scalabrini Father
CSS	Stigmatine
CSSp	Spiritan
CSSR	Redemptorist
FDP	Son of Divine Providence
IC	Rosminian (Institute of Charity)
IMC	Consolata Father
LMO	Lebanese Maronite Order
MAfr	Missionary of Africa (White Father)
MHM	Mill Hill Missionary
Mccl	Comboni Missionary
MIC	Marian Father
MPS	Missionary Community of Divine Providence
MSC	Missionary of the Sacred Heart
MSFS	Fransalian
MSP	Missionary Society of St Paul
MSU	Monaci Studiti Ucraini
OAR	Augustinian Recollect
OCarm	Carmelite
ODC	Carmelite (Discalced)
OFM	Franciscan (Friar Minor)
OFMCap	Capuchin Friar
OMI	Oblate of Mary Immaculate
OP	Dominican
OSA	Augustinian
OSB	Benedictine
OSM	Servite
SAC	Pallottine
SChr	Society of Christ
SCJ	Sacred Heart Father
SDS	Salvatorian
SDV	Society of Divine Vocations
SJ	Jesuit
SM	Marist
SMA	Society of African Missions
SMM	Montfort Missionary
SSC	Columban Father
SS.CC	Sacred Hearts Congregation
SSP	Society of St Paul
SVD	Divine Word Missionary

SECTION 4

BISHOP

Lonchyna (MSU, Eparch, Titular Bishop of Bareta) Hlib; **22 Binney Street W1K 5BQ Tel 020 7629 1073 (Eparchy of the Holy Family, Ukrainian Cathedral))**

RETIRED BISHOPS

Campbell (OSA, Bishop Emeritus of Lancaster) Michael; **55 Fulham Palace Road W6 8AU (Hammersmith)**

Jabalé (OSB, Bishop Emeritus of Menevia) Mark; **14 Egerton Gardens NW4 4BA Tel: 020 3686 0096**

PRIESTS

Adayi (CSSp) Daniel; **94 Bath Road, Hounslow TW3 3EH Tel: 020 8570 1693 (Hounslow, also Chaplaincy, Heathrow Airport)**

Addison (OSM) Paul; 264 Fulham Road SW10 9EL (Fulham Road)
Ahimbisibwe (SMM) John Mary; 27 St Gabriel's Road NW2 4DS (Willesden Green)
Akoeso (OSB) Bernard M; 51 Nether Street N12 7NN (Finchley North)
Alex (OMI) Angodage Don Joseph; 30 Prescot Street E1 8BB (Tower Hill)
Alexander (Keralan Chaplaincy) Johnson; 373 Bowes Road N11 1AA
Tel 07438 182888 (New Southgate)
Anzioli (MCCJ) Angelo; 16 Dawson Place W2 4TJ (Bayswater)
Armstrong (CM) Raymond; 2 Flower Lane NW7 2JB Tel: 020 8959 1021 (Mill Hill)
Audu (Nigerian Chaplaincy) Peter Babangida; 8 King Henry's Walk N1 4PB
Tel: 07710 512244 (Kingsland)
Axelrod (CSsR) OBE, Cyril;
Azagra (Opus Dei) PhL, MEng, Dancho; Netherhall House, Nutley Terrace NW3 5SA (Swiss Cottage)
Azzi (LMO) Aziz; 6 Dobson Close NW6 4RS Tel: 020 7586 1801 (Lebanese Maronite Church)

Baczewski (SJ) Adam; 182 Walm Lane NW2 3AX Tel: 020 8452 4304 (Willesden Green)
Bansi (SDS) Fortunatus; 191 High Road, Harrow Weald HA3 5EE (Wealdstone)
Barnes (SS.CC) Kenneth; 372 Uxbridge Road W5 3LH (Acton West)
Beattie (SJ) Michael; 114 Mount Street W1K 3AH (Farm Street)
Beebwa (MAfr) Aloysius; 64 Little Ealing Lane W5 4XF (Brentford)
Bermingham (SJ) Edward; 27 High Road N15 6ND (Stamford Hill)
Bevan (OSB) Alexander; Ealing Abbey, Charlbury Grove W5 2DY (Ealing)
Biernacki (MIC) Jakub; 2 Windsor Road W5 5PD Tel: 020 8567 1746 (Polish 3)
Blaj (Iasi, Romanian Chaplaincy) Marcelin; Presbytery, 22 Hay Lane NW9 0NG (Kingsbury Green)
Blum (Cologne) Andreas; 47 Adler Street E1 1EE (German Church)
Boidin (SM) Pascal; 5 Leicester Place WC2H 7BX (French Church)
Bonelli (IMC) Carlo; 3 Salisbury Avenue N3 3AJ (Finchley Church End)
Bonnet-Eymard (SM) Hubert; 5 Leicester Place WC2H 7BX (French Church)
Borovsky (Slovak & Czech Chaplaincy) Tibor; 22 Cortayne Road SW6 3QA (Parsons Green)
Bossy (SJ) Michael; 27 High Road N15 6ND (Stamford Hill)
Bowen (Oratorian) George; The Oratory, Brompton Road SW7 2RP (Oratory)
Bristow (Opus Dei) MA, STD, Peter; 8 Orme Court W2 4RL (Queensway)
Brunet (CCN) Christophe; 29 Bramley Road N14 4HE (Cockfosters)
Buba Leszek; 2 Devonia Road N1 8JJ Tel: 020 7226 9944 (Polish 1)
Burns (OSB) BA, STB, Peter; Ealing Abbey, Charlbury Grove W5 2DY (Ealing)
Burrows (Plymouth) Peter; White House, Watford Road, Northwood HA6 3PW (Northwood)
Byron (SJ) Timothy; Copleston House, 221 Goldhurst Terrace NW6 3EP (Kilburn)

Calcutt (MAfr) Richard; 64 Little Ealing Lane W5 4XF (Brentford)

Cameron-Mowat (SJ) Andrew; **27 High Road N15 6ND (Stamford Hill)**
Camilleri (OFM, Maltese Chaplaincy) Victor; **47 Adler Street E1 1EE Tel: 07930 198251 Email: camilleri_victor@hotmail.com (German Church)**
Carmody (SJ) Brendan; **114 Mount Street W1K 3AH (Farm Street, Tyburn Convent)**
Chaim Krzysztof; **Holy Family of Nazareth Convent, 52 London Road, Enfield EN2 6EN Tel: 07902 432343 (Enfield)**
Chamakala John (Syro-Malabar Eparchy of Great Britain) Sebastian; **165 Arlington Road NW1 7EX (Camden Town)**
Chantry (MHM) Anthony; **23 Eccleston Square SW1V 1NU (Pimlico)**
Chillman (OSB) BEd, Gregory; **Ealing Abbey, Charlbury Grove W5 2DY (Ealing)**
Chinery (Ordinariate) Simon; **19 Broadcroft, Hemel Hempstead HP2 5YX Tel: 01442 387195 Email: simon.chinery@ordinariate.org.uk (Hemel Hempstead North)**
Choi (OSA) Jacob; **55 Fulham Palace Road W6 8AU (Hammersmith)**
Choma Very Rev Andrew B; **22 Binney Street W1K 5BQ Tel: 020 7629 1073 (Ukrainian Cathedral)**
Ciebien Krzysztof; **2 Devonia Road N1 8JJ Tel: 020 7704 7662 (Polish 1)**
Clarke (OCD) Christopher; **41 Kensington Church Street W8 4BB (Kensington 2)**
Clifford (OSA) Barry; **19 Hoxton Square N1 6NT (Hoxton)**
Cooper (OSB) Vincent; **Ealing Abbey, Charlbury Grove W5 2DY (Ealing)**
Creighton-Jobe (Oratorian) Ronald; **The Oratory, Brompton Road SW7 2RP (Oratory)**
Crotty (SS.CC) Fintan; **5 Berrymead Gardens W3 8AA (Acton)**
Csicsó (Pecs) János; **62 Little Ealing Lane W5 4EA (Brentford)**
Cullen (CP) Timothy; **Nazareth House, East End Road N2 0RU (East Finchley)**
Cummins (MAfr) Joseph; **64 Little Ealing Lane W5 4XF (Brentford)**
Cummins (MAfr) Thomas; **64 Little Ealing Lane W5 4XF (Brentford)**
Curci (MCCJ) Carmine; **16 Dawson Place W2 4TJ (Bayswater)**
Cussen (SMA) Anthony; **White House, Watford Road, Northwood HA6 3PW (Northwood)**

Dabre (OSA) Gladson; **55 Fulham Palace Road W6 8AU (Hammersmith)**
Dako (Chaldean Catholic Chaplaincy) Nadheer; **38 Cavendish Avenue W13 0JQ (Northfields)**
Daly (SAC) Thomas; **358 Greenford Road, Greenford UB6 9AN (Greenford)**
Dampson (SMA) Anthony; **White House, Watford Road, Northwood HA6 3PW (Northwood)**
Deidun (IC) Tom; **14 Ely Place EC1N 6RY (Ely Place)**
De Caro (SAC) Giuseppe; **4 Back Hill, Clerkenwell Road EC1R 5EN (Italian Church)**
De Marchi (MCCJ) Benito; **16 Dawson Place W2 4TJ (Bayswater)**
Devereux (OMI) Thomas; **New Priory, Quex Road NW6 4PS (Kilburn)**
Diaper (Opus Dei) MA, JCD, Paul; **Presbytery, Maresfield Gardens NW3 5SU (Swiss Cottage)**
Dilke (Oratorian) Charles; **The Oratory, Brompton Road SW7 2RP (Oratory)**
Dillon (OMI) Paschal; **237 Goldhurst Terrace NW6 3EP (Kilburn)**

Diouf (SM) Damien; 5 Leicester Place WC2H 7BX (French Church)
Doherty (SDS) Michael; 9 Breakspear, Stevenage SG2 9SQ
Tel: 01438 352182 (Stevenage Parishes)
Doherty (CP) Tiernan; St Joseph's Retreat, Highgate Hill N19 5NE (Highgate)
Donaghy (OSA) George; 19 Hoxton Square N1 6NT (Hoxton)
Donnelly (SVD) Eamonn; 8 Teignmouth Road NW2 4HN (Willesden Green)
Doyle (Oratorian) Patrick; The Oratory SW7 2RP (Oratory)
Duffy (SM) Kevin; 5 Leicester Place WC2H 7BX (French Church) *from Jan 2019*
Dunn (OP) Michael; St Dominic's Priory, Southampton Road NW5 4LB (Haverstock Hill)

Edgar (OP) Leo; St Dominic's Priory, Southampton Road NW5 4LB (Haverstock Hill)
Egboo (Nigerian Chaplaincy) Peter Tochukwu; 8 King Henry's Walk N1 4PB
Tel: 07440 653821 (Kingsland)
Elias (SJ) Harold 2 Chandler Street E1W 2QT (Wapping)
Elliott-Smith (Ordinariate) MA, DipRAM, GRSM, LRAM, Mark; 165 Arlington Road NW1 7EX
Tel: 020 7485 2727 / 07815 320761 Email: markelliottsmith@rcdow.org.uk (Warwick Street)
Escoto (SVD) Albert; 8 Teignmouth Road NW2 4HN (Willesden Green)
Ezechukwu (OCD) Alexander; 41 Kensington Church Street W8 4BB (Kensington 2)

Fasakin (CSSp) James Ademola; 63 Somerset Road, New Barnet EN5 1RF (New Barnet)
Fernando (OMI) Lylie; New Priory, Quex Road NW6 4PS (Kilburn)
Fitzgerald (CP) Patrick; St Joseph's Retreat, Highgate Hill N19 5NE (Highgate)
Fitzharris (SVD) Kieran; 8 Teignmouth Road NW2 4HN (Willesden Green)
Flynn (SMM) Kieran; 27 St Gabriel's Road NW2 4DS (Willesden Green)
Fordham (Oratorian) John; The Oratory, Brompton Road SW7 2RP (Oratory)
Frances (OAR) Jose; 18 Cheniston Gardens W8 6TQ (Kensington 1)
Fulco (SAC) Andrea; 4 Back Hill, Clerkenwell Road EC1R 5EN (Italian Church)

Gallagher (SJ) Peter; Copleston House, 221 Goldhurst Terrace NW6 3EP (Kilburn)
Gałuszka Marek; Priests House, Gravel Hill N3 3RJ Tel: 07523 545493 (Finchley Church End)
Ganeri (OP) Martin St Dominic's Priory, Southampton Road NW5 4LB (Haverstock Hill)
Gerrard (MAfr) John; 15 Corfton Road W5 2HP (Ealing)
Gomes (MPS, Brazilian Chaplaincy) Jose Flavio; St Anne's Church, Underwood Road E1 5AW Tel: 020 7247 7833 (Underwood Road)
Gorham (OSB) STB, Timothy; Ealing Abbey, Charlbury Grove W5 2DY (Ealing)
Gowkielewicz (MIC) Andrzej; 1 Courtfield Gardens W13 0EY (Ealing)
Graham (OSA) Paul; 19 Hoxton Square N1 6NT (Hoxton)
Griffin (Ordinariate) Alan; 24 Cinnamon Street E1W 3NJ
Tel: 020 7265 1851 Email: a.h.f.griffin@gmail.com
Gucevicius (Vilnius) Petras; 21 The Oval, Hackney Road E2 9DT Tel: 020 7739 8735 (Lithuanian Church)
Gumienny (MIC) Wiktor; 2 Windsor Road W5 5PD Tel: 020 8567 1746 (Polish 3)

Halman (FDP) Henryk; 25 Lower Teddington Road, Hampton Wick KT1 4HB (Teddington)
Hannon (MAfr) Matthew; 64 Little Ealing Lane W5 4XF (Brentford)
Harries (OP) BSc, BD, Peter; St Dominic's Priory, Southampton Road NW5 4LB (Haverstock Hill)
Harris (SDS) Paul; 191 High Road, Harrow Weald HA3 5EE (Wealdstone)
Hassan (OSA) Gabriel; 19 Hoxton Square N1 6NT (Hoxton)
Hayward (Opus Dei) LLB, JCD, Paul; 4 Orme Court W2 4RL (Queensway)
Heap (MAfr) Michael; 15 Corfton Road W5 2HP (Ealing)
Hemer (MHM) John; 28 Beaufort Street SW3 5AA Tel: 020 7349 5618 (Seminary)
Hewitt Stephen; St Joseph's, Oxhey Drive, South Oxhey, Watford WD19 7SW Tel: 020 8428 2774 (Carpenders Park)
Hnylycia (Opus Dei) BSc, PGCE, Stefan; The Presbytery, Maresfield Gardens NW3 5SU (Swiss Cottage)
Holman (SJ) Michael; Copleston House, 221 Goldhurst Terrace NW6 3EP (Kilburn)
Homer (Ordinariate, School Chaplain) Antony; Email: antonyhomer@rcdow.org.uk
Howard (SJ) Damian; 114 Mount Street W1K 3AH (Farm Street)
Hughes (OSB) Andrew; Ealing Abbey, Charlbury Grove W5 2DY (Ealing)
Hume (SJ) Patrick; 114 Mount Street W1K 3AH (Farm Street)

Igbe (CSSp) Terkura; 63 Somerset Road, New Barnet EN5 1RF (New Barnet, School Chaplain)
Ikwuka (CSSp) Ugo; 15 St John's Villas N19 3EE Tel: 020 7272 8195 (Archway)

James (SDV) Vipin; 15 The Green, Heston Road, Heston TW5 0RL (Heston)
Januszkiewicz Canon Jerzy; Tel: 07899 992648 (Retired)
Johnson (Focolare Movement) Francis Thomas; 138 Parkway, Welwyn Garden City AL8 6HP Tel: 01707 339242 (Welwyn Garden City)
Jones Bryan; 377 Mile End Road E3 4QS Tel: 020 8980 1845 (Mile End)
Joseph (Quilon) Sebastian; 73 Pembroke Road, Ruislip HA4 8NN Tel: 01895 632739 (Ruislip)

Kaduthanam (CMI) Joseph; St Joseph's Presbytery, 339 High Road, Wembley HA9 6AG (Wembley 1)
Kasereka (a.a.) Justin; Assumption Priory, Victoria Park Square E2 9PB (Bethnal Green)
Katsuva Kasine (a.a.) Euloge; 16 Nightingale Road, Hitchin SG5 1QS (Hitchin)
Katthula (CMF) Joseph (from Dec 2018); Botwell House, Botwell Lane, Hayes UB3 2AB (Hayes)
Kattiyangal (Knanaya Chaplaincy) Mathew; The Presbytery, Esdaile Lane, Hoddesdon EN11 8DS Tel: 01992 440986 (Hoddesdon)
Keane (SDS) Noel; Salvatorian Community House, 189 High Street, Wealdstone, Harrow HA3 5DY (Wealdstone)
Keeley (Lancaster) Stewart; Presbytery, 22 Hay Lane NW9 0NG Tel: 020 8204 2834 (Kingsbury Green)

Keenan (OP) Oliver; St Dominic's Priory, Southampton Road NW5 4LB (Haverstock Hill)
Kelly (CP) Christopher; Nazareth House, East End Road N2 0RU (East Finchley)
Kelly (MAfr) Peter; 64 Little Ealing Lane W5 4XF (Brentford)
Kołodziej Bogdan; 2 Devonia Road N1 8JJ Tel: 020 7226 9944 (Polish 1)
Koloth (CP) George; St Joseph's Retreat, Highgate Hill N19 5NE (Highgate)
Konopinski (SJ) Mateusz; St Ignatius Church, 27 High Road N15 6ND (Stamford Hill)
Kouevi Adjétey (MCCJ) Louis Mawoulolo; 16 Dawson Place W2 4TJ (Bayswater)
Kozak (MIC) Michał; 2 Windsor Road W5 5PD Tel: 020 8567 1746 (Polish 3)
Kraiczyi (OSBM) Irineu; 22 Binney Street W1K 5BQ Tel: 020 7629 1534 / 07772 111963 (Ukrainian Cathedral)
Krzyskow (SVD) Krzysztof; 8 Teignmouth Road NW2 4HN (Willesden Green)
Kukla Mgr Tadeusz; 120A Fairway, Northolt UB5 4SW Tel: 07976 728716 Web: www.dalondon.org.uk

Lambert (a.a.) Michael; 16 Nightingale Road, Hitchin SG5 1QS (Hitchin)
Lang (Oratorian) Michael; The Oratory, Brompton Road SW7 2RP (Oratory)
Large (Oratorian) Julian; The Oratory, Brompton Road SW7 2RP (Oratory)
Laverty (SS.CC) Derek; 372 Uxbridge Road W5 3LH (Acton West)
Leachman (OSB) James; Ealing Abbey, Charlbury Grove W5 2DY (Ealing)
Leggett (MAfr) Raymond; 15 Corfton Road W5 2HP (Ealing)
Lesniak(SJ) Bogdan; 27 High Road N15 6ND (Stamford Hill)
Leszczyk (MIC) Grzegorz; 2 Windsor Road W5 5PD Tel: 020 8567 1746 (Polish 3)
Lew (OP) Lawrence; St Dominic's Priory, Southampton Road NW5 4LB (Haverstock Hill)
Liang (Jianxi, Chinese Chaplaincy) Joseph; Assumption Priory, Victoria Park Square E2 9PB Tel: 07753 471611 (Bethnal Green)
Lobo Ratu (SVD) Nicodemus; 8 Teignmouth Road NW2 4HN (Willesden Green)
Loewenstein (OP) Rudolf; St Dominic's Priory, Southampton Road NW5 4LB (Haverstock Hill)
Lodge (CP) Benedict; St Joseph's Retreat, Highgate Hill N19 5NE (Highgate)
Longo Francischini (MPS, Brazilian Chaplaincy) Patrick; St Anne's Church, Underwood Road E1 5AW Tel: 020 7247 7833 (Underwood Road)
Luoga (SDS) Christopher; The Presbytery, 96 The Crescent, Abbots Langley, Watford WD5 0DS (Abbots Langley, Chipperfield)
Lynch (SAC) Eugene; 358 Greenford Road, Greenford UB6 9AN (Greenford)

McAneny (SS.CC) Christopher; 372 Uxbridge Road W5 3LH (Acton East)
McCambridge (OSB) Ambrose; Ealing Abbey, Charlbury Grove W5 2DY (Ealing)
McCarthy (SVD) John; 8 Teignmouth Road NW2 4HN (Willesden Green)
McCaul (SMA) Dermot; White House, Watford Road, Northwood HA6 3PW (Northwood)
McClorry (SJ) Brian; 2 Chandler Street E1W 2QT (Wapping)
McCormick (OCD) Fabian; 41 Kensington Church Street W8 4BB (Kensington 2)

McCullagh (CM) Michael; 2 Flower Lane NW7 2JB (Mill Hill)
McDade (SJ) Pedro; Copleston House, 221 Goldhurst Terrace NW6 3EP (Kilburn)
McFadden (OMI) John; New Priory, Quex Road NW6 4PS (Kilburn, University Chaplaincy)
McFlynn (Irish Chaplaincy) Gerry; Tel: 020 7482 5528 (Kentish Town)
McGowan (OCD) John; 41 Kensington Church Street W8 4BB (Kensington 2)
McHardy (Oratorian) Rupert; The Oratory, Brompton Road SW7 2RP (Oratory)
McLoughlin (SAC) Joseph; 358 Greenford Road, Greenford UB6 9AN (Greenford)
McMillan (SJ) Keith; 2 Chandler Street E1W 2QT (Wapping)
McPake (SVD) Martin; 8 Teignmouth Road NW2 4HN (Willesden Green)
Madden (MAfr) Terence; 64 Little Ealing Lane W5 4XF Tel: 020 8799 5012 (Brentford)
Madewa (Nigerian Chaplaincy) Matthew Gbenga; 8 King Henry's Walk N1 4PB (Kingsland)
Magugu (Zimbabwean Chaplaincy) Jabulani Cletus; 4 Lady Margaret Road NW5 2XT Tel: 020 7485 4023 (Kentish Town)
Maguire (SS.CC) Fergal; 85 Old Oak Common Lane W3 7DD (Acton East)
Mahoney (SJ) John; 114 Mount Street W1K 3AH (Farm Street)
Manivelil (SJ) Aneesh Joseph; Copleston House, 221 Goldhurst Terrace NW6 3EP (Kilburn)
Markey (SSC) Gerard; 12 Blakesley Avenue W5 2DW (Ealing)
Markowski (MAfr) Antoni; St Vincent's Nursing Home, Wiltshire Lane, Eastcote HA5 2NB Tel: 020 8429 4778 Email: JAM5331@protonmail.com
Marsh (Opus Dei) DIC, STD, Bernard; 8 Orme Court W2 4RL Tel: 020 7243 9411 (Queensway)
Marsh (OSA) Robert; 55 Fulham Palace Road W6 8AU (Hammersmith)
Matwijiwskyj Very Rev Mykola; 22 Binney Street W1K 5BQ Tel: 020 7629 1073 (Ukrainian Cathedral)
Mazewski (MIC) Dariusz; 1 Courtfield Gardens W13 0EY Tel: 07427 748605 (Ealing)
Mazzotta (FDP) Carlo; 25 Lower Teddington Road, Hampton Wick KT1 4HB (Teddington)
Mboko (Congolese Chaplaincy) Julien Matondo; 2 Lukin Street E1 0AA (Commercial Road)
Mekekiuk Carlos; 22 Binney Street W1K 5BQ Tel: 020 7629 1073 (Ukrainian Cathedral)
Menonkari (CMI) John; 339 High Road, Wembley HA9 6AG (Wembley 1)
Michalek Maciej; 1 Leysfield Road W12 9JF Tel: 07973 923026 (Polish 2)
Mignolli (CSS) Natalino; 2 Leigh Gardens NW10 5HP (Kensal Rise)
Milby (Buffalo, NY) Lawrence; 39 Duncan Terrace N1 8AL (Islington)
Minihane (OSA) Mark; 55 Fulham Palace Road W6 8AU (Hammersmith)
Mitchell (SJ) Gerard; St Anselm's Rectory, The Green, Southall UB2 4BE (Southall)
Moffatt (SJ) John; 2 Chandler Street E1W 2QT (Wapping)
Moller (SJ) Philip; Copleston House, 221 Goldhurst Terrace NW6 3EP (Kilburn)
Montanez (a.a.) Ricky; Assumption Priory, Victoria Park Square E2 9PB (Bethnal Green)
Morrish (Opus Dei) MA, STD, Mgr Nicholas; 4 Orme Court W2 4RL (Queensway)
Morrone (SDV) Luigi; 15 The Green, Heston Road, Heston TW5 0RL (Heston)
Mudereri (Zimbabwean Chaplaincy) John Rufaro; 24 Bouverie Road N16 0AJ (Stoke Newington)
Munitiz (SJ) Joseph; Copleston House, 221 Goldhurst Terrace NW6 3EP (Kilburn)
Murray (SDS) John; Nazareth House, 169-175 Hammersmith Road W6 8DB (Brook Green)

SECTION 4

Murray (OMI) Terence; New Priory, Quex Road NW6 4PS (Kilburn)
Mway-Zeng (SDS) Richard; The Presbytery, 96 The Crescent, Abbots Langley, Watford WD5 0DS (Abbots Langley, Chipperfield)

Naughton (SS.CC) Ultan; 5 Berrymead Gardens W3 8AA (Acton)
Neville (MSC) Alan; 14 Beaconsfield Road, St Albans AL1 3RB (St Albans)
Newman (CMF) Chris; Botwell House, Botwell Lane, Hayes UB3 2AB (Hayes)
Newton (Ordinariate) Mgr Keith; 24 Golden Square W1F 9JR
Tel: 020 7440 5750 (Warwick Street)
Nguyen (Vietnamese Chaplaincy) Tam Huu; 117 Bow Common Lane E3 4AU
Tel: 020 7987 3477 (Bow Common)
Nguyen (Vietnamese Chaplaincy) Van Dien; 117 Bow Common Lane E3 4AU
Tel: 020 7987 3477 (Bow Common)
Nicholson (SJ) Paul; 114 Mount Street W1K 3AH (Farm Street)
Nogoy (SJ) Patrick Vance; Copleston House, 221 Goldhurst Terrace NW6 3EP (Kilburn)
Nolan (MAfr) Francis; 64 Little Ealing Lane W5 4XF (Brentford)
Notarianni (OSA) Gianni; 55 Fulham Palace Road W6 8AU (Hammersmith)
Nunn (OSB) MMus, Alban; Ealing Abbey, Charlbury Grove W5 2DY (Ealing)
Nwosu (CSSp) Augustine; 94 Bath Road, Hounslow TW3 3EH Tel: 020 8570 1693 (Hounslow)
Nyarko Clement; 17 Churchfield Path, off Church Lane, Cheshunt EN8 9EG (Cheshunt)

O'Brien (OSM) Chris; 264 Fulham Road SW10 9EL (Fulham Road)
O'Brien (SSC) Eamonn; 12 Blakesley Avenue W5 2DW (Ealing)
O'Brien (a.a.) Tom; 16 Nightingale Road, Hitchin SG5 1QS (Hitchin)
O'Byrne (CMF) John; Botwell House, Botwell Lane, Hayes UB3 2AB (Hayes)
O'Connell (OSM) Patrick; 264 Fulham Road SW10 9EL (Fulham Road)
O'Connor (OMI) Michael; New Priory, Quex Road NW6 4PS (Kilburn)
O'Dell (a.a.) Andrew; 16 Nightingale Road, Hitchin SG5 1QS (Hitchin)
O'Donovan (SAC) Liam; 358 Greenford Road, Greenford UB6 9AN (Greenford)
O'Halpin (SSC) Aodh; 12 Blakesley Avenue W5 2DW (Ealing)
O'Malley (SSC) Daniel; 12 Blakesley Avenue W5 2DW (Ealing)
O'Reilly (OMI) Lorcan; 14 Quex Road NW6 4PL (Kilburn)
O'Reilly (SJ) Paul; 27 High Road N15 6ND (Stamford Hill)
Ofere (Warri) Albert; The Presbytery, Chalkhill Road, Wembley Park HA9 9EW
Tel: 020 8904 2306 (Wembley 2)
Ogunnaike (MSP) Emmanuel; 115 Hertford Road N9 7EN (Edmonton)
Onwe (OCD) Luke Dominic; 41 Kensington Church Street W8 4BB (Kensington 2)
Onwu (Okigwe) Emmanuel; 60 Rylston Road SW6 7HW Tel: 020 7385 4040 (Fulham 1)
Onyebuchi (MSP) Livinus; St Peter's Presbytery, Bishop's Rise, Hatfield, Herts AL10 9HN (Hatfield Marychurch and Hatfield South, also University Chaplaincy)
Ostrynski (CCN) Sebastian; 29 Bramley Road N14 4HE (Cockfosters)
Otoaye (MSP) Julius; St Peter's Presbytery, Bishop's Rise, Hatfield, Herts AL10 9HN (Hatfield South, also University Chaplaincy)

Owens (OSB) Elijah; Newman House, 111 Gower Street WC1E 6AR Tel: 020 7387 6370
Email: frelijahosb@gmail.com

Paluku (AA) Jean-Marie Meso; 16 Nightingale Road, Hitchin SG5 1QS
Tel: 01462 459126 (Hitchin)
Panato (MCCJ) Pasquino; 16 Dawson Place W2 4TJ (Bayswater)
Parayadyil (MST) Mgr Thomas; 373 Bowes Road N11 1AA Tel: 020 8368 1638 (New Southgate)
Paunon Agustin (Filipino/Hospital Chaplaincy, based at London North West Healthcare NHS Trust HA1 3UJ); Room 235, Block 4, Hodgson Court, Nightingale Avenue, Harrow HA1 3GH Tel: 020 8869 2112 Pager: 07659 136452 Mobile: 07880 558225 (Harrow-on-the-Hill)
Pedley (SJ) Christopher; 114 Mount Street W1K 3AH (Farm Street)
Pereiro (Opus Dei) PhD, STD James; 1 Leopold Road W5 3PB (Gunnersbury)
Perera (Colombo) Sudham; Clergy House, Peter Avenue NW10 2DD Tel: 020 8451 4677 (Willesden Green)
Perrotta (FDP) John; 25 Lower Teddington Road, Hampton Wick KT1 4HB (Teddington)
Phelan (OMI) Michael; New Priory, Quex Road NW6 4PS (Kilburn)
Plower (MSC) Tom; 14 Beaconsfield Road, St Albans AL1 3RB (St Albans)
Porter (SJ) Adrian; 114 Mount Street W1K 3AH (Farm Street)
Preston (SDS) Peter; 189 High Street, Wealdstone, Harrow HA3 5DY (Wealdstone)
Puthenpurackal (CMI) Tebin; 339 High Road, Wembley HA9 6AG (Wembley 1)

Quaicoe (Cape Coast) Michael K A; Cathedral Clergy House, 42 Francis Street SW1P 1QW (Cathedral)

Raftery (CM) Eamon; 2 Flower Lane NW7 2JB (Mill Hill)
Rajewski Bartosz; 120A Fairway, Northolt UB5 4SW Tel: 07449 801752
Email: chaplaincy@pcmew.org.uk Web: www.dalondon.org.uk
Reczek, Marek; 1 Leysfield Road W12 9JF Tel: 07973 923026 (Polish 2)
Riezu (OAR) Robert; 18 Cheniston Gardens W8 6TQ (Kensington 1)
Robinson (SJ) Dominic; 114 Mount Street W1K 3AH (Farm Street)
Rockey (CP) Thomas; St Joseph's Retreat, Highgate Hill N19 5NE (Highgate)
Rossiter (OSB) JCL, DD, Abbot Francis; Ealing Abbey, Charlbury Grove W5 2DY (Ealing)
Rout (OFM) Paul; 15 The Green, Heston Road, Heston TW5 0RL Tel: 020 8570 1818 (Heston)
Ryall (OSM) Patrick; 264 Fulham Road SW10 9EL (Fulham Road)
Ryan (SSC) Thomas; 12 Blakesley Avenue W5 2DW (Ealing)

Saba (LMO) Johnny; 6 Dobson Close NW6 4RS Tel: 020 7586 1801 (Lebanese Maronite Church)
Sagar (FDP) Sidon; 25 Lower Teddington Road, Hampton Wick KT1 4HB (Teddington)
Sagwanti (SMM) Oscar; 27 St Gabriel's Road NW2 4DS (Willesden Green)
Salmi (SJ) Richard; Copleston House, 221 Goldhurst Terrace NW6 3EP (Kilburn)

Salter (Antioch) John A T; 1 St James Close, Bishop Street N1 8PH Tel: 020 7359 0250 (Islington)
Samson (a.a.) Erik; Assumption Priory, Victoria Park Square E2 9PB (Bethnal Green)
Sandambongo (CSSp) David 94 Bath Road, Hounslow TW3 3EH
Tel: 020 8570 1693 (Hounslow)
Satur (OSM) Allan; 264 Fulham Road SW10 9EL (Fulham Road)
Sawadogo (MAfr) Augustin; 15 Corfton Road W5 2HP (Ealing)
Semaan (Syriac Catholic Chaplaincy) Mgr Nizar; 41 Brook Green W6 7BL (Brook Green)
Serra (Italian Mission) Antonio; 197 Durants Road, Enfield EN3 7DE
Tel: 020 8804 2307 (Ponders End)
Sheehan (Opus Dei) MA, STD, Gerard; 8 Orme Court W2 4RL
Tel: 020 7243 9411 (Queensway)
Shipperlee (OSB) BD, BA, Abbot Martin; Ealing Abbey, Charlbury Grove W5 2DY (Ealing)
Shorter (MAfr) Aylward; 64 Little Ealing Lane W5 4XF (Brentford)
Skeats (OP) Thomas; St Dominic's Priory, Southampton Road NW5 4LB (Haverstock Hill)
Smith (MAfr) George; 64 Little Ealing Lane W5 4XF (Brentford)
Smith (SJ) Michael; 2 Chandler Street E1W 2QT (Wapping)
Smyth (CMF) Paul; Botwell House, Botwell Lane, Hayes UB3 2AB (Hayes)
Soane (Opus Dei) BSc, STD, Andrew; 4 Orme Court W2 4RL (Queensway)
Soyombo Charles; 47 Cumberland Street SW1V 4LY (Pimlico)
Stachyra (SChr) Wojciech; 16 Wellington Road, Hampton Hill TW12 1JR (Hampton Hill)
Stapleford (OSB) BA, Thomas; Ealing Abbey, Charlbury Grove W5 2DY (Ealing)
Starkey (MAfr) Denis; 64 Little Ealing Lane W5 4XF (Brentford)
Stasievich (Belarusian) Serge; Marian House, Holden Avenue N12 8HY (Finchley North)
Stawicki (CMF) Krzysztof; Botwell House, Botwell Lane, Hayes UB3 2AB (Hayes)
Stewart (SJ) David; 27 High Road N15 6ND (Stamford Hill)
Stones (MAfr) Gerry; 64 Little Ealing Lane W5 4XF (Brentford)
Stork (Opus Dei) MSc, STD, Mgr Richard; 18 Netherhall Gardens NW3 5TH (Swiss Cottage)
Strange Mgr Roderick; St Mary's University, Waldegrave Road, Twickenham TW1 4SX
Tel: 020 8240 8288 Email: roderick.strange@stmarys.ac.uk (Twickenham)
Stubbs (MSC) Jimmy; 14 Beaconsfield Road, St Albans AL1 3RB (St Albans)
Styles (SJ) Robert; 114 Mount Street W1K 3AH (Farm Street)
Szuta (SJ) Leszek; 182 Walm Lane NW2 3AX Tel: 020 8452 4304 (Willesden Green)

Tadeo (Davao City) Arnel; 82 Union Street, Barnet EN5 4HZ Tel: 020 8449 3338 (Barnet)
Tangonyire (SJ) Raymond; Copleston House, 221 Goldhurst Terrace NW6 3EP (Kilburn)
Taylor (OSB) Dominic; Ealing Abbey, Charlbury Grove W5 2DY (Ealing)
Thayriam (SJ) George Stephen; St Anselm's Rectory, The Green, Southall UB2 4BE (Southall)
Tomas (IMC) Luis; 3 Salisbury Avenue N3 3AJ (Finchley Church End)
Tomaszewski (SJ) Adam; 182 Walm Lane NW2 3AX Tel: 020 8452 4304 (Willesden Green)

Trad (LMO) Charbel; 6 Dobson Close NW6 4RS Tel: 020 7586 1801 (Lebanese Maronite Church)
Travers (CM) Noel; 2 Flower Lane NW7 2JB (Mill Hill)
Tverijonas MA, Petras; 21 The Oval, Hackney Road E2 9DT (Lithuanian Church)
Tworek Mgr Janusz; 2 Devonia Road N1 8JJ Tel: 07970 150712 (Polish 1)
Tyliszczak Canon Krzysztof; 2 Devonia Road N1 8JJ Tel: 07710 198765 (Polish 1)

Ugwu (CSSp) Oliver; 15 St John's Villas N19 3EE Tel: 020 7272 8195 (Archway, Hospital Chaplaincy)

van den Bergh (Oratorian) Edward; The Oratory, Brompton Road SW7 2RP (Oratory)
Vico (CS) Alberto; Villa Scalabrini, Green Street, Shenley WD7 9BB
Tel: 020 8207 5713 (Borehamwood North)
Vincent (OCD) Paul; 41 Kensington Church Street W8 4BB (Kensington 2)

Waiga (CSSp) Vincent: 15 St John's Villas N19 3EE (Archway) Tel: 020 7272 8195
Wallbank (MAfr), Christopher; 64 Little Ealing Lane W5 4XF (Brentford)
Walsh (Albanian Chaplaincy) Gary; 8 Ogle Street W1W 6HS
Tel: 020 7636 2883 (Ogle Street)
Waters (SDS) Francis; St Joseph's Presbytery, 191 High Road, Harrow Weald HA3 5EE (Wealdstone)
Wildsmith (MAfr) Edward; 15 Corfton Road W5 2HP (Ealing)
Williamson (OCD) John; 41 Kensington Church Street W8 4BB (Kensington 2)
Woo (MAfr) Edward; 64 Little Ealing Lane W5 4XF (Brentford)
Woollen (Lyons) Nigel; The Presbytery, 100a Balls Pond Road N1 4AG
Tel: 020 7254 4378 (Kingsland)
Wrobel (SAC) Ryszard; 4 Back Hill EC1R 5EN (Italian Church)
Wylezek Mgr Stefan; 2 Devonia Road N1 8JJ Tel: 020 7226 3439 (Polish 1)

Xavior (OCD) Tijo; 41 Kensington Church Street W8 4BB (Kensington 2)

Yacub (SJ) Chester; Copleston House, 221 Goldhurst Terrace NW6 3EP (Kilburn)

RELIGIOUS CONGREGATIONS AND SOCIETIES OF APOSTOLIC LIFE (MEN)

A place name in italics refers to a parish entry, where further details may be found.

African Missions, Society of (SMA)
White House, Watford Road, Northwood HA6 3PW *(Northwood)*
Burrows, Peter **(Plymouth Diocese)**
Cussen, Anthony
Dampson, Anthony
McCaul, Dermot

Assumptionists (a.a.)
(1) Assumptionist Priory, Victoria Park Square E2 9PB *(Bethnal Green)*
(2) 16 Nightingale Road, Hitchin SG5 1QS *(Hitchin)*
Kasereka, Justin (1)
Katsuva Kasine, Euloge (2)
Lambert, Michael (2)
Montanez, Ricky (1)
O'Brien, Tom (2)
O'Dell, Andrew (2)
Samson, Erik (1)
Brother:
Tran, Joseph Quoc Cuong

Augustinians (OSA)
(1) 55 Fulham Palace Road W6 8AU *(Hammersmith)*
(2) 19 Hoxton Square N1 6NT *(Hoxton)*
Campbell, Bishop Michael (1)
Choi, Jacob (1)
Clifford, Barry (2) **(Prior)**
Dabre, Gladson (1)
Donaghy, George (2)
Hassan, Gabriel (2) **(Parish Priest)**
Marsh, Robert (1) **(Provincial)**
Minihane, Mark (1) **(Prior)**
Notarianni, Gianni (1) **(Parish Priest)**

Augustinian Recollects (OAR)
18 Cheniston Gardens W8 6TQ *(Kensington 1)*
Riezu, Robert **(Prior)**

Benedictines (OSB - English Congregation)
Charlbury Grove W5 2DY *(Ealing)*
Bevan, Alexander
Burns, Peter
Chillman, Gregory
Cooper, Vincent
Gorham, Timothy
Hughes, Andrew
Leachman, James
McCambridge, Ambrose
Nunn, Alban
Rossiter, Francis
Shipperlee, Martin **(Abbot)**
Stapleford, Thomas
Taylor, Dominic **(Prior)**

Carmelites, Discalced (OCD)
41 Kensington Church Street W8 4BB *(Kensington 2)*
Clarke, Christopher **(Prior)**
McCormick, Fabian
McGowan, John
Onwe, Luke Dominic
Vincent, Paul
Williamson, John **(Parish Priest)**
Xavior, Tijo

Carmelites of Mary Immaculate (CMI)
St Joseph's Presbytery 339 High Road, Wembley HA9 6AG *(Wembley 1)*
Kaduthanam, Joseph
Menonkari, John
Puthenpurackal, Tebin

SECTION 4

Charity, Institute of (IC - Rosminians)
14 Ely Place EC1N 6RY *(Ely Place)*
Deidun, Tom

Chemin Neuf Community (CCN)
29 Bramley Road N14 4HE
(Cockfosters)
Brunet, Christophe **(Parish Priest)**
Ostrynski, Sebastian **(Community Leader)**

Claretian Missionaries (CMF - Missionary Sons of the Immaculate Heart of Mary)
Botwell House, Botwell Lane, Hayes UB3 2AB *(Hayes)*
Katthula, Joseph
Newman, Chris
O'Byrne, John
Smyth, Paul **(Major Superior)**
Stawicki, Krzysztof

Columban Fathers (SSC)
12 Blakesley Avenue W5 2DW *(Ealing)*
Markey, Gerard
O'Brien, Eamonn
O'Halpin, Aodh
O'Malley, Daniel **(Superior)**
Ryan, Thomas

Comboni Missionaries (MCCI - Verona Fathers)
Comboni House, 16 Dawson Place W2 4TJ
(Bayswater)
Anzioli, Angelo **(Superior)**
Curci, Carmine
De Marchi, Benito
Kouevi Adjétey, Louis Mawoulolo
Panato, Pasquino

Congregation of the Sacred Hearts (SS.CC)
(1) 372 Uxbridge Road W5 3LH *(Acton West)*
(2) 5 Berrymead Gardens W3 8AA *(Acton)*
(3) St Aidan of Lindisfarne W3 7DD *(Acton East)*
Barnes, Kenneth (1)
Crotty, Fintan (2)
Laverty, Derek (1)
Leahy, John (2)
McAneny, Christopher (3), (1)
Maguire, Fergal (3), (2)
Naughton, Ultan (2)

Consolata Fathers (IMC)
3 Salisbury Avenue N3 3AJ
(Finchley Church End)
Bonelli, Carlo
Tomas, Luis **(Superior)**

Divine Providence, Sons of (FDP)
25 Lower Teddington Road, Hampton Wick KT1 4HB *(Teddington)*
Halman, Henryk
Mazzotta, Carlo
Perrotta, John C **(Superior)**
Sagar, Sidon

Divine Word Missionaries (SVD)
(1) 8 Teignmouth Road NW2 4HN
(Willesden Green)
(2) 112 Twickenham Road, Isleworth TW7 6DL *(Isleworth)*
Donnelly, Eamonn (1)
Escoto, Albert (1) **(Praeses)**
Fitzharris, Kieran (2)
Krzyskow, Krzysztof (1)
Lobo Ratu, Nicodemus (2)
McCarthy, John (1)
McPake, Martin (1)

Dominicans (OP - The Order of Preachers)
St Dominic's Priory, Southampton Road NW5 4LB *(Haverstock Hill)*
Dunn, Michael
Edgar, Leo
Ganeri, Martin **(Provincial)**
Harries, Peter
Keenan, Oliver
Lew, Lawrence
Loewenstein, Rudolf

Skeats, Thomas **(Prior and Parish Priest)**

Franciscans (OFM)
Camilleri, Victor *(German Church)*
Rout, Paul *(Heston)*

Hospitaller Order of St John of God (OH)
52 Kenneth Crescent NW2 4PN
(Willesden Green)
Brothers:
Brannigan, Malachy **(Prior)**
Gerrard, Bonaventure
O'Neil, John
Zach, Andrzej

Jesuits (SJ - Society of Jesus)
(1) Provincial Curia, 114 Mount Street W1K 3AH *(Farm Street)*
(2) Farm Street Church, 114 Mount Street W1K 3AH *(Farm Street)*
(3) St Ignatius Church, 27 High Road N15 6ND *(Stamford Hill)*
(4) Polish Jesuits, 182 Walm Lane NW2 3AX *(Willesden Green)*
(5) Copleston House, 221 Goldhurst Terrace NW6 3EP *(Kilburn)*
(6) St Anselm's Rectory, The Green, Southall UB2 4BE *(Southall)*
(7) Hurtado Jesuit Centre, 2 Chandler Street E1W 2QT *(Wapping)*
(8) Tyburn Convent, 8 Hyde Park Place W2 2LJ *(Marylebone)*
Baczewski, Adam (4)
Beattie, Michael (2)
Bermingham, Edward (3)
Bossy, Michael (3)
Cameron-Mowat, Andrew (3)
Carmody, Brendan (2,8)
Elias, Harold (7)
Gallagher, Peter (5)
Holman, Michael (5)
Howard, Damian (1,2) **(Provincial)**
Hume, Patrick (2)
Konopinski, Mateusz (3)
Lesniak, Bogdan (3)
McClorry, Brian (7)
McDade, Pedro (5)
McMillan, Keith (7)
Mahoney, John (2)
Manivelil, Aneesh Joseph (5)
Mitchell, Gerard (6)
Moffatt, John (7)
Moller, Philip (5)
Munitiz, Joseph (5)
Nicholson, Paul (2)
Nogoy, Patrick Vance (5)
O'Reilly, Paul (3)
Pedley, Christopher (2)
Porter, Adrian (2)
Robinson, Dominic (2)
Salmi, Richard (5)
Smith, Michael (7)
Stewart, David (3)
Styles, Robert (2)
Szuta, Leszek (4)
Tangonyire, Raymond (5)
Thayriam, George Stephen (6)
Tomaszewski, Adam (4)
Yacub, Chester (5)
Power, Br Stephen (7)

Lebanese Maronite Order (LMO)
6 Dobson Close NW6 4RS
(Lebanese Church)
Azzi, Aziz
Saba, Johnny
Trad, Charbel

Malta, Order of (SMOM)
13 Deodar Road SW15 2NP

Marian Fathers (MIC)
(1) 2 Windsor Road W5 5PD *(Polish Church 3)*
(2) 1 Courtfield Gardens W13 0EY *(Ealing)*
Biernacki, Jakub (1)
Gowkielewicz, Andrzej (2)
Gumienny, Wiktor (1)

SECTION 4

Kozak, Michał (1) **(Parish Priest)**
Leszczyk, Grzegorz (1)
Mazewski, Dariusz (1,2) **(Provincial Delegate)**

Marist Fathers (SM)
5 Leicester Place WC2H 7BX
(French Church)
Boidin, Pascal **(Parish Priest)**
Bonnet-Eymard, Hubert **(Superior)**
Diouf, Damien
Duffy, Kevin
Vodopivec, Br Ivan

Mill Hill Missionaries
Chantry, Anthony *(Missio)*
Hemer, John *(Allen Hall Seminary)*

Missionaries of Africa (MAfr - White Fathers)
(1)15 Corfton Road W5 2HP *(Ealing)*
(2) 64 Little Ealing Lane W5 4XF *(Brentford)*
Beebwa, Aloysius (2)
Calcutt, Richard (2)
Cummins, Joseph (2)
Cummins, Thomas (2)
Gerrard, John (1) **(Superior)**
Hannon, Matthew (2)
Heap, Michael (1)
Kelly, Peter (2)
Madden, Terence (2) **(Provincial)**
Markowski, Antoni *(St Vincent's, Eastcote)*
Nolan, Francis (2)
Sawadogo, Augustin (1)
Shorter, Aylward (2)
Smith, George (2)
Starkey, Denis (2)
Stones, Gerry (2)
Wallbank, Christopher (2) **(Superior)**
Wildsmith, Edward (1)
Woo, Edward (2)
Brothers:
Murphy, Nicholas (1)
O'Reilly, Patrick (2)

Missionary Community of Divine Providence (MPS)
St Anne's Church, Underwood Road E1 5AW
(Underwood Road)
Francischini, Patrick Longo
Gomes, Jose Flavio

Missionary Society of St Paul (MSP)
(1) 115 Hertford Road N9 7EN
(Edmonton)
(2) St Peter's Presbytery, Bishop's Rise, Hatfield AL10 9HN *(Hatfield Marychurch & Hatfield South)*
Ogunnaike, Emmanuel (1)
Onyebuchi, Livinus (2)
Otoaye, Julius (2)

Montfort Missionaries (SMM)
27 St Gabriel's Road NW2 4DS
(Willesden Green)
Ahimbisibwe, John Mary
Flynn, John K
Sagwanti, Oscar

Oblates of Mary Immaculate (OMI)
(1) New Priory, Quex Road NW6 4PS
(Kilburn)
(2) 237 Goldhurst Terrace NW6 3EP
(Kilburn)
(3) 1 Stafford Road NW6 5RS *(Kilburn West)*
(4) 30 Prescot Street E1 8BB *(Tower Hill)*
(5) Denis Hurley House, 14 Quex Road NW6 4PL *(Kilburn)*
Alex, Angodage Don Joseph (4) **(Parish Priest)**
Devereux, Thomas (1)
Dillon, Paschal (2)
Fernando, Lylie (1)
McFadden, John (3)
Murray, Terence (1)
O'Connor, Michael (1,3) **(Parish Priest)**
O'Reilly, Lorcan (5)
Phelan, Michael (1)
Moore, Br Michael (3)

Oratorians
The Oratory, Brompton Road SW7 2RP
(Oratory)
van den Bergh, Edward
Bowen, George
Creighton-Jobe, Ronald
Dilke, Charles
Doyle, Patrick
Fordham, John
Lang, Michael **(Parish Priest)**
Large, Julian **(Provost)**
McHardy, Rupert

Pallottine Fathers (SAC)
(1) 358 Greenford Road, Greenford UB6 9AN *(Greenford)*
(2) 4 Back Hill EC1R 5EN *(St Peter's Italian Church)*
Daly, Thomas (1)
De Caro, Giuseppe (2)
Fulco, Andrea (2)
Lynch, Eugene (1)
McLoughlin, Joseph (1)
O'Donovan, Liam (1)
Wrobel, Ryszard (2)

Passionists (CP)
St Joseph's Retreat, Highgate Hill, N19 5NE *(Highgate)*
Cullen, Timothy *(Nazareth House, Finchley)*
Doherty, Tiernan **(Rector)**
Fitzgerald, Patrick **(Parish Priest)**
Kelly, Christopher *(Nazareth House, Finchley)*
Koloth, George
Lodge, Benedict
Rockey, Thomas

Sacred Heart, Brothers of the (SC)
8 King Harry Lane, St Albans AL3 4AW
(St Albans South)
Brothers:
Dionne, Nelson
Pelletier, Clement
St Jacques, Daniel
Vaillancourt, Paul **(Superior)**

Sacred Heart, Missionaries of the (MSC)
14 Beaconsfield Road, St Albans AL1 3RB
(St Albans)
Neville, Alan
Plower, Tom
Stubbs, Jimmy

Salvatorians (SDS - Society of the Divine Saviour)
(1) 96 The Crescent, Abbots Langley WD5 0DS *(Abbots Langley, Chipperfield)*
(2) Salvatorian Community House, 189 High Street, Wealdstone, Harrow HA3 5DY and **The Presbytery, 191 High Street, Wealdstone HA3 5EA** *(Wealdstone)*
(3) 9 Breakspear, Stevenage SG2 9SQ *(Stevenage Shephall)*
Bansi, Fortunatus (2)
Doherty, Michael (3) **(Superior)**
Harris, Paul (2)
Keane, Noel (2)
Luoga, Christopher (1)
Murray, John *(Nazareth House, Brook Green)*
Mway-Zeng, Richard (1) **(Provincial)**
Preston, Peter
Waters, Frank (2)

Scalabrini Fathers (CS)
Green Street, Shenley WD7 9BB
(Borehamwood North)
Vico, Alberto

Servites (OSM - Friar Servants of Mary)
264 Fulham Road SW10 9EL *(Fulham Road)*
Addison, Paul **(Prior Provincial)**
O'Brien, Chris
O'Connell, Patrick
Ryall, Patrick **(Prior)**
Satur, Allan

Society of Christ (SChr)
16 Wellington Road, Hampton Hill TW12 1JR *(Hampton Hill)*
Stachyra, Wojciech

Society of Divine Vocations (SDV)
15 The Green, Heston Road, Heston TW5 0RL *(Heston)*
James, Vipin
Morrone, Luigi

Spiritans (CSSp - Congregation of the Holy Spirit)
(1) 63 Somerset Road, New Barnet EN5 1RF *(New Barnet)*
(2) 15 St John's Villas N19 3EE *(Archway)*
(3) 94 Bath Road, Hounslow TW3 3EH *(Hounslow)*
Adayi, Daniel (3)
Fasakin, James Ademola (1)
Igbe, Terkura (1)
Ikwuka, Ugo (2)
Nwosu, Augustine (3)
Sandambongo, David (3)
Waiga, Vincent (2)

Stigmatine Fathers (CSS)
2 Leigh Gardens NW10 5HP *(Kensal Rise)*
Mignolli, Natalino

Vincentians (CM - Congregation of the Mission)
2 Flower Lane NW7 2JB *(Mill Hill)*
Armstrong, Raymond
McCullagh, Michael **(Superior)**
Raftery, Eamon
Travers, Noel

RELIGIOUS CONGREGATIONS AND SOCIETIES OF APOSTOLIC LIFE (WOMEN)

Place-names refer to a parish entry, where further details may be found.

Adoratrices, Handmaids of the Blessed Sacrament and of Charity (AASC): Kensington 2

Adorers of the Sacred Heart (OSB) - Tyburn Nuns: Marylebone

Capitanio Sisters (CS): Ealing

Carmelites (ODC): St Charles Square, Ware

Carmelite Missionaries (CM): St John's Wood

Columban Sisters (MSSC): Bow

Comboni Missionary Sisters (CMS): Chiswick

Congregation of Jesus (CJ): Willesden Green

Congregation of Our Lady (Canonesses of St Augustine) (CSA): Oratory

Congregation of Our Lady of the Missions (RNDM): New Southgate, Wealdstone

Congregation of La Sainte Union des Sacrés Coeurs (LSU): Holloway, Kentish Town, Wembley 3

Congregation of the Sisters of Nazareth (CSN): Brook Green, Finchley East

Daughters of Charity of St Vincent de Paul (DC): Cathedral, Kensal Rise, Mill Hill, Northwood, Pinner

Daughters of the Cross (Liege) (FC): Bishop's Stortford, Chelsea 1

Daughters of Divine Love (DDL): Borehamwood North, Wood Green

Daughters of Mary, Mother of Mercy DMMM): Edgware

Daughters of Providence (St Brieuc) : Palmers Green

Daughters of St Paul (FSP): Kensington 1

Dominican Sisters (Congr. of Newcastle, Natal) (OP): Bushey, Cricklewood, Edgware, Harpenden

Faithful Companions of Jesus (FCJ): Isleworth, Poplar, Somers Town

Franciscan Sisters of the Heart of Jesus (FCJ): Pimlico

Franciscan Missionaries of Mary (FMM): Acton West, Shepherds Bush

Franciscan Sisters of Mill Hill (OSF): Mill Hill

Franciscan Sisters of Our Lady of Victories: Cathedral

Handmaids of the Holy Child Jesus (HHCJ): Edmonton

Handmaids of the Sacred Heart of Jesus (ACI): St John's Wood

Institute of the Blessed Virgin Mary (Loreto Sisters) (IBVM): Acton West

Institute of Our Lady of Mercy: Highbury

Little Company of Mary (LCM): Ealing, Gunnersbury

Little Sisters of Jesus: Hoxton, St Charles Square

Little Sisters of the Poor (LSP): Stoke Newington

Marist Sisters (SM): Archway, White City

Medical Missionaries of Mary (MMM): Ealing

Medical Mission Sisters (Society of Catholic Medical Missionaries - SCMM): Acton, Hanwell, Northfields

Missionary Community of Divine Providence (MPS): Underwood Road

SECTION 4

Missionaries of Charity (MC): Kensal New Town, Southall

Missionary Sisters of Christ the King (MChR): Willesden Green

Missionary Sisters of the Immaculate (PIME): Chiswick

Missionary Sisters of Our Lady of Africa (White Sisters) (MSOLA): Ealing

Missionary Sisters of the Society of Mary (SMSM): French Church

Pallottine Missionary Sisters (SAC): Clerkenwell

Poor Clares (OSC): Barnet

Poor Handmaids of Jesus Christ (PHJC): Hendon

Poor Servants of the Mother of God (PSMG): Brentford, Hampton-on-Thames, Somers Town

Religious of the Assumption (RA): Bayswater, Kensington 2, Twickenham

Religious of Mary Immaculate (RMI): Kensington 2

Religious of the Sacred Heart of Mary (RSHM): Northfields

Religious Sisters of Charity (RSC): Acton, Hackney

School Sisters of Notre Dame (SSND): Copenhagen Street

Servants of Mary (OSM): Clapton, Stamford Hill

Sisters of Charity of Jesus and Mary (SCJM): Letchworth, Stevenage

Sisters of Charity of St Jeanne Antide (S de C); Sisters of St Martha: Ealing, Potters Bar

Sisters of Charity of St Paul (Selly Park) (SP): Hackney

Sisters of Christian Instruction (St Gildas) (SCI): Barnet, Stroud Green

Sisters of the Cross and Passion (CP) Fulham Road, Islington

Sisters of the Holy Cross (HC): Ealing

Sisters of the Holy Family of Bordeaux (HFB): Kilburn, Willesden Green

Sisters of the Holy Family of Nazareth (CSFN): Enfield

Sisters of the Holy Name of Jesus: Polish Church 3

Sisters Hospitallers of the Sacred Heart (HSC): Fulham Road

Sisters of the Infant Jesus (IJS): Acton East

Sisters of Jesus and Mary (rjm): Kensal Rise

Sisters of Jesus in the Temple (SJT): Notting Hill

Sisters of Mercy (RSM): Clapton Park, Commercial Road, Cricklewood, Feltham, Hillingdon, Kensal New Town, St John's Wood, Twickenham

Sisters of Notre Dame de Namur (SND): Pimlico

Sisters of Our Lady of the Missions: Wealdstone

Sisters of Our Lady of Sion (NDS): Bayswater

Sisters of Providence (of the Immaculate Conception): Royston

Sisters of Providence (Rosminian) (SPR): Lincoln's Inn Fields

Sisters of Providence (Ruille-sur-Loir): Stroud Green

Sisters of the Resurrection (CR): Ealing, Polish 3

Sisters of the Sacred Heart of Jesus (St Jacut) (SSCJ): Whetstone

Sisters of the Sacred Hearts of Jesus and Mary (Chigwell): Uxbridge

Sisters of St Dorothy (SSD): Hampstead

Sisters of St John of God (SSJG): West Green

Sisters of St Joseph of Peace (CSJ): Cricklewood, Hanwell

Sisters of St Louis (SSL): Cockfosters, Harrow South, New Southgate

Sisters of St Marcellina (IM) : Hampstead

Sisters of Saint Mary of Namur (SSMN): Harrow-on-the-Hill

Sisters of St Paul de Chartres (SPC): Highbury

Society of the Holy Child Jesus (SHCJ): Brook Green

Society of Marie Auxiliatrice: Muswell Hill

Society of the Sacred Heart (RSCJ): Brook Green

Ursulines of Jesus (UJ): Kingsland, Manor House, Stamford Hill

Verbum Dei Missionary Fraternity (FMVD): West Green

Wisdom (La Sagesse) Daughters of (DW): Archbishop's House, Willesden Green

Conference of Religious in England and Wales (COREW) - 'Providing Strength through Unity'
The association supports the leaders of the religious communities of England and Wales. COR aims to help men and women Religious face the challenges and needs of 21st century society. The aim is to focus on agreed initiatives and provide religious leaders with the support and educational resources that enable them to serve their individual communities better. Over the past 50 years the Conference has identified key needs for its members who themselves have worked tirelessly serving our communities to improve the lives of parishioners through their educational, healthcare and prayer roles, social justice and pastoral work.
Contacts
Br James A Boner OFM Cap **General Secretary**
Tel: 020 8566 7009 Email: gensec@corew.org
Ray Wilson **Technical Manager/Administrator**
Tel: 020 8566 7025 Email: adviser@corew.org
Bernadette Kehoe **Communications & Development Lead**
Tel: 020 3255 1085 Email: communications@corew.org
Ravina Saluja **Administrative Co-ordinator**
Tel: 020 3255 1085 Email: admin@corew.org
3 Montpelier Avenue W5 2XP Web: www.corew.org

Consecrated Hermit (Code c. 603) Sr Marianne **P.O. Box 14945 London W5 3ZZ**

Consecrated Women
See *Conscecrated Women* under Catholic Societies and Organisations, Section 6

The Grail A grant-making body, supporting activities consonant with the aims of the former Grail Secular Institute. See *Grail, The* under Catholic Societies and Organisations, Section 6

The Leaven A Carmelite way of life for single or widowed Catholic women
See *Carmelite Secular Institute* under Catholic Societies and Organisations, Section 6

St Boniface Secular Institute (English Region) 44 Exeter Road NW2 4SB
Tel: 020 8438 9628 Email: info.house42@yahoo.com Web: www.hostel-lioba-house.de
See *German Church* and *Willesden Green* parish entries

Servants of the Word (SW) An ecumenical congregation based in Acton at **31a Lynton Road W3 9HL Tel: 020 8993 8113**

Servite Secular Institute (SSI) A life of service through vows of chastity, poverty and obedience in union with others of like mind, remaining in their own circumstances. Women of prayer living in the world as Servants of Mary.
Contact Regional Director **27 Glengate, South Wigston, Leicestershire LE18 4SQ**
Email: vocations@ssi.org.uk Web: www.ssi.org.uk

Section 5

CATHOLIC SCHOOLS

All schools are listed under the local authority area in which they are situated, and, for primary schools, the name of the parish is also indicated. In the case of secondary schools and colleges the name of the deanery is only given where that is different from the local authority area in which the school or college is situated. The Parish Priest normally acts as Chaplain for primary schools. In secondary schools and colleges, the name of the Chaplain is given.

Unless stated otherwise, all schools are voluntary aided and co-educational, and all primary schools are junior and infant. (A) indicates that the school is an Academy. (+N) indicates that the school has a nursery. (RO) indicates that the school is in the trusteeship of a Religious Order. (R) indicates that it is recognised as Catholic by the Cardinal Archbishop; all other schools are in the trusteeship of the Diocese. All schools with websites are to be found listed at **www.rcdow.org.uk.**

Statistics	
Primary (Aided & Academy)	153
Primary (Independent)	9
Secondary (Aided & Academy)	40
Secondary (Independent)	2
All-age (Non-maintained Special)	2
All-age (Independent)	3
VI Form Colleges	2
Total	**211**

CITY OF WESTMINSTER (213)

PRIMARY SCHOOLS

Our Lady of Dolours: (+N) (3381) **19 Cirencester Street W2 5SR**
Tel: 020 7641 4326 Fax: 020 7641 4389 Email: head@ourladydolours.co.uk
Head Mrs Sarah Alley (Paddington)

St Edward: (+N) (3432) **Lisson Grove NW1 6LH**
Tel: 020 7723 5911 Fax: 020 7723 5250 Email: office@stedwardsprimary.co.uk
Head Miss Clare O'Connor (St John's Wood) (RO)

St Joseph, Maida Vale: (+N) (3473) **Lanark Road W9 1DF**
Tel: 020 7286 3518 Fax: 020 7286 2303 Email: head@stjosephsschool.org.uk
Head Mrs Katharine Maria Husain (St John's Wood)

St Mary of the Angels: (+N) (3532) **Shrewsbury Road W2 5PR**
Tel: 020 7792 1883 Fax: 020 7641 4484 Email: head@stmaryangels.co.uk
Head Mrs Mary Wilson (Bayswater)

SECTION 5

St Vincent, Marylebone: (+N) (3610) **St Vincent Street W1U 4DF**
Tel: 020 7641 6110 Fax: 020 7641 6116 Email: head@stvincentsprimary.org.uk
Head Miss Marina Coleman (Spanish Place)

St Vincent de Paul: (+N) (3611) **Morpeth Terrace SW1P 3EP**
Tel: 020 7641 5990 Fax: 020 7641 5901 Email: head@svpschool.co.uk
Head Mr Nathaniel Scott-Cree (Cathedral)

Westminster Cathedral: (3623) **Bessborough Place SW1V 3SE**
Tel: 020 7641 5915 Fax: 020 7821 9349 Email: office@westcathsch.co.uk
Head Mrs Alexandra Stacey (Pimlico)

Independent

St Christina (6225) (Girls) **25 St Edmund's Terrace NW8 7PY**
Tel: 020 7722 8784 Fax: 020 7586 4961 Email: secretary@saintchristinas.org.uk
Interim Head Mr Alistair Gloag (St John's Wood) (RO)

Westminster Cathedral Choir School: (6197) (Boys) **Ambrosden Avenue SW1P 1QH**
Tel: 020 7798 9081 Fax: 020 7798 9060 Email: office@choirschool.com
Head Mr Neil McLaughlan (Cathedral)

SECONDARY SCHOOL

St George: (A) (4809) **Lanark Road W9 1RB**
Tel: 020 7328 0904 Fax: 020 7624 6083 Email: s.williams@stgeorgesrc.org
Executive Head Mr Martin Tissott **Acting Deputy Executive Head** Mr James Martin
Acting Head of School Ms Michelle Henderson
Chaplain Bernard Dadswell (Marylebone Deanery)

LONDON BOROUGH OF BARNET (302)

PRIMARY SCHOOLS

The Annunciation: (Infants +N) (3500) **Thirleby Road, Edgware HA8 0HQ**
Tel: 020 8959 2325 Fax: 020 8906 4116 Email: head@annunciationinf.barnetmail.net
Head Miss Teresa Lynch BA (Burnt Oak)

The Annunciation: (Junior) (3514) **The Meads, Edgware HA8 9HQ**
Tel: 020 8906 0723 Fax: 020 8906 0377 Email: head@annunciationjnr.barnetmail.net
Head Miss Carol Minihan (Burnt Oak)

Blessed Dominic: (+N) (3511) **Lanacre Avenue NW9 5FN**
Tel: 020 8205 3790 Fax: 020 8205 9341 Email: office@blesseddominic.barnetmail.net
Head Mrs Geraldine Pears (Grahame Park)

Our Lady of Lourdes, Finchley: (+N) (3501) **Bow Lane N12 0JP**
Tel: 020 8346 1681 Fax: 020 8346 0579 Email: office@olol.barnetmail.net
Head Miss Barbara Costa (Finchley East)

Sacred Heart, Whetstone: (3510) 2 Oakleigh Park South N20 9JU
Tel: 020 8445 3854 Fax: 020 8445 0862 Email: office@sacredheart.barnetmail.net
Head Mrs Catherine McMahon (Whetstone)

St Agnes, Cricklewood: (+N) (3502) Thorverton Road NW2 1RG
Tel: 020 8452 4565 Fax: 020 8830 6709 Email: office@stagnes.barnetmail.net
Head Mrs Susan O'Reilly (Cricklewood)

St Catherine, Barnet: (+N) (3504) Vale Drive, Barnet EN5 2ED
Tel: 020 8440 4946 Fax: 020 8441 3436 Email: head@stcatherines.barnetmail.net
Head Miss Maureen Kelly (Barnet)

St Joseph, Hendon: (3509) Watford Way NW4 4TY
Tel: 020 8202 5229 Fax: 020 8202 5530 Email: head@stjosephs.barnet.sch.uk
Executive Head Dr James Lane (Hendon)

St Theresa: (3507) East End Road N3 2TD
Tel: 020 8346 8826 Fax: 020 8346 0215 Email: office@sttheresas.barnetmail.net
Head Mrs Linda O'Melia (Finchley Church End)

St Vincent, Mill Hill: (3506) The Ridgeway NW7 1EJ
Tel: 020 8959 3417 Fax: 020 8906 9733 Email: head@stvincents.barnet.sch.uk
Head Miss Marie Tuohy (Mill Hill)

Independent

St Anthony School for Girls: (6008) (Girls) Ivy House, 94-96 North End Road NW11 7SX
Tel: 020 3869 3070 Email: info@stanthonysgirls.co.uk
Head Mrs Laura Martin (Golders Green)

SECONDARY SCHOOLS

Bishop Douglass Catholic High: (5408) Hamilton Road N2 0SQ
Tel: 020 8444 5211/3 Fax: 020 8444 0416 Email: head@bishopdouglass.barnet.sch.uk
Head Mr Martin Tissot Chaplain Fr Kevin Ryan

Finchley Catholic High: (5405) (Boys) Woodside Lane N12 8TA
Tel: 020 8445 0105 Fax: 020 8446 0691 Email: narnull@finchleycatholic.org.uk
Head Mrs Niamh Arnull Chaplain Rebecca Parsons

St James Catholic High: (5407) Great Strand NW9 5PE
Tel: 020 8358 2800 Fax: 020 8358 2801 Email: admin@st-james.barnet.sch.uk
Head Mrs Carolyn Laws Chaplain Jennifer Whelan

St Michael Catholic Grammar: (5404) (Girls) Nether Street N12 7NJ
Tel: 020 8446 2256 Fax: 020 8343 9598 Email: office@st-michaels.barnet.sch.uk
Head Mr Michael Stimpson Chaplain Awaiting appointment (RO)

LONDON BOROUGH OF BRENT (304)

PRIMARY SCHOOLS

The Convent of Jesus & Mary: (Infants +N) (3507) **21 Park Avenue NW2 5AN**
Tel: 020 8459 5890 Fax: 020 8451 9499 Email: admin@conventinf.brent.sch.uk
Head Miss Elsa Fonseca (Willesden Green)

Our Lady of Grace, Dollis Hill: (Infants +N) (3510) **Dollis Hill Avenue NW2 6EU**
Tel: 020 8450 6757 Fax: 020 8452 1501 Email: philbourne@ologinfants.brent.sch.uk
Head Mrs Philomena Bourne (Dollis Hill)

Our Lady of Grace, Dollis Hill: (Junior) (3500) **Dollis Hill Lane NW2 6HS**
Tel: 020 8450 6002 Fax: 020 8208 3430 Email: head@ologjuniors.brent.sch.uk
Head Mr Stephen McGrath (Dollis Hill)

Our Lady of Lourdes, Willesden: (+N) (3508) **Wesley Road NW10 8PP**
Tel: 020 8961 5037 Fax: 020 8963 1197 Email: mbickerstaff@lourdes.brent.sch.uk
Head Miss Mary Bickerstaff (Stonebridge)

Federation of St Joseph Infant and Junior Schools, Wembley:
St Joseph, Wembley: (Infants +N) (3509) **Waverley Avenue, Wembley HA9 6TA**
Tel: 020 8903 6032 Fax: 020 8903 5263 Email: mwhelan@sjinf.brent.sch.uk
Executive Head Mrs Amanda Whelan (Wembley 1)

St Joseph, Wembley: (Junior) (3501) **Chatsworth Avenue, Wembley HA9 6BE**
Tel: 020 8902 3438 Fax: 020 8903 5482 Email: admin@sjjnr.brent.sch.uk
Executive Head Mrs Amanda Whelan **Associate Head** Mr Mark Betts (Wembley 1)

St Joseph, Willesden: (+N) (5203) **Goodson Road NW10 9LS**
Tel: 020 8965 5651 Fax: 020 8961 9022 Email: dtitus@stjo.brent.sch.uk
Head Miss Dawn Titus (Willesden)

St Margaret Clitherow, Neasden: (+N) (3511) **Quainton Street NW10 0BG**
Tel: 020 8450 3631 Fax: 020 8450 3729 Email: head@clitherow.brent.sch.uk
Head Mrs Ewa McSperrin BEd (Wembley 2)

St Mary, Kilburn: (+N) (3602) **Canterbury Road NW6 5ST**
Tel: 020 7624 3830 Fax: 7372 4932 Email: admin@marycps.brent.sch.uk
Head Mrs Bridget Pratley (Kilburn)

St Mary Magdalen: (Junior) (3505) **Linacre Road NW2 5BB**
Tel: 020 8459 3159 Fax: 020 8459 0108 Email: mnowicka@marymag.brent.sch.uk
Head Miss Maria Nowicka (Willesden Green)

St Robert Southwell: (+N) (3506) **Slough Lane NW9 8YD**
Tel: 020 8204 6148 Fax: 020 8905 0287 Email: admin@robsouth.brent.sch.uk
Head Miss Honor Beck (Kingsbury Green)

SECONDARY SCHOOLS

Convent of Jesus & Mary Language College: (A) (5404) (Girls) **Crownhill Road NW10 4EP**
Tel: 020 8965 2986 Fax: 020 8838 0071 Email: office@cjmlc.co.uk
Head Mrs Louise McGowan **Chaplain** Ann-Marie Sylvestercha

Newman Catholic College: (5407) (Boys) **Harlesden Road NW10 3RN**
Tel: 020 8965 3947 Fax: 020 8965 3430 Email: office@ncc.brent.sch.uk
Head Mr Daniel Coyle **Chaplain** John Roche

St Gregory Catholic Science College: (5406) **Donnington Road, Harrow HA3 0NB**
Tel: 020 8907 8828 Fax: 020 8909 1161 Email: cryan@stgregorys.harrow.sch.uk
Head Mr Andrew Prindiville **Chaplain** Michael Coughlan

LONDON BOROUGH OF CAMDEN (202)

PRIMARY SCHOOLS

Our Lady, Camden: (+N) (3655) **Pratt Street NW1 0DP**
Tel: 020 7485 7997 Fax: 020 7428 9426 Email: head@ourladys.camden.sch.uk
Executive Head Mrs Juliette Jackson **Associate Head** Ms Moya Richardson (Camden Town)

Rosary: (+N) (3391) **238 Haverstock Hill NW3 2AE**
Tel: 020 7794 6292 Fax: 020 7794 6292 Email: admin@rosary.camden.sch.uk
Interim Head Mr Peter Keane (Haverstock Hill)

St Aloysius: (+N) (3400) **Aldenham Street NW1 1PS**
Tel: 020 7387 3551 Email: executivehead@acps.camden.sch.uk
Executive Head Miss Clare McFlynn **Head of School** Mrs Bronagh McCann (Somers Town)

St Dominic, Camden: (+N) (3429) **Southampton Road NW5 4JS**
Tel: 020 7485 5918 Fax: 020 7284 0961 Email: head@stdominics.camden.sch.uk
Head Ms Jennifer O'Prey (Haverstock Hill)

St Eugene de Mazenod: (3649) **Mazenod Avenue, Quex Road NW6 4LS**
Tel: 020 7624 4837 Fax: 020 7328 2280 Email: head@steugene.camden.sch.uk
Executive Head Mrs Juliette Jackson (Kilburn)

St Joseph, Macklin Street: (+N) (3482) **Macklin Street, Drury Lane WC2B 5NA**
Tel: 020 7242 7712 Fax: 020 7430 1834 Email: head@stjosephs.camden.sch.uk
Head Miss Helen Tyler (Lincoln's Inn Fields)

St Patrick, Kentish Town: (+N) (3560) **Holmes Road NW5 3AH**
Tel: 020 7267 1200 Fax: 020 7485 4691 Email: head@stpatricks.camden.sch.uk
Head Mr Sean Cranitch (Kentish Town)

Independent

St Anthony's Preparatory: (6181) (Boys) **90 Fitzjohn's Avenue NW3 6AA**
Tel: 020 7431 1066 Fax: 020 7435 9223 Email: sadhna.halai@stanthonysprep.co.uk
Head Mr Paul Keyte (Hampstead) **Chaplain** Mgr Phelim Rowland (R)

St Mary's, Hampstead: (6084) (Girls) **47 Fitzjohn's Avenue NW3 6PG**
Tel: 020 7435 1868 Fax: 020 7794 7922 Email: office@stmh.co.uk
Head Mrs Harriet Connor-Earl (Swiss Cottage) (R)

SECONDARY SCHOOLS

La Sainte Union: (5041) (Girls) **Highgate Road NW5 1RP**
Tel: 020 7428 4600 Fax: 020 7267 7647 Email: sfegan@lsu.camden.sch.uk
Head Mrs Sophie Fegan **Chaplain** Shirley Taylor (RO)

Maria Fidelis: (4652) (Girls) **34 Phoenix Road NW1 1TA**
Tel: 020 7387 3856 Fax: 020 7388 9558 Email: office@mariafidelis.camden.sch.uk
Head Mrs Helen Gill **Chaplain** Awaiting appointment (RO)

LONDON BOROUGH OF EALING (307)

PRIMARY SCHOOLS

Holy Family School: (2000) **Vale Lane W3 0DY**
Tel: 020 8992 3980 Email: head@holyfamily.ealing.sch.uk
Head Mr Thomas Doherty (Acton West)

Mount Carmel: (+N) (3500) **Little Ealing Lane W5 4EA**
Tel: 020 8567 4646 Fax: 020 8579 5362 Email: admin@mountcarmel.ealing.sch.uk
Head Mrs Clare Walsh (Brentford)

Our Lady of the Visitation: (3503) **Greenford Road, Greenford UB6 9AN**
Tel: 020 8575 5344 Fax: 020 8575 6734 Email: admin@olovrc.com
Head Miss Kathleen Coll (Greenford)

St Anselm, Southall: (3505) **Church Avenue, Southall UB2 4BH**
Tel: 020 8574 3906 Fax: 020 8571 6308 Email: head@st-anselms.ealing.sch.uk
Head Mrs Ruth Sykes (Southall)

St Gregory, Ealing: (+N) (3506) **Woodfield Road W5 1SL**
Tel: 020 8997 7550 Fax: 020 8810 6506 Email: admin@st-gregorys.ealing.sch.uk
Head Ms Margaret Kolanowska (Ealing)

St John Fisher, Perivale: (+N) (3504) **Sarsfield Road, Perivale UB6 7AF**
Tel: 020 8799 0970 Fax: 020 8998 6618 Email: head@st-johnfisher.ealing.sch.uk
Head Mrs Tracey Brosnan (Perivale)

St Joseph, Hanwell: (+N) (3507) **York Avenue W7 3HU**
Tel: 020 8567 6293 Fax: 020 8840 0278 Email: admin@stjosephs.ealing.sch.uk
Head Mr Julian Rakowski (Hanwell)

St Raphael: (3508) **Hartfield Avenue, Northolt UB5 6NL**
Tel: 020 8841 0848 Fax: 020 8842 4617 Email: head@st-raphaels.ealing.sch.uk
Head Ms Evelyn Ward (Yeading)

St Vincent, Ealing: (3509) 1 Pierrepoint Road W3 9JR
Tel: 020 8992 6625 Fax: 020 8896 0623 Email: head@st-vincents.ealing.sch.uk
Head Mrs Monica McCarthy (Acton)

Independent

St Benedict Junior: (6606) 5 Montpelier Avenue W5 2XP
Tel: 020 8862 2054 Fax: 020 8862 2058 Email: jssecretary@stbenedicts.org.uk
Head Mr Robert Simmons BA (Hons) Chaplain Dom Andrew Hughes OSB (R)

SECONDARY SCHOOL

The Cardinal Wiseman School: (4603) Greenford Road, Greenford UB6 9AW
Tel: 020 8575 8222 Fax: 020 8575 9963 Email: info@wiseman.ealing.sch.uk
Head Mr Michael Kiely Chaplain Megan James

Independent

St Benedict Senior: (6006) 54 Eaton Rise W5 2ES
Tel: 020 8862 2254 Fax: 020 8862 2199 Email: headmaster@stbenedicts.org.uk
Head Mr Andrew Johnson Chaplain Dom Alexander Bevan OSB (RO)

PRIMARY & SECONDARY SCHOOL

Independent

St Augustine Priory School: (6005) (Girls) Hillcrest Road W5 2JL
Tel: 020 8997 2022 Fax: 020 8810 6501 Email: head@sapriory.com
Head Mrs Sarah Raffray Chaplain Mari King (R)

LONDON BOROUGH OF ENFIELD (308)

PRIMARY SCHOOLS

Our Lady of Lourdes: (3504) The Limes Avenue N11 1RD
Tel: 020 8361 0767 Fax: 020 8361 6682 Email: headteacher@ololschool.enfield.sch.uk
Head Mr Declan Meehan (New Southgate)

St Edmund, Enfield: (3501) Hertford Road N9 7HJ
Tel: 020 8807 2664 Fax: 020 8807 8877 Email: mhanley3.308@lgflmail.org
Head Mrs Margaret Hanley (Edmonton)

St George, Enfield: (3502) Gordon Road, Enfield EN2 0QA
Tel: 020 8363 3729 Fax: 020 8367 2275 Email: headteacher@st-georges.enfield.sch.uk
Head Mr Paul O'Rourke (Enfield)

St Mary, Enfield: (+N) (5403) Durants Road, Enfield EN3 7DE
Tel: 020 8804 2396 Fax: 020 8805 8847 Email: office@stmarys.enfield.sch.uk
Head Miss Maeve Creed (Ponders End)

St Monica, Enfield: (3503) Cannon Hill, Cannon Road N14 7HE
Tel: 020 8886 4647 Fax: 020 8882 8424 Email: office@st-monicas.enfield.sch.uk
Head Mrs Kate Baptiste (Palmers Green)

Independent

Vita et Pax Preparatory School: (6056) **Priory Close, Green Road N14 4AT**
Tel: 020 8449 8336 Fax: 020 8440 0483 Email: info@vitaetpax.co.uk
Head Mrs Gillian Chumbley (Cockfosters) (RO)

SECONDARY SCHOOLS

St Anne Catholic High for Girls: (4706) (Girls) **Oakthorpe Road N13 5TY**
Tel: 020 8886 2165 Fax: 020 8886 6552 Email: admin@st-annes.enfield.sch.uk
Head Ms Siobhan Gilling **Chaplain** John Ravi

St Ignatius College: (3500) (Boys) **Turkey Street, Enfield EN1 4NP**
Tel: 01992 717835 / 760520 Fax: 01992 652070 Email: head@stignatius.enfield.sch.uk
Head Mrs Mary O'Keeffe **Chaplain** John Dawson (RO)

LONDON BOROUGH BOROUGH OF HACKNEY (204)

PRIMARY SCHOOLS

Our Lady and St Joseph: (+N) (3371) **Buckingham Road N1 4DG**
Tel: 020 7254 7353 Fax: 020 7249 3870 Email: seanjflood@yahoo.co.uk
Head Mr Sean Flood MA BEd (Hons) (Kingsland)

St Dominic, Hackney: (+N) (2900) **Ballance Road E9 5SR**
Tel: 020 8985 0995 Fax: 020 8985 2915 Email: dfinan@stdominics.hackney.sch.uk
Head Mrs Deirdre Finan BEd (Hons) MA (Homerton)

St Monica, Hackney: (+N) (3553) **Hoxton Square N1 6NT**
Tel: 020 7739 5824 Fax: 020 7613 4465 Email: office@st-monicas.hackney.sch.uk
Head Mrs Amanda Ruthven (Hoxton)

St Scholastica (+N) (3659) **Kenninghall Road E5 8BS**
Tel: 020 8985 3466 Fax: 020 8533 0014 Email: nmulholland@st-scholasticas.hackney.sch.uk
Head Mrs Naomi Mulholland (Clapton)

SECONDARY SCHOOLS

Cardinal Pole: (4714) **205 Morning Lane E9 6LG**
Tel: 020 8985 5150 Fax: 020 8533 7325 Email: tracymortimer@cardinalpole.co.uk
Head Ms Jane Heffernan **Chaplain** James Ryan

Our Lady's Convent High: (4641) (Girls) **6-16 Amhurst Park N16 5AF**
Tel: 020 8800 2158 Fax: 020 8809 8898 Email: jmcdonald@ourladys.hackney.sch.uk
Head Ms Justine McDonald **Chaplain** Sr Dominico Savio(RO)

LONDON BOROUGH OF HAMMERSMITH & FULHAM (205)

PRIMARY SCHOOLS

The Good Shepherd: (+N) (3602) **Gayford Road W12 9BY**
Tel: 020 8743 5060 Fax: 020 8740 1626 Email: head@goodshepherdrc.lbhf.sch.uk
Head Mrs Imogen Lavelle (Shepherds Bush)

Holy Cross, Fulham: (+N) (3354) **Basuto Road SW6 4BL**
Tel: 020 7736 1447 **Fax:** 020 7371 9954 **Email:** admin@holycross.lbhf.sch.uk
Executive Head Mrs Kathleen Williams **Associate Head** Mrs Catherine MacGonigal (Parsons Green)

Larmenier & Sacred Heart: (+N) (3649) **41a Brook Green W6 8DH**
Tel: 020 8748 9444 **Fax:** 020 8748 2387 **Email:** head@larshrc.lbhf.sch.uk
Head Miss Jennifer McGinty (Brook Green)

St Augustine: (3378) **Disbrowe Road W6 8QE**
Tel: 020 7385 4333 **Fax:** 020 7386 7751 **Email:** admin@staugustinesrc.lbhf.sch.uk
Head Miss Mary Kelliher (Hammersmith)

St John XXIII: (+N) (3645) **1 India Way W12 7QT**
Tel: 020 8743 9428 **Fax:** 020 8749 7117 **Email:** head@stjohnxxiii.lbhf.sch.uk
Head Mrs Karen Cunningham (White City)

St Mary: (+N) (3529) **Masbro Road W14 0LT**
Tel: 020 7603 7717 **Fax:** 020 7602 7432 **Email:** head@stmarysrc.lbhf.sch.uk
Head Ms Robina Maher (Brook Green)

St Thomas of Canterbury: (3648) **Estcourt Road SW6 7HB**
Tel: 020 7385 8165 **Fax:** 020 7385 0918 **Email:** admin@stthomasrc.lbhf.sch.uk
Executive Head Mrs Karen Wyatt **Head of School** Miss Jo Breslin (Fulham 1)

SECONDARY SCHOOLS

The London Oratory: (A) (5400) (Boys) **Seagrave Road SW6 1RX**
Tel: 020 7385 0102 **Fax:** 020 7381 3836 **Email:** admin@los.ac
Head Mr Daniel Wright **Chaplain** Fr George Bowen (RO)

Sacred Heart High: (A) (3394) (Girls) **212 Hammersmith Road W6 7DG**
Tel: 020 8748 7600 **Fax:** 020 8748 0392 **Email:** mdoyle@sacredh.lbhf.sch.uk
Head Mrs Marian Doyle **Chaplain** Angela Gregory (RO)

LONDON BOROUGH OF HARINGEY (309)

PRIMARY SCHOOLS

Our Lady of Muswell: (+N) (3500) **Pages Lane N10 1PS**
Tel: 020 8444 6894 **Fax:** 020 8365 4620 **Email:** office@ourladymuswell.haringey.sch.uk
Head Mrs Angela McNicholas (Muswell Hill)

Federation of St Francis de Sales Infant and Junior Schools, Haringey:
St Francis de Sales: (Infants+N) (3507) **Brereton Road N17 8DA**
Tel: 020 8808 2923 **Email:** head.federation@sfds.haringey.sch.uk
Head Dr James Lane (Tottenham)

St Francis de Sales: (Junior) (3501) **Brereton Road N17 8DA**
Tel: 020 8808 2923 **Email:** admin.junior@sfds.haringey.sch.uk
Head Dr James Lane (Tottenham)

SECTION 5

St Gildas: (Junior) (3509) **1 Oakington Way N8 9EP**
Tel: 020 8348 1902 Fax: 020 8340 7805 Email: admin@st-gildas.haringey.sch.uk
Head Mrs Gillian Hood (Stroud Green)

St Ignatius: (+N) (3502) **St Ann's Road N15 6ND**
Tel: 020 8800 2771 Fax: 020 8802 7156 Email: head@st-igs.haringey.sch.uk
Head Mr Con Bonner (Stamford Hill)

St John Vianney: (+N) (3510) **Stanley Road N15 3HD**
Tel: 020 8889 8421 Fax: 020 8881 2528 Email: head@st-johnvianney.haringey.sch.uk Head Mr Stephen McNicholas (West Green)

St Martin de Porres: (+N) (3508) **Blake Road N11 2AF**
Tel: 020 8361 1445 Fax: 020 8361 5849 Email: head@st-martinporres.haringey.sch.uk
Head Mrs Louise Fleming (Wood Green)

Federation of St Mary Priory Infant and Junior Schools:
St Mary Priory: (Infants +N) (3505) **Hermitage Road N15 5RE**
Tel: 020 8800 9305 Fax: 020 8800 1142 Email: fcollins@stmarysrcpriory.haringey.sch.uk
Head Mrs Florence Collins (Stamford Hill) (RO)

St Mary Priory: (Junior) (3503) **Hermitage Road N15 5RE**
Tel: 020 8800 9305 Fax: 020 8880 1142 Email: admin@stmarysrcpriory.haringey.sch.uk
Head Mrs Florence Collins (Stamford Hill) (RO)

St Paul: (3504) **Bradley Road N22 4SZ**
Tel: 020 8888 7081 Fax: 020 8889 1397 Email: headteacher@st-pauls.haringey.sch.uk
Executive Head Mrs Louise Fleming **Head of School** Mr Peter O'Shaughnessy (Wood Green)

St Peter-in-Chains: (Infants) (3506) **3 Elm Grove N8 9AJ**
Tel: 020 8340 6789 Fax: 020 8340 3653 Email: head@st-peter-in-chains-rc.haringey.sch.uk
Head Miss Margaret Falvey BEd Hons (Stroud Green)

SECONDARY SCHOOL

St Thomas More: (A) (4703) **Glendale Avenue N22 5HN**
Tel: 020 8888 7122 Fax: 020 8826 9370 Email: headteacher@stthomasmoreschool.org.uk
Executive Head Mr Martin Tissot **Head of School** Mr Mark Rowland
Chaplain Awaiting appointment

LONDON BOROUGH OF HARROW (310)

PRIMARY SCHOOLS

St Anselm, Harrow: (3501) **Roxborough Park, Harrow HA1 3BE**
Tel: 020 8422 1600 Fax: 020 8422 3564 Email: monahana@st-anselms.harrow.sch.uk
Head Mrs Anne Monahan (Harrow-on-the-Hill)

St Bernadette, Harrow: (3500) Clifton Road, Kenton, Harrow HA3 9NS
Tel: 020 8204 8902 Fax: 020 8905 0738 Email: head@stbernadette.harrow.sch.uk
Head Mr David O'Farrell (Kenton)

St George, Harrow: (3508) Sudbury Hill, Harrow HA1 3SB
Tel: 020 8422 1272 Fax: 020 8864 5540 Email: head@stgeorges.harrow.sch.uk
Head Mrs Deirdre Monaghan (Sudbury)

St John Fisher: (3505) Melrose Road, Pinner HA5 5RA
Tel: 020 8868 2961 Fax: 020 8866 5882 Email: conlon@st-johnfisher.harrow.sch.uk
Head Mrs Maria Conlon (Harrow North)

St Joseph, Harrow: (3507) Dobbin Close, Belmont, Harrow HA3 7LP
Tel: 020 8863 8531 Fax: 020 8863 3341 Email: office@stjosephs.harrow.sch.uk
Head Mr Christopher Briggs (Wealdstone)

St Teresa, Harrow: (+N) (3504) Long Elmes, Harrow Weald HA3 6LE
Tel: 020 8428 8640 Fax: 020 8420 1571 Email: llowney1@st-teresas.harrow.sch.uk
Head Miss Laura Lowney (Headstone Lane)

SECONDARY SCHOOLS

Sacred Heart Language College: (4700) (Girls) 186 High Street ,Wealdstone HA3 7AY
Tel: 020 8863 9922 Fax: 020 8861 5051 Email: ghiggins@tshlc.harrow.sch.uk
Head Miss Geraldine Higgins Chaplain Marie Wright

Salvatorian College: (A) (5400) (Boys) High Road, Harrow Weald HA3 5DY
Tel: 020 8863 2706 Fax: 020 8863 3435 Email: admin@salvatorian.harrow.sch.uk
Executive Head Mr Martin Tissot Chaplain Awaiting appointment (RO)

SIXTH FORM COLLEGE

St Dominic: (8600) Mount Park Avenue, Harrow-on-the-Hill HA1 3HX
Tel: 020 8422 8084 Fax: 020 8422 3759 Email: ap@stdoms.ac.uk
Principal Mr Andrew Parkin Chaplain Angela O'Brien

LONDON BOROUGH OF HILLINGDON (312)

PRIMARY SCHOOLS

Botwell House: (+N) (3401) Botwell Lane, Hayes UB3 2AB
Tel: 020 8573 2229 Fax: 020 8569 0286 Email: pglancy@ibotwell.co.uk
Head Miss Pauline Glancy (Hayes)

Sacred Heart, Ruislip: (+N) (3405) Herlwyn Avenue, Ruislip HA4 6EZ
Tel: 01895 633240 Fax: 01895 625 772 Email: office@shpsruislip.org
Head Mrs Theresa McManus (Ruislip)

St Bernadette, Hillingdon: (+N) (3402) 160 Long Lane, Hillingdon UB10 0EH
Tel: 01895 232298 Fax: 01895 230086 Email: office@stbernadetteschool.co.uk
Head Mrs Colette Acres (Hillingdon)

St Catherine, West Drayton: (+N) (3403) Money Lane, West Drayton UB7 7NX
Tel: 01895 442839 Fax: 01895 442631 Email: office@stcatherine.co.uk
Head Miss Elizabeth Doonan (West Drayton)

St Mary, Uxbridge: (+N) (3404) Rockingham Close, Uxbridge UB8 2UA
Tel: 01895 232814 Fax: 01895 235403 Email: ashevlin@stmarysuxbridge.org.uk
Head Miss Ann Shevlin (Uxbridge)

St Swithun Wells: (+N) (3400) Hunters Hill, South Ruislip HA4 9HS
Tel: 01895 808194 Fax: 020 8845 1611 Email: kdavis@ssw.school
Head Mrs Kristy Davis (Ruislip South)

SECONDARY SCHOOL

The Douay Martyrs: (A) (5408) Edinburgh Drive, Ickenham, Uxbridge UB10 8QY
Tel: 01895 679400 Fax: 01895 679401 Email: tcorish@douaymartyrs.co.uk
Head Mr Anthony Joseph Corish Chaplain Luisa Foley

NON-MAINTAINED SPECIAL SCHOOL

Pield Heath House: (7006) Pield Heath Road, Hillingdon UB8 3NW
Tel: 01895 258507 Fax: 01895 256497 Email: admin@pieldheathschool.org.uk
Head Sr Julie Rose Chaplain Eryl D'Souza (RO)

LONDON BOROUGH OF HOUNSLOW (313)

PRIMARY SCHOOLS

Our Lady & St John: (+N) (3502) Boston Park Road, Brentford TW8 9JF
Tel: 020 8560 7477 Fax: 020 8568 8806 Email: head@stjohnrc.hounslow.sch.uk
Head Mrs Susan Cunningham (Brentford)

The Rosary: (3941) 10 The Green, Heston TW5 0RL
Tel: (Key Stage 1) 020 8570 4942 (Key Stage 2) 020 8581 0066 Fax: 020 8581 0065
Email: head@rosary.hounslow.sch.uk
Head Awaiting appointment (Heston)

St Lawrence: (+N) (3503) Victoria Road, Feltham TW13 4AF
Tel: 020 8890 3878 Fax: 020 8883 1885 Email: head@st-lawrence.hounslow.sch.uk
Head Mr Leo Duggan (Feltham)

St Mary, Chiswick: (+N) (3505) Duke Road W4 2DF
Tel: 020 8994 5606 Fax: 020 8742 7630 Email: head@stmarys.hounslow.sch.uk
Executive Head Miss Joan Harte (Chiswick)

St Mary, Isleworth: (+N) (3504) South Street, Isleworth TW7 7EE
Tel: 020 8560 7166 Fax: 020 8232 8820 Email: head@smi.hounslow.sch.uk
Head Mr Farley Marsh (Isleworth)

St Michael's and St Martin's: (+N) (3507) Belgrave Road, Hounslow TW4 7AG
Tel: 020 8572 9658 Fax: 020 8572 1982 Email: head@stmichaelrc.hounslow.sch.uk
Head Mrs Nicola Duggan (Hounslow)

SECONDARY SCHOOLS

Gumley House: (A) (5400) (Girls) St John's Road, Isleworth TW7 6XF
Tel: 020 8568 8692 Fax: 020 8758 2674 Email: cbraggs@gumley.hounslow.sch.uk
Head Mrs Caroline Braggs Chaplain Celia Hannigan (RO)

Gunnersbury: (5401) (Boys) The Ride, Boston Manor Road, Brentford TW8 9LB
Tel: 020 8568 7281 Fax: 020 8569 7946 Email: headteacher@gunnersbury.hounslow.sch.uk
Head Mr Kevin Burke Chaplain Amy Jachulski

St Mark: (A) (4800) 106 Bath Road, Hounslow TW3 3EJ
Tel: 020 8577 3600 Fax: 020 8577 0559 Email: waughlucasa@st-marks.hounslow.sch.uk
Head Mrs Andrea Waugh-Lucas Chaplain Ivan Cižmárik

LONDON BOROUGH OF ISLINGTON (206)

PRIMARY SCHOOLS

Blessed Sacrament: (+N) (3643) Boadicea Street N1 0UF
Tel: 020 7278 2187 Fax: 020 7278 0015
Email: norah.flatley@blessedsacrament.islington.sch.uk
Head Mrs Norah Flatley (Copenhagen Street)

Christ the King: (+N) (3633) 55 Tollington Park N4 3QW
Tel: 020 7272 5987 Fax: 020 7272 7780 Email: admin@ctks.co.uk
Executive Head Mr John Lane Head of School Ms Romy Hoster (Tollington Park)

Sacred Heart, Islington: (3384) 68 George's Road N7 8JN
Tel: 020 7607 3407 Fax: 020 7606 4906 Email: john.lane@sacredheart.islington.sch.uk
Head Mr John Lane (Holloway)

St Joan of Arc, Highbury: (+N) (3631) Northolme Road N5 2UX
Tel: 020 7226 3920 Fax: 020 7704 9220 Email: headteacher@st-joanofarc.islington.sch.uk
Head Miss Clare Campbell (Highbury)

St John the Evangelist: (+N) (3456) Duncan Street N1 8BL
Tel: 020 7226 1314 Fax: 020 7226 5563 Email: office@stjohnevangelist.islington.sch.uk
Head Miss Stephanie Day (Islington)

St Joseph: (+N) (3483) Highgate Hill N19 5NE
Tel: 020 7272 1270 Fax: 020 7272 9728 Email: head@st-josephs.islington.sch.uk
Head Miss Clare McFlynn (Highgate) (RO)

St Peter and St Paul, Islington: (+N) (3575) Compton Street EC1V 0EU
Tel: 020 7253 0839 Fax: 020 7336 7226 Email: tpeters9.206@lgflmail.org
Head Miss Tracey Peters (Clerkenwell)

SECONDARY SCHOOL

St Aloysius: (4651) (Boys) **Hornsey Lane N6 5LY**
Tel: 020 7561 7800 Fax: 020 7263 5963 Email: loderick.d@sta.islington.sch.uk
Executive Head Mrs Jane Heffernan **Chaplain** Awaiting appointment

ROYAL BOROUGH OF KENSINGTON AND CHELSEA (207)

PRIMARY SCHOOLS

Oratory: (3379) **Bury Walk, Cale Street SW3 6QH**
Tel: 020 7589 5900 Fax: 020 7581 5220 Email: head@oratory.rbkc.sch.uk
Head Mrs Jane Griffiths (Oratory) (RO)

Our Lady of Victories: (+N) (5200) **Clareville Street SW7 5AQ**
Tel: 020 7373 4491 Fax: 020 7244 0591 Email: allyson.hodnett@olov.rbkc.sch.uk
Head Mr Christopher McPhilemy (Kensington 1)

St Charles: (+N) (5201) **83 St Charles Square W10 6EB**
Tel: 020 8969 5566 Fax: 020 8960 4338 Email: ann.slavin@st-charles.rbkc.sch.uk
Head Miss Ann Slavin (St Charles Square)

St Francis of Assisi: (+N) (3437) **Treadgold Street W11 4BJ**
Tel: 020 7727 8523 Fax: 020 7229 2174 Email: info@franassisi.rbkc.sch.uk
Executive Head Mrs Kathleen Williams (Notting Hill)

St Joseph, Chelsea: (+N) (3477) **Cadogan Street SW3 2QT**
Tel: 020 7589 2438 Fax: 020 7581 9489 Email: Karen.wyatt@stjosephs.rbkc.sch.uk
Executive Head Mrs Karen Wyatt (Chelsea 1)

St Mary, East Row: (+N) (3542) **East Row W10 5AW**
Tel: 020 8969 0321 Fax: 020 8964 3122 Email: joan.harte@st-marys.rbkc.sch.uk
Executive Head Mrs Joan Harte (Kensal New Town)

The Servite: (+N) (3613) **252 Fulham Road SW10 9NA**
Tel: 020 7352 2588 Fax: 020 7351 4024 Email: kathleen.williams@servite.rbkc.sch.uk
Head Mrs Kathleen Williams (Fulham Road) (RO)

Independent

St Philip's Preparatory School: (6104) (Boys) **6 Wetherby Place SW7 4NE**
Tel: 020 7373 3944 Fax: 020 7244 9766 Email: info@stphilipschool.co.uk
Head Mr Alexander Wulffen-Thomas (Kensington 2) (RO)

SECONDARY SCHOOLS

The Cardinal Vaughan Memorial School: (5402) (Boys) **89 Addison Road W14 8BZ**
Tel: 020 7603 8478 Fax: 7602 3124 Email: StubbinP@cvms.co.uk
Head Mr Paul Stubbings **Chaplain** Fr Dominic Allain

All Saints Catholic College: (4801) St Charles Square W10 6EL
Tel: 020 8969 7111 Fax: 020 8969 5119 Email: a.oneill@allsaintscc.org.uk
Head Mr Andrew O'Neill Chaplain Therese Teevan (North Kensington Deanery)

St Thomas More Language College, Chelsea: (4861) Cadogan Street SW3 2QS
Tel: 020 7589 9734 Fax: 020 7823 7868 Email: info@stm.rbkc.sch.uk
Head Dr Trevor Papworth Chaplain Fr Anthony Homer

Independent

More House School: (6202) (Girls) 22 Pont Street SW1X 0AA
Tel: 020 7235 2855 Fax: 020 7259 6782 Email: office@morehouse.org.uk
Head Mrs Amanda Leach Chaplain Awaiting appointment (RO)

SIXTH FORM COLLEGE

St Charles Catholic Sixth Form College: (8600) 74 St Charles Square W10 6EY
Tel: 020 8968 7755 Fax: 020 8968 1061 Email: principal@stcharles.ac.uk
Principal Mrs Elaine Taylor Chaplain Heather Jameson (North Kensington Deanery)

LONDON BOROUGH OF RICHMOND (318)

PRIMARY SCHOOLS

The Sacred Heart, Teddington: (3320) St Mark's Road, Teddington TW11 9DO
Tel: 020 8977 6591 Fax: 020 8943 2449 Email: bsmith@sacredheart.richmond.sch.uk
Head Mrs Bernadette Smith (Teddington)

St Edmund, Whitton: (3315) St Edmund's Lane, Nelson Road, Whitton TW2 7BB
Tel: 020 8894 7898 Fax: 020 8898 3032 Email: g.nicholl@st-edmunds.richmond.sch.uk
Head Mrs Carmel Moreland (Whitton)

St James, Twickenham: (+N) (3316) 260 Stanley Road, Twickenham TW2 5NP
Tel: 020 8898 4670 Fax: 020 8893 3032 Email: info@st-james.richmond.sch.uk
Head Mrs Louise Yarnell (Twickenham)

PRIMARY AND SECONDARY SCHOOL

St Richard Reynolds Catholic College Federation:
St Richard Reynolds (Primary): (2000) Clifden Road, Twickenham TW1 4LT
Tel: 020 8325 4630 Email: rburke@srrcc.org.uk
Head Mr Richard Burke BSc MA (Twickenham)

St Richard Reynolds Catholic College: (4000) Clifden Road, Twickenham TW1 4LT
Tel: 020 8325 4630 Email: rburke@srrcc.org.uk
Head Mr Richard Burke BSc MA Chaplain Molly Bayliss-Conway (Upper Thames Deanery)

Independent

St Catherine Catholic School: (6008) (Girls) Cross Deep, Twickenham TW1 4QJ
Tel: 020 8891 2898 Fax: 020 8744 9629 Email: admissions@stcatherineschool.co.uk
Head Mrs Johneen McPherson Chaplain Awaiting appointment (RO) (Upper Thames Deanery)

LONDON BOROUGH OF TOWER HAMLETS (211)

PRIMARY SCHOOLS

English Martyrs: (+N) (3619) St Mark Street E1 8DJ
Tel: 020 7709 0182 Fax: 020 7680 9395 Email: head@englishmartyrs.towerhamlets.sch.uk
Head Ms Bronagh Nugent (Tower Hill)

Guardian Angels: (3346) Whitman Road E3 4RB
Tel: 020 8980 3939 Fax: 020 8983 4210 Email: head@guardianangels.towerhamlets.sch.uk
Head Miss Elizabeth Worrell (Mile End)

Our Lady and St Joseph: (+N) (3667) Wade's Place E14 0DE
Tel: 020 3764 8860 Fax: 020 3764 8861 Email: patrick.devereux@olsj.co.uk
Head Mr Patrick Devereux (Poplar)

St Agnes, Bow: (+N) (3397) Rainhill Way E3 3ES
Tel: 020 8980 3076 Fax: 020 8983 1770 Email: admin@st-agnes.towerhamlets.sch.uk
Head Ms Brid McDaid (Bow)

St Anne, Whitechapel: (+N) (3411) Underwood Road E1 5AW
Tel: 020 7247 6327 Fax: 020 7377 5024 Email: head@st-annes.towerhamlets.sch.uk
Head Mrs Sheila Mouna (Underwood Road)

St Edmund, Millwall: (+N) (3431) 299 West Ferry Road E14 3RS
Tel: 020 7987 2546 Fax: 020 7538 0332 Email: head@st-edmunds.towerhamlets.sch.uk
Head Ms Gail O'Flaherty (Millwall)

St Elizabeth: (+N) (2003) Bonner Road E2 9JY
Tel: 020 8980 3964 Fax: 020 8983 3377 Email: head@st-elizabeth.towerhamlets.sch.uk
Head Miss Angelina John (Bethnal Green)

St Mary and St Michael: (+N) (2002) Sutton Street E1 0BD
Tel: 020 7790 4986 Fax: 020 7790 9343
Email: admin@st-marymichael.towerhamlets.sch.uk
Head Mrs Rachel Mahon (Commercial Road)

SECONDARY SCHOOLS

Bishop Challoner Catholic Federation of Schools:
Bishop Challoner: (4726) (Girls) 352 Commercial Road E1 0LB
Tel: 020 7791 9500 Fax: 020 7791 9589 Email: dwhelan@bishop.towerhamlets.sch.uk
Executive Head Mr Richard Fitzgerald Chaplain Scott Hanlon
Bishop Challoner: (4298) (Boys) 352 Commercial Road E1 0LB
Tel: 020 7791 9500 Fax: 020 7791 9589 Email: dwhelan@bishop.towerhamlets.sch.uk
Executive Head Mr Richard Fitzgerald Head of School Mr Bryan Young
Chaplain Scott Hanlon

COUNTY OF HERTFORDSHIRE (919)

PRIMARY SCHOOL (ENFIELD DEANERY)

Pope Paul: (3975) Baker Street, Potters Bar EN6 2ES
Tel: 01707 659755 Fax: 01707 665431 Email: head@popepaul.herts.sch.uk
Head Mrs Elizabeth Heymoz (Potters Bar)

PRIMARY SCHOOLS (LEA VALLEY DEANERY)

Sacred Heart, Ware: (3424) Broadmeads, Ware SG12 9HY
Tel: 01920 461678 Fax: 01920 461418 Email: head@sacredheart312.herts.sch.uk
Head Mrs Michelle Fusi (Ware)

St Augustine, Hoddesdon: (+N) (3345) Riversmead, Hoddesdon EN11 8DP
Tel: 01992 463549 Email: head@staugustines.herts.sch.uk
Head Mrs Gillian Napier (Hoddesdon)

St Cross: (3408) Upper Marsh Lane, Hoddesdon EN11 8BN
Tel: 01992 467309 Fax: 01992 450362 Email: admin@stcross.herts.sch.uk
Head Mrs Kathryn Hall (Hoddesdon)

St Joseph, Bishop's Stortford: (+N) (3318) Great Hadham Road, Bishop's Stortford CM23 2NL
Tel: 01279 652576 Fax: 01279 466519 Email: head@stjosephs207.herts.sch.uk
Head Mr Peter Coldwell (Bishop's Stortford)

St Joseph, Hertford: (+N) (3341) North Road, Hertford SG14 2BY
Tel: 01992 583148 Fax: 01992 550503 Email: head@stjosephs255.herts.sch.uk
Head Mrs Justine Page (Hertford)

St Joseph, Waltham Cross: (+N) (3327) Royal Avenue, Waltham Cross EN8 7EN
Tel: 01992 629503 Fax: 01992 628824 Email: head@stjosephs351.herts.sch.uk
Head Mr Tony Gorton; Mrs Barbara O'Connor (from 1/1/19) (Waltham Cross)

St Paul, Cheshunt: (+N) (3423) Park Lane, Cheshunt EN7 6LR
Tel: 01992 635060 Fax: 01992 625215 Email: head@stpauls373.herts.sch.uk
Head Mrs Yvonne Devereux (Cheshunt)

St Thomas of Canterbury: (3367) High Street, Puckeridge, near Ware SG11 1RZ
Tel: 01920 821450 Fax: 01920 822534 Email: head@stcanterbury.herts.sch.uk
Head Mrs Michelle Keating (Old Hall Green and Puckeridge)

SECTION 5

PRIMARY SCHOOLS (ST ALBANS DEANERY)

St Adrian: (+N) (3389) Watling View, St Albans AL1 2PB
Tel: 01727 852687 Fax: 01727 850822 Email: head@stadrians.herts.sch.uk
Head Mr Dominic Bedford (St Albans South)

St Alban & St Stephen: (Infants +N) (3362) **Vanda Crescent, St Albans AL1 5EX**
Tel: 01727 854643 Email: head@ssasinfants.herts.sch.uk
Acting Head Mrs Aisling Cannon (St Albans)

St Alban & St Stephen: (Junior) (3421) **Cecil Road, St Albans AL1 5EG**
Tel: 01727 866668 Fax: 01727 810710 Email: head@ssasjm.herts.sch.uk
Acting Head Mrs Aideen Porter (St Albans)

St Albert the Great: (3391) **Acorn Road, Rant Meadow, Hemel Hempstead HP3 8DW**
Tel: 01442 264835 Fax: 01442 246418 Email: head@albertthegreat.herts.sch.uk
Head Mrs Kathryn Jane Little (Hemel Hempstead East)

St Bernadette, London Colney: (+N) (3416) **Walsingham Way, London Colney AL2 1NL**
Tel: 01727 822489 Fax: 01727 823327 Email: head@stbernadette.herts.sch.uk
Head Mrs Sandra Lavelle-Murphy (London Colney)

St Cuthbert Mayne: (Junior) (3386) **Clover Way, Gadebridge, Hemel Hempstead HP1 3EA**
Tel: 01442 253347 Fax: 01442 230320 Email: head@cuthbertmayne.herts.sch.uk
Head Mrs Fionnuala Smith (Hemel Hempstead Boxmoor, North & West)

St Dominic, Harpenden: (+N) (3401) **Southdown Road, Harpenden AL5 1PF**
Tel: 01582 760047 Fax: 01582 760047 Email: head@stdominic.herts.sch.uk
Head Miss Clare O'Sullivan (Harpenden)

St John Fisher, St Alban's: (3403) **Hazelmere Road, Marshalwick, St Albans AL4 9RW**
Tel: 01727 861077 Fax: 01727 831163 Email: head@sjfisher.herts.sch.uk
Head Miss Patricia O'Donnell (St Albans)

St Rose: (Infants +N) (3409) **Green End Road, Boxmoor, Hemel Hempstead HP1 1QW**
Tel: 01442 398855 Fax: 01442 398835 Email: head@stroses.herts.sch.uk
Acting Head Mrs Ella Ryan (Hemel Hempstead Boxmoor)

St Teresa, Borehamwood: (+N) (3384) **Brook Road, Borehamwood WD6 5HL**
Tel: 020 8953 3753 Fax: 020 8381 5273 Email: head@stteresas.herts.sch.uk
Head Mrs Teresa McBride (Borehamwood)

St Thomas More, Berkhamsted: (+N) (3402) **Greenway, Berkhamsted HP4 3LF**
Tel: 01442 385060 Fax: 01442 385061 Email: head@stmore.herts.sch.uk
Executive Head Mrs Kathryn Little (Berkhamsted)

Independent

St Columba's College: (6136) (Boys) **Preparatory School, 8 King Harry Lane, St Albans AL3 4AW**
Tel: 01727 862616 Fax: 01727 892025 Email: Coakley.b@stcolumbascollege.org
Head Mrs Ruth Loveman (St Albans South) (RO)

PRIMARY SCHOOLS (STEVENAGE DEANERY)

Holy Family, Welwyn Garden City (+N) (3404) Crookhams, Welwyn Garden City AL7 1PG
Tel: 01707 375518 Email: head@holyfamily.herts.sch.uk
Head Miss Ginnette Stevens (Welwyn Garden City Digswell)

Our Lady, Hitchin: (A) (3399) Old Hale Way, Hitchin SG5 1XT
Tel: 01462 622555 Fax: 01462 622777 Email: head@ourladys.herts.sch.uk
Head Mrs Ciara Nicholson (Hitchin)

Our Lady, Welwyn Garden City: (+N) (3382) Woodhall Lane, Welwyn Garden City AL7 3TF
Tel: 01707 324408 Fax: 01707 391005 Email: admin@ourladys527.herts.sch.uk
Head Mr Richard Curry (Welwyn Garden City East)

St John, Baldock: (A) (+N) (3413) Providence Way, Baldock SG7 6TT
Tel: 01462 892478 Fax: 01462 892683 Email: head@stjohns4.herts.sch.uk
Head Ms Alex Hanou (Baldock)

St Margaret Clitherow, Stevenage: (3397) Monkswood Lane SG2 8RH
Tel: 01438 352863 Fax: 01438 352553 Email: head@clitherow.herts.sch.uk
Head Miss Carmela Puccio (Stevenage Shephall)

St Mary, Royston: (A) (+N) (5200) Melbourn Road, Royston SG8 7DB
Tel: 01763 246021 Fax: 01763 248825 Email: head@st-marys-royston.herts.sch.uk
Head Mrs Julia Pearce (Royston)

St Philip Howard (3388) Woods Avenue, Hatfield AL10 8NN
Tel: 01707 263969 Fax: 01707 263969 Email: head@sphoward.herts.sch.uk
Head Mrs Mairead Ann Waugh (Hatfield)

St Thomas More, Letchworth: (A) (3400) Highfield, Letchworth Garden City SG6 3QB
Tel: 01462 620670 Fax: 01462 620670 Email: admin@strcjmi.herts.sch.uk
Head Mrs Jane Perry (Letchworth)

St Vincent de Paul, Stevenage: (+N) (3977) Bedwell Crescent, Stevenage SG1 1NJ
Tel: 01438 729555 Fax: 01438 358122 Email: head@stvincent.herts.sch.uk
Head Mr Jonathan White (Stevenage Bedwell)

PRIMARY SCHOOLS (WATFORD DEANERY)

Divine Saviour: (+N) (3410) Broomfield Rise, Abbots Langley WD5 0HW
Tel: 01923 265607 Fax: 01923 291632 Email: head@divinesaviour.herts.sch.uk
Executive Head Mr Stephen Wheatley (Abbots Langley)

The Holy Rood: (+N) (3985) Greenbank Road, Watford WD17 4FS
Tel: 01923 223785 Fax: 01923 481342 Email: head@holyrood.herts.sch.uk
Executive Head Mr Stephen Wheatley Head of School Mrs Emma Brand (Watford)

SECTION 5

Sacred Heart, Bushey: (3415) **Merryhill Road, Bushey WD23 1SU**
Tel: 01923 493040 Fax: 01923 493041 Email: head@sacredheart682.herts.sch.uk
Head Mrs Rebecca Tregear (Bushey and Oxhey)

St Anthony: (+N) (3428) **Croxley View, Watford WD18 6BW**
Tel: 01923 226987 Fax: 01923 234645 Email: head@stanthonys.herts.sch.uk
Head Mrs Pauline Wilson MA (Watford)

St Catherine of Siena: (A) (5211) **Horseshoe Lane, Garston, Watford WD25 7HP**
Tel: 01923 676022 Fax: 01923 893497 Email: head@st-catherine.herts.sch.uk
Head Ms Nicola Kane (Garston)

St John, Rickmansworth: (3398) **Berry Lane, Mill End, Rickmansworth WD3 7HG**
Tel: 01923 774004 Fax: 01923 710915 Email: head@stjohns705.herts.sch.uk
Executive Head Mr Peter Sweeney **Head of School** Mr Tony Hall (Mill End)

St Joseph, South Oxhey: (+N) (3383) **Ainsdale Road, South Oxhey, Watford WD19 7DW**
Tel: 020 8428 5371 Fax: 020 8421 0568 Email: head@stjosephs775.herts.sch.uk
Head Mrs Linda Payne (Carpenders Park)

SECONDARY SCHOOLS (HERTFORDSHIRE)

John F Kennedy: (4619) **Hollybush Lane, Hemel Hempstead HP1 2PH**
Tel: 01442 266150 Fax: 01442 200014 Email: admin@jfk.herts.sch.uk
Head Mr Paul Neves **Chaplain** Awaiting appointment (St Albans Deanery)

John Henry Newman: (A) (5413) **Hitchin Road, Stevenage SG1 4AE**
Tel: 01438 314643 Fax: 01438 747882 Email: admin@jhn.herts.sch.uk
Head Mr Clive Mathew MSc **Chaplain** Fr Philip Law
(Stevenage Deanery)

Loreto: (A) (4620) (Girls) **Hatfield Road, St Albans AL1 3RQ**
Tel: 01727 856206 Fax: 01727 833794 Email: admin@loreto.herts.sch.uk
Head Mrs Maire Lynch **Chaplain** Shane McCarthy (RO) (St Albans Deanery)

Nicholas Breakspear: (A) (5412) **Colney Heath Lane, St Albans AL4 0TT**
Tel: 01727 860079 Fax: 01727 848912 Email: admin@nbs.herts.sch.uk
Head Mr Declan Linnane **Chaplain** Barry O'Sullivan (St Albans Deanery)
St Joan of Arc: (A) (5418) **High Street, Rickmansworth WD3 1HG**
Tel: 01923 773881 Fax: 01923 897545 Email: admin@joa.herts.sch.uk
Head Mr Peter Sweeney BEd (Hons) MA NPQH **Chaplain** Liam Lynch (Watford Deanery)

St Mary, Bishop's Stortford: (5422) **Windhill, Bishop's Stortford CM23 2NQ**
Tel: 01279 654901 Fax: 01279 653889 Email: a.celano@stmarys.net
Head Mr Andrew Celano **Chaplain** Awaiting appointment (Lea Valley Deanery)

St Michael: (A) (5417) High Elms Lane, Garston, Watford WD25 0SS
Tel: 01923 673760 Fax: 01923 680511 Email: admin@stmichaelscatholichighschool.co.uk
Head Mr Edward Conway STB MA BA(Psych) Chaplain Fr Terkura Igbe CSSp (Watford Deanery)

Independent

St Columba College: (6025) (Boys) King Harry Lane, St Albans AL3 4AW
Tel: 01727 855185 Fax: 01727 892024 Email: Coakley.b@stcolumbascollege.org
Head Mr David Buxton Chaplain Awaiting appointment (RO) (St Albans Deanery)

NON-MAINTAINED SPECIAL SCHOOL

St Elizabeth Centre: (7006) South End, Much Hadham SG10 6EW
Tel: 01279 843451 Fax: 01279 843903 Email: school@stelizabeths.org.uk
Director of Education Mrs Sharon Wallin Head of School Mrs Samantha Steinke-Sanderson
Head of College Awaiting appointment Chaplain Fr Paul Arnold (RO) (Lea Valley Deanery)

PRIMARY AND SECONDARY SCHOOL

Independent

St Edmund's College: (6115) Old Hall Green, Ware SG11 1DS
Tel: 01920 821504 Fax: 01920 823011 Email: head@stedmundscollege.org
Head Mr Paolo Durán
Priest-in-Residence Fr Peter Lyness Lay Chaplain Paula Pierce (Lea Valley Deanery)

COUNTY OF SURREY (936)

PRIMARY SCHOOLS

Our Lady of the Rosary: (3461) Park Avenue, Staines-upon-Thames TW18 2EF
Tel: 01784 453539 Fax: 01784 449485 Email: head@ourlady.surrey.sch.uk
Head Miss Lisa Wallage (Staines-upon-Thames)

St Ignatius, Sunbury: (3459) Green Street, Sunbury-on-Thames TW16 6QG
Tel: 01932 785396 Fax: 01932 771418 Email: handrews@st-ignatius.surrey.sch.uk
Head Mrs Helen Andrews (Sunbury)

St Michael, Ashford: (3915) Feltham Hill Road, Ashford TW15 2DG
Tel: 01784 253333 Fax: 01784 240834 Email: head@st-michaels.surrey.sch.uk
Head Mr John Anthony Lane (Ashford)

SECONDARY SCHOOL

St Paul College: (5411) Manor Lane, Sunbury-on-Thames TW16 6JE
Tel: 01932 783811 Fax: 01932 786485 Email: jmcnulty@st-pauls.surrey.sch.uk
Head Mr James McNulty Chaplain Rebecca Walker (Upper Thames Deanery)

Section 6

CATHOLIC SOCIETIES AND ORGANISATIONS

Organisations in this section have a membership widely distributed in the Diocese and a fundamental commitment to the teaching of the Catholic Church, particularly as expressed by the documents of the Second Vatican Council and the Catechism of the Catholic Church.

AID TO THE CHURCH IN NEED

ACN is a Pontifical Foundation directly under the Holy See. As a Catholic charity, it supports the faithful wherever they are persecuted, oppressed or in need, through information, prayer, and action. Founded in 1947 by Fr Werenfried van Straaten, whom Pope St John Paul II named 'an outstanding Apostle of Charity', the organisation is now at work in 140 countries throughout the world. Undertaking thousands of projects every year, the charity provides emergency support for people experiencing persecution, transport for clergy and lay Church workers, Children's Bibles, media and evangelisation projects, churches, Mass stipends and other support for priests and nuns, and training for seminarians.

Aid to the Church in Need UK is a registered charity in England and Wales [1097984] and Scotland [SC040748]. The UK office is in Sutton, Surrey and there is a Scottish office in Motherwell, near Glasgow and another office based in Lancaster that covers the North-West.

National Director Neville Kyrke-Smith **Aid to the Church in Need UK, 12-14 Benhill Avenue, Sutton SM1 4DA Tel: 020 8662 8668 Email: acn@acnuk.org**

ANSCOMBE BIOETHICS CENTRE

A national Catholic Research Centre, established by the Catholic Bishops of England and Wales in 1977. It seeks to promote understanding of Catholic teaching on healthcare and biotechnology issues through research and educational outreach. The Centre engages in scholarly dialogue with academics and practitioners of different traditions, and contributes to public policy debates and consultations. In addition to academic conferences and seminars, it also runs educational programmes for, and gives advice to, healthcare professionals, biomedical scientists, students and the wider Catholic community.

Director Prof David Albert Jones **17 Beaumont Street, Oxford OX1 2NA**
Tel: 01865 610212 Email: admin@bioethics.org.uk Web: www.bioethics.org.uk

APOSTLESHIP OF THE SEA

AoS is the official maritime and welfare mission agency of the Catholic Church in Great Britain, as well as a registered charity wholly reliant on voluntary contributions. Ninety percent of world trade is carried by ship; however, seafarers often work in dangerous conditions suffering loneliness, deprivation and even exploitation. AoS deploys chaplains and ship visitors who welcome vulnerable merchant seafarers to our shores and provide for their pastoral and practical needs – regardless of creed or nationality. Catholic seafarers are also given the opportunity to receive the sacraments. AoS also provides chaplains on board cruise ships, works ecumenically to maintain ecumenical seafarers' centres inside ports, and collaborates with industry bodies to speak for seafarers' rights. AoS relies on a network of valued parish contacts and volunteers to sustain its development.

Director Martin Foley **Apostleship of the Sea, 39 Eccleston Square SW1V 1BX**
Tel: 020 7901 1931 Email: info@apostleshipofthesea.org.uk
Web: www.apostleshipofthesea.org.uk

ARCHCONFRATERNITY OF ST STEPHEN

The Archconfraternity of St Stephen exists to promote and encourage high standards of altar serving. Servers can be enrolled into the Guild with permission of their Parish Priest once they have been serving for at least six months and made their First Communion. Please contact the Hon Secretary or Diocesan Director for details on how a parish can be affiliated to the Guild.

National Director Fr Dennis F P Touw Tempelmans-Plat (Fulham I)
Diocesan Director Fr Keith Stoakes (Poplar / Limehouse)
Hon President Michael O'Leary
Hon Secretary Michael Malone **PO Box 568, London WC1A 1YT**
Email: archconfraternitysecretary@hotmail.com

ASSOCIATION FOR LATIN LITURGY

(Under the patronage of the Bishops' Conference of England & Wales)
We promote the use of Latin in the Ordinary Form and the richness of the Church's heritage of chant and polyphony, working especially to enable the faithful to participate fully in them. We arrange meetings with sung Masses, Vespers and Benediction in Latin, talks, chant days, publish our journal *Latin Liturgy*, engage in liturgical studies, liaise with the hierarchy, and produce liturgical booklets for congregations. Our latest publication, the *Graduale Parvum*, provides simple but authentic settings of the Introits for all Sundays of the year, in Latin and English, suitable for small choirs and for congregations. Other chants of the Propers will follow.

Membership Secretary **173 Davidson Road, Croydon CR0 6DP**
General enquiries **Email: enquiries@latin-liturgy.org Web: www.latin-liturgy.org / www.facebook.com/latinliturgy twitter.com/latinliturgyuk**

ASSOCIATION FOR THE PROPAGATION OF THE FAITH (APF)

Part of the Missio network, the Association for the Propagation of the Faith (APF) builds much needed infrastructure in predominantly impoverished, remote areas – from chapels and schools, to orphanages, clinics and dispensaries. Requested by the local community, our support transforms lives and creates a hub from which the young Church can flourish and grow, spreading the Good News of the Gospel, ministering to the faithful and delivering essential services in health and education through the Red Mission boxes and the World Mission Sunday annual collection.

Diocesan Director Fr Philip Knights **Email: philipknights@rcdow.org.uk**
Mill Hill Appealer for the Diocese Fr John Hemer MHM
Tel: 020 7349 5609 Email: johnhemer@gmail.com
National Office for Missio 23 Eccleston Square SW1V 1NU (Reg. Charity No. 1056651)
Tel: 020 7821 9755 Email: apf@missio.org.uk Web: www.missio.org.uk

ASSOCIATION OF MARY HELP OF CHRISTIANS

To promote personal devotion to, and public honour of Our Lady under the title 'Help of Christians'. A prayer meeting is held on the fourth Saturday of each month at 3.30pm at **9 Henry Road N4 2LH** **Contact** Rev Deacon Kassa Tsegaye **120 Seaford Road N15 5DT Tel: 07930 416927,** Fr Hugh Preston SDB **Tel: 07806 803683**

ASSOCIATION OF SRI LANKAN CATHOLICS

To promote spiritual and temporal advancement, reconciliation and understanding among all Sri Lankans and work for peace.

c/o Ss Michael and Martin Parish, 94 Bath Road, Hounslow TW3 3EH

ASSUMPTION VOLUNTEERS

Assumption Volunteers (age 20+) spend one year in a culture very different from their own, sharing their lives and skills with the young in poor communities in India, the Philippines, Rwanda, Lithuania and England. The Assumption Sisters subsidise 10 placements each year. 'Everyone has a mission'; in giving and receiving, discover the meaning of your life.

Contact Volunteer Co-ordinator **20 Kensington Square W8 5HH Tel: 020 7361 4752**
Email: vc@assumptionvolunteers.org.uk Web: www.assumptionvolunteers.org.uk
Facebook: Assumption Volunteers

BANNEUX ND. INTERNATIONAL UNION OF PRAYER

Promulgates the message given by Our Lady at Banneux under the title 'Virgin of the Poor' by showing films and leading retreats and pilgrimages.

Secretary Lisa Pirie **1 Lines Road, Stevenage SG1 3DJ Tel: 07500 288384**
Email: banneuxndgb@gmail.com

BEGINNING EXPERIENCE

A Catholic ministry for men and women who find themselves single again following divorce, separation or the death of a partner. It offers a weekend programme which seeks to encourage participants to close the door gently on the past and to approach life with more confidence and hope in the future.

Contact Freda Bacon **Tel: 01322 838415**, Sandra Maishman **Tel: 01293 783965** or John Brotherton **Email: johnabrotherton@hotmail.co.uk**
Web: www.beginningexperience.org

CAFOD (CATHOLIC AGENCY FOR OVERSEAS DEVELOPMENT)

This international development and relief agency of the Church in England and Wales builds partnerships with local organisations in over 30 countries across Africa, Asia and Latin America, supporting them to build a better world for people living in extreme poverty. CAFOD focuses on sustainable livelihoods, clean water and sanitation, combating HIV/AIDS, and peace-building. In emergencies it provides immediate relief and long-term programmes to rebuild people's lives. Support can be offered through donations, prayer, volunteering and campaigning.

CAFOD's Lent Family Fast Day is on 15 March and Harvest Fast Day is on 4 October and donation envelopes will be available in churches weekends before and after.
Contact Tony Sheen **CAFOD Westminster Volunteer Centre, 29 Bramley Road N14 4HE**
Tel: 020 8449 6970 Email: westminster@cafod.org.uk Web: cafod.org.uk
Blog: cafodwestminster.wordpress.com

CARITAS CHRISTI

International secular institute for women living a celibate life. For the single or widowed.
Web: www.ccinfo.org

CARITAS SOCIAL ACTION NETWORK

CSAN is the official agency of the Catholic Bishops' Conference of England and Wales for domestic social action. We support and facilitate our network of over 40 Catholic dioceses and independent charities. Our members provide help for families and children, the elderly, homeless people, refugees, the disabled, and prisoners. The national team strives to develop the network, to advance the education, training, practice and formation of those active in Catholic social action, and to offer a coherent Catholic voice on social justice in the public arena. CSAN is a member of *Caritas Internationalis*, within the *Caritas Europa* group.
Chairman of Trustees Rt Rev Terence Drainey **Vice-Chairman** Sr Lynda Dearlove
CEO Dr Philip McCarthy **Romero House, 55 Westminster Bridge Road SE1 7JB**
Tel: 020 7633 4973 Email: admin@csan.org.uk Web: www.csan.org.uk

CARMELITES OF THE DISCALCED CARMELITE SECULAR ORDER

Carmelite Seculars, together with the friars and nuns, are sons and daughters of the Order of Our Lady of Mount Carmel and St Teresa of Jesus. They share the same charism. It is one family with the same spiritual possessions, the same call to holiness and the same apostolic mission. There are four groups that meet regularly within the Westminster diocese.
Contact Mark Courtney **Tel: 020 8288 0536 Email: mark.courtney@oxon.org**
Web: www.carmeldiscalcedsecular.org.uk

CARMELITE SECULAR INSTITUTE (THE LEAVEN)

The Leaven, the Secular Institute of Our Lady of Mount Carmel, is a secular institute for single women and widows founded in 1949. There are currently members in England, Scotland, Namibia and Australia. The individual apostolate of members is rooted in a life of prayer drawing on the rich heritage of the Carmelites and each member lives her everyday life wherever she finds herself: alone, with family or friends. The commitment to service and contemplation is shown in the vows they take of poverty, celibacy and obedience.
Contact Angela Kneale **8 Fulwell Court, St Leger Drive, Great Linford, Milton Keynes MK14 5HB Tel: 01908 231209 Email: theleavensi@gmail.com**

CARMELITE THIRD ORDER (ANCIENT OBSERVANCE)

Carmel-in-London offers laity and diocesan clergy the opportunity to deepen their following of Christ within one of the Church's most ancient spirituality traditions, combining contemplative

reflection with prophetic service and action for justice. Drawing inspiration from the prophet Elijah, the Blessed Virgin Mary and the Saints of Carmel, we form praying communities in the heart of the Church at the service of all God's people, through formal Carmelite Third Order gatherings and more diverse Carmelite Spirituality Groups. A Carmelite Third Order Group of the Ancient Observance (O.Carm) meets regularly in Westminster Diocese, alongside the monthly Carmel-in-the-City Spirituality Group. **Contact** Sylvia Lucas
Email: sylvia@carmelinthecity.org.uk Web: www.carmelinthecity.org.uk

CATENIAN ASSOCIATION

International Association of Catholic men, with over 250 local groups in the UK including 20+ in Westminster diocese. Catenians support each other, their families and friends, their clergy and parishes, vocations, young people, and many charities each year. We share our faith as friends and meet monthly to renew friendships, share a meal, organise events, and unload the daily stresses and strains of modern living.
Contact Declan O'Farrell (Director) **Tel: 07866 523092 Email: declanofarrell@hotmail.com**

CATHOLIC ARCHIVES SOCIETY

The Catholic Archives Society promotes and advises on listing, management and preservation of records of dioceses, religious foundations and institutions of the Catholic Church. It does not collect or store archives.
Secretary Sarah Maspero **38 Crawford Drive, Fareham PO16 7RW**
Email: sarah.maspero@gmail.com Web: www.catholicarchivesociety.org

CATHOLIC ASSOCIATION FOR RACIAL JUSTICE

The Catholic Association for Racial Justice is an independent charity, and a membership organisation. CARJ works with people of diverse backgrounds, in Church and society, to create a more just, more equal, more co-operative community. We do this through education, advocacy and facilitating mutual support among:

- schools, families and young people in marginalised communities
- Gypsies, Roma and Traveller communities
- those working in poor urban communities
- those suffering discrimination based on race, caste, religion and social class.

Wherever possible, CARJ works in formal or informal partnership with members, friends and fellow citizens who share our basic values.
Chair Mrs Yogi Sutton **Catholic Association for Racial Justice, 9 Henry Road N4 2LH**
Tel: 020 8802 8080 Fax: 020 8211 0808 Email: info@carj.org.uk Web: www.carj.org.uk

CATHOLIC ASSOCIATION OF PERFORMING ARTS (FORMERLY CATHOLIC STAGE GUILD)

Open to everyone with an interest in the performing arts, enabling them to use their talents to help others, work with like-minded professionals, enjoy social and networking opportunities and explore and develop their spiritual side.
Chaplain Fr Alan Robinson **Secretary** Molly Steele **1 Maiden Lane WC2E 7NB**
Tel: 020 7240 1221 Email: secretary@caapa.org.uk Web: www.caapa.org.uk

CATHOLIC BIBLICAL ASSOCIATION

To promote knowledge and love of the Bible.
Web: http://cbagb.org.uk

CATHOLIC CHARISMATIC RENEWAL

Information Centre on behalf of the National Service Committee (NSC) about Catholic Charismatic Renewal, with contacts for prayer groups and communities, and details of Goodnews, our quarterly magazine. **Contact** Goodnews, **CCR Centre, PO Box 67138 London SW11 9FD Tel: 07932 457767**
Email: ccrcentre.goodnews@gmail.com Web: www.ccr.org.uk

CATHOLIC CONCERN FOR ANIMALS

(Registered Charity 231022) CCA is the principal animal welfare organisation within the Catholic Church worldwide and we exist to promote and care for the well-being and protection of all of God's creation and work within the spirit of *Laudato Si'*, the Encyclical on the Environment by Pope Francis.
Contact Chris Fegan **Tel: 07817 730472 Email: chrisfegancca@gmail.com**
Web: www.catholic-animals.com

CATHOLIC EDUCATION SERVICE

Acts as the agent of the Bishops of England and Wales on matters of national strategy and policy, negotiating on their behalf with Government and other agencies.
Chair Archbishop Malcolm McMahon OP
Director Paul Barber **39 Eccleston Square SW1V 1BX**
Tel: 020 7901 1900 Fax: 020 7901 1939
Email: general@catholiceducation.org.uk Web: www.catholiceducation.org.uk

CATHOLIC EVANGELISATION SERVICES

Produce Catholic teaching resources on DVD to equip parishes, schools and colleges. A wide range of CaFE (Catholic Faith Exploration) resources are available for sacramental preparation, parish renewal, chaplaincy groups and to support the RE curriculum in secondary schools.
Director David Payne **PO Box 333, St Albans AL2 1EL Tel: 0845 050 9428**
Email: info@faithcafe.org Web: www.faithcafe.org www.youthcafe.org

CATHOLIC EVIDENCE GUILD

For the training and provision of public speakers on the Catholic Faith.
Enquiries Mr Phil Gough **84 Grove Green Road E11 4EL**

CATHOLIC FAMILY HISTORY SOCIETY

The Society exists to help and encourage those who have Catholic ancestry in England, Wales and Scotland to research their family history. Details of membership, publications and resources are obtainable through the website or by email.
Email: cfhsrecords@gmail.com Web: http://catholicfhs.online

CATHOLIC GRANDPARENTS ASSOCIATION

The Catholic Grandparents Association is a global organisation of the faithful. An integral part of the Catholic Grandparents Association is setting up branches at the parish level. These act as prayer and support groups for grandparents. Grandparents have a unique vocation that must be fostered and cherished in the spirit of St Joachim and St Anne, the grandparents of Jesus and parents of Mary. **PO Box 90, Walsingham, Norfolk NR21 1AQ Tel: 01328 560333**

CATHOLICS IN FUNDRAISING

A network to share best practice amongst Catholics working in fundraising for charities. Meets twice a year in London for a topical presentation, discussion and networking. There is also a LinkedIn group 'Catholics in Fundraising, UK'

Contact John Green **Email: johngreen@apostleshipofthesea.org.uk**

CATHOLIC MEDICAL ASSOCIATION

For Catholic members of the medical and healthcare professions

39 Eccleston Square SW1V 1BX Tel: 020 7901 4895 Fax: 020 7901 4819

Chairman of Westminster Branch Rev Dr Michael Jarmulowicz **337 Harrow Road W9 3RB**

Tel: 020 7286 2170 Email: secretary@catholicmedicalassociation.org.uk

Web: www. catholicmedicalassociation.org.uk

CATHOLIC MISSIONARY UNION OF ENGLAND AND WALES

The national forum and information centre of the missionary societies and congregations-lay and religious-working in mission and human development projects overseas. It promotes mission, coordinates the annual parish mission appeals by the member societies and is a consultative body to the Bishops' Conference.

Secretary Richard Owens **CMU, 37-39 Shakespeare Street, Southport PR8 5AB**

Tel: 01704 533708 Email: secretariat@cmu.org.uk Web: www.cmu.org.uk

CATHOLIC NATIONAL LIBRARY

In 2015 the Catholic National Library was gifted to Durham University, to form part of Durham University Library's collection to support research within the Centre for Catholic Studies and the wider Faculty of Arts and Humanities. Together with the collections of Ushaw College, Durham Cathedral and the University, it forms a rich resource base for theological research. Once the collection is fully assessed and catalogued, it will be accessed via the University Library catalogue: **www.durham.ac.uk/library**.

Contact Christine Purcell **Email: c.w.purcell@durham.ac.uk**

CATHOLIC PEOPLE'S WEEKS

Established in 1945, CPW run educational, residential weeks which provide the opportunity for people to combine study of their faith with thoughtful joyous liturgy, time to reflect and relax, community experience and a holiday for young and old. Chaplains serve on each week. New programme each January.

Hon Secretary Lizzy Allerton **8 Kings Close, Prestwich, Manchester M25 1QE**
Tel: 0161 773 2410 Email: secretary@catholicpeoplesweeks.org.uk
Web: www.catholicpeoplesweeks.org.uk

CATHOLIC RECORD SOCIETY

Founded in 1904 to make available material for study of the Catholic history of England and Wales since the Reformation, publishing transcripts of diaries; letters and biographies; legal, court and official papers; and records of old Catholic missions, seminaries, colleges and convents. Since then its purview has broadened considerably; it hosts an annual conference and its peer-reviewed academic journal, British Catholic History, is published twice a year by Cambridge University Press.
Contact Hon Secretary Dr Serenhedd James **Oriel College, Oxford, OX1 4EW**
Email: serenhedd.james@theology.ox.ac.uk Web: www.catholicrecordsociety.co.uk

CATHOLIC TRUTH SOCIETY

CTS supports the constant spiritual renewal of the Church and faithful, helping people to deepen their faith and share it with others by explaining the faith, teaching and life of the Catholic Church. As publisher to the Holy See, CTS publishes the official documents of the Church as they are issued, and offers authentic Catholic teaching at affordable prices.
Chair Rt Rev Paul Hendricks MA PhL VG, Auxiliary Bishop in Southwark Archdiocese
General Secretary Fergal Martin LLB, LLM
Publishing Office 42-46 Harleyford Road SE11 5AY Tel: 020 7640 0042 Fax: 020 7640 0046
Bookshop Tel: 020 7834 1363 Fax: 020 7821 7398 Email: orders@CTSbooks.org
Web: www.CTSbooks.org

CATHOLIC UNION OF GREAT BRITAIN AND C.U. CHARITABLE TRUST

CUGB is the consistent voice of the laity working to promote and develop the values of Catholic social teaching by working with the Bishops' Conference and Parliament. This is to ensure that our values are presented to key decision makers who determine legislation and social policy. We also work to promote the common good in public life and it is vital that the Catholic voice continues to be proclaimed in public. We liaise with the wider Christian community on issues of common interest. Funding is through annual individual membership subscription.
The Catholic Union Charitable Trust (CUCT) was launched in February 2015, to develop and strengthen the role of advancing Catholic moral and spiritual principles by means of conferences, lectures, training, seminars on education and by the implementation of a social media strategy. CUCT is funded is by donation through the gift aid scheme.
President Sir Edward Leigh MP **The Catholic Union, St Maximilian Kolbe House, 63 Jeddo Road W12 9EE Tel: 020 8749 1321 Email: info@catholicunion.org.uk**
Web: www.catholicunion.org.uk

CATHOLIC VOICES

An Apologetics project that has spread to 22 countries. Set up to train spokespersons for radio and TV interviews, it now also offers speakers to parishes, chaplaincies, and schools. It holds topical briefings when the Church is in the news, runs a blog (www.cvcomment.org) and has led to publications, including 'How to Defend the Faith Without Raising Your Voice'. It offers bespoke media trainings for dioceses and Catholic organisations in the UK and abroad. Independent of the Bishops' Conference, it is supported as part of their 'Confidently Catholic' agenda, encouraging lay people 'to know and live their faith with courage and give witness to it with confidence'.

Contacts Austen Ivereigh, Jack Valero, Kathleen Griffin and Eileen Cole
Email: info@catholicvoices.org.uk **Web:** www.catholicvoices.org.uk
Twitter: @CatholicVoices.

CATHOLIC WOMEN'S LEAGUE

The Catholic Women's League was founded in 1906. It is a Catholic agency uniting Catholic women in a bond of friendship and encouraging them to use their talents in the service of the Church and the community, reaching out to every area of concern.

Contact Veronica Comparini, President Westminster Branch **Tel:** 01442 258684
Email: veedotcomp@gmail.com, Jean Clarke, National Secretary **Email:** natsec@cwlhq.org.uk
Web: catholicwomensleaguecio.org.uk

CHRISTIAN LIFE COMMUNITY

Small groups of Christians who meet regularly to help each other deepen their life of prayer. CLC's special characteristic is the spirituality of St Ignatius, helping members to integrate prayer with action in their daily lives.

National Chaplain Br Alan Harrison SJ **Diocesan Representative** Jackie Gill **(Administrator)**
114 Mount Street W1K 3AH Email: president@clcew.org.uk

COMMUNITY OF SANT'EGIDIO

The Community of Sant'Egidio is a 'Church Public Lay Association' which began in Rome in 1968. The different communities, spread across 73 countries, share the same spirituality and principles which characterise the way of Sant'Egidio: Prayer, Communicating the Gospel, Solidarity with the Poor, Ecumenism, and Dialogue.

The Community regularly gathers for common prayer, as a pathway to becoming familiar with Jesus' words, presenting to the Lord the needs of poor people, our own needs and the needs of the whole world. The Community of Sant'Egidio, in London as elsewhere, lives in service to the poor in friendship and familiarity, considering them as brothers and sisters, especially the homeless and the elderly in nursing homes.

Email: cse.london@gmail.com **Web:** www.santegidio.org.uk, www.santegidio.org

COMMUNITY OF THE RISEN LORD

The mission of the Community of the Risen Lord (CRL) UK is to bring life-transforming renewal both to parishes and Dioceses, with outreach and pastoral activities based on the teaching of the Catholic Church. Meetings are held at St. Joseph's Pastoral Centre, Hendon, from 3.30-5.30 pm on 2nd and 4th Sundays.

Contact: Sonia Tissera **(UK Co-ordinator),** Niru Fernando **and** Eric Jeevaraj **(Co-Group Team)**
70 Roxeth Green Avenue, South Harrow HA2 8AG Tel: 07957 117928
Email: ericc2210@gmail.com Web: www.crlmain.org

CONSECRATED WOMEN

Vatican II restored the Order of Virgins, which dates from the early Church. Canon 604 speaks of this form of consecrated life, mentioned in the Catechism (paras 922-4). We are consecrated publicly by the Bishop to live an independent life within the local church community. Each woman is autonomous, and her pattern of life is planned by herself and approved by the Bishop. She is responsible for her own finances. Other women are consecrated as widows; our vow is for life. Those who wish meet annually for a week at Hyning monastery. This kind of religious life combines freedom with commitment.

Contact: Gosia Brykczynska OCV **148 Carlyle Road W5 4BJ Tel: 020 8560 0120**
Email: gosia.brykczynska@talktalk.net

CONSTANTINIAN ORDER OF ST GEORGE

Internationally recognised ancient and charitable Catholic Order of Knighthood under the custodianship of the Royal House of Bourbon Two Sicilies.

Grand Master HRH The Duke of Castro **Prior** HE Vincent, Cardinal Nichols, Archbishop of Westminster **Sub-Prior** Most Rev George Stack, Archbishop of Cardiff; **Chief Chaplain for Ireland** Most Rev Dr Raymond Field, Auxiliary to the Archbishop of Dublin; **Delegate for Britain and Ireland** HE Mr Anthony Bailey;
Vice-Delegates HE Mr John Bruton **(Ireland),** The Rt Hon Lord Murphy of Torfaen **(Great Britain),** The Hon Sir Peter Caruana **(Gibraltar)**
Contact Sacred Military Constantinian Order of St George
12 Queen's Gate Gardens SW7 5LY Tel: 020 7594 0275 Fax: 020 7594 0265
Email: chancery@constantinian.org.uk Web: www.constantinian.org.uk

COUPLES FOR CHRIST (CFC)

Renewing the face of the earth, moved by the Holy Spirit, one with the Catholic Church, and blessed to witness to Christ's love and service, Couples for Christ is a united global community of family evangelizers that sets the world on fire with the fullness of God's transforming love.

Contact Bong Nidea **UK Head Tel: 07576 227725 Email: nideabong@gmail.com**
Joel Rama **UK Elder Co-ordinator Tel: 07584 414290**
Email: marku2much@yahoo.com Web: http://couplesforchristuk.weebly.com

DOMINICAN LAITY

For those called to spread the Gospel in the tradition of St Dominic. The Fraternity meets monthly at St Dominic's Priory, Southampton Road NW5 4LB.

Chaplain Fr Leo Edgar OP **Secretary** Alison Fincham **5 New Street, Canterbury CT2 8AU Email: alison_fincham@yahoo.co.uk**

DOMINICAN SECULAR INSTITUTE

A life consecrated to God through vows, offering challenge and mutual support, helping to develop our apostolate and service to others. **Moderator** Miss Janet Wiltshire **19 Broomfield Place, Earlsdon, Coventry CV5 6GY Email: Janetwilts@aol.com**

EMMANUEL COMMUNITY

A Public Association of the Faithful, recognised by the Holy See, for lay people, priests, deacons and consecrated men and women. **Web: www.emmanuel.info**

ENGLISH CATHOLIC HISTORY ASSOCIATION

To promote interest and encourage research into English and Welsh Catholic history. Helps preserve relevant documents. Arranges regular meetings/visits. Members' quarterly newsletter. **Secretary** Mrs Angela Hodges **45 High Street, Stoke sub Hamdon, Somerset TA14 6PR Tel: 01935 823928 Email: secretary@echa.org.uk Web: www.echa.org.uk**

FOCOLARE MOVEMENT

An international ecclesial movement started by Chiara Lubich in 1943 at Trent in N. Italy. Its principal aim is to help bring about the fulfilment of the prayer of Jesus 'That all may be one'. **Focolare Centre for Unity, 69 Parkway, Welwyn Garden City AL8 6JG Tel: 01707 323620 Email: cfu@focolare.org.uk Web: www.focolare.org/gb**

FRIENDS OF THE HOLY FATHER

To pray for the Holy Father's intentions, study and promote his teaching. Supports a fund assisting in defraying expenses of his Apostolic Ministry. **Chair** John Dean DipLaw, DipLP **Secretary** Dr Michael Straiton MB, KCSG **23a Vincent House, Vincent Square SW1P 2NB Email: fhfenquiries@gmail.com Web: www.thefriendsoftheholyfather.org**

FRIENDS OF THE HOLY LAND

FHL (Registered Charity 1130054) helps Christians to flourish in the land of their birth, securing a presence where Christianity began. We raise awareness of the challenges Christians face, encourage prayers for them, generate funds towards a sustainable future, and encourage Holy Land pilgrims to meet local Christians. Projects include repairs to deteriorating homes; developing a Day Care Centre for the elderly in Bethlehem; offering help with medical bills and school fees; and supporting families in desperate need.

FHL is organised to suit parishes in both Catholic and Anglican dioceses and is frequently represented through parish groups which meet regularly to pray, share information about the Holy Land and organise fundraising. Cardinal Vincent Nichols is one of the Charity's Patrons.

Chair Jim Quinn **Vice-Chair** Peter Rand **Hon Treasurer** Tony Stokes

Contact Karen Baxter **(Office Manager) Friends of the Holy Land, Farmer Ward Road, Kenilworth, Warwickshire CV8 2DH Tel: 01926 512980 Email: office@friendsoftheholyland.org.uk Web: www.friendsoftheholyland.org.uk**

FRIENDS OF THE ORDINARIATE OF OUR LADY OF WALSINGHAM

The aim of the Friends is to raise money from across the Catholic community to support the work and mission of the Ordinariate. In particular we assist with the training and support of priests and invest in churches owned or used by the Ordinariate..

Contact Peter Sefton-Williams **c/o 24 Golden Square W1F 9JR**

Email: peter@seftonwilliams.com Web: http://friendsoftheordinariate.org.uk/

FRIENDS OF THE *VENERABILE* (THE ENGLISH COLLEGE IN ROME)

The Friends (Charity no. 1075141) support students of the College, who will be our future priests, with prayers, encouragement and financial help. **Contact** Mike Lang **Tel: 01364 644811**

Email: mikelang537@btinternet.com Web: www.friendsofenglishcollegerome.org.uk

GOOD COUNSEL NETWORK

A Catholic, pro-life pregnancy centre in central London providing friendship and practical help and ongoing support of all kinds to assist women to choose life for their children. We have Daily Mass and Adoration in our Centre. We provide speakers and run a monthly day of prayer and fasting for the end of abortion. We provide post-abortion counselling, too. We welcome volunteers who wish to help us in our work.

Director Clare McCullough **The Good Counsel Network, PO Box 46679 NW9 8ZT**

Tel: 020 7723 1740 Email: info@goodcounselnetwork.com

Web: www.goodcounselnetwork.com Blog: mariastopsabortion.blogspot.com

GRAIL, THE

The Grail has always worked to share its Christian inspiration and values with the world by encouraging awareness of God's presence in the individual, communities and creation, in the belief that to help one person to grow is to help to build the world. Today this work is being continued through the making of small grants to other charities or groups whose work embodies these values. For full details of eligibility and application forms **contact**

Email: president@grailsociety.org.uk Web: www.grailsociety.org.uk

GUILD OF OUR LADY OF RANSOM

Founded 29th November 1887 with a threefold mission: 1. The conversion of England and Wales; 2. The restoration of the lapsed; and 3. Praying for the forgotten dead.

The Guild has moved its administration to Walsingham. To support its work **contact**

The Guild of Our Lady of Ransom **Catholic National Shrine of Our Lady, Pilgrim Bureau, Friday Market Place, Walsingham, Norfolk NR22 6EG Tel: 01328 800999**

E-mail: info@guild-ransom.co.uk Web: www.guild-ransom.co.uk

GUILD OF OUR LADY OF WILLESDEN

The Guild is open to all and meets every Tuesday at **Our Lady of Willesden, Nicoll Road NW10 9AX** after the 7pm Mass. Its purpose is to pray for the intentions and protection of London through the intercession of Our Lady of Willesden.

Guild Master Fr Stephen Willis

GUILD OF ST AGATHA

Catholic Association of Bellringers. **Guild Office, 1 Albert Road, Bournemouth BH1 1BZ**
Diocesan Representative Canon Shaun Lennard **243 Mutton Lane, Potters Bar EN6 2AT**
Tel: 01707 654359

HERALDS OF THE GOSPEL

Association of Pontifical Right formed mainly by young people who alternate a life of recollection, study and prayer with evangelising activities. Their spirituality is based on devotion to the Holy Eucharist, love for Mary and fidelity to the Pope. **Contact** Rev Deacon Arthur Hlebnikian **29 Lower Teddington Road, Hampton Wick KT1 4EU Tel: 020 8943 4159**
Email: lumenmaria@aol.com Web: www. arautos.org

HOLY SEPULCHRE, EQUESTRIAN ORDER OF THE

To strengthen in its members the Christian life, in fidelity to the Pope and the teachings of the Church, observing the principles of charity for assistance to the Holy Land; to aid the charitable, cultural and social works and institutions of the Church in the Holy Land, particularly those of and in the Latin Patriarchate of Jerusalem, with which the Order maintains ties; to support the propagation of the Faith there, involving in this work Catholics scattered throughout the world, united in charity by the symbol of the Order, and also all brother Christians; and to sustain the rights of the Catholic Church in the Holy Land.
Contact Roland Hayes **Email: khswestminsterpres@gmail.com Web: www.khs.org.uk**

HOME MISSION OFFICE

CBCEW's Department of Evangelisation and Catechesis helps the local Church to make the joy of the Gospel a reality in England and Wales. The Priorities are:
* To inspire the faithful to deepen and share their faith
* To facilitate formation of those engaged in evangelisation in local dioceses
* To develop outreach to people who do not subscribe to any faith

The Home Mission Office engages with the local Church to achieve these priorities, working with Diocesan evangelisation personnel, leaders of New Movements, CYMFed and Catholic resource providers who support evangelisation and catechesis in a parish context. It also produces resources for Home Mission Sunday and National Youth Sunday.
Chair Bishop Mark O'Toole **Development Officer** Teresa Carvalho
Catechetical Development Officer Victoria Seed **Executive Assistant** Sylvia Ideh
Tel: 020 7901 4882 Email: home.mission@cbcew.org.uk
The Catholic Enquiry Office exists to respond to those enquiring about the Catholic Faith and helping them to connect with their local parish. This is supported by the staff in the Home Mission Office **Email: ceo@cbcew.org.uk**

HOUSING JUSTICE

Through national membership we offer advice and training on delivering services to people who are homeless or in housing need; facilitate and co-ordinate frontline services, including a London-wide winter shelters forum; and campaign for better legislation. We support the development of services nationwide and champion alternative solutions, notably housing cooperatives and community land trusts. Members are available to speak to groups or after Masses about homelessness and housing. We also co-ordinate the annual Homeless Sunday, on the 4th Sunday in January.

Chief Executive Kathy Mohan **256 Bermondsey Street SE1 3UJ Tel: 020 3544 8094 Email: info@housingjustice.org.uk Web: www.housingjustice.org.uk**

IMPACT

Young people making a difference (13-17 year-olds) trains young people to become leaders in life using the 'See, Judge, Act' method. See '**Young Christian Workers**' for more details.

JOHN PAUL II FOUNDATION FOR SPORT (JP2F4S)

Launched by Pope Benedict XVI during his visit to Britain, to honour the memory of St John Paul II and his vision for sport, this charity enables the setting up of clubs in parishes and schools, supports clubs in need of advice and guidance and produces educational materials for schools and parishes. Catholic in inspiration, working with all and for all, its purpose is summed up in its strapline: 'Educating young people through sport'.

Contact Mgr Vladimir Felzmann CEO **John Paul II Foundation for Sport, Vaughan House, 46 Francis Street SW1P 1QN Email: info@jp2f4s.org**

KNIGHTS OF ST COLUMBA

Fraternal order of Catholic men supporting the mission of the Church and the spiritual, intellectual and material welfare of its members and their families.

Head Office, 75 Hillington Road South, Glasgow G52 2AE Tel: 0141 883 5700
Email: headoffice@ksc.org.uk
Provincial Grand Knights: Province 11 Roger Khan, **Province 29** Benjamin Agwunobi **Province 30** Rosario Fichardo

LATIN MASS SOCIETY

Founded in 1965, LMS is an association of Catholic faithful and a registered charity with around 2,000 members, predominantly lay, drawn from every age, group and walk of life. It is dedicated to promoting the use and wider provision of the Traditional Latin Mass (the Extraordinary Form) and other Sacraments. Working with its network of local representatives, the Society organises pilgrimages, retreats, days of recollection, training conferences for priests and servers, conferences for the general public, research and campaigning. It is a supporter of the Gregorian Chant Network (**www.gregorianchantnetwork.org**). Details of its sodality for altar servers, the Society of St Tarcisius (**www.liturgialatina.org/tarcisius**), and family and youth affiliates can be obtained from the London office. It also publishes a quarterly magazine, Mass of Ages. Its online shop offers books and DVDs on the Traditional Mass and devotions.

Contact National Office **11-13 Macklin Street WC2B 5NH Tel: 020 7404 7284 Email: info@lms.org.uk Web: lms.org.uk**

LAY MISSIONARY AND VOLUNTEER NETWORK

An informal group of Catholic missionary and volunteer organisations which offer faith-based volunteering overseas. Co-ordinators meet to share ideas and resources and each summer run a residential week-long pre-departure training course for volunteers. This training course is also open to those going to volunteer abroad with religious orders who may not have access to training.

Each organisation has its own charism and sending practice (opportunities, countries, length of service, age range). If you'd like to volunteer with one of us contact details for each website can be found on **Facebook page LMVN**

LIFE ASCENDING MOVEMENT (FORMERLY THE ASCENT)

For Christians in middle and later life helping them grow spiritually and to take up their responsibilities as members of the Church through friendship, spirituality and mission, with parish-based regular meeings.

National President Mr Ross Roberts **77 Bingham Road, Addiscombe, Croydon CRO 7EJ Tel: 020 8656 6873 Email: rosscharlesroberts@yahoo.com**

National Secretary Mrs Marylyn Duncan **29 Middle Lane N8 8PJ Tel: 020 8342 9392 Email: maazaa@hotmail.co.uk**

LONDON CATHOLIC WORKER

LCW is part of the international Catholic Worker movement founded in 1933 by Dorothy Day and Peter Maurin. CW communities are houses of hospitality for the poor as well as places to perform the works of mercy and organise resistance to the works of war, injustice and violence. The movement practises hospitality, active non-violence, gentle personalism and voluntary poverty. Each community is independent, with no HQ. We need full-time live-in community members and volunteers, as well as part-time volunteers and donations in cash or in kind. **Contact** London Catholic Worker **49 Mattison Road N4 1BG Tel: 020 8348 8212 Email: londoncatholicworker@yahoo.co.uk Web: www.londoncatholicworker.org**

MALTA, ORDER OF (BRITISH ASSOCIATION)

A British charity and a religious order of the Church, supporting in the UK, inter alia, The Orders of St John Care Trust, soup kitchens in London, Oxford, Cambridge, Colchester and St Andrews and pilgrimages for the sick to Lourdes and Walsingham.

British Association Sovereign Military Order of Malta, Craigmyle House, 13 Deodar Road SW15 2NP Tel: 020 7286 1414 Email: basmom@btconnect.com.

MARIST WAY

The Marist Way is the lay branch of the Marist Congregation, bringing together people who wish to participate in the life and mission of the Church in the `Spirit of Mary', a way envisaged by Jean-Claude Colin, founder of the Marists, who are Priests, Sisters, Brothers and Laity.

Marists endeavour to think, feel, judge and act as Mary did, at Nazareth and at Pentecost All Marists believe that Mary maintains a special interest in bringing the women and men of our time into contact with her Son, Jesus. They feel called to share in this concern of Mary's and to become part of her family to work on her behalf. The term `the work of Mary' describes this essentially missionary spirit.

Contact Mrs Pat O'Connor **12 Harrow Road, Linthorpe, Middlesbrough TS5 5PD Tel: 01642 814486 Email: patriciaoconnor@ntlworld.com**

MARRIAGE CARE

We provide marriage preparation and relationship counselling to thousands of couples each year through a network of centres and professionally accredited volunteers. Ring our appointments service to book a place on a marriage preparation course for those marrying in the Catholic Church or for a counselling appointment. If you are interested in helping us support couples in your community we'd love to hear from you, please go to our website.
Family Lives line: 0808 800 2222
Registered office (Charity number 218159): Marriage Care, Huntingdon House, 278 Huntingdon Street, Nottingham NG1 3LY Tel: 0800 389 3801
Email: info@marriagecare.org.uk Web: www.marriagecare.org.uk

MARRIAGE ENCOUNTER

Provides weekends for couples and those who are engaged, in association with priests and religious, to enrich their lives through improving communication.
Contact Phil and Rita Jackson **Web: http://wwme.org.uk/**

MARY POTTER CENTRE

Offering counselling, coaching, spiritual direction, talks, courses, and workshops to build self-understanding, confidence, deal with stress, difficult relationships, loss, bereavement, anxiety and distress; also psychometric testing. EFT, Tips for prevention of age-related memory loss.
Director Sr Josephine Bugeja LCM, MA, RGN, RMN **Flat 10 Berkeley Court, 33 Gordon Road W5 2AE Tel: 020 8810 4432 Email: jbugeja@aol.com**

MING-AI (LONDON) INSTITUTE

A lifelong education centre having close links with Caritas-Hong Kong, providing MA in Chinese Cultural Heritage Management and a wide range of leisure, cookery, health, business, oriental language classes, as well as community projects. It promotes links between our Diocese and the Church in Hong Kong and China. **Chairman** Professor Jonathan Liu
Dean Ms Chungwen Li **Ming-Ai (London) Institute, 1 Cline Road N11 2LX**
Tel: 020 8361 7161 Email: enquiry@ming-ai.org.uk Web: www.ming-ai.org.uk

MISSIO

The Pope's official charity for overseas mission, with 120 offices worldwide under the co-ordination of the Pontifical Mission Societies in Rome. We are the Holy Father's chosen instrument for sharing the Gospel and building the Church throughout the world.
Together, the Missio offices globally support 1,069 dioceses in 157 countries. It is the only Catholic charity which supports the 40% of the Universal Church that is too new, young or poor to support itself. We aim to follow Christ's example by helping everyone in need, regardless of background or belief.
Missio comprises four branches which work together: the Association for the Propagation of the Faith (APF), the Society of St Peter the Apostle (SPA), Mission Together (MT), and the Pontifical Missionary Union (PMU).

National Director Fr Anthony Chantry MHM
National Office for Missio 23 Eccleston Square SW1V 1NU (Reg. Charity No. 1056651)
Tel: 020 7821 9755 Email: info@missio.org.uk Web: www.missio.org.uk

MISSION TOGETHER (HOLY CHILDHOOD)

Part of the Missio network, Mission Together (MT) provides such things as healthcare and education for the world's poorest children, regardless of background or belief. It supports vulnerable children via educational, medical and welfare projects through schools, orphanages, health centres, children's homes and nutrition programmes. The food, education, medications, shelter, and formation that MT provides fulfil both the children's spiritual and practical needs.
National Office for Missio 23 Eccleston Square SW1V 1NU (Reg. Charity No. 1056651)
Tel: 020 7821 9755 Email: missiontogether@missio.org.uk Web: www.missio.org.uk

NATIONAL BOARD OF CATHOLIC WOMEN

A consultative body to the Bishops' Conference of England & Wales with consultative status within the United Nations, with representatives from 32 Catholic organisations and the dioceses. A forum in which women are enabled to share their views and concerns and make recommendations at all levels.
Tel: 07724 685780 Email: nbcwpres@gmail.com Web: nbcw.co.uk

NATIONAL COUNCIL FOR LAY ASSOCIATIONS (ENGLAND AND WALES)

A consultative body to the Bishops' Conference, consisting of lay apostolic national organisations, 8 liaison representatives, advisors & executive. **Adviser** Bishop Tom Williams
President John Smart **Tel: 07711 148907 Email: president@ncla.org.uk**
Secretary Debbie Cottam **Email: secretary@ncla.org.uk**

NEWMAN ASSOCIATION

National association of Catholic laity and clergy. Local circles **London** Patricia Donald **Tel: 020 8504 2017; Ealing** Martin Redfern **6 Tudor Way W3 9AG Email: MartinTRedfern@gmail.com; Herts** Maggy Swift **Email: maggy.swift@btinternet.com**

OUR LADY'S CATECHISTS (SPECIAL COMMITTEE OF THE CATHOLIC WOMEN'S LEAGUE)

An association of men and women who are qualified to give religious instruction. We work in parishes and also by distance learning. Postal and online courses include our Foundation Course, leading to a qualification certificate for training parish catechists or as a personal development course only; our Diploma Course, which provides more academic training enabling catechists to lead parish programmes; the Catholicism Made Simple Course, which is a basic introduction to the faith for adults and youth; and the Children's Section, which provides courses and lesson leaflets for parents or catechists working with children attending non-Catholic schools and in preparation for the first Sacraments. Our latest course is Mysteries of the Christian Life, based on the 20 decades of the Rosary.
Contact Charmaine Jayasuriya **Tel: 01442 267035 Email: dcharmainej@gmail.com**
Web: www.ourladyscatechists.wordpress.com

PAX CHRISTI

Pax Christi is a gospel-based international movement for peace, open to all. We strive to help the Church and wider community to proclaim and make peace through its work for reconciliation and the promotion of a culture of peace and non-violence. We offer a wide range of materials for education, reflection and campaigning for peace. Pax Christi also produces material for parishes each year to encourage support for Peace Sunday (the Pope's World Peace Message), celebrated on the 2nd Sunday in Ordinary Time.

National President Archbishop Malcolm McMahon OP **General Secretary** Patricia Gaffney
St Joseph's, Watford Way NW4 4TY Tel: 020 8203 4884 Email: info@paxchristi.org.uk
Web: www.paxchristi.org.uk

PONTIFICAL MISSIONARY UNION (PMU)

Part of the Missio network, the Pontifical Mission Union (PMU) is responsible for encouraging all the faithful to have passion for mission and evangelisation. As Catholics we are encouraged to share the love of God through our words and actions with our global family.

National Office for Missio 23 Eccleston Square SW1V 1NU (Reg. Charity No. 1056651)
Tel: 020 7821 9755 Email: info@missio.org.uk Web: www.missio.org.uk

POPE'S WORLDWIDE PRAYER NETWORK

The Network (formerly the Apostleship of Prayer) is based with the Jesuit Community at St Ignatius church in Stamford Hill, where the National Director, Fr David Stewart SJ is resident. Its renewal was mandated by Pope Benedict, then by Pope Francis. The 175 year-old ministry is active in almost 100 countries, inviting the faithful to pray the Monthly Intentions of the Holy Father. It offers the Daily Prayer Pathway, expanding the traditional Morning Offering, whilst the new 'Way of the Heart' renews the much-loved devotion to the Sacred Heart. All parishes are invited and encouraged to pray with the Pope. Office hours: Monday and Tuesday only.

PWPN National Office, 27 High Road N15 6ND Tel: 020 8442 5232 / 07432 591117
Email: prayernetwork@jesuit.org.uk Twitter: @PraywiththePope Skype: jdstewartsj

PRAY AS YOU GO

A daily prayer session produced by the Jesuits in Britain and designed for use on portable MP3 players. Visit **www.pray-as-you-go.org** to listen to the daily sessions, explore other resources, and find out how to subscribe to the podcast or download apps for iOS and Android.

114 Mount Street W1K 3AH Tel: 020 7499 0285 Email: feedback@pray-as-you-go.org

PRISON ADVICE & CARE TRUST (FORMERLY THE BOURNE TRUST)

Pact is the national Catholic charity working to support prisoners, people with convictions and their families. We work in courts, prisons and in the community to support people to make a fresh start, and to minimise the harm that can be caused by imprisonment to people who have committed offences, on families and on communities. If you or someone you know needs support, call free, confidential helpline **0808 808 3444**, email **helpline@prisonadvice.org.uk** or fill in the webform at **prisonadvice.org.uk/forms/contact-our-helpline**. If interested in the criminal justice system, please get in touch for information about volunteer opportunities.

29 Peckham Road SE5 8UA Tel: 020 7735 9535 Email: ParishAction@prisonadvice. org.uk Web: www.prisonadvice.org.uk

PROJECT 2030

Our group enables Catholics in their 40s to get together at a social and spiritual level. Events include Masses, retreats, walks, meals, museum visits, pilgrimages, holidays, and other opportunities to meet up together.

National office: St John's, 266 Wellington Road North, Heaton Chapel SK4 2QR
Contact Rev Hugh Hanley SCJ **Email: project2030@btinternet.com**

RETROUVAILLE

A lifeline for troubled marriages, helping heal and renew marriages in distress. For couples who are finding it difficult to communicate; who argue about everything or live in silence; who feel alone, lonely and distant; who may think separation and divorce are their only options.

Contact Michael and Frances Hyland (Co-ordinators) **Tel: 07887 296983**
Julie and Gearoid MacAmhlaoibh **Tel: 07973 380443**
Email: info@retrouvaille.org.uk Web: www.retrouvaille.org.uk

ST BARNABAS SOCIETY (SUCCESSOR TO THE CONVERTS' AID SOCIETY)

For the assistance of needy former clergy and religious received into the Catholic Church.

Secretary Fr Paul Martin **Windsor House, Heritage Gate, East Point Business Park, Sandy Lane West, Oxford OX4 6L Tel: 01865 513377 Email: directorstbarnabas@gmail.com Web: www.StBarnabasSociety.org.uk**

ST FRANCIS LEPROSY GUILD

SFLG's mission since 1895 has been the alleviation of the suffering caused by Leprosy. We give material support to leprosy hospitals, clinics, residential and outreach centres for leprosy sufferers and former patients and their dependents who are unable to return to their communities through disability or cultural prejudices.

Hon Secretary Sr Helen McMahon FMM **73 St Charles Square W10 6EJ**
Tel: 020 8969 1345 Email: enquiries@stfrancisleprosy.org

ST FRANCIS OF ASSISI CATHOLIC RAMBLERS CLUB

Organises Sunday walks in London and the Home Counties throughout the year. Rambles on additional days and further afield are occasionally provided, plus other social activities. **Contact** Antoinette Adkins **Tel: 020 8769 3643** or **Email: antoinette_adkins2000@yahoo.co.uk** for an information pack or for further details go to **www.stfrancisramblers.ukwalkers.com**

ST JOSEPH'S SOCIETY (FORMERLY THE AGED POOR SOCIETY)

Provides accommodation for elderly Catholics in need and of limited means.

Secretary S Dolan **St Joseph's Almshouse, 42 Brook Green W6 7BW**
Tel: 020 7603 9817 Email: stjosephssociety@yahoo.co.uk

ST VINCENT DE PAUL SOCIETY

The St Vincent de Paul Society (SVP) is an international Christian society, Catholic in character and origin. The Society's mission is to bear witness to Christ's love and to put his teaching into practice. With mutual support, friendship and encouragement, members seek to reach out and extend their commitment through person-to-person care for those disadvantaged, neglected or in need. They seek to identify the causes of need, provide items of furniture, clothing and food where appropriate and offer the hand of friendship. In these ways members aim to develop their own spiritual lives, strengthening their own faith and deepening their love of God and their neighbour.

Contact St Vincent de Paul Society **Romero House, 55 Westminster Bridge Road SE1 7JB**
Tel: 020 7703 3030 Email: info@svp.org.uk Web: www.svp.org.uk

ST VINCENT'S FAMILY PROJECT

The Project provides direct support to families in Westminster and beyond. Family Space supports 130+ families, offering free accredited parenting programmes, Drop-In, Crèche, Speech & Language assessment, Specialised Advice & Healthy Living classes. In addition, Creative Arts Therapy, via Art, Drama and Dance & Movement provides for 28+ local children experiencing emotional difficulties. Our 40+ Volunteering and Student Intern opportunities are via the Volunteer Space programme. Our six Vincentian values are: being respectful, inspired, travellers together, professional, holistic and compassionate.

St Vincent's Family Project, Methodist Central Hall, Storey's Gate
SW1H 9NH Tel: 020 7654 5351 Email: info@svfp.org.uk Web: www.svfp.org.uk

SECULAR CLERGY COMMON FUND

Secretary Michael O'Shea **St Mary's Cemetery, 679-681 Harrow Road NW10 5NU**
Tel: 020 8969 1145

SECULAR CLERGY NEW COMMON FUND

Chief Administrator Mgr Canon Nicholas Rothon **Tel: 020 8852 5420**
Diocesan Representative (Provisional) Fr Graham Stokes **Tel: 020 8868 7531**

SECULAR FRANCISCAN ORDER

St Francis of Assisi left us 'a Dream to dream and a Journey to challenge everyone'. All Franciscans are inspired by him to follow Christ. The Secular Franciscan Order belongs to this family. In their secular state, members permanently commit themselves to live the Gospel as Francis did, following his Rule approved by the Pope. The OFS is open to the laity and diocesan clergy. There are more than 850 Secular Franciscans in Great Britain. Gathering in fraternities, they strive to grow in the love of God and in peace with each other. In this way, they aspire to be faithful disciples of Christ.

Contact National Secretary Pam Thornton **5 Palmerston Road, Liverpool L18 8AJ**
Email: natsec@ofsgb.org Web: ofsgb.org

SION CENTRE FOR DIALOGUE & ENCOUNTER

A centre for study and growth in mutual understanding between Christians and Jews, as well

as other faiths and cultures. As a place to listen, learn, reflect and respect we offer a regular programme of courses and lectures, as well as times for reflection and prayer. Our specialist library has staff available to assist with research. Outside groups also use our facilities for their own seminars, training and meetings. The Centre is run by the Sisters of Our Lady of Sion.
Director Sr Margaret Shepherd nds **34 Chepstow Villas W11 2QZ Tel: 020 7313 8286**
Email: sioncentrefordialogue@gmail.com Web: www.sioncentre.com

SOCIETY OF CATHOLIC ARTISTS

Aims to encourage high standards in Church art, to assist prospective patrons in the selection of suitable artists and craftsmen and to provide fellowship to those who have the arts and Catholicism in common.
Email: mj.sibtain@virgin.net Web: www.catholicartists.co.uk

SOCIETY OF OUR LADY OF LOURDES

To promote devotion to Our Lady, organise services and pilgrimages and assist sick pilgrims, financially and otherwise, to go to Lourdes. **c/o Church of the Immaculate Heart of Mary, Botwell Lane, Hayes UB3 2AB Tel: 020 8848 9833 Fax: 020 8848 9844**
Email: enquiries@soll-lourdes.com Web: www.soll-lourdes.com

SOCIETY OF ST AUGUSTINE OF CANTERBURY

Promotion and advancement of the Roman Catholic religion in England and Wales, principally through assistance in the maintenance of Archbishop's House, Westminster.
Secretary Richard Collyer-Hamlin **77 Gibbon Road, Kingston upon Thames, Surrey KT2 6AE Tel: 07970 401731 Email: richardcollyerhamlin@hotmail.com**
Web: www.staugustineofcanterbury.org.uk

SOCIETY OF ST GREGORY

The national Catholic society promoting understanding, active participation and good practice in the celebration of the liturgy. It organises summer schools, lectures and study for all who are engaged in liturgy and music. The journal Music and Liturgy (available by subscription) contains articles, news, reviews and a practical liturgy planner.
Diocesan representative John Ainslie **76 Great Bushey Drive N20 8QL Tel: 020 8445 5724**
Email: john.ainslie@ssg.org.uk Web: www.ssg.org.uk

SOCIETY OF ST JOHN CHRYSOSTOM

Founded in 1926 to encourage greater knowledge, understanding and appreciation of the tradition of the Eastern Churches, to promote Catholic-Orthodox unity and to support the Eastern Catholic Churches. Publishes *Chrysostom* three times a year.
Email: johnchrysostom@btinternet.com Web: www.orientalelumen.org.uk
President Cardinal Vincent Nichols, Archbishop of Westminster
Chair Fr Mark Woodruff **Tel: 07710 024505 Email: as above**
Membership & General Enquiries Mrs Ola Stayne **22 Esher Avenue, Walton on Thames KT12 2TA Email: miss_ola0127@yahoo.pl**

SOCIETY OF ST PETER THE APOSTLE (SPA)

Part of the Missio network, the Society of St Peter the Apostle trains the Church leaders of tomorrow, bringing the love of Christ to vulnerable communities, and passing on the gift of faith to future generations in over 157 countries around the world. Every year Missio's SPA supports the training of 30,000 future priests and 11,000 religious sisters in the mission dioceses. Only SPA, as the Pope's own charity, has this unique role throughout the world.

Diocesan Director for Missio Fr Philip Knights **Email: philipknights@rcdow.org.uk**
National Office for Missio 23 Eccleston Square SW1V 1NU (Reg. Charity No. 1056651)
Tel: 020 7821 9755 Email: spa@missio.org.uk Web: www.missio.org.uk

TEAMS (EQUIPES NOTRE-DAME)

International movement for married couples of all ages whose purpose is to help couples live fully the Sacrament of Marriage. Groups of 4-6 couples, with a chaplain or spiritual advisor, meet monthly in each others' homes to support, pray and discuss Scripture. There are over 13,500 such Teams around the world.

Contact Piotr and Dzidzia Chodzko-Zajko **49 Ravenor Park Road, Greenford UB6 9QY**
Tel: 020 8575 5421 Email: central@teamsgb.org.uk Web: www.teamsgb.org.uk

THINKING FAITH

The online journal of the Jesuits in Britain. Articles, film reviews and book reviews to help you think about your faith and think, through your faith, about the world. Visit **www.thinkingfaith.org** to see latest content, search the archive and subscribe to regular email alerts.

114 Mount Street W1K 3AH Tel: 020 7499 0285 Email: editor@thinkingfaith.org

UNION OF CATHOLIC MOTHERS

National organisation for the preservation of the family and sanctification of the home.

Diocesan President Mrs Iona De Souza **47 Redfern Avenue, Whitton TW4 5NA**
Tel: 020 8894 2366 Email: ionadesouza@aol.com
Spiritual Director Awaiting appointment

VINCENTIAN VOLUNTEERS

A challenging and fulfilling Gap Year in the UK for 18-35 year olds of any nationality, living in small communities serving people who are vulnerable, in the spirit of St. Vincent de Paul.

Contact Marion Osuide **St. Matthew's Presbytery, Worsley Road, Eccles, Manchester M30 8BL Tel: 07708 314996 Email: marion@vincentianvolunteers.org.uk**
Web: www.vincentianvolunteers.org.uk

YOUNG CHRISTIAN WORKERS & IMPACT

A movement of apostolic formation, for young people between 13 and 30. Through a programme of enquiry in small groups in parishes and schools, YCW educates and trains young people for their mission of Christian service in everyday life. It enables them to become apostles to other young people and prepares them for the responsibilities of adult Christian life. YCW also produces educative enquiry discussion material and arranges numerous training events, including residential weekends.

Contact YCW HQ **St Anthony's Presbytery, Eleventh Street, Trafford Park, Manchester M17 1JF Tel: 0161 872 6017 Email: info@ycwimpact.com Web: www.ycwimpact.com**

YOUTH 2000

Seeks to enable young people to encounter Jesus Christ, at the heart of the Catholic Church. This is primarily through weekend Prayer Festivals, where young people are introduced to the essentials of the catholic faith: Mass, Eucharistic Adoration, Confession, Scripture and Devotion to Our Lady. These are opportunities to build friendships, experience God's love, receive the grace of conversion and begin living anew the christian life. **Charity No. 1000371**

Contact Youth 2000 **Pilgrim Bureau, Friday Market Place, Walsingham NR22 6EG**
Tel: 01328 821153 / 07585 039442 Email: admin@youth2000.org
Web: http://youth2000.org

WORLD APOSTOLATE OF FATIMA

A Public Association of the Faithful which promotes Our Lady's call to live the Gospel more profoundly through prayer, penance, offering up daily duties in a spirit of sacrifice, daily recitation of the Rosary and the Five First Saturdays Communion of Reparation to the Immaculate Heart of Mary. Every July a week-long National Pilgrimage to Fatima is organised.

Acting National President Oliver Abasolo **42 Blenheim Gardens, Kingston upon Thames KT2 7BW Tel: 020 8274 8261 / 07782 661922 Email: abasolo35@gmail.com**
Web: www.worldfatima-englandwales.org.uk

Spiritual Director for Westminster Fr Richard Nesbitt **The Catholic Presbytery, Commonwealth Avenue W12 7QR Tel: 020 8743 8334 Email: whitecity@rcdow.org.uk**

WORLD COMMUNITY FOR CHRISTIAN MEDITATION

Promotes the prayer of Christian meditation as taught by John Main, monk of Ealing Abbey, simple practical wisdom that brings the truths of faith alive in our own experience. There is a full programme of prayer, teaching and days of recollection at the Meditatio Centre, St Mark's, Myddelton Square EC1R 1XX, where the International Office is based. A small resident community lives at Meditatio House in the spirit of the Rule of St Benedict. Meditation times (7am, noon & 6pm) are open to all.

Director Fr Laurence Freeman OSB **Meditatio House, 10 Cloudesley Square N1 0HT**
Tel: 020 7837 8567 Email: MeditatioHouse@wccm.org Web: www.wccm.org

OTHER USEFUL ADDRESSES

Catholic Communications Network
39 Eccleston Square SW1V 1BX Tel: 020 7901 4800 Email: ccn@cbcew.org.uk

Catholic Safeguarding Advisory Service (CSAS)
39 Eccleston Square SW1V 1BX Tel: 020 7901 1920 Email: admin@csas.uk.net
Web: www.csas.uk.net

Catholic Spirituality Network (CSN, formerly CNRS, NRM)
A national network of individuals and groups including prayer guides, spiritual companions, chaplains, Retreat Centre teams, pastoral workers and clergy. We are the Catholic member group of the Ecumenical Retreat Association. We produce two newsletters a year and organize an annual conference, open to all, and day events around the country.
Contact Membership Secretary Margaret Palladino **Catholic Spirituality Network (CSN), c/o St George's Cathedral, Westminster Bridge Road SE1 7HY Tel: 07756 864754**
Email: catholicspiritualitynetwork@gmail.com Web: www.csn.retreats.org.uk

Churches Together in England
27 Tavistock Square WC1H 9HH Tel: 020 7529 8131

Independent Catholic News - the UK's first daily on-line Catholic news service
Tel: 020 7267 3616 Web: www.indcatholicnews.com

Jesuit Refugee Service [JRS-UK]
Hurtado Jesuit Centre, 2 Chandler Street E1W 2QT Tel: 020 7488 7310
Fax: 020 7488 7329 Email: uk@jrs.net

Mary's Meals
Sets up school feeding programmes in some of the world's poorest communities where poverty and hunger prevent children from gaining an education. Currently 1.257 million children are fed one good nutritious meal every school day in countries such as Malawi, Liberia, Haiti, India, South Sudan, Lebanon and Syria.
13 Hippodrome Place W11 4SF Tel: 020 7221 5745
Email: London.admin@marysmeals.org Web: www.marysmeals.org.uk

National Catholic Safeguarding Commission (NCSC)
Box 91, 95 Wilton Road SW1V 1BZ Tel: 07530 972830
Email: admin@catholicsafeguarding.org.uk Web: www.catholicsafeguarding.org.uk

The Retreat Association
Clare Charity Centre, Wycombe Road, Saunderton, Bucks HP14 4BF
Tel: 01494 569056 Email: info@retreats.org.uk Web: www.retreats.org.uk

Society for the Protection of Unborn Children (SPUC)
Unit B, 3 Whitacre Mews, Stannary Street SE11 4AB
Tel: 020 7091 7091 Fax 020 7820 3131
Email: information@spuc.org.uk Web: www.spuc.org.uk

women@thewell
Provides services for the most vulnerable women caught up in multiple cycles of abuse, particularly those involved in street-based prostitution and those who struggle with substance abuse.
54/55 Birkenhead Street WC1H 8BB Tel: 020 7520 1710
Email: info@watw.org.uk Web: www.watw.org.uk

Section 7

THE CYCLE OF PRAYER

The liturgical year has been divided into six periods. We are asked to use the intentions during the current period, both corporately and in personal prayer, as well as on specific Days of Prayer. Parish Priests are asked to make the Cycle known by displaying and distributing copies in their churches, and to issue a reminder when a new period of the Cycle begins. When a Day of Special Prayer occurs on a Sunday, it is sufficient to announce the Day at the beginning of Mass and to include a suitable petition in the Universal Prayer. An introductory leaflet and leaflets for the seasons as well as model intercessions are available on the Bishops' Conference Liturgy Office website: **www.liturgyoffice.org.uk** .

ADVENT/CHRISTMAS 2018

Intentions: Openness to the Word of God; Migrants and Refugees; Expectant Mothers.

Migrants' Day	Monday 3 December	
Bible Sunday	Sunday 9 December	2nd Sunday of Advent
Expectant Mothers	especially on 23 December	4th Sunday of Advent

ORDINARY TIME: TO SPRING 2019

Intentions: Peace on Earth; Christian Unity; The Sick and Those who care for them; Victims of Trafficking and Those who work to combat it; Racial Justice; The Unemployed.

Octave of Prayer for Christian Unity		18 – 25 January
Peace Day	Sunday 20 January	2nd Sunday in O.T.
Day for Victims of Trafficking	Friday 8 February	St Josephine Bakhita
World Day for the Sick	Monday 11 February	Our Lady of Lourdes
Europe	Thursday 14 February	Ss Cyril and Methodius
Racial Justice Day	Sunday 17 February	3 Sundays before Lent I
Day for the Unemployed	Sunday 3 March	Sunday before Lent I

LENT 2019

Intentions: Candidates for the Sacraments (especially on the Sundays of Lent); Women; The Needy and Hungry of the World; Penitents and Wanderers.

Women's World Day of Prayer	Friday 1 March	Ist Friday in March
Lent Fast Day	Friday 15 March	Friday, 1st Week of Lent
Day of Prayer for Victims and Survivors of Sexual Abuse	Friday 12 April	Friday, 5th Week of Lent

EASTER 2019

Intentions: New Members of the Church; Vocations; The Right Use of the Media; The Church; Human Work.

World Day of Prayer for Vocations	Sunday 12 May	4th Sunday of Easter
Europe	Monday 29 April	St Catherine of Siena
Human Work	Wednesday 1 May	St Joseph the Worker
World Communications Day	Sunday 2 June	7th Sunday of Easter
The Church	Sunday 9 June	Pentecost

ORDINARY TIME: SUMMER 2019 (until September)

Intentions: A Deeper Understanding between Christians and Jews; Those who suffer Persecution, Oppression and Denial of Human Rights; Europe; Human Life; Seafarers.

Day for Life	Sunday 16 June	3rd Sunday in June
Those who suffer persecution	Saturday 22 June	Ss John Fisher and Thomas More
Europe	Thursday 11 July	St Benedict
Sea Sunday	Sunday 14 July	2nd Sunday in July
Europe	Tuesday 23 July	St Bridget of Sweden
Europe	Friday 9 August	St Teresa Benedicta of the Cross

ORDINARY TIME: AUTUMN 2019 (September to OLJC, King of the Universe)

Intentions: Students and Teachers; The Spread of the Gospel; The Harvest; The Fruits of Human Work, and the Reverent Use of Creation; Justice and Peace in the World; All Victims of War; Young People; Prisoners and their Families.

The Care of Creation	Sunday 1 September	1 September
Education Day	Sunday 8 September	2nd Sunday in September
Home Mission Day	Sunday 15 September	3rd Sunday in September
The Harvest	Sunday 22 September or whenever harvest festivals are held	Sunday 22–28 September,
Harvest Fast Day	Friday 4 October	1st Friday in October
Prisons Week	13-19 October	2nd Week in October
World Mission Day	Sunday 20 October	penultimate Sunday in October
Remembrance Day	Sunday 10 November	2nd Sunday in November
World Day of the Poor	Sunday 17 November	33rd Sunday in O.T.
Youth Day	Sunday 24 November	Christ the King

ADVENT/CHRISTMAS 2019

Intentions: Openness to the Word of God; Migrants and Refugees; Expectant Mothers.

Migrants' Day	Tuesday 3 December	St Francis Xavier
Bible Sunday	Sunday 8 December	2nd Sunday of Advent
Expectant Mothers	especially on 22 December	4th Sunday of Advent

Dated Days of Prayer are also repeated against the relevant date; the symbol § indicates a reference to the Cycle of Prayer.

THE HOLY FATHER'S PRAYER INTENTIONS 2018/19

DECEMBER 2018

Evangelisation: In the Service of the Transmission of Faith
That people, who are involved in the service and transmission of faith, may find, in their dialogue with culture, a language suited to the conditions of the present time.

JANUARY 2019

Evangelisation: That young people, especially in Latin America, follow the example of Mary and respond to the call of the Lord to communicate the joy of the Gospel to the world.

FEBRUARY 2019

Universal: For a generous welcome of the victims of human trafficking, of enforced prostitution, and of violence.

MARCH 2019

Evangelisation: That Christian communities, especially those who are persecuted, feel that they are close to Christ and have their rights respected.

APRIL 2019

Universal: For doctors and their humanitarian collaborators in war zones, who risk their lives to save the lives of others.

MAY 2019

Evangelisation: That the Church in Africa, through the commitment of its members, may be the seed of unity among her peoples and a sign of hope for this continent.

JUNE 2019

Universal: That priests, through the modesty and humility of their lives, commit themselves actively to a solidarity with those who are most poor.

JULY 2019

Evangelisation: That those who administer justice may work with integrity, and that the injustice which prevails in the world may not have the last word.

AUGUST 2019

Universal: That families, through their life of prayer and love, become ever more clearly 'schools of true human growth'.

SEPTEMBER 2019

Universal: That politicians, scientists and economists work together to protect the world's seas and oceans.

OCTOBER 2019

Evangelisation: That the breath of the Holy Spirit engender a new missionary 'spring' in the Church.

NOVEMBER 2019

Universal: That a spirit of dialogue, encounter, and reconciliation emerge in the Near East, where diverse religious communities share their lives together.

DECEMBER 2019

Evangelisation: That every country determine to take the necessary measures to make the future of the very young, especially those who suffer, a priority.

SPECIAL COLLECTIONS 2019

Collection	Announce	Collect	Send to
Racial Justice *	10 Feb	17 Feb	CaTEW via Finance, Vaughan House
Cardinal's Lenten Appeal ****	3 Mar	During Lent	Finance, Vaughan House
CAFOD Family Fast Day * (Friday 15 Mar)	10 Mar	17 Mar	CAFOD, Romero House, 55 Westminster Bridge Road SE1 7JB
Holy Places ** (Good Friday)	14 Apr	19 Apr	Finance, Vaughan House
Priest Training Fund ****	12 May	19 May	Finance, Vaughan House
Catholic Communications Network **	26 May	2 June	CaTEW via Finance, Vaughan House
Day for Life ***	9 Jun	16 Jun	CaTEW Finance Department, CBCEW, 39 Eccleston Square SW1V 1BX
Peter's Pence **	23 Jun	30 Jun	Finance, Vaughan House
Apostleship of the Sea ***	7 Jul	14 Jul	Apostleship of the Sea, 39 Eccleston Square SW1V 1PX
Catholic Education Service *	1 Sep	8 Sep	Finance, Vaughan House
Home Mission Appeal ***	8 Sep	15 Sep	CaTEW via Finance, Vaughan House
CAFOD Harvest Fast Day * (Friday 4 Oct)	29 Sep	6 Oct	CAFOD, Romero House, 55 Westminster Bridge Road SE1 7JB
World Mission Sunday **	13 Oct	20 Oct	Missio, 23 Eccleston Square SW1V 1NU
Sick & Retired Priests ****	3 Nov	10 Nov	Finance, Vaughan House
Missionary Orders Annual Appeal *		Any time	The Order concerned

* Optional
** Mandatory, Holy See
*** Mandatory, CBCEW
****Mandatory, Diocesan

LITURGICAL INFORMATION

Universal Calendar

Announcements from the Congregation for Divine Worship:

(1) The celebrations of St John XXIII, Pope, and St John Paul II, Pope, (http://www.liturgyoffice.org.uk/Calendar/National/JPII-E.pdf) become Optional Memorials on 11 October and 22 October respectively. St John Paul II therefore appears no longer in the list for the National Calendar.

(2) St Mary Magdalene, hitherto celebrated as an Obligatory Memorial, is now kept as a Feast. Texts for Mass and the Office remain as hitherto, except for a new Preface, which will receive *Confirmatio* in English translation in due course.

(3) The Obligatory Memorial of the Blessed Virgin Mary, Mother of the Church, with Proper Readings (http://www.liturgyoffice.org.uk/Calendar/Sanctoral/May.shtml#MMC), is now celebrated on the Monday after Pentecost.

Variations from the Universal Calendar

Where no indication of rank is given, the celebration is an Optional Memorial.

(1) National

Proper prayers are found in the Proper of Saints in the Roman Missal; readings are taken from the appropriate Common in the Lectionary.

12 January	St Aelred of Rievaulx	
19 January	St Wulstan, Bishop	
14 February	**Ss Cyril, Monk and Methodius, Bishop, Patrons of Europe**	Feast
1 March	**St David, Bishop, Patron of Wales**	Feast
17 March	**St Patrick, Bishop, Patron of Ireland**	Feast
21 April	St Anselm, Bishop & Doctor	
23 April	**St George, Martyr, Patron of England**	Solemnity
24 April	St Adalbert, Bishop & Martyr St Fidelis of Sigmaringen, Priest & Martyr	
29 April	**St Catherine of Siena, Virgin & Doctor, Patron of Europe**	Feast
4 May	**The English Martyrs**	Feast
19 May	St Dunstan, Bishop	
25 May	St Bede the Venerable, Priest & Doctor	Memorial
27 May	**St Augustine of Canterbury**	Feast
5 June	St Boniface, Bishop & Martyr	Memorial
9 June	St Columba, Abbot	
16 June	St Richard of Chichester, Bishop	
20 June	St Alban, Protomartyr	
22 June	**Ss John Fisher, Bishop, and Thomas More, Martyrs**	Feast

23 June	St Etheldreda (Audrey), Abbess	
1 July	St Oliver Plunkett, Bishop & Martyr	
11 July	**St Benedict, Abbot, Patron of Europe**	Feast
23 July	**St Bridget, Religious, Patron of Europe**	Feast
9 August	**St Teresa Benedicta of the Cross (Edith Stein), Virgin & Martyr, Patron of Europe**	Feast
26 August	Blessed Dominic of the Mother of God, Priest	
30 August	Ss Margaret Clitherow, Anne Line and Margaret Ward, Martyrs	
31 August	St Aidan, Bishop, and the Saints of Lindisfarne	
3 September	**St Gregory the Great, Pope & Doctor**	Feast
4 September	St Cuthbert, Bishop	
19 September	St Theodore of Canterbury, Bishop	
24 September	Our Lady of Walsingham	Memorial
9 October	Blessed John Henry Newman	
10 October	St Paulinus of York, Bishop	
12 October	St Wilfrid, Bishop	
13 October	St Edward the Confessor	
26 October	Ss Chad and Cedd, Bishops	
3 November	St Winifride, Virgin	
7 November	St Willibrord, Bishop	
16 November	St Edmund of Abingdon, Bishop	
	St Margaret of Scotland	
17 November	St Hilda, Abbess	
	St Hugh of Lincoln, Bishop	
	St Elizabeth of Hungary, Religious	
30 November	**St Andrew, Apostle, Patron of Scotland**	Feast
29 December	**St Thomas Becket, Bishop & Martyr Patron of the Parish Clergy**	Feast

Thursday after Pentecost

Our Lord Jesus Christ, the Eternal High Priest Feast

(see www.liturgyoffice.org.uk/Calendar/Sanctoral/May.shtml#OLJC)

(2) Diocesan

Proper prayers are found in the Diocesan Proper (either in booklet form or available online) or National Proper in the Missal; readings are taken from the appropriate Lectionary Common.

3 February	Ss Laurence, Dunstan, Theodore, Archbishops of Canterbury	Memorial
19 April	St Alphege, Bishop	Memorial
24 April	Ss Erkenwald and Mellitus, Bishops	Memorial
20 June	St Alban, Protomartyr	Memorial

27 June	St John Southworth, Priest & Martyr **(Solemnity in the Cathedral)**	Memorial
1 July	Dedication of the Cathedral **(Solemnity in the Cathedral)**	Feast
13 October	St Edward the Confessor **(Solemnity in the City of Westminster)**	Feast
29 October	Blessed Martyrs of Douai College	Memorial
16 November	St Edmund of Abingdon, Bishop	Memorial

(3) Local

Each church celebrates as a Solemnity its Feast of Title, and, if it is consecrated, the Anniversary of Dedication. Falling on a Sunday of Ordinary Time or Sunday in the octave of Christmas they may replace the liturgy of that Sunday. On Sundays of Advent, Lent or Easter or on another Solemnity they are transferred to the following day. These celebrations may also, for pastoral reasons, be transferred to an ordinary Sunday or other suitable day.

(4) Holy Days of Obligation for England and Wales in 2019

By Prot. N.180/17 of 4 August 2017, the Congregation for Divine Worship approved the Bishops' Conference's request that the Epiphany be henceforth celebrated on 6 January, unless this falls on a Saturday or Monday, in which case it is celebrated on the Sunday. The Ascension of the Lord will henceforth be celebrated on the Thursday in Week 6 of Eastertide.

Epiphany of the Lord	Sunday 6 January
Ascension of the Lord	Thursday 30 May
Corpus Christi	Sunday 23 June
Ss Peter and Paul	Sunday 30 June
Assumption BVM	Thursday 15 August
All Saints	Friday 1 November
Christmas	Wednesday 25 December

(5) Calendar for the Extraordinary Form

The basic Calendar for the Extraordinary Form according to the Missale Romanum 1962 is given on the website of the Liturgy Office for England and Wales.

Following a request for information, the Bishops' Conference of England and Wales submitted a *dubium* to the Pontifical Commission *Ecclesia Dei,* which confirmed that in the Roman Rite, whichever Form of the liturgy is being celebrated, the Holy Days of Obligation are held in common. When the Holy Day is transferred to the Sunday, this is to be followed in both Ordinary and Extraordinary Form celebrations of Mass.

(6) Additional Days of Prayer

(1) The World Day of Prayer for the Care of Creation is kept on 1 September. Liturgical resources are available at www.liturgyoffice.org.uk/Calendar/Cycle/AutumnCP.shtml#Harvest

(2) The Day of Prayer for Victims and Survivors of Abuse is kept on Friday of the 5th Week of Lent. The Pontifical Commission has produced resources on its website: http://www.protectionofminors.va/content/tuteladeiminori/en.html .

SECTION 7: LITURGICAL INFORMATION

Choice of Mass to be celebrated

(1) Mass *ad libitum* in Ordinary Time

Where a Mass is to be celebrated *ad libitum*, the priest may choose:

from the Mass formula of the preceding Sunday or any one of the Sundays in Ordinary Time, even with some of the prayers taken from any another Sunday in Ordinary Time or from the prayers for Various Needs and Occasions; or

from the Mass of a Saint noted in the calendar as an optional memorial, or of a saint noted in the Martyrology for that day; or

from any Mass for the dead, although the formulas of the daily Mass for the dead may only be used if the Mass is actually said for the dead; or

a Mass for Various Needs; or

a Votive Mass.

(2) Occasions when Mass texts of the day may be replaced

<table>
<tr><th></th><th>V1</th><th>V2</th><th>V3</th><th>D1</th><th>D2</th><th>D3</th></tr>
<tr><td>1. Solemnities of precept</td><td rowspan="3">✗</td><td rowspan="3">✗</td><td rowspan="3">✗</td><td rowspan="3">✗</td><td rowspan="3">✗</td><td rowspan="3">✗</td></tr>
<tr><td>2. Sundays in the seasons of Advent, Lent and Easter</td></tr>
<tr><td>3. Holy Thursday, Easter Triduum</td></tr>
<tr><td>4. Solemnities not of precept, All Souls</td><td rowspan="3">✗</td><td rowspan="3">✗</td><td rowspan="3">✗</td><td rowspan="3">✓</td><td rowspan="3">✗</td><td rowspan="3">✗</td></tr>
<tr><td>5. Ash Wednesday, weekdays of Holy Week</td></tr>
<tr><td>6. Days in the octave of Easter</td></tr>
<tr><td>7. Sundays of Christmas and Sundays in Ordinary Time</td><td rowspan="2">✓</td><td rowspan="2">✗</td><td rowspan="2">✗</td><td rowspan="2">✓</td><td rowspan="2">✗</td><td rowspan="2">✗</td></tr>
<tr><td>8. Feasts</td></tr>
<tr><td>9. Weekdays in the season of Advent from 17 to 24 December</td><td rowspan="3">✓</td><td rowspan="3">✗</td><td rowspan="3">✗</td><td rowspan="3">✓</td><td rowspan="3">✓</td><td rowspan="3">✗</td></tr>
<tr><td>10. Days in the octave of Christmas</td></tr>
<tr><td>11. Weekdays in the season of Lent</td></tr>
<tr><td>12. Obligatory memorials</td><td rowspan="4">✓</td><td rowspan="4">✓</td><td rowspan="4">✗</td><td rowspan="4">✓</td><td rowspan="4">✓</td><td rowspan="4">✗</td></tr>
<tr><td>13. Weekdays in the season of Advent to 16 December</td></tr>
<tr><td>14. Weekdays in the season of Christmas from 2 January</td></tr>
<tr><td>15. Weekdays in the season of Easter</td></tr>
<tr><td>16. Weekdays in Ordinary Time</td><td>✓</td><td>✓</td><td>✓</td><td>✓</td><td>✓</td><td>✓</td></tr>
</table>

The table of rubrics inserted here governs when celebrations using the formularies from Ritual Masses, Masses for Various Needs and Occasions, Votive Masses, and Masses for the Dead are permitted within the liturgical year.

V1 = Ritual Masses (General Instruction of the Roman Missal [hereafter, GIRM], no. 372). Masses for various needs and occasions and votive Masses, in cases of serious need or pastoral advantage, at the direction of the local Ordinary or with his permission (GIRM, no. 374).

V2 = Masses for various needs and occasions and votive Masses, in cases of serious need or pastoral advantage, at the discretion of the rector of the church or the priest celebrant (GIRM, no. 376).

V3 = Masses for various needs and occasions and votive Masses chosen by the priest celebrant in favour of the devotion of the people (GIRM, nn. 373, 375).
D1 = Funeral Mass (GIRM, no. 380).
D2 = Mass on the occasion of news of a death, final burial, or the first anniversary (GIRM, no. 381).
D3 = Daily Mass for the dead (GIRM, no. 381). When D1 and D2 are not permitted, neither is D3.
✓ = permitted.
✗ = not permitted.

(3) Funeral Mass

A Funeral Mass may be celebrated on any day, except solemnities which are Holy Days of Obligation, Maundy Thursday, the Triduum, and the Sundays of Advent, Lent, and Eastertide.

(4) Prefaces of the Eucharistic Prayer

Solemnities, Feasts and certain other days are provided with Prefaces (either Proper or Common). These are indicated in the Calendar and are always used.
On Memorials either a seasonal Preface or an appropriate Preface of Saints may be used, according to the desire of the priest.
Prayers I and II for Reconciliation have their own Prefaces, but may be used with other appropriate Prefaces that refer to penance, e.g. the Prefaces of Lent.
Prayers I-IV for Use in Masses for Various Needs have their own Prefaces which may not be replaced.

(5) Choice of Eucharistic Prayer

Prayer I (The Roman Canon) may always be used, and particularly on days for which proper texts or insertions are provided; the feasts of apostles and saints mentioned in the Prayer; and on Sundays.
Prayer II is more appropriately used on weekdays and in special circumstances. Its own Preface may always be replaced by another. It is also suitable for a Mass for the Dead, with the optional formula for naming the deceased.
Prayer III is preferred for Sundays and feasts of the saints, who may be named within it. It also offers a formula for the dead, making it appropriate for occasions commemorating Christian Death.
Prayer IV is an integral text, with an invariable preface. It may only be used on Sundays and ferial days of Ordinary Time, when a Mass has no Proper Preface of its own.
Prayers I and II for Reconciliation and Prayers I-IV for Use in Masses for Various Needs may be used in association with the Votive and other Masses noted in the rubrics for each Prayer.

Fulfilment of Obligation

The obligation of participating in the Mass is satisfied by assisting at Mass wherever it is celebrated in a Catholic rite, either on the Sunday or Holy Day itself or on the evening of the previous day. (Canon 1248.1)

Reception of the Eucharist a Second Time on the Same Day

It is permitted to receive Holy Communion twice on one day, provided this takes place during the celebration of Mass (Canon 917). This provision is to be observed except in the case of Viaticum for the dying.

Eucharistic Fast

Whoever is to receive the blessed Eucharist is to abstain for at least one hour before Holy Communion from all food and drink, with the sole exception of water and medicine (Canon 919.1).

A priest who, on the same day, celebrates Mass twice or three times may consume something before the second or third celebration, even though there is not an hour's interval (Canon 919.2).

The elderly, and those who are suffering from some illness, as well as those who care for them, may receive the blessed Eucharist even if within the preceding hour they have consumed something (Canon 919.3).

Abstinence

(1) The Bishops of England and Wales recognise that simple acts of witness, accompanied by sincere prayer, can be a powerful call to faith. Traditional Catholic devotions such as making the sign of the cross with care and reverence, praying the Angelus and saying a prayer before and after meals, are straightforward actions which both dedicate certain moments in our daily lives to Almighty God and demonstrate our love and trust in His goodness and providence. If these devotions have been lost or even forgotten, particularly in our homes and schools, we have much to gain from learning and living them again.

(2) Every Friday is set aside as a special day of penitence, as it is the day of the suffering and death of the Lord. It is important that all the faithful again be united in a common, identifiable act of Friday penance since the virtue of penitence is best acquired as part of a common resolve and witness. The law of the Church requires Catholics on Fridays to abstain from meat, or some other form of food, or to observe some other form of penance laid down by the Bishops' Conference. The Bishops have decided that this penance be fulfilled simply by abstaining from meat and by uniting this to prayer. Those who cannot or choose not to eat meat as part of their normal diet should abstain from some other food of which they regularly partake. This decision came into effect on Friday 16 September 2011.

(3) Re-emphasising the importance of penitence is but one of the responses the Bishops wish to make to the growing desire of people to deepen and give identity to the spiritual aspects of their lives. It is also clear that many of us forget our obligation to do penance on a Friday. On a Sunday our prayer is in thanksgiving to God for the new and eternal life brought to us by Christ's resurrection from the dead. On a Friday our prayer is in thanksgiving for the gift of the mortal life that we have been given; a life which Christ willingly sacrificed on the cross for our sake. A fitting prayer then, as part of our Friday penance, would be to ask Almighty God to turn away all threats to mortal life. The act of abstinence itself can be offered consciously as a prayer for life and in reparation for sins against life. It can also be put at the service of others if we make a sacrifice and give the financial savings made from our abstention (or fasting) to charities which assist those who are poor or suffering. If we are unable to make that financial sacrifice, we can still perform a 'work of charity', an act of kindness and love to another person who is in need or suffering in some way.

(4) Canon 1251 states: 'Abstinence from eating meat or another food according to the prescriptions of the Conference of Bishops is to be observed on Fridays throughout the year unless they are solemnities; abstinence and fast are to be observed on Ash Wednesday and on the Friday of the Passion and Death of Our Lord Jesus Christ'.

Canon 1252 states: 'The law of abstinence binds those who have completed their fourteenth year. The law of fasting binds those who have attained their majority, until the beginning of their sixtieth year. Pastors of souls and parents are to ensure that even those who by reason of their age are not bound by the law of fasting and abstinence, are taught the true meaning of penance'.

Those under fourteen years of age, the sick, the elderly and frail, pregnant women, seafarers, manual workers according to need, guests at a meal who cannot excuse themselves without giving great offence to their hosts or causing friction, and those in other situations of moral or physical impossibility are not required to observe abstention from meat; in other words, we should act prudently.

(5) The Holy See has noted that the 'gravity' of the obligation applies to our intention to observe penance as a regular and necessary part of our spiritual lives as a whole. Therefore, the 'gravity' of the obligation does not relate to observing the specific act of penance (abstaining from meat) prescribed by the Conference of Bishops. The 'gravity' of the obligation applies to the intention to do penance during the prescribed penitential days and seasons of the Church's year. Failure to abstain from meat on a particular Friday then would not constitute a sin.

KEY TO THE CALENDAR

RANKS OF CELEBRATION

There are three ranks of celebration: Solemnity, Feast, Memorial. These are indicated in the calendar by the typeface used, thus:

SOLEMNITY FEAST Memorial

ABBREVIATIONS

\+ indicates that attendance at Mass fulfils the Sunday or Holy Day obligation

Ps on the right of the page indicates the Week of the Psalter

§ indicates a reference to the Cycle of Prayer

CELEBRATION OF FIRST VESPERS

These are noted for Vigil Masses which have proper readings and/or prayers, for Solemnities and for Feasts falling on Sundays, which would otherwise not have First Vespers.

Solemnities and all Sundays other than Easter Day have First Vespers, unless these are impeded by Second Vespers of a higher-ranking Solemnity.

LITURGICAL COLOURS

B	Black
G	Green
P	Purple
R	Red
RP	Rose Pink
W	White

When the Saturday Mass of the Blessed Virgin Mary is celebrated in Ordinary Time, either White or Green vestments may be used.
When vestments of the appropriate colour are not available, White may always be substituted.

TABLE OF MOVEABLE FEASTS

	2019	2020	2021
Lectionary (Sunday/Weekday)	C/1	A/2	B/1
First Sunday of Advent	2 December 2018	1 December 2019	29 November 2020
Nativity of the Lord	25 December	25 December	25 December
Epiphany	6 January	5 January	6 January
Ash Wednesday	6 March	26 February	17 February
Easter Sunday	21 April	12 April	4 April
Ascension	30 May	21 May	13 May
Pentecost	9 June	31 May	23 May
Corpus Christi	23 June	14 June	6 June
Ss Peter and Paul	30 June	28 June	29 June
Assumption BVM	15 August	16 August	15 August
All Saints	1 November	1 November	31 October
First Sunday of Advent	1 December	29 November	28 November

- **Bold entries** denote Holydays of Obligation in England and Wales. The Epiphany, Ss Peter & Paul, the Assumption BVM and All Saints, falling on Saturday or Monday are transferred to the Sunday.
- Table supplied by CBCEW Liturgy Office for England and Wales: **www.liturgyoffice.org.uk**

DECEMBER 2018

LECTIONARY FOR SUNDAYS: YEAR C

ADVENT

Advent has a twofold character: as a season to prepare for Christmas, when Christ's first coming to us is remembered; and as a season when that remembrance directs the mind and heart to await Christ's Second Coming at the end of time. Advent is thus a period for devout and joyful expectation.

The playing of the organ and other musical instruments, and the decoration of the altar with flowers should be done in a moderate manner, as is consonant with the character of the season, without anticipating the full joy of the Nativity of the Lord. The same moderation should be observed in the celebration of Matrimony.

Eucharistic Prayer 4 is not used in this season.

DECEMBER 2018

Sat evening	P	First Vespers (Divine Office Volume I)	
2 Sun	P	+ Ist SUNDAY OF ADVENT *Creed, Advent Preface I (and on following days)* Mass & Office of the day	*Ps Week I*
3 Mon	W	St Francis Xavier, Priest: Mass & Office of the Memorial § Migrants' Day	
4 Tue	P W	Advent feria, First Week of Advent: Mass & Office of the day *or* St John Damascene, Priest & Doctor: Mass & Office of the Memorial	
5 Wed	P	Advent feria: Mass & Office of the day	
6 Thu	P W	Advent feria: Mass & Office of the day *or* St Nicholas, Bishop: Mass & Office of the Memorial	
7 Fri	W	St Ambrose, Bishop & Doctor: Mass & Office of the Memorial	*Friday abstinence*
evening	W	First Vespers	*Abstinence ends*
8 Sat	W	**THE IMMACULATE CONCEPTION OF THE BLESSED VIRGIN MARY, Patron of the Diocese** *Gloria, Creed, Proper Preface* Mass, Lauds & Lesser Hours of the Solemnity	

DECEMBER 2018

evening	P	First Vespers
9 Sun	P	+ 2nd SUNDAY OF ADVENT *Ps Week 2* *Creed, Advent Preface I* Mass & Office of the day § Bible Sunday
10 Mon	P	Advent feria, Second Week of Advent: Mass & Office of the Day
11 Tue	P W	Advent feria: Mass & Office of the day *or* St Damasus I, Pope: Mass & Office of the Memorial
12 Wed	P W	Advent feria: Mass & Office of the day *or* Our Lady of Guadalupe: Mass & Office of the Memorial
13 Thu	R	St Lucy, Virgin & Martyr: Mass & Office of the Memorial
14 Fri	W	St John of the Cross, Priest & Doctor: *Friday abstinence* Mass & Office of the Memorial
15 Sat	P	Advent feria: Mass & Office of the day
evening	RP or P	First Vespers
16 Sun	RP or P	+ 3rd SUNDAY OF ADVENT (Gaudete Sunday) *Ps Week 3* *Creed, Advent Preface I* Mass & Office of the day

Memorials which occur on days between 17 and 31 December may be commemorated at Mass by using the collect of the saint in place of the collect of the day. In the Office of Readings the proper hagiographical reading and responsory may be added after the Patristic reading and responsory; the collect of the saint concludes the office. At Lauds and Vespers the antiphon (proper or common) and collect of the saint may be added after the collect of the day.

At Mass, proper texts and readings are given for the weekdays from 17-24 December, and these should be used instead of those indicated for the weekdays of the third or fourth week of Advent.

17 Mon	P	Advent feria: Mass & Office of 17 December *Advent Preface II (and on following days)*
18 Tue	P	Advent feria: Mass & Office of 18 December
19 Wed	P	Advent feria: Mass & Office of 19 December

DECEMBER 2018

20 Thu	P	Advent feria: Mass & Office of 20 December
21 Fri	P	Advent feria: Mass & Office of 21 December *Friday abstinence* (St Peter Canisius, Priest & Doctor)
22 Sat	P	Advent feria: Mass & Office of 22 December
evening	P	First Vespers: Magnificat antiphon of 22 December
23 Sun	P	+ 4th SUNDAY OF ADVENT *Ps Week 4* *Creed, Advent Preface II* Mass of the day; Office of the day, with readings, also Benedictus & Magnificat antiphons of 23 December (see Divine Office Vol I, page 161 ff) § Expectant Mothers Announce Holy Day of Obligation
24 Mon	P	Advent feria: Mass & Office of 24 December
		CHRISTMAS SEASON After the annual celebration of the Paschal Mystery there is no more ancient feast day for the Church than the recalling of the memory of the Nativity of the Lord and of the mysteries of his first appearing. Eucharistic Prayer 4 is not used in this season.
evening	W W	First Vespers + Proper Vigil Mass of Christmas precedes or follows *Gloria, Proper Readings (Short form Gospel), Creed, (kneel at* Incarnatus*),* *a Preface of the Nativity* & Communicantes *in the Roman Canon* For pastoral reasons, readings at the following Christmas Masses may be chosen from among all those provided for the Solemnity. It is appropriate that a Solemn Vigil be kept by celebrating the Office of Readings before the Mass during the Night. Compline is omitted by those attending that Mass.
	W	+ Mass during the Night *Gloria, Proper Readings, Creed (kneel at* Incarnatus*), a Preface of the Nativity* & Communicantes *in the Roman Canon*
25 Tue	W	**+ THE NATIVITY OF THE LORD (CHRISTMAS)** *Gloria, Proper Readings Short form Gospel), Creed (kneel at* Incarnatus*), a Preface of the Nativity* & Communicantes *in the Roman Canon* Mass & Office of the Solemnity All priests may celebrate or concelebrate three Masses today, provided that they are celebrated at their proper time.

DECEMBER 2018

26 Wed	R	ST STEPHEN, The First Martyr *Gloria, Proper Readings, a Preface of the Nativity & Communicantes in the Roman Canon* Mass, Lauds & Lesser Hours of St Stephen; Vespers of the Octave
	R	*(In parishes dedicated to ST STEPHEN, The First Martyr, his Solemnity is observed:* *Gloria, 1st Reading Proper, 2nd Reading from the Common of Martyrs, Gospel Proper, Creed, a Preface of the Nativity & Communicantes in the Roman Canon,* Second Vespers of the Solemnity)
27 Thu	W	ST JOHN, Apostle & Evangelist *Gloria, Proper Readings, a Preface of the Nativity & Communicantes in the Roman Canon* Mass, Lauds & Lesser Hours of St John; Vespers of the Octave
	W	*(In parishes dedicated to ST JOHN, Apostle & Evangelist, his Solemnity is observed:* *Gloria, 1st Reading from the Proper of All Saints, 2nd Reading & Gospel Proper, Creed, a Preface of the Nativity & Communicantes in the Roman Canon,* First & Second Vespers of the Solemnity)
28 Fri	R	THE HOLY INNOCENTS, Martyrs *No Friday abstinence* *Gloria, Proper Readings, a Preface of the Nativity & Communicantes in the Roman Canon* Mass, Lauds & Lesser Hours of the Holy Innocents; Vespers of the Octave
29 Sat	R	ST THOMAS BECKET, Bishop & Martyr, Patron of the Parish Clergy *National* *Gloria, Proper National Readings, a Preface of the Nativity & Communicantes in the Roman Canon* Mass, Lauds & Lesser Hours of St Thomas Becket
	R	*(In parishes dedicated to ST THOMAS BECKET Bishop & Martyr, his Solemnity is observed:* *Gloria, 1st Reading from the Common of Martyrs, 2nd Reading & Gospel Proper, Creed, a Preface of the Nativity & Communicantes in the Roman Canon,* First & Second Vespers of the Solemnity, also + Evening Mass)
	W	First Vespers
30 Sun	W	+ THE HOLY FAMILY OF JESUS, MARY AND JOSEPH *Gloria, 1st and 2nd Readings, Gospel of Year C or ad lib Readings of Year C, Creed, a Preface of the Nativity & Communicantes in the Roman Canon* Mass & Office of the Feast Announce Holy Day of Obligation

DECEMBER 2018/JANUARY 2019

31 Mon	W	7th DAY IN THE OCTAVE OF CHRISTMAS *Gloria, a Preface of the Nativity* & Communicantes *in the Roman Canon* Mass & Office of the Octave (St Sylvester I, Pope)
evening	W	First Vespers

JANUARY 2019

1 Tue	W	**SOLEMNITY OF MARY, THE HOLY MOTHER OF GOD** THE OCTAVE DAY OF THE NATIVITY OF THE LORD *Gloria, Creed, Preface I of Blessed Virgin Mary* & Communicantes *in the Roman Canon* Mass & Office of the Solemnity
		A Preface of the Nativity is used on weekdays of the Christmas season, unless other provision is made.
2 Wed	W	Ss Basil the Great and Gregory Nazianzen, Bishops & Doctors — *Ps Week I* *Readings of 2 January* Mass & Office of the Memorial
3 Thu	W	Christmas feria *First Collect, Readings of 3 January* Mass & Office of the Day *or*
	W	The Most Holy Name of Jesus: Mass & Office of the Memorial
4 Fri	W	Christmas feria — *Friday abstinence* *First Collect, Readings of 4 January* Mass & Office of the Day
5 Sat	W	Christmas feria *First Collect, Readings of 5 January* Mass & Office of the Day
evening	W	First Vespers
	W	+ Proper Vigil Mass of the Epiphany precedes or follows *Gloria, Epiphany Readings, Creed, Proper Preface* & Communicantes *of the Epiphany in the Roman Canon*

JANUARY 2019

6 Sun	W	**+ THE EPIPHANY OF THE LORD** *Gloria, Creed, Proper Preface & Communicantes of the Epiphany in the Roman Canon; an increased display of lights is recommended.* *At today's Mass, after the Gospel, the announcement may be made of moveable feasts according to the formula given in the Roman Pontifical, on page 1247 of the* Missale Romanum, editio typica tertia *and page 1505 of the Roman Missal.* Mass & Office of the Solemnity
		A Preface of the Nativity or of the Epiphany is used until the Christmas season ends, unless other provision is made.
7 Mon	W	Christmas feria — *Ps Week 2* *Second Collect, Readings of 7 January* Mass & Office of the day *or*
	W	St Raymond of Penyafort, Priest: Mass & Office of the Memorial
8 Tue	W	Christmas feria *Second Collect, Readings of 8 January* Mass & Office of the day
9 Wed	W	Christmas feria *Second Collect, Readings of 9 January* Mass & Office of the day
10 Thu	W	Christmas feria *Second Collect, Readings of 10 January* Mass & Office of the day
11 Fri	W	Christmas feria — *Friday abstinence* *Second Collect, Readings of 11 January* Mass & Office of the day
12 Sat	W	Christmas feria *Second Collect, Readings of 12 January* Mass & Office of the day *or*
	W	St Aelred of Rievaulx: — *National* Mass & Office of the Memorial
evening	W	First Vespers
13 Sun	W	+ THE BAPTISM OF THE LORD *Gloria, (Alternative Collect), 1st and 2nd Reading, Gospel of Year C or* ad lib *Readings for Year C, Creed, Proper Preface* Mass & Office of the Feast
		Christmas Time ends.

JANUARY 2019

LECTIONARY FOR SUNDAYS: YEAR C
WEEKDAY LECTIONARY: YEAR I
Eucharistic Prayer 4 may be used in this Season
The choice of Masses which may be celebrated *ad libitum* is shown in the Liturgical Information on page 292.
On ferial days in Ordinary Time the Office of a saint included for that day in the Roman Martyrology may be celebrated. Occasional Votive Offices are permitted, although care to observe the four-week cycle of the Office should be maintained.

14 Mon	G	feria, First Week of Year 1: Mass ad lib; Office of the day	*Ps Week 1*
15 Tue	G	feria: Mass ad lib; Office of the day	
16 Wed	G	feria: Mass ad lib; Office of the day	
17 Thu	W	St Anthony, Abbot: Mass & Office of the Memorial	
		From 18-25 January the Octave of Prayer for Christian Unity takes place. A Mass for the Unity of Christians may be celebrated on any ferial day during the Octave.	
18 Fri	G	feria: Mass ad lib; Office of the day	*Friday abstinence*
19 Sat	G W W	feria: Mass ad lib; Office of the day *or* St Wulstan, Bishop: Mass & Office of the Memorial *or* Blessed Virgin Mary on Saturday: Mass & Office of the Memorial	 *National*
evening	G	First Vespers	
20 Sun	G	+ 2nd SUNDAY IN ORDINARY TIME *Gloria, Creed, a Preface of Sundays in O.T.* Mass & Office of the day § Peace Day	*Ps Week 2*
21 Mon	R	St Agnes, Virgin & Martyr: Mass & Office of the Memorial	
22 Tue	G R	feria, Second Week of Year 1: Mass ad lib; Office of the day *or* St Vincent, Deacon & Martyr: Mass & Office of the Memorial	
23 Wed	G	feria: Mass ad lib; Office of the day	

SECTION 7: LITURGICAL CALENDAR

JANUARY/FEBRUARY 2019

24 Thu	W	St Francis de Sales, Bishop & Doctor: Mass & Office of the Memorial Anniversary of the Episcopal Ordination of Cardinal Vincent Nichols (1992). An intention may be included in the Universal Prayer and the Mass 'For the Bishop' (Roman Missal page 1306) may be celebrated.
25 Fri	W	THE CONVERSION OF ST PAUL THE APOSTLE *Friday abstinence* *Gloria, (Alternative 1st Reading), Preface I of Apostles* Mass & Office of the Feast
26 Sat	W	Ss Timothy and Titus, Bishops *(Proper Alternative 1st Readings)* Mass & Office of the Memorial
evening	G	First Vespers
27 Sun	G	+ 3rd SUNDAY IN ORDINARY TIME *Ps Week 3* *Gloria, (Short form 2nd Reading), Creed, a Preface of Sundays in O.T.* Mass & Office of the day
28 Mon	W	St Thomas Aquinas, Priest & Doctor: Mass & Office of the Memorial
29 Tue	G	feria, Third Week of Year 1: Mass ad lib; Office of the day
30 Wed	G	feria: Mass ad lib; Office of the day
31 Thu	W	St John Bosco, Priest: Mass & Office of the Memorial
FEBRUARY 2019		
1 Fri	G	feria: Mass ad lib; Office of the day *Friday abstinence*
2 Sat	W	THE PRESENTATION OF THE LORD *Blessing of candles with Procession or Solemn Entry, no Penitential Act, Gloria, 1st or 2nd Reading, (Short form Gospel), Proper Preface* Mass & Office of the Feast, 2nd Vespers and
	W	+ Evening Mass *as above, but 1st and 2nd Readings, Creed also*
3 Sun	G	+ 4th SUNDAY IN ORDINARY TIME *Ps Week 4* *Gloria, (Short form 2nd Reading), Creed, a Preface of Sundays in O.T.* Mass & Office of the day *The blessing of St Blaise on throats may be given today or transferred to another suitable day.*

FEBRUARY 2019			
4 Mon	G	feria, Fourth Week of Year I: Mass ad lib; office of the day	
5 Tue	R	St Agatha, Virgin & Martyr: Mass & Office of the Memorial	
6 Wed	R	St Paul Miki and Companions, Martyrs: Mass & Office of the Memorial	
7 Thu	G	feria: Mass ad lib; Office of the day	
8 Fri	G W W	feria: Mass ad lib; office of the day *or* St Jerome Emiliani: Mass & Office of the Memorial *or* St Josephine Bakhita: Mass & Office of the Memorial § Day for Victims of Trafficking and those who work to combat it	*Friday abstinence*
9 Sat	G W	feria: Mass ad lib; Office of the day *or* Blessed Virgin Mary on Saturday: Mass & Office of the Memorial	
evening	G	First Vespers	
10 Sun	G	+ 5th SUNDAY IN ORDINARY TIME *Gloria, (Short form 2nd Reading), Creed, a Preface of Sundays in O.T.* Mass & Office of the day Announce Special Collection	*Ps Week I*
11 Mon	G	feria, Fifth Week of Year I: Mass ad lib; Office of the day *or* Our Lady of Lourdes: Mass & Office of the Memorial § World Day for the Sick	
12 Tue	G	feria: Mass ad lib; Office of the day	
13 Wed	G	feria: Mass ad lib; Office of the day	
14 Thu	W	Ss CYRIL, Monk & METHODIUS, Bishop, Patrons of Europe *Gloria, Proper Readings, Preface of Holy Pastors* Mass & Office of the Feast § Europe	*National*
15 Fri	G	feria: Mass ad lib; Office of the day	*Friday abstinence*
16 Sat	G W	feria: Mass ad lib; Office of the day *or* Blessed Virgin Mary on Saturday: Mass & Office of the Memorial	
evening	G	First Vespers	

FEBRUARY/MARCH 2019

17 Sun	G	+ 6th SUNDAY IN ORDINARY TIME *Gloria, Creed, a Preface of Sundays in O.T.* Mass & Office of the day § Racial Justice Collection for Racial Justice	*Ps Week 2*
18 Mon	G	feria, Sixth Week of Year 1: Mass ad lib; Office of the day	
19 Tue	G	feria: Mass ad lib; Office of the day	
20 Wed	G	feria: Mass ad lib; Office of the day	
21 Thu	G W	feria: Mass ad lib; Office of the day *or* St Peter Damian, Bishop & Doctor: Mass & Office of the Memorial	
22 Fri	W	THE CHAIR OF ST PETER THE APOSTLE *Gloria, Preface I of Apostles* Mass & Office of the Feast	*Friday abstinence*
23 Sat	R	St Polycarp, Bishop & Martyr: Mass & Office of the day	
evening	G	First Vespers	
24 Sun	G	+ 7th SUNDAY IN ORDINARY TIME *Gloria, Creed, a Preface of Sundays in O.T.* Mass & Office of the day	*Ps Week 3*
25 Mon	G	feria, Seventh Week of Year 1: Mass ad lib; Office of the day	
26 Tue	G	feria: Mass ad lib; Office of the day	
27 Wed	G	feria: Mass ad lib; Office of the day	
28 Thu	G	feria: Mass ad lib; Office of the day	
MARCH 2019			
1 Fri	W	ST DAVID, Bishop, Patron of Wales *Gloria, Proper National Readings,* *Preface of Holy Pastors* Mass & Office of the Feast § Women's World Day of Prayer	*National* *Friday abstinence*
2 Sat	G W	feria: Mass ad lib; Office of the day *or* Blessed Virgin Mary on Saturday: Mass & Office of the Memorial	
evening	G	First Vespers	

MARCH 2019

3 Sun G + 8th SUNDAY IN ORDINARY TIME *Ps Week 4*
Gloria, Creed, a Preface of Sundays in O.T.
Mass & Office of the day
§ Day for the Unemployed
Announce Ash Wednesday, Day of Fast and Abstinence
Announce Mandatory Diocesan Lenten Alms Appeal

4 Mon G feria, Eighth Week of Year I: Mass ad lib: Office of the day *or*
W St Casimir: Mass & Office of the Memorial

5 Tue G feria: Mass ad lib; Office of the day

LENT

The season of Lent is a preparation for the celebration of Easter. The liturgy prepares the catechumens for the celebration of the Paschal Mystery by the various stages of Christian initiation; it also prepares the faithful, who recall their baptism and do penance in preparation for Easter.

Memorials which occur on a weekday may only be commemorated at Mass by using the collect of the saint in place of the collect of the day. In the Office of Readings the proper hagiographical reading and responsory may be added after the Patristic reading and responsory; the collect of the saint concludes the office. At Lauds and Vespers the antiphon (proper or common) and collect of the saint may be added after the collect of the day.

The *Alleluia* is always omitted, both in the Office and in Mass.

It is not permitted to adorn the altar with flowers, and the organ and other instruments may only be played for the purpose of sustaining the singing. An exception is made for *Laetare* Sunday, and for Solemnities and Feasts.

During the Lenten season the Apostles' Creed may suitably be used as an alternative when the Creed is appointed to be said.

For the celebration of marriage, the parish priest should alert spouses to the need to take account of the particular penitential character of this season.

Eucharistic Prayer 4 is not used in this Season; Eucharistic Prayers for Reconciliation may appropriately be used during Lent.
(Divine Office Volume II)

6 Wed P **ASH WEDNESDAY** *Fast & Abstinence* *Ps Week 4*
Penitential Act omitted, Blessing and distribution of ashes after the homily, Preface III or IV of Lent
The ashes, according to custom, are from branches blessed the previous year. The blessing and distribution of ashes may take place outside Mass, in a Liturgy of the Word after the homily; the celebration then concludes with the Universal Prayer, Blessing and Dismissal.
Mass & Office of the day; at Lauds, Pss and Canticle of Friday, Week 3 may be used

MARCH 2019

		On ferial days of the Lenten season one of the four Lenten prefaces is used, unless other provision is made.	
7 Thu	P	Lent feria: Mass & Office of the day (Ss Perpetua & Felicity, Martyrs)	
8 Fri	P	Lent feria: Mass & Office of the day (St John of God, Religious)	*Friday abstinence*
9 Sat	P	Lent feria: Mass & Office of the day (St Frances of Rome, Religious)	
in Cathedral		3 pm Rite of Election (First Service)	
evening	P	First Vespers	
10 Sun	P	+ 1st SUNDAY OF LENT *Creed, Preface of First Sunday of Lent* Mass & Office of the day	*Ps Week 1*
in Cathedral		3pm Rite of Election (Second Service) § Candidates for the Sacraments Announce Optional CAFOD Family Fast Day	
11 Mon	P	Lent feria, First Week of Lent: Mass & Office of the day	
12 Tue	P	Lent feria: Mass & Office of the day	
13 Wed	P	Lent feria: Mass & Office of the day Anniversary of the Election of Pope Francis (2013). In England and Wales, by decision of the Bishops' Conference, this is observed on the Solemnity of Ss Peter and Paul, Sunday 30 June.	
14 Thu	P	Lent feria: Mass & Office of the day	
15 Fri	P	Lent feria: Mass & Office of the day § Family Fast Day	*Friday abstinence*
16 Sat	P	Lent feria: Mass & Office of the day	
evening	P	First Vespers	
17 Sun	P	+ 2nd SUNDAY OF LENT *(Short form 2nd Reading), Creed, Preface of Second Sunday of Lent* Mass & Office of the day § Candidates for the Sacraments Collect Family Fast Day Offerings for CAFOD	*Ps Week 2*

MARCH 2019		
18 Mon	P	Lent feria, Second Week of Lent: Mass & Office of the day (St Cyril of Jerusalem, Bishop & Doctor)
	W	First Vespers
19 Tue	W	**ST JOSEPH, Spouse of the Blessed Virgin Mary, Patron of the Diocese** *Gloria, Proper Readings (Alternative Gospel Reading), Creed, Preface of St Joseph* Mass & Office of the Solemnity
20 Wed	P	Lent feria, Second Week of Lent: Mass & Office of the day
21 Thu	P	Lent feria: Mass & Office of the day
22 Fri	P	Lent feria: Mass & Office of the day *Friday abstinence*
23 Sat	P	Lent feria: Mass & office of the day (St Turibius of Mogrovejo, Bishop)
evening	P	First Vespers
24 Sun	P	+ 3rd SUNDAY OF LENT *Ps Week 3* *Creed, Preface I or II of Lent; Year A Readings (Short form Gospel) may be used, with the matching Preface and Communion Antiphon* Mass & Office of the day, including 2nd Vespers and
	P	+ Evening Mass RCIA - First Scrutiny: the Ritual Mass (pages 1177-9) with Year A Readings (Short form Gospel), Proper Preface (pages 260-1) and Insertions in the Eucharistic Prayer. § Candidates for the Sacraments
		The Gospel of the Samaritan Woman may be used on a ferial weekday, with 1st Reading and Psalm as in Year A of the Lectionary. The matching Preface and Communion Antiphon should also be used. The Alternative Readings (Vol I, page 258 ff) may also be used.
25 Mon	W	**THE ANNUNCIATION OF THE LORD** *Gloria, Proper Readings, Creed (kneel at* Incarnatus*), Proper Preface* Mass & Office of the Solemnity
26 Tue	P	Lent feria, Third Week of Lent: Mass & Office of the day
27 Wed	P	Lent feria: Mass & Office of the day

MARCH/APRIL 2019

28 Thu	P	Lent feria: Mass & Office of the day
29 Fri	P	Lent feria: Mass & Office of the day *Friday abstinence*
30 Sat	P	Lent feria: Mass & Office of the day
		The Lenten discipline in the use of organ, other musical instruments and flowers does not apply to Laetare Sunday.
evening	RP or P	First Vespers
31 Sun	RP or P	+ 4th SUNDAY OF LENT (Laetare Sunday) *Ps Week 4* *Creed, Preface I or II of Lent; Year A Readings (Short form Gospel) may be used, with the matching Preface and Communion Antiphon* Mass & Office of the day RCIA - Second Scrutiny: the Ritual Mass (pages 1179-80) with Year A Readings (Short form Gospel), Proper Preface (pages 270-1) and Insertions in the Eucharistic Prayer. § Candidates for the Sacraments
		The Gospel of the Man born Blind may be used on a ferial weekday, with 1st Reading and Psalm as in Year A of the Lectionary. The matching Preface and Communion Antiphon should also be used. The Alternative Readings (Vol I, page 287 ff) may also be used.
APRIL 2019		
1 Mon	P	Lent feria, Fourth Week of Lent: Mass & Office of the day
2 Tue	P	Lent feria: Mass & Office of the day (St Francis of Paola, Hermit)
3 Wed	P	Lent feria: Mass & Office of the day
4 Thu	P	Lent feria: Mass & Office of the day (St Isidore, Bishop & Doctor)
5 Fri	P	Lent feria: Mass & Office of the day *Friday abstinence* (St Vincent Ferrer, Priest)
6 Sat	P	Lent feria: Mass & Office of the day
		The practice of covering crosses and images in the church may be observed. Crosses remain covered until the end of the celebration

APRIL 2019

		of the Lord's Passion on Good Friday; images until the beginning of the Easter Vigil.
evening	P	First Vespers
7 Sun	P	+ 5th SUNDAY OF LENT *Ps Week I* *Creed, Preface I or II of Lent; Year A Readings (Short form Gospel) may be used, with the matching Preface and Communion Antiphon* Mass & Office of the day RCIA - Third Scrutiny: the Ritual Mass (pages 1180-1) with Year A Readings (Short form Gospel), Proper Preface (pages 281-2) and Insertions in the Eucharistic Prayer. § Candidates for the Sacraments
		The Gospel of Lazarus may be used on a ferial weekday, with 1st Reading and Psalm as in Year A of the Lectionary. The matching Preface and Communion Antiphon should also be used. The Alternative Readings (Vol I, page 316 ff) may also be used.
8 Mon	P	Lent feria, Fifth Week of Lent *(Short form 1st Reading, Alternative Gospel), Preface I of the Passion of the Lord (and on following days)* Mass & Office of the day
9 Tue	P	Lent feria: Mass & Office of the day
10 Wed	P	Lent feria: Mass & Office of the day
11 Thu	P	Lent feria: Mass & Office of the day (St Stanislaus, Bishop & Martyr)
12 Fri	P	Lent feria *Friday abstinence* *Alternative Collect* Mass & Office of the day § Day of Prayer for the Victims and Survivors of Abuse
13 Sat	P	Lent feria: Mass & Office of the day (St Martin I Pope & Martyr)
		HOLY WEEK In Holy Week the Church celebrates the mysteries of salvation accomplished by Christ in the last days of his earthly life, from his messianic entry into Jerusalem, until his blessed Passion and glorious Resurrection. Lent continues until Maundy Thursday.
evening	R	First Vespers

APRIL 2019

14 Sun R **+ PALM SUNDAY OF THE PASSION OF THE LORD**

Ps Week 2

Blessing of Palms and Procession or Solemn Entrance before the Principal Mass; the latter may be repeated or the Simple Entrance used before other Masses, Narrative of the Lord's Passion (Short form), Creed, Proper Preface

Mass & Office of the day

§ Candidates for the Sacraments

Announce Good Friday, Day of Fast and Abstinence

Announce Mandatory Holy See Good Friday collection

---

15 Mon P MONDAY OF HOLY WEEK: Mass & Office of the day

Preface II of the Passion of the Lord

---

16 Tue P TUESDAY OF HOLY WEEK: Mass & Office of the day

Preface II of the Passion of the Lord

W Chrism Mass in the Cathedral

---

17 Wed P WEDNESDAY OF HOLY WEEK: Mass & Office of the day

Preface II of the Passion of the Lord

THE PASCHAL TRIDUUM

In the Sacred Triduum, the Church solemnly celebrates the greatest mysteries of our redemption, keeping by means of special celebrations the memorial of her Lord, crucified, buried and risen.

The Paschal Fast should also be kept sacred. It is to be celebrated everywhere on the Friday of the Lord's Passion and, where appropriate, prolonged also through Holy Saturday as a way of coming, with spirit uplifted, to the joys of the Lord's Resurrection.

18 Thu P **MAUNDY THURSDAY**: Office of the day

Vespers are not said by those attending the Evening Mass.

Holy Communion may be distributed to the faithful only during the Mass of the Lord's Supper. The sick, however, may receive Communion at any hour. The celebration of Mass without a congregation is prohibited.

W **Evening Mass of the Lord's Supper**

Gloria, during which bells are rung; the Washing of Feet may be carried out; Preface I of the Most Holy Eucharist and insertions in the Roman Canon. Procession & Reposition of the Blessed Sacrament take place if the Celebration of the Lord's Passion is to take place in the Church; watching before the Altar of Repose then follows with solemnity until midnight and may conclude with Compline II of Sunday.

APRIL 2019

19 Fri | R | **GOOD FRIDAY**: Office of the Day | *Fast & Abstinence*

It is highly appropriate that the Office of Readings and Lauds be celebrated solemnly with the people.
Vespers are not said by those attending the Afternoon Liturgy.
Compline II of Sunday may conclude the day.
Holy Communion is distributed to the faithful only during the Celebration of the Lord's Passion, but may be taken at any time to the sick who are unable to take part in this liturgy. Only the Sacraments of Penance and of the Anointing of the Sick may be celebrated.

R | **The Celebration of the Passion of the Lord**

This takes place in the afternoon, at about 3pm (or at least not before noon and not after 9pm).
Collection for the Holy Places

---

20 Sat | P | **HOLY SATURDAY**: Office of the day | *Fast as desired*

It is highly appropriate that the Office of Readings and Lauds be celebrated solemnly with the people. Vespers are of Holy Saturday. Compline (II of Sunday) is not said by those attending the Easter Vigil.
The Church today abstains completely from the celebration of Mass. Holy Communion may only be given as Viaticum. Only the Sacraments of Penance and of the Anointing of the Sick may be celebrated.

EASTER SEASON

Throughout the Easter season, the *Angelus* is replaced by *Regina Caeli*. The Apostles' Creed may suitably be used as an alternative on days when the Creed is appointed to be said.

Eucharistic Prayer 4 is not used in this Season.

at night | W | **+ The Easter Vigil in the Holy Night**

The entire celebration of the Easter Vigil must take place during the night, so that it begins after nightfall and ends before daybreak. The celebration of a Mass without the rites of the Easter Vigil is not permitted.
Gloria, Year C Gospel, Preface I of Easter, Proper Insertions in the Roman Canon, Commemoration of the Baptised in the Eucharistic Prayer (pages 1183-4), double Alleluia *added to* Ite, missa est
The Office of Readings is omitted by those who attend the Vigil.
The Paschal candle should be placed near the ambo or altar, and kept there for the whole Easter season until the end of Pentecost Sunday. It is lit for the more solemn liturgical celebrations during this time.

APRIL 2019

21 Sun	W	**+ EASTER SUNDAY OF THE RESURRECTION** *Either: In place of the Penitential Act,* Vidi aquam *is sung and all are sprinkled with water blessed at the Vigil to recall their Baptism; in this case the Creed is used.* *Or: If the Renewal of Baptismal Promises is desired, this takes place after the homily and the Creed is omitted.* *Gloria, (Alternative 2nd Reading, Alternative Gospel Readings of the Vigil or Easter Wednesday* [latter Evening Mass only]*), Sequence, Creed or Renewal of Baptismal Promises, Preface I of Easter, Proper Insertions in the Roman Canon, Commemoration of the Baptised in the Eucharistic Prayer (pages 1183-4), double* Alleluia *added to* Ite, missa est . Mass & Office of the Solemnity
22 Mon	W	**MONDAY WITHIN THE OCTAVE OF EASTER** *Gloria, Sequence ad lib, Preface I of Easter, Proper Insertions in the Roman Canon, double* Alleluia *added to* Ite, missa est Mass & Office of the Solemnity
23 Tue	W	**TUESDAY WITHIN THE OCTAVE OF EASTER** *Gloria, Sequence ad lib, Preface I of Easter, Proper Insertions in the Roman Canon, double* Alleluia *added to* Ite, missa est Mass & Office of the Solemnity
24 Wed	W	**WEDNESDAY WITHIN THE OCTAVE OF EASTER** *Gloria, Sequence ad lib, Preface I of Easter, Proper Insertions in the Roman Canon, double* Alleluia *added to* Ite, missa est Mass & Office of the Solemnity
25 Thu	W	**THURSDAY WITHIN THE OCTAVE OF EASTER** *Gloria, Sequence ad lib, Preface I of Easter, Proper Insertions in the Roman Canon, double* Alleluia *added to* Ite, missa est Mass & Office of the Solemnity
26 Fri	W	**FRIDAY WITHIN THE OCTAVE OF EASTER** *Gloria, Sequence ad lib, Preface I of Easter, Proper Insertions in the Roman Canon, double* Alleluia *added to* Ite, missa est Mass & Office of the Solemnity *No Friday abstinence*
27 Sat	W	**SATURDAY WITHIN THE OCTAVE OF EASTER** *Gloria, Sequence ad lib, Preface I of Easter, Proper Insertions in the Roman Canon, double* Alleluia *added to* Ite, missa est Mass & Office of the Solemnity
evening	W	First Vespers

APRIL/MAY 2019		
28 Sun	W	+ **SECOND SUNDAY OF EASTER** (or of DIVINE MERCY) *Gloria, Sequence ad lib, Creed, Preface I of Easter, Proper Insertions in the Roman Canon, double* Alleluia *added to* Ite, missa est Mass & Office of the Solemnity
		Throughout the Easter season, particular attention should be paid to the mystagogical formation of the newly baptised. On ferial days of the Easter season one of the five Easter prefaces is said, unless other provision is made.
29 Mon	W	ST CATHERINE OF SIENA, Virgin & Doctor, Patron of Europe *National* *Gloria, Proper Readings, Preface of Holy Virgins & Religious* Mass & Office of the Feast § Europe
	R	First Vespers
30 Tue	R	**ST GEORGE, Martyr, Patron of England** *Gloria, 1st Reading from Common 2nd Reading & Gospel from National Proper, (Alternative Gospel Reading), Creed, Preface I or II of Holy Martyrs* Mass & Office of the Solemnity
MAY 2019		
1 Wed	W	Easter feria, Second Week of Easter: *Ps Week 2* Mass & Office of the day *or*
	W	St Joseph the Worker: Mass & Office of the Memorial *Proper Gospel Reading, Preface of St Joseph* § Human Work
2 Thu	W	St Athanasius, Bishop & Doctor: Mass & Office of the Memorial
3 Fri	R	Ss PHILIP and JAMES, Apostles *Friday abstinence* *Gloria, Proper Readings, Preface I or II of Apostles* Mass & Office of the Feast
4 Sat	R	THE ENGLISH MARTYRS *National* *Gloria, Either the Readings for today's former Feast of the Beatified Martyrs or those for the former Feast of the Forty Martyrs on 25 October, given in the current editions of the Lectionary, may be used, Preface I or II of Holy Martyrs* Mass & Office of the Feast
evening	W	First Vespers

MAY 2019

5 Sun	W	+ 3rd SUNDAY OF EASTER *Gloria, (Short form Gospel), Creed, a Preface of Easter* Mass & Office of the day	*Ps Week 3*
6 Mon	W	Easter feria, Third Week of Easter: Mass & Office of the day	
7 Tue	W	Easter feria: Mass & Office of the day	
8 Wed	W	Easter feria: Mass & Office of the day	
9 Thu	W	Easter feria: Mass & Office of the day	
10 Fri	W	Easter feria: Mass & Office of the day	*Friday abstinence*
11 Sat	W	Easter feria: Mass & Office of the day	
evening	W	First Vespers	
12 Sun	W	+ 4th SUNDAY OF EASTER *Gloria, Creed, a Preface of Easter* Mass & Office of the Day § World Day of Prayer for Vocations Announce Mandatory Diocesan PTF Collection	*Ps Week 4*
13 Mon	W W	Easter feria, Fourth Week of Easter: Mass & Office of the day *or* Our Lady of Fatima: Mass & Office of the Memorial	
14 Tue	R	ST MATTHIAS, Apostle *Gloria, Proper Readings, Preface I or II of Apostles* Mass & Office of the Feast	
15 Wed	W	Easter feria: Mass & Office of the day	
16 Thu	W	Easter feria: Mass & Office of the day	
17 Fri	W	Easter feria: Mass & Office of the day	*Friday abstinence*
18 Sat	W R	Easter feria: Mass & Office of the day *or* St John I, Pope & Martyr: Mass & Office of the Memorial	
evening	W	First Vespers	
19 Sun	W	+ 5th SUNDAY OF EASTER *Gloria, Creed, a Preface of Easter* Mass & Office of the day Collection for Priests' Training Fund	*Ps Week 1*

MAY 2019

20 Mon	W W	Easter feria, Fifth Week of Easter: Mass & Office of the day *or* St Bernadine of Siena, Priest: Mass & Office of the Memorial	
21 Tue	W R	Easter feria: Mass & Office of the day *or* St Christopher Magallanes, Priest, and Companions, Martyrs: Mass & Office of the Memorial Anniversary of the Installation of Cardinal Vincent Nichols, Eleventh Archbishop of Westminster (2009). An intention may be included in the Universal Prayer.	
22 Wed	W W	Easter feria: Mass & Office of the day *or* St Rita of Cascia, Religious: Mass & Office of the Memorial	
23 Thu	W	Easter feria: Mass & Office of the day	
24 Fri	W	Easter feria: Mass & Office of the day	*Friday abstinence*
25 Sat	W	St Bede the Venerable, Priest & Doctor Mass & Office of the Memorial	*National*
evening	W	First Vespers	
26 Sun	W	+ 6th SUNDAY OF EASTER *Gloria, Creed, a Preface of Easter* Mass & Office of the day Announce Mandatory Holy See CCN Collection Announce Holy Day of Obligation	*Ps Week 2*
27 Mon	W	ST AUGUSTINE OF CANTERBURY, Bishop *Gloria, Proper National Readings, Preface of Holy Pastors* Mass & Office of the Feast	*National*
28 Tue	W	Easter feria, Sixth Week of Easter: Mass & Office of the day	
29 Wed	W	Easter feria: Mass & Office of the day	
evening	W W	First Vespers + Proper Vigil Mass of the Ascension precedes or follows *Gloria, Ascension Readings, Creed, Preface I or II of the Ascension &* Communicantes *in the Roman Canon*	
30 Thu	W	+ **THE ASCENSION OF THE LORD** *Gloria, (Alternative Collect), (Alternative 2nd Reading), Creed, Preface I or II of the Ascension &* Communicantes *in the Roman Canon* Mass & Office of the Solemnity	

MAY/JUNE 2019

On ferial days until Pentecost a preface of Easter or of the Ascension is used, unless other provision is made.

31 Fri	W	THE VISITATION OF THE BLESSED VIRGIN MARY *Gloria, Proper Readings (Alternative 1st Reading), Preface II of the Blessed Virgin Mary* Mass & Office of the Feast *Friday abstinence*

JUNE 2019

1 Sat	R	St Justin, Martyr: Mass & Office of the Memorial *1st or 2nd Gospel Acclamation*
	W	First Vespers
2 Sun	W	+ 7th SUNDAY OF EASTER — *Ps Week 3* *Gloria, Creed, a Preface of Easter or of the Ascension* Mass & Office of the day § World Communications Day Collection for Catholic Communications Network
3 Mon	R	Ss Charles Lwanga and Companions, Martyrs Mass & Office of the Memorial
4 Tue	W	Easter feria, Seventh Week of Easter: Mass & Office of the day
5 Wed	R	St Boniface, Bishop & Martyr — *National* Mass & Office of the Memorial
6 Thu	W W	Easter feria: Mass & Office of the day *or* St Norbert, Bishop: Mass & Office of the Memorial
7 Fri	W	Easter feria: Mass & Office of the day — *Friday abstinence*
8 Sat	W	Easter feria: Mass & Office of the day

The fifty days of the sacred season of Easter conclude with Pentecost Sunday, when the Church recalls the gift of the Holy Spirit to the Apostles, the beginnings of the Church, and the start of her mission to all tongues and peoples and nations.

It is appropriate that the Vigil Mass of Pentecost be celebrated in the extended form, using the readings and prayers to be found in the liturgical books. This Mass, however, does not have a baptismal character, as does the Easter Vigil, but instead is a celebration of more intense prayer, after the example of the Apostles and disciples, who together with Mary, the Mother of Jesus, were one in persevering prayer, as they awaited the outpouring of the Holy Spirit.

JUNE 2019

evening	R	First Vespers
	R	+ Proper Vigil Mass of Pentecost precedes, follows or incorporates *Gloria, (Two Alternative Collects), (Choice of Old Testament Readings), Creed, Proper Preface &* Communicantes *in the Roman Canon, double* Alleluia *added to* Ite, missa est
9 Sun	R	+ **PENTECOST SUNDAY** *Gloria, (Alternative 2nd & Gospel Readings), Sequence, Creed, Proper Preface &* Communicantes *in the Roman Canon, double* Alleluia *added to* Ite, missa est Mass & Office of the Solemnity § The Church Announce Mandatory CBCEW Day for Life Collection

The Easter season ends. After today, the Paschal Candle is no longer kept in the sanctuary, but moved to the baptistry, where it is lit at baptisms. At funerals it is placed and lit near the coffin, to signify that Christian death is a true Passover.
From tomorrow, the recitation of the *Angelus* is resumed.

[R] When Monday or Tuesday after Pentecost are days on which it is customary for the faithful to attend Mass, the Mass of Pentecost Sunday or the Votive Mass of the Holy Spirit may be used.

ORDINARY TIME - AFTER THE EASTER SEASON

The weeks of Ordinary Time celebrate no particular aspect of Christ. Instead, celebration is made of the mystery of Christ in all its fullness.

LECTIONARY FOR SUNDAYS: YEAR C
WEEKDAY LECTIONARY: YEAR I
ORDINARY TIME: WEEK 10
(Divine Office Volume III)
Eucharistic Prayer 4 may be used in this Season.
The choice of Masses which may be celebrated *ad libitum* is shown in the Liturgical Information on page 292.
On ferial days in Ordinary Time the Office of a saint included for that day in the Roman Martyrology may be celebrated. Occasional Votive Offices are permitted, although care to observe the four-week cycle of the Office should be maintained.

10 Mon	W	The Blessed Virgin Mary, Mother of the Church *Ps Week 2* Mass & Office of the Memorial (Roman Missal, Votive Mass 10 B, page 1411 ff; texts for the Office *ad interim* from the Common of the BVM)

JUNE 2019

11 Tue	R	St Barnabas, Apostle *Proper 1st Reading, Preface I or II of Apostles* Mass & Office of the Memorial	
12 Wed	G	feria, Tenth Week of Year 1: Mass ad lib; Office of the day	
13 Thu	W	OUR LORD JESUS CHRIST, THE ETERNAL HIGH PRIEST *Gloria, Proper Year C Readings (Alternative 1st Reading), Preface of the Priesthood of Christ and of the Church [see Chrism Mass, page 324 ff]* Mass and Office of the Feast *[see Liturgical information, National Calendar, page 290]*	*National*
14 Fri	G	feria: Mass ad lib; Office of the day	*Friday abstinence*
15 Sat	G W	feria: Mass ad lib; Office of the day *or* Blessed Virgin Mary on Saturday: Mass & Office of the Memorial	
evening	W	First Vespers	
16 Sun	W	+ **THE MOST HOLY TRINITY** *Gloria, Creed, Proper Preface* Mass & Office of the Solemnity § Day for Life Collection for Life Announce Holy Day of Obligation	
17 Mon	G	feria, Eleventh Week of Year 1: Mass ad lib; Office of the day	*Ps Week 3*
18 Tue	G	feria: Mass ad lib; Office of the day	
19 Wed	G W	feria: Mass ad lib; Office of the day *or* St Romuald, Abbot: Mass & Office of the Memorial	
20 Thu	R	St Alban, Protomartyr *Proper National Collect* Mass & Office of the Memorial	*Diocesan*
21 Fri	W	St Aloysius Gonzaga, Religious: Mass & Office of the Memorial	*Friday abstinence*
22 Sat	R	Ss JOHN FISHER, Bishop and THOMAS MORE, Martyrs *Gloria, Proper National Readings, Preface I or II of Holy Martyrs* Mass & Office of the Feast § Those who suffer persecution	*National*

JUNE 2019

evening	W	First Vespers
23 Sun	W	+ **THE MOST HOLY BODY AND BLOOD OF CHRIST (CORPUS CHRISTI)** *Gloria, Sequence* ad lib, *Creed, Preface II of the Most Holy Eucharist (Preface I may be used)* Mass & Office of the Solemnity, 2nd Vespers and + Evening Mass Announce Holy Day of Obligation Announce Mandatory Holy See Peter's Pence Collection
24 Mon	W	**THE NATIVITY OF ST JOHN THE BAPTIST** *Gloria, Creed, Preface of St John the Baptist* Mass & Office of the Solemnity
25 Tue	G	feria, Twelfth Week of Year I: *Ps Week 4* Mass ad lib; Office of the day
26 Wed	G	feria: Mass ad lib; Office of the day
in Cathedral	R	First Vespers
27 Thu	R	St John Southworth, Priest & Martyr *Diocesan* see *Diocesan Supplement Book or online, (Short form 1st Reading)* Mass, Lauds & Lesser Hours of the Memorial
in Cathedral	R	**ST JOHN SOUTHWORTH, Priest & Martyr** *Diocesan* *Gloria, 1st, 2nd & Gospel Readings all from the Common, Creed, Preface I or II of Holy Martyrs; see Diocesan Supplement Book or online* Mass, Lauds & Lesser Hours of the Solemnity
evening	W	First Vespers
28 Fri	W	**THE MOST SACRED HEART OF JESUS (Diocese consecrated to the Sacred Heart, 17 June 1873)** *No Friday abstinence* *Gloria, Creed, Proper Preface* Mass & Office of the Solemnity
29 Sat	W	The Immaculate Heart of Mary *Proper Gospel, Preface I of the Blessed Virgin Mary*
evening	R	First Vespers
	R	+ Proper Vigil Mass of Ss Peter and Paul precedes or follows *Gloria, Proper Readings, Creed, Preface of Ss Peter and Paul*

JUNE/JULY 2019		
30 Sun	R	**+ Ss PETER and PAUL, Apostles** **St Peter, Prince of Apostles, Patron of the Diocese** *Gloria, Creed, Preface of Ss Peter & Paul* Mass & Office of the Solemnity The anniversary of the election of Pope Francis is observed today, by decision of the Bishops' Conference. A special intention for the Holy Father should be included in the Universal Prayer. Collection for Peter's Pence
JULY 2019		
1 Mon	W	DEDICATION OF THE CATHEDRAL *Diocesan* *Gloria, Readings Lectionary Vol. 2, page 1392, Common of the Dedication of a Church II, page 1095* Mass & Office of the Feast
in Cathedral	W	**DEDICATION OF THE CATHEDRAL (1910)** *Diocesan* *Mass in the Dedicated Church: Gloria, 1st & 2nd Readings and Gospel from Lectionary Vol. 2, page 1392, Creed, Common of the Dedication of a Church I, page 1091* Mass & Office of the Solemnity
2 Tue	G	feria, Thirteenth Week of Year I: *Ps Week I* Mass ad lib; Office of the day
3 Wed	R	ST THOMAS, Apostle *Gloria, Proper Readings, Preface I or II of Apostles* Mass & Office of the Feast
4 Thu	G W	feria: Mass ad lib; Office of the day *or* St Elizabeth of Portugal: Mass & Office of the Memorial
5 Fri	G W	feria: Mass ad lib; Office of the day *or* *Friday abstinence* St Anthony Zaccaria, Priest: Mass & Office of the Memorial
6 Sat	G R W	feria: Mass ad lib; Office of the day *or* St Maria Goretti, Virgin & Martyr: Mass & Office of the Memorial *or* Blessed Virgin Mary on Saturday: Mass & Office of the Memorial
evening	G	First Vespers
7 Sun	G	+ 14th SUNDAY IN ORDINARY TIME *Ps Week 2* *Gloria, (Short form Gospel), Creed, a Preface of Sundays in O.T.* Mass & Office of the day Announce Mandatory CBCEW Collection for AoS

JULY 2019

8 Mon	G	feria, Fourteenth Week of Year 1: Mass ad lib; Office of the day
9 Tue	G R	feria: Mass ad lib; Office of the day *or* St Augustine Zhao Rong, Priest, and Companions, Martyrs: Mass & Office of the Memorial
10 Wed	G	feria: Mass ad lib; Office of the day
11 Thu	W	ST BENEDICT, Abbot, Patron of Europe *National* *Gloria, Proper Readings, Preface of Holy Pastors or Holy Virgins and Religious* Mass & Office of the Feast § Europe
12 Fri	G	feria: Mass ad lib; Office of the day *Friday abstinence*
13 Sat	G W W	feria: Mass ad lib; Office of the day *or* St Henry: Mass & Office of the Memorial *or* Blessed Virgin Mary on Saturday: Mass & Office of the Memorial
evening	G	First Vespers
14 Sun	G	+ 15th SUNDAY IN ORDINARY TIME *Ps Week 3* *Gloria, (Alternative Psalm), Creed, a Preface of Sundays in O.T.* Mass & Office of the day § Sea Sunday Collection for Apostleship of the Sea
15 Mon	W	St Bonaventure, Bishop & Doctor: Mass & Office of the Memorial
16 Tue	G W	feria, Fifteenth Week of Year 1: Mass ad lib; Office of the day *or* Our Lady of Mount Carmel: Mass & Office of the Memorial
17 Wed	G	feria: Mass ad lib; Office of the day
18 Thu	G	feria: Mass ad lib; Office of the day
19 Fri	G	feria: Mass ad lib; Office of the day *Friday abstinence*
20 Sat	G R W	feria: Mass ad lib; Office of the day *or* St Apollinaris, Bishop & Martyr: Mass & Office of the Memorial *or* Blessed Virgin Mary on Saturday: Mass & Office of the Memorial
evening	G	First Vespers
21 Sun	G	+16th SUNDAY IN ORDINARY TIME *Ps Week 4* *Gloria, Creed, a Preface of Sundays in O.T.* Mass & Office of the day

JULY/AUGUST 2019

22 Mon	W	ST MARY MAGDALENE *Gloria, Proper Readings (Alternative First Reading), Proper Preface (presently Latin only)* Mass & Office of the Feast
23 Tue	W	ST BRIDGET OF SWEDEN, Patron of Europe *National* *Gloria, Proper Readings, Preface of Holy Virgins and Religious* Mass & Office of the Feast § Europe
24 Wed	G W	feria, Sixteenth Week of Year I: Mass ad lib; Office of the day *or* St Sharbel Makhluf, Priest: Mass & Office of the Memorial
25 Thu	R	ST JAMES, Apostle *Gloria, Proper Readings, Preface I or II of Apostles* Mass & Office of the Feast
26 Fri	W	Ss Joachim and Anne, *Friday abstinence* Parents of the Blessed Virgin Mary Mass & Office of the Memorial
27 Sat	G W	feria: Mass ad lib; Office of the day *or* Blessed Virgin Mary on Saturday: Mass & Office of the Memorial
evening	G	First Vespers
28 Sun	G	+ 17th SUNDAY IN ORDINARY TIME *Ps Week I* *Gloria, Creed, a Preface of Sundays in O.T.* Mass & Office of the day
29 Mon	W	St Martha *Proper Alternative Gospels* Mass & Office of the Memorial
30 Tue	G W	feria, Seventeenth Week of Year I: Mass ad lib; Office of the day *or* St Peter Chrysologus, Bishop & Doctor: Mass & Office of the Memorial
31 Wed	W	St Ignatius of Loyola, Priest: Mass & Office of the Memorial
AUGUST 2019		
1 Thu	W	St Alphonsus Liguori, Bishop & Doctor: Mass & Office of the Memorial

On 2nd August the plenary indulgence ('the Portiuncula') may be acquired in minor basilicas, shrines and parish churches.

AUGUST 2019

		Requirements: a devout visit to a church and the recitation there of the Lord's Prayer and Creed, in addition to sacramental confession, Holy Communion and prayer for the intentions of the Holy Father. This indulgence may be gained only once. The visit may be made from noon the previous day to midnight on the day itself.
2 Fri	G W W	feria: Mass ad lib; Office of the day *or* *Friday abstinence* St Eusebius of Vercelli, Bishop: Mass & Office of the Memorial *or* St Peter Julian Eymard, Priest: Mass & Office of the Memorial
3 Sat	G W	feria: Mass ad lib; Office of the day *or* Blessed Virgin Mary on Saturday: Mass & Office of the Memorial
evening	G	First Vespers
4 Sun	G	+18th SUNDAY IN ORDINARY TIME *Ps Week 2* *Gloria, (Alternative Psalm), Creed, a Preface of Sundays in O.T.* Mass & Office of the day
5 Mon	G W	feria, Eighteenth Week of Year 1: Mass ad lib; Office of the day *or* The Dedication of the Basilica of St Mary Major: Mass & Office of the Memorial
6 Tue	W	THE TRANSFIGURATION OF THE LORD *Gloria, 1st or 2nd Reading, Year C Gospel, Proper Preface* Mass & Office of the Feast
7 Wed	G R W	feria: Mass ad lib; Office of the day *or* Ss Sixtus II, Pope, and Companions, Martyrs: Mass & Office of the Memorial *or* St Cajetan, Priest: Mass & Office of the Memorial
8 Thu	W	St Dominic, Priest: Mass & Office of the Memorial
9 Fri	R	ST TERESA BENEDICTA OF THE CROSS, *National* Virgin & Martyr, Patron of Europe *Friday abstinence* *Gloria, Proper Readings as indicated in the Lectionary for St Cecilia (22 November), Preface I or II of Holy Martyrs* Mass & Office of the Feast § Europe
10 Sat	R	ST LAWRENCE, Deacon & Martyr *Gloria, Proper Readings, Preface I or II of Holy Martyrs* Mass & Office of the Feast
evening	G	First Vespers

SECTION 7: LITURGICAL CALENDAR

AUGUST 2019		
11 Sun	G	+ 19th SUNDAY IN ORDINARY TIME *Ps Week 3* *Gloria, (Short form 2nd & Gospel Readings), Creed, a Preface of Sundays in O.T.* Mass & Office of the day Announce Holy Day of Obligation
12 Mon	G W	feria, Nineteenth Week of Year 1: Mass ad lib; Office of the day *or* St Jane Frances de Chantal, Religious: Mass & Office of the Memorial *[see Divine Office for 12 December, Vol I, p 33* ff]*
13 Tue	G R	feria: Mass ad lib; Office of the day *or* Ss Pontian, Pope, & Hippolytus, Priest, Martyrs: Mass & Office of the Memorial
14 Wed	R	St Maximilian Mary Kolbe, Priest & Martyr: Mass & Office of the Memorial
evening	W W	First Vespers + Proper Vigil Mass of the Assumption precedes or follows *Gloria, Proper Readings, Creed, Proper Preface*
15 Thu	W	**+ THE ASSUMPTION OF THE BLESSED VIRGIN MARY** *Gloria, Creed, Proper Preface* Mass & Office of the Solemnity
16 Fri	G W	feria: Mass ad lib; Office of the day *or* *Friday abstinence* St Stephen of Hungary: Mass & Office of the Memorial
17 Sat	G W	feria: Mass ad lib; Office of the day *or* Blessed Virgin Mary on Saturday: Mass & Office of the Memorial
evening	G	First Vespers
18 Sun	G	+ 20th SUNDAY IN ORDINARY TIME *Ps Week 4* *Gloria, Creed, a Preface of Sundays in O.T.* Mass & Office of the day
19 Mon	G W	feria, Twentieth Week of Year 1: Mass ad lib; Office of the day *or* St John Eudes, Priest: Mass & Office of the Memorial
20 Tue	W	St Bernard, Abbot & Doctor: Mass & Office of the Memorial
21 Wed	W	St Pius X, Pope: Mass & Office of the Memorial

AUGUST 2019			
22 Thu	W	The Queenship of the Blessed Virgin Mary *Proper Readings, Preface I or II of the Blessed Virgin Mary* Mass & Office of the Memorial	
23 Fri	G W	feria: Mass ad lib; Office of the day *or* St Rose of Lima, Virgin: Mass & Office of the Memorial	*Friday abstinence*
24 Sat	R	ST BARTHOLOMEW, Apostle *Gloria, Proper Readings, Preface I or II of Apostles* Mass & Office of the Feast	
evening	G	First Vespers	
25 Sun	G	+ 21st SUNDAY IN ORDINARY TIME *Gloria, Creed, a Preface of Sundays in O.T.* Mass & Office of the day	*Ps Week I*
26 Mon	G W	feria, Twenty-First Week of Year I: Mass ad lib; Office of the day *or* Blessed Dominic of the Mother of God, Priest: Mass & Office of the Memorial	
27 Tue	W	St Monica: Mass & Office of the Memorial	
28 Wed	W	St Augustine, Bishop & Doctor: Mass & Office of the Memorial	
29 Thu	R	The Passion of St John the Baptist *Proper Gospel, Preface of St John the Baptist* Mass & Office of the Memorial	
30 Fri	G R	feria: Mass ad lib; Office of the day *or* Ss Margaret Clitherow, Anne Line and Margaret Ward, Martyrs: Mass & Office of the Memorial	*Friday abstinence* *National*
31 Sat	G W W	feria: Mass ad lib; Office of the day *or* St Aidan, Bishop, and the Saints of Lindisfarne: Mass & Office of the Memorial *or* Blessed Virgin Mary on Saturday: Mass & Office of the Memorial	*National*
evening	G	First Vespers	

SEPTEMBER 2019

SEPTEMBER 2019

1 Sun	G	+ 22nd SUNDAY IN ORDINARY TIME *Gloria, Creed, a Preface of Sundays in O.T.* Mass & Office of the day Anniversary of the Death of Cardinal Cormac Murphy O'Connor, Tenth Archbishop of Westminster (2017) § World Day of Prayer for the Care of Creation Annouce Optional Catholic Education Service Collection	*Ps Week 2*
2 Mon	G	feria, Twenty-Second Week of Year 1: Mass ad lib; Office of the day	
3 Tue	W	ST GREGORY THE GREAT, Pope & Doctor *Gloria, Proper National Readings, Preface of Holy Pastors* Mass & Office of the Feast	*National*
4 Wed	G W	feria: Mass ad lib; Office of the day *or* St Cuthbert, Bishop: Mass & Office of the Memorial	 *National*
5 Thu	G	feria: Mass ad lib; Office of the day	
6 Fri	G	feria: Mass ad lib; Office of the day	*Friday abstinence*
7 Sat	G W	feria: Mass ad lib; Office of the day *or* Blessed Virgin Mary on Saturday: Mass & Office of the Memorial	
evening	G	First Vespers	
8 Sun	G	+ 23rd SUNDAY IN ORDINARY TIME *Gloria, Creed, a Preface of Sundays in O.T.* Mass & Office of the day § Education Sunday Collection for Catholic Education Service Announce Mandatory CBCEW Home Mission Appeal collection	*Ps Week 3*
9 Mon	G W	feria, Twenty-Third Week of Year 1: Mass ad lib; Office of the day *or* St Peter Claver, Priest: Mass & Office of the Memorial	
10 Tue	G	feria: Mass ad lib; Office of the day	
11 Wed	G	feria: Mass ad lib; Office of the day	
12 Thu	G W	feria: Mass ad lib; Office of the day *or* The Most Holy Name of Mary: Mass & Office of the Memorial	

SEPTEMBER 2019			
13 Fri	W	St John Chrysostom, Bishop & Doctor: Mass & Office of the Memorial	*Friday abstinence*
14 Sat	R	THE EXALTATION OF THE HOLY CROSS *Gloria, 1st or 2nd Reading, Preface of the Holy Cross (Preface I of the Passion of the Lord may be used)* Mass & Office of the Feast	
evening	G	First Vespers	
15 Sun	G	+ 24th SUNDAY IN ORDINARY TIME *Gloria, (Short form Gospel), Creed, a Preface of Sundays in O.T.* Mass & Office of the day § Home Mission Day Collection for Home Mission Appeal	*Ps Week 4*
16 Mon	R	Ss Cornelius, Pope, and Cyprian, Bishop, Martyrs: Mass & Office of the Memorial	
17 Tue	G W	feria, Twenty-Fourth Week of Year I: Mass ad lib; Office of the day *or* St Robert Bellarmine, Bishop & Doctor: Mass & Office of the Memorial	
18 Wed	G	feria: Mass ad lib; Office of the day	
19 Thu	G R	feria: Mass ad lib; Office of the day *or* St Januarius, Bishop & Martyr: Mass & Office of the Memorial *The Proper Calendar for England gives today as an optional memorial of St Theodore of Canterbury, Bishop, but the Westminster Diocesan Calendar has the Memorial of Ss Laurence, Dunstan & Theodore on 3 February.*	
20 Fri	R	Ss Andrew Kim Tae-gŏn, Priest, Paul Chŏng Ha-sang, and Companions, Martyrs: Mass & Office of the Memorial	*Friday abstinence*
21 Sat	R	ST MATTHEW, Apostle & Evangelist *Gloria, Proper Readings, Preface I or II of Apostles* Mass & Office of the Feast	
evening	G	First Vespers	
22 Sun	G	+ 25th SUNDAY IN ORDINARY TIME *Gloria, (Short form Gospel), Creed, a Preface of Sundays in O.T.* Mass & Office of the day Annual Mass Count – 1 § The Harvest	*Ps Week 1*

SEPTEMBER/OCTOBER 2019

23 Mon	W	St Pius of Pietrelcina, Priest: Mass & Office of the Memorial	
24 Tue	W	Our Lady of Walsingham: Mass & Office of the Memorial	*National*
25 Wed	G	feria, Twenty-Fifth Week of Year I: Mass ad lib; Office of the day	
26 Thu	G R	feria: Mass ad lib; Office of the day *or* Ss Cosmas and Damian, Martyrs: Mass & Office of the Memorial	
27 Fri	W	St Vincent de Paul, Priest: Mass & Office of the Memorial	*Friday abstinence*
28 Sat	G R R W	feria: Mass ad lib; Office of the day *or* St Wenceslaus, Martyr: Mass & Office of the Memorial *or* St Lawrence Ruiz and Companions, Martyrs: Mass & Office of the Memorial *or* Blessed Virgin Mary on Saturday: Mass & Office of the Memorial	
evening	G	First Vespers	
29 Sun	G	+ 26th SUNDAY IN ORDINARY TIME *Gloria, Creed, a Preface of Sundays in O.T.* Mass & Office of the day Annual Mass Count – 2 Announce Optional CAFOD Harvest Fast Day collection	*Ps Week 2*
30 Mon	W	St Jerome, Priest & Doctor: Mass & Office of the Memorial	

OCTOBER 2019

The Rosary should be recommended to the faithful, and its nature and importance explained. A plenary indulgence may be gained by reciting five decades of the Rosary in church, as a family at home, as a religious community, or as a pious fraternity, or in general whenever several persons have gathered for a good purpose; in other circumstances a partial indulgence may be gained.

1 Tue	W	St Thérèse of the Child Jesus, Virgin & Doctor: Mass & Office of the Memorial
2 Wed	W	The Holy Guardian Angels *Proper Gospel Reading, Preface of the Angels* Mass & Office of the Memorial

OCTOBER 2019

3 Thu	G	feria, Twenty-Sixth Week of Year 1: Mass ad lib; Office of the day
4 Fri	W	St Francis of Assisi: *Friday abstinence* Mass & Office of the Memorial § Harvest Fast Day
5 Sat	G W	feria: Mass ad lib; Office of the day *or* Blessed Virgin Mary on Saturday: Mass & Office of the Memorial
evening	G	First Vespers
6 Sun	G	+ 27th SUNDAY IN ORDINARY TIME *Ps Week 3* *Gloria, Creed, a Preface of Sundays in O.T.* Mass & Office of the day Annual Mass Count – 3 Collect Harvest Fast Day Offerings for CAFOD
7 Mon	W	Our Lady of the Rosary: Mass & Office of the Memorial
8 Tue	G	feria, Twenty-Seventh Week of Year 1: Mass ad lib; Office of the day
9 Wed	G R W W	feria: Mass ad lib; Office of the day *or* St Denis, Bishop, and Companions, Martyrs: Mass & Office of the Memorial *or* St John Leonardi, Priest: Mass & Office of the Memorial *or* Blessed John Henry Newman, Priest: *National* Mass & Office of the Memorial
10 Thu	G W	feria: Mass ad lib; Office of the day *or* St Paulinus of York, Bishop: *National* Mass & Office of the Memorial
11 Fri	G W	feria: Mass ad lib; Office of the day *or* *Friday abstinence* St John XXIII, Pope *Common of Pastors: For a Pope* Mass & Office of the Memorial
12 Sat	G W W	feria: Mass ad lib; Office of the day *or* St Wilfrid, Bishop: Mass & Office of the Memorial *or National* Blessed Virgin Mary on Saturday: Mass & Office of the Memorial
evening	G	First Vespers
in City of Westminster	W	First Vespers

SECTION 7: LITURGICAL CALENDAR

OCTOBER 2019

13 Sun	G	+ 28th SUNDAY IN ORDINARY TIME *Gloria, Creed, a Preface of Sundays in O.T.* Mass & Office of the day	*Ps Week 4*
in City of Westminster	W	**ST EDWARD THE CONFESSOR, Patron of the Diocese and of the City of Westminster** *Gloria, Proper National Readings (1st from Common), Creed, Preface I or II of Saints; see Diocesan Supplement Book or online [also National Collect]* Mass & Office of the Solemnity Annual Mass Count – 4 § Week of Prayer for Prisoners and their Families Announce Mandatory Holy See World Mission Sunday collection	*Diocesan*
14 Mon	G R	feria, Twenty-Eighth Week of Year 1: Mass ad lib; Office of the day *or* St Callistus I, Pope & Martyr	
15 Tue	W	St Teresa of Jesus, Virgin & Doctor: Mass & Office of the Memorial	
16 Wed	G W W	feria: Mass ad lib; Office of the day *or* St Hedwig, Religious: Mass & Office of the Memorial *or* St Margaret Mary Alacoque, Virgin: Mass & Office of the Memorial	
17 Thu	R	St Ignatius of Antioch, Bishop & Martyr: Mass & Office of the Memorial	
18 Fri	R	ST LUKE, Evangelist *Gloria, Proper Readings, Preface II of Apostles* Mass & Office of the Feast	*Friday abstinence*
19 Sat	G R W W	feria: Mass ad lib; Office of the day *or* Ss John de Brébeuf and Isaac Jogues, Priests, and Companions, Martyrs: Mass & Office of the Memorial *or* St Paul of the Cross, Priest: Mass & Office of the Memorial *or* Blessed Virgin Mary on Saturday: Mass & Office of the Memorial	
evening	G	First Vespers	
20 Sun	G	+ 29th SUNDAY IN ORDINARY TIME *Gloria, Creed, a Preface of Sundays in O.T.* Mass & Office of the day § World Mission Day (One Mass for the Evangelisation of Peoples is permitted today or on a subsequent ferial day) Collection for World Mission Sunday	*Ps Week 1*

OCTOBER 2019			
21 Mon	G	feria, Twenty-Ninth Week of Year 1: Mass ad lib; Office of the day	
22 Tue	G	feria: Mass ad lib; Office of the day *or*	
	W	St John Paul II, Pope	
		Common of Pastors: For a Pope	
		Mass & Office of the Memorial	
23 Wed	G	feria: Mass ad lib, Office of the day *or*	
	W	St John of Capistrano, Priest: Mass & Office of the Memorial	
24 Thu	G	feria: Mass ad lib; Office of the day *or*	
	W	St Anthony Mary Claret, Bishop: Mass & Office of the Memorial	
25 Fri	G	feria: Mass ad lib; Office of the day	*Friday abstinence*
26 Sat	G	feria; Mass ad lib; Office of the day *or*	
	W	Ss Chad and Cedd, Bishops:	*National*
		Mass & Office of the Memorial *or*	
	W	Blessed Virgin Mary on Saturday: Mass & Office of the Memorial	
evening	G	First Vespers	
27 Sun	G	+ 30th SUNDAY IN ORDINARY TIME	*Ps Week 2*
		Gloria, Creed, a Preface of Sundays in O.T.	
		Mass & Office of the day	
		Announce Holy Day of Obligation	
28 Mon	R	Ss SIMON and JUDE, Apostles	
		Gloria, Proper Readings, Preface I or II of Apostles	
		Mass & Office of the Feast	
29 Tue	R	Blessed Martyrs of Douai College	*Diocesan*
		see Diocesan Supplement Book or online	
		Mass & Office of the Memorial	
30 Wed	G	feria, Thirtieth Week of Year 1: Mass ad lib; Office of the day	
31 Thu	G	feria: Mass ad lib; Office of the day	
evening	W	First Vespers	

NOVEMBER 2019

NOVEMBER 2019

A plenary indulgence, applicable only to the souls in Purgatory, is granted to any of the faithful who (1) on one of the days from 1-8 November visit devoutly a cemetery or simply pray mentally for the dead; (2) on All Souls' Day visit a church or chapel with devotion and there recite the Our Father and the Creed.
A partial indulgence, applicable only to the souls in Purgatory, is granted to any of the faithful who (1) visit devoutly a cemetery or who simply pray mentally for the dead; (2) recite devoutly Lauds or Vespers of the Office of the Dead, or the invocation 'Eternal rest grant unto them, O Lord...'

1 Fri	W	**+ ALL SAINTS** *Gloria, Creed, Proper Preface* Mass & Office of the Solemnity	*No Friday abstinence*
2 Sat	P or B	THE COMMEMORATION OF ALL THE FAITHFUL DEPARTED (ALL SOULS' DAY) *The altar is not decorated with flowers and the organ is used only to sustain the singing.* Mass & Office of the Dead *Readings selected from Masses for the Dead, a Preface for the Dead* All priests are permitted to say three Masses today, with an interval of time between one Mass and the next, and on condition that while one of the Masses may be applied in favour of any person, the second Mass should be applied for all the faithful departed, and the third for the intentions of the Holy Father.	
evening	P or B	Vespers of the Dead + Mass for the Dead *1st, 2nd & Gospel Readings from Masses for the Dead, Creed, a Preface for the Dead.*	
3 Sun	G	+ 31st SUNDAY IN ORDINARY TIME *Gloria, Creed, a Preface of Sundays in O.T.* Mass & Office of the day Announce Mandatory Diocesan Sick & Retired Priests collection	*Ps Week 3*
4 Mon	W	St Charles Borromeo, Bishop: Mass & Office of the Memorial	
5 Tue	G	feria, Thirty-First Week of Year 1: Mass ad lib; Office of the day	
6 Wed	G	feria: Mass ad lib; Office of the day	

NOVEMBER 2019

7 Thu	G W	feria: Mass ad lib; Office of the day *or* St Willibrord, Bishop: Mass & Office of the Memorial *National*
8 Fri	G	feria: Mass ad lib; office of the day *Friday abstinence*
9 Sat	W	THE DEDICATION OF THE LATERAN BASILICA *Gloria, 1st or 2nd Reading, Proper Preface* Mass & Office of the Feast
evening	G	First Vespers
10 Sun	G P or B	+ 32nd SUNDAY IN ORDINARY TIME *Ps Week 4* *Gloria, (Short form Gospel), Creed, a Preface of Sundays in O.T.* Mass & Office of the day + One Requiem Mass permitted (REMEMBRANCE SUNDAY) *1st, 2nd & Gospel Readings from Masses for the Dead, Creed, a Preface for the Dead* Collection for Sick and Retired Priests
11 Mon	W	St Martin of Tours, Bishop: Mass & Office of the Memorial
12 Tue	R	St Josaphat, Bishop & Martyr: Mass & Office of the Memorial
13 Wed	G	feria, Thirty-Second Week of Year 1: Mass ad lib; Office of the day
14 Thu	G	feria: Mass ad lib; Office of the day
15 Fri	G W	feria: Mass ad lib; Office of the day *or* *Friday abstinence* St Albert the Great, Bishop & Doctor: Mass & Office of the Memorial
16 Sat	W	St Edmund of Abingdon, Bishop *Diocesan* *see Diocesan Supplement Book or online [also National Collect]* Mass & Office of the Memorial
evening	G	First Vespers
17 Sun	G	+ 33rd SUNDAY IN ORDINARY TIME *Ps Week 1* *Gloria, Creed, a Preface of Sundays in O.T.* Mass & Office of the day § World Day of the Poor
18 Mon	G W	feria, Thirty-Third Week of Year 1: Mass ad lib; Office of the day *or* The Dedication of the Basilicas of Ss Peter and Paul, Apostles *Proper Readings* Mass & Office of the Memorial

NOVEMBER/DECEMBER 2019

19 Tue	G	feria: Mass ad lib; Office of the day	
20 Wed	G	feria: Mass ad lib; Office of the day	
21 Thu	W	The Presentation of the Blessed Virgin Mary *Preface I or II of the Blessed Virgin Mary* Mass and Office of the Memorial	
22 Fri	R	St Cecilia, Virgin & Martyr: Mass & Office of the Memorial	*Friday abstinence*
23 Sat	G R W W	feria: Mass ad lib; Office of the day *or* St Clement I, Pope & Martyr: Mass & Office of the Memorial *or* St Columban, Abbot: Mass & Office of the Memorial *or* Blessed Virgin Mary on Saturday: Mass & Office of the Memorial	
evening	W	First Vespers	
24 Sun	W	**+ OUR LORD JESUS CHRIST, King of the Universe** *Gloria, Creed, Proper Preface* Mass & Office of the Solemnity § Youth Day	
25 Mon	G R	feria, Thirty-Fourth Week of Year I: Mass ad lib; Office of the day *or* St Catherine of Alexandria, Virgin & Martyr: Mass & Office of the Memorial	*Ps Week 2*
26 Tue	G	feria: Mass ad lib, Office of the day	
27 Wed	G	feria: Mass ad lib; office of the day	
28 Thu	G	feria: Mass ad lib; Office of the day	
29 Fri	G	feria; Mass ad lib; Office of the day	*Friday abstinence*
30 Sat	R	ST ANDREW, Apostle, Patron of Scotland *Gloria, Preface I or II of Apostles* Mass & Office of the Feast	*National*

DECEMBER 2019

LECTIONARY FOR SUNDAYS: YEAR A

ADVENT

Advent has a two-fold character: as a season to prepare for Christmas, when Christ's first coming to us is remembered; and as a season when

DECEMBER 2019

that remembrance directs the mind and heart to await Christ's coming at the end of time. Advent is thus a period for devout and joyful expectation.
The playing of the organ and other musical instruments, and the decoration of the altar with flowers should be done in a moderate manner, as is consonant with the character of the season, without anticipating the full joy of the Nativity of the Lord. The same moderation should be observed in the celebration of marriage.
Eucharistic Prayer 4 is not used in this Season.

evening	P	First Vespers (Divine Office Volume I)	
1 Sun	P	+ 1st SUNDAY OF ADVENT *Creed, Advent Preface I (and on following days)* Mass & Office of the day	*Ps Week 1*
2 Mon	P	Advent feria, First Week of Advent: Mass & Office of the day *(Alternative 1st Reading)*	
3 Tue	W	St Francis Xavier, Priest: Mass & Office of the Memorial § Migrants' Day	
4 Wed	P W	Advent feria, First Week of Advent: Mass & Office of the day *or* St John Damascene, Priest & Doctor: Mass & Office of the Memorial	
5 Thu	P	Advent feria: Mass & Office of the day	
6 Fri	P W	Advent feria: Mass & Office of the day *or* St Nicholas, Bishop: Mass & Office of the Memorial	*Friday abstinence*
7 Sat	W	St Ambrose, Bishop & Doctor: Mass & Office of the Memorial	
evening	P	First Vespers	
8 Sun	P P	+ 2nd SUNDAY OF ADVENT *Creed, Advent Preface I* Mass & Office of the day, 2nd Vespers and + Evening Mass § Bible Sunday	*Ps Week 2*
9 Mon	W	**THE IMMACULATE CONCEPTION OF THE BLESSED VIRGIN MARY, Patron of the Diocese** *Gloria, Creed, Proper Preface* Mass & Office of the Solemnity	
10 Tue	P	Advent feria, Second Week of Advent: Mass & Office of the day	

DECEMBER 2019			
11 Wed	P W	Advent feria: Mass & Office of the day *or* St Damasus I, Pope: Mass & Office of the Memorial	
12 Thu	P W	Advent feria: Mass & Office of the day *or* Our Lady of Guadalupe: Mass & Office of the Memorial	
13 Fri	R	St Lucy, Virgin & Martyr: Mass & Office of the Memorial	*Friday abstinence*
14 Sat	W	St John of the Cross, Priest & Doctor: Mass & Office of the Memorial	
evening	RP or P	First Vespers	
15 Sun	RP or P	+ 3rd SUNDAY OF ADVENT (Gaudete Sunday) *Creed, Advent Preface I* Mass & Office of the day	*Ps Week 3*
16 Mon	P	Advent feria, Third Week of Advent: Mass & Office of the day	
		Memorials which occur on days between 17 and 31 December may be commemorated at Mass by using the collect of the saint in place of the collect of the day. In the Office of Readings the proper hagiographical reading and responsory may be added after the Patristic reading and responsory; the collect of the saint concludes the office. At Lauds and Vespers the antiphon (proper or common) and collect of the saint may be added after the collect of the day. At Mass, proper texts and readings are given for the weekdays from 17-24 December, and these should be used instead of those indicated for the weekdays of the third or fourth week of Advent.	
17 Tue	P	Advent feria *Advent Preface II (and on following days)* Mass & Office of 17 December	
18 Wed	P	Advent feria: Mass & Office of 18 December	
19 Thu	P	Advent feria: Mass & Office of 19 December	
20 Fri	P	Advent feria: Mass & Office of 20 December	*Friday abstinence*
21 Sat	P	Advent feria: Mass & Office of 21 December *(Alternative 1st Reading)* (St Peter Canisius, Priest and Doctor)	
evening	P	First Vespers: Magnificat antiphon of 21 December	

DECEMBER 2019

22 Sun	P	+ 4th SUNDAY OF ADVENT *Ps Week 4* *Creed, Advent Preface II* Mass of the day; Office of the day, with readings, also Benedictus & Magnificat antiphons of 22 December (see Divine Office Vol I, page 154 ff) § Expectant Mothers Announce Holy Day of Obligation
23 Mon	P	Advent feria: Mass & Office of 23 December (St John of Kanty, Priest)
24 Tue	P	Advent feria: Mass & Office of 24 December

CHRISTMAS SEASON

After the annual celebration of the Paschal Mystery there is no more ancient feast day for the Church than the recalling of the memory of the Nativity of the Lord and of the mysteries of his first appearing.

Eucharistic Prayer 4 is not used in this season.

evening	W W	First Vespers + Proper Vigil Mass of Christmas precedes or follows *Gloria, Proper Readings (Short form Gospel), Creed, (kneel at* Incarnatus*), a Preface of the Nativity &* Communicantes *in the Roman Canon*
		For pastoral reasons, readings at the following Christmas Masses may be chosen from among all those provided for the Solemnity. It is appropriate that a Solemn Vigil be kept by celebrating the Office of Readings before the Mass during the Night. Compline is omitted by those attending that Mass.
	W	+ Mass during the Night *Gloria, Proper Readings, Creed (kneel at* Incarnatus*), a Preface of the Nativity &* Communicantes *in the Roman Canon*
25 Wed	W	**+ THE NATIVITY OF THE LORD (CHRISTMAS)** *Gloria, Proper Readings (Short form Gospel), Creed (kneel at* Incarnatus*), a Preface of the Nativity &* Communicantes *in the Roman Canon* Mass & Office of the Solemnity All priests may celebrate or concelebrate three Masses today, provided that they are celebrated at their proper time.
26 Thu	R	ST STEPHEN, The First Martyr *Gloria, Proper Readings, a Preface of the Nativity &* Communicantes *in the Roman Canon* Mass, Lauds & Lesser Hours of St Stephen; Vespers of the Octave

DECEMBER 2019

	R	*(In parishes dedicated to ST STEPHEN, The First Martyr, his Solemnity is observed:* *Gloria, 1st Reading Proper, 2nd Reading from the Common of Martyrs, Proper Gospel, Creed, a Preface of the Nativity & Communicantes in the Roman Canon,* Second Vespers of the Solemnity
27 Fri	W	ST JOHN, Apostle & Evangelist *Gloria, Proper Readings, a Preface of the Nativity & Communicantes in the Roman Canon* Mass, Lauds & Lesser Hours of St John; Vespers of the Octave *No Friday abstinence*
	W	*(+ In parishes dedicated to ST JOHN, Apostle & Evangelist, his Solemnity is observed:* *Gloria, 1st Reading from the Proper of All Saints, Other Readings Proper, Creed, a Preface of the Nativity & Communicantes in the Roman Canon* First and Second Vespers of the Solemnity)
28 Sat	R	THE HOLY INNOCENTS, Martyrs *Gloria, Proper Readings, a Preface of the Nativity & Communicantes in the Roman Canon* Mass, Lauds & Lesser Hours of the Holy Innocents
evening	W	First Vespers
29 Sun	W	+ THE HOLY FAMILY OF JESUS, MARY AND JOSEPH *Gloria, 1st and 2nd Readings, Gospel of Year A, Creed, a Preface of the Nativity & Communicantes in the Roman Canon* Mass & Office of the Feast
	R	*(In parishes dedicated to ST THOMAS BECKET, Bishop & Martyr, his Solemnity is observed:* *Gloria, 1st Reading from the Common of Martyrs, 2nd Reading & Gospel Proper, Creed, a Preface of the Nativity & Communicantes in the Roman Canon,* 1st and 2nd Vespers of the Solemnity, also + Evening Mass Announce Holy Day of Obligation
30 Mon	W	6th DAY IN THE OCTAVE OF CHRISTMAS *Gloria, a Preface of the Nativity & Communicantes in the Roman Canon* Mass & Office of the Octave
31 Tue	W	7th DAY IN THE OCTAVE OF CHRISTMAS *Gloria, a Preface of the Nativity & Communicantes in the Roman Canon* Mass & Office of the Octave (St Sylvester I, Pope)
evening	W	First Vespers

JANUARY 2020

JANUARY 2020

1 Wed	W	**SOLEMNITY OF MARY, THE HOLY MOTHER OF GOD** THE OCTAVE DAY OF THE NATIVITY OF THE LORD *Gloria, Creed, Preface I of Blessed Virgin Mary &* Communicantes *in the Roman Canon* Mass & Office of the Solemnity
		A Preface of the Nativity is used on weekdays of the Christmas season, unless other provision is made.
2 Thu	W	Ss Basil the Great and Gregory Nazianzen, Bishops & Doctors *Ps Week I* *Readings of 2 January* Mass & Office of the Memorial
3 Fri	W	Christmas feria *Friday abstinence* *Readings of 3 January* Mass & Office of the Day *or*
	W	The Most Holy Name of Jesus: Mass & Office of the Memorial
4 Sat	W	Christmas feria *Readings of 4 January* Mass & Office of the Day
evening	W	First Vespers
	W	+ Proper Vigil Mass of the Epiphany precedes or follows *Gloria, Epiphany Readings, Creed, Proper Preface &* Communicantes *of the Epiphany in the Roman Canon*
5 Sun	W	**+ THE EPIPHANY OF THE LORD** *Gloria, Creed, Proper Preface &* Communicantes *of the Epiphany in the Roman Canon; an increased display of lights is recommended.* *At today's Mass, after the Gospel, the announcement may be made of moveable feasts according to the formula given in the Roman Pontifical, on page 1247 of the* Missale Romanum, editio typica tertia *and page 1505 of the Roman Missal.* Mass & Office of the Solemnity
		A Preface of the Nativity or of the Epiphany is used until the Christmas season ends, unless other provision is made.
6 Mon	W	Christmas feria *Ps Week 2* *Second Collect, Readings of Monday after Epiphany*

SECTION 7: LITURGICAL CALENDAR

JANUARY 2020

7 Tue	W	Christmas feria *Second Collect, Readings of Tuesday after Epiphany* Mass & Office of the day
8 Wed	W	Christmas feria *Second Collect, Readings of Wednesday after Epiphany* Mass & Office of the day
9 Thu	W	Christmas feria *Second Collect, Readings of Thursday after Epihany* Mass & Office of the day
10 Fri	W	Christmas feria *Friday abstinence* *Second Collect, Readings of Friday after Epiphany* Mass & Office of the day
11 Sat	W	Christmas feria *Second Collect, Readings of Saturday after Epiphany* Mass & Office of the day
evening	W	First Vespers
12 Sun	W	+ THE BAPTISM OF THE LORD *Gloria, (Alternative Collect), 1st and 2nd Reading, Gospel of Year A, Creed, Proper Preface* Mass & Office of the Feast
		Christmas Time ends.

INDEX OF ADVERTISEMENTS

Further advertisements which may be helpful can be found in the monthly **Westminster Record.**

INDEX

NOTES

NOTES

NOTES

NOTES

NOTES

NOTES

Calendar 2019

JANUARY

S	M	T	W	T	F	S
		1	2	3	4	5
6	7	8	9	10	11	12
13	14	15	16	17	18	19
20	21	22	23	24	25	26
27	28	29	30	31		

FEBRUARY

S	M	T	W	T	F	S
					1	2
3	4	5	6	7	8	9
10	11	12	13	14	15	16
17	18	19	20	21	22	23
24	25	26	27	28		

MARCH

S	M	T	W	T	F	S
					1	2
3	4	5	6	7	8	9
10	11	12	13	14	15	16
17	18	19	20	21	22	23
24	25	26	27	28	29	30
31						

APRIL

S	M	T	W	T	F	S
	1	2	3	4	5	6
7	8	9	10	11	12	13
14	15	16	17	18	19	20
21	22	23	24	25	26	27
28	29	30				

MAY

S	M	T	W	T	F	S
			1	2	3	4
5	6	7	8	9	10	11
12	13	14	15	16	17	18
19	20	21	22	23	24	25
26	27	28	29	30	31	

JUNE

S	M	T	W	T	F	S
						1
2	3	4	5	6	7	8
9	10	11	12	13	14	15
16	17	18	19	20	21	22
23	24	25	26	27	28	29
30						

JULY

S	M	T	W	T	F	S
	1	2	3	4	5	6
7	8	9	10	11	12	13
14	15	16	17	18	19	20
21	22	23	24	25	26	27
28	29	30	31			

AUGUST

S	M	T	W	T	F	S
				1	2	3
4	5	6	7	8	9	10
11	12	13	14	15	16	17
18	19	20	21	22	23	24
25	26	27	28	29	30	31

SEPTEMBER

S	M	T	W	T	F	S
1	2	3	4	5	6	7
8	9	10	11	12	13	14
15	16	17	18	19	20	21
22	23	24	25	26	27	28
29	30					

OCTOBER

S	M	T	W	T	F	S
		1	2	3	4	5
6	7	8	9	10	11	12
13	14	15	16	17	18	19
20	21	22	23	24	25	26
27	28	29	30	31		

NOVEMBER

S	M	T	W	T	F	S
					1	2
3	4	5	6	7	8	9
10	11	12	13	14	15	16
17	18	19	20	21	22	23
24	25	26	27	28	29	30

DECEMBER

S	M	T	W	T	F	S
1	2	3	4	5	6	7
8	9	10	11	12	13	14
15	16	17	18	19	20	21
22	23	24	25	26	27	28
29	30	31				